doubt!!™
volume one

doubt!!™

volume one
shôjo edition

Story & Art by Kaneyoshi Izumi

English Adaptation/Kelly Sue DeConnick
Translation/Naomi Kokubo
Touch-up Art & Lettering/Freeman Wong
Design/Amy Martin
Editor/Frances E. Wall

Managing Editor/Annette Roman
Director of Production/Noboru Watanabe
Editorial Director/Alvin Lu
Sr. Director of Acquisitions/Rika Inouye
Vice President of Sales & Marketing/Liza Coppola
Executive Vice President/Hyoe Narita
Publisher/Seiji Horibuchi

Printed in the U.S.A.

Published by VIZ, LLC
P.O. Box 77010
San Francisco, CA 94107

10 9 8 7 6 5 4 3 2 1
First printing, February 2005

www.viz.com   store.viz.com

doubt!!™

volume one

story and art by

Kaneyoshi Izumi

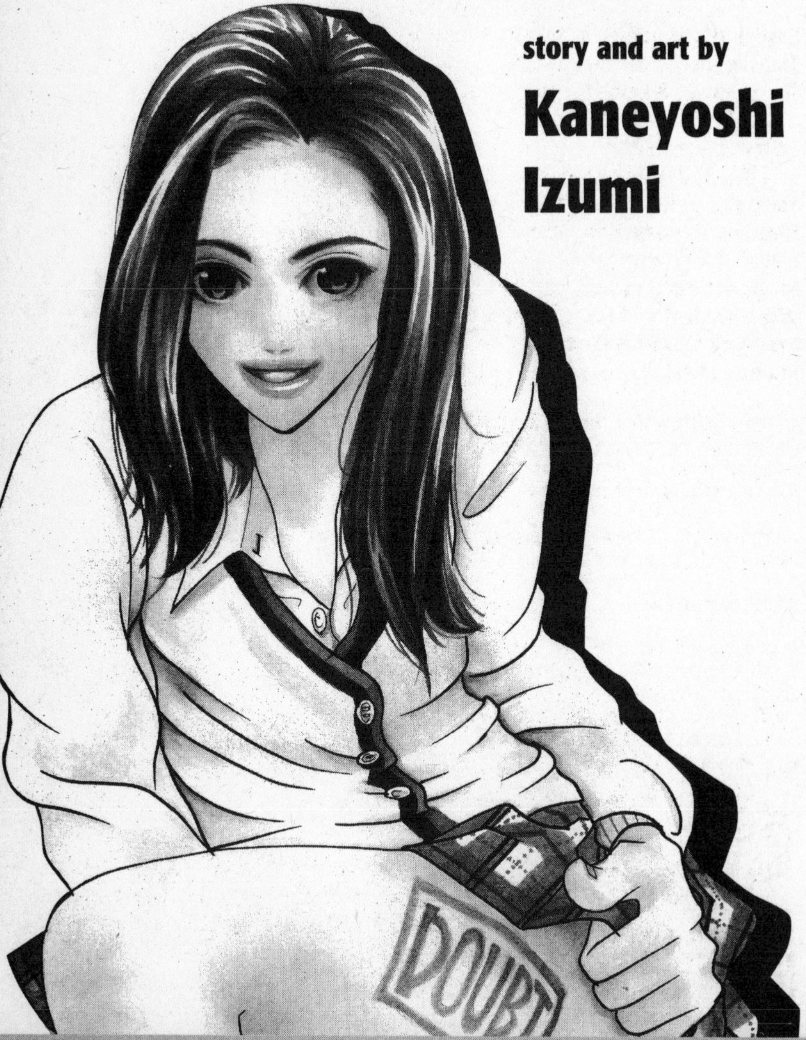
DOUBT

doubt!!™ 1 contents

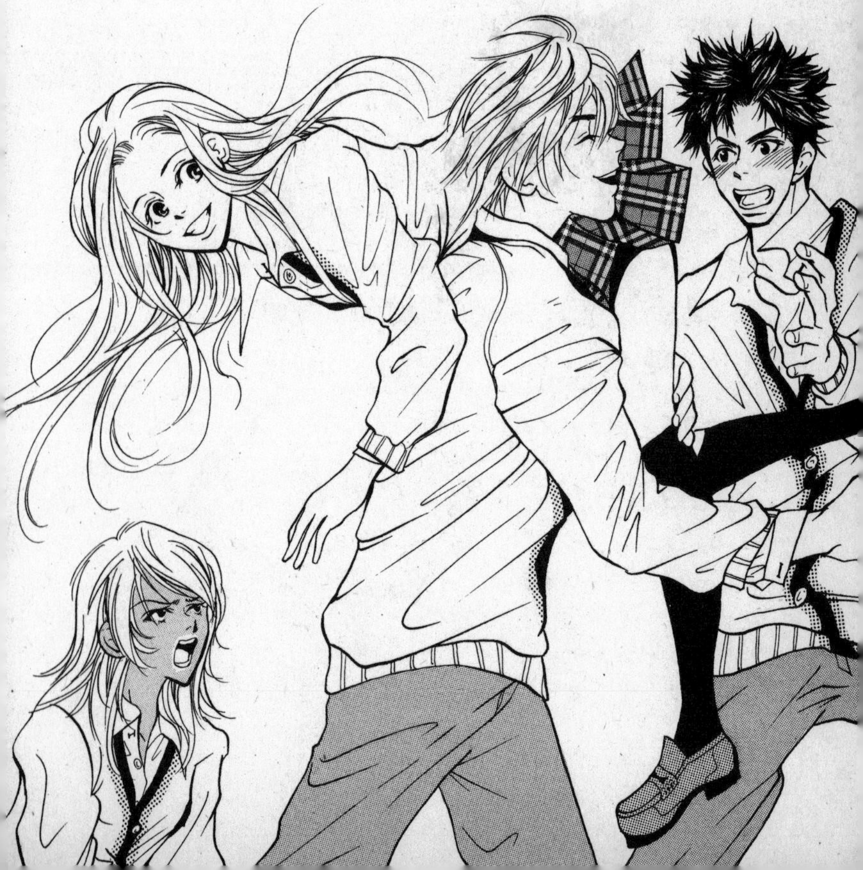

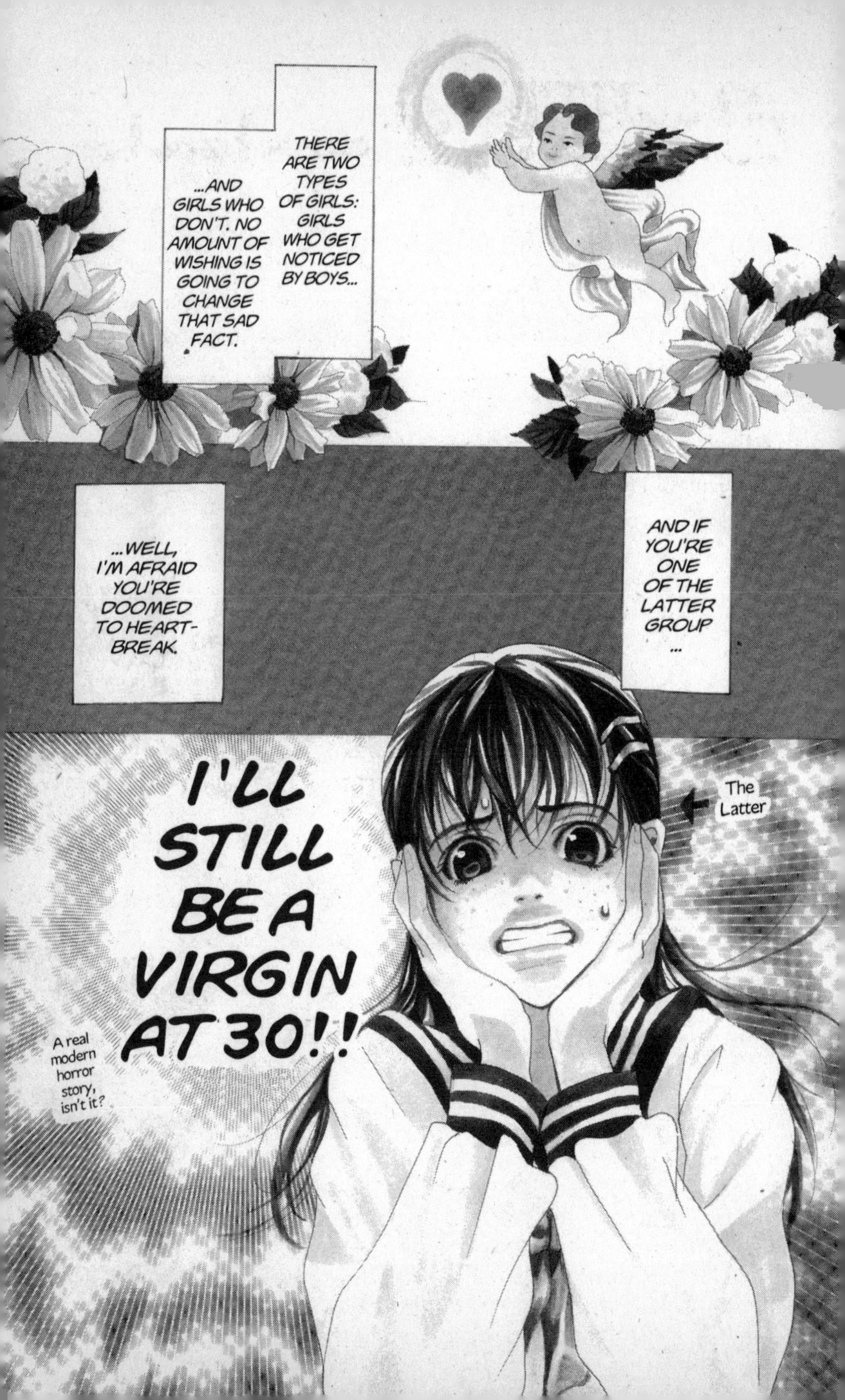
THERE ARE TWO TYPES OF GIRLS: GIRLS WHO GET NOTICED BY BOYS...
...AND GIRLS WHO DON'T. NO AMOUNT OF WISHING IS GOING TO CHANGE THAT SAD FACT.
AND IF YOU'RE ONE OF THE LATTER GROUP...
...WELL, I'M AFRAID YOU'RE DOOMED TO HEART-BREAK.
The Latter
I'LL STILL BE A VIRGIN AT 30!!
A real modern horror story, isn't it?

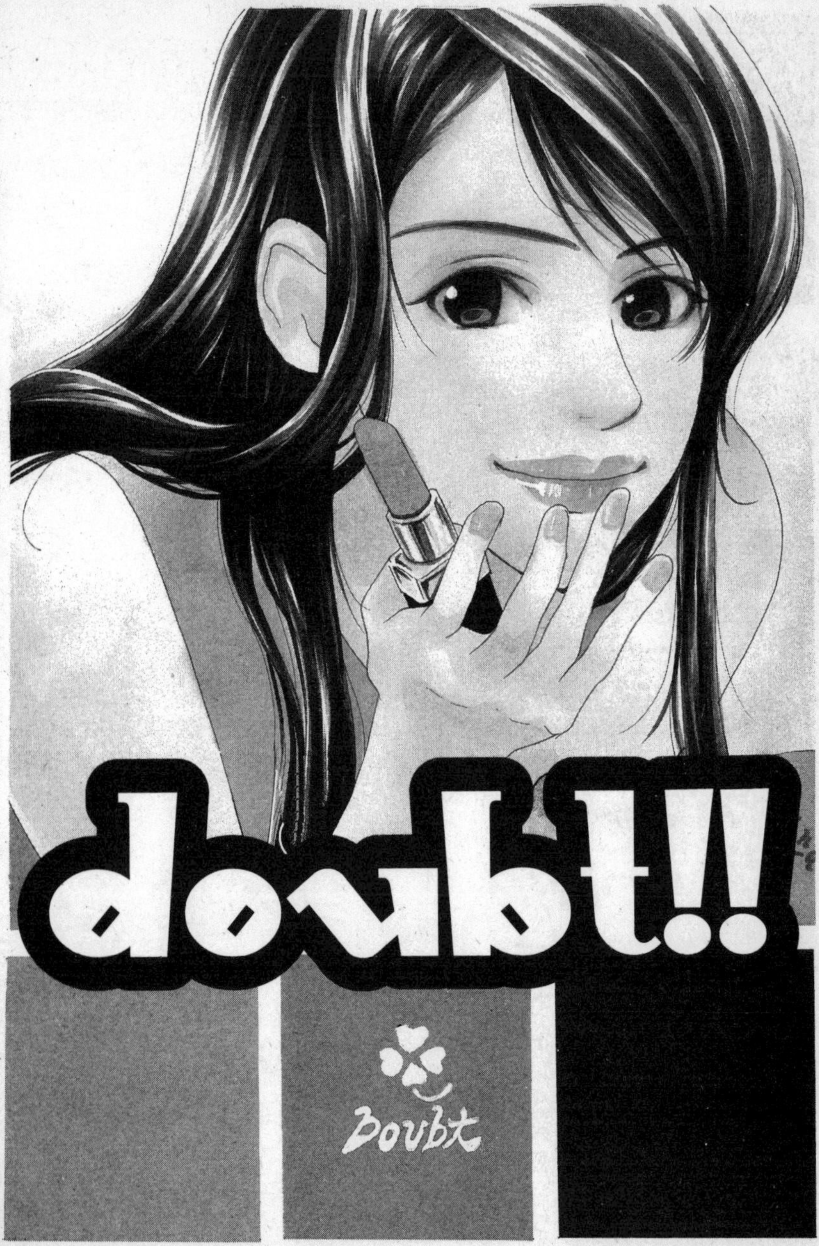
doubt!!
Doubt

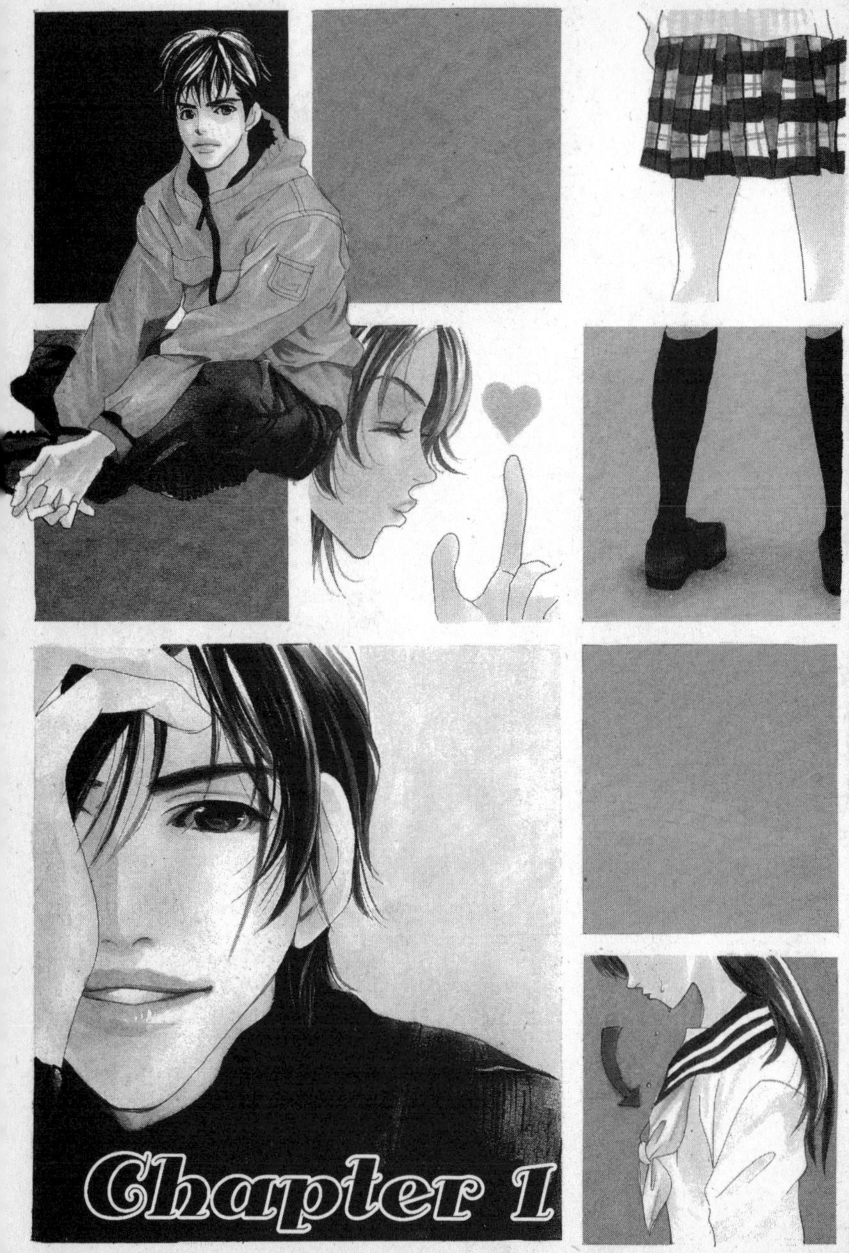
Chapter 1

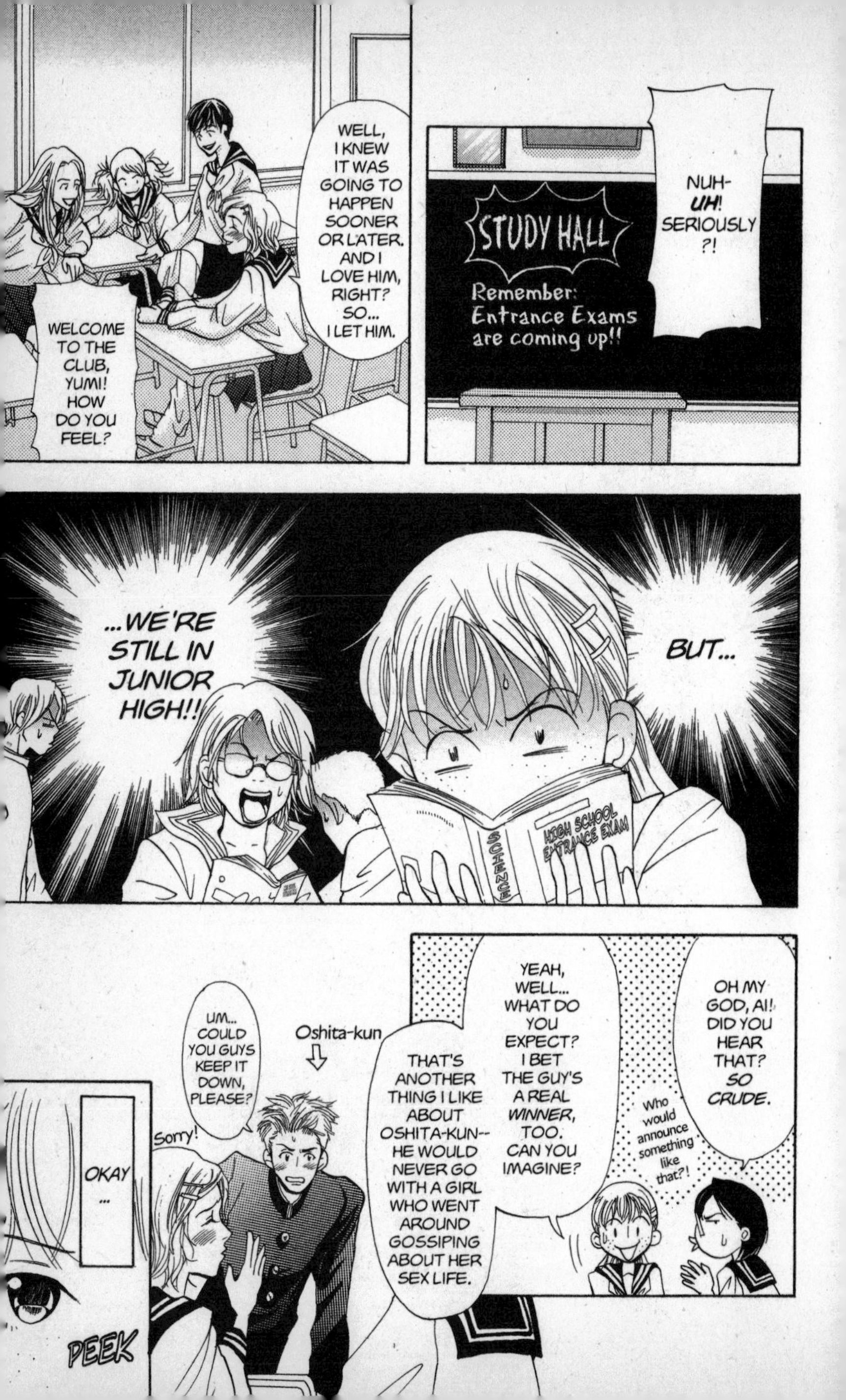
NUH-*UH*! SERIOUSLY?!
STUDY HALL
Remember: Entrance Exams are coming up!!
WELL, I KNEW IT WAS GOING TO HAPPEN SOONER OR LATER. AND I LOVE HIM, RIGHT? SO... I LET HIM.
WELCOME TO THE CLUB, YUMI! HOW DO YOU FEEL?
BUT...
...WE'RE STILL IN JUNIOR HIGH!!
SCIENCE
HIGH SCHOOL ENTRANCE EXAM
OH MY GOD, AI! DID YOU HEAR THAT? *SO CRUDE.*
Who would announce something like that?!
YEAH, WELL... WHAT DO YOU EXPECT? I BET THE GUY'S A REAL *WINNER*, TOO. CAN YOU IMAGINE?
THAT'S ANOTHER THING I LIKE ABOUT OSHITA-KUN-- HE WOULD NEVER GO WITH A GIRL WHO WENT AROUND GOSSIPING ABOUT HER SEX LIFE.
UM... COULD YOU GUYS KEEP IT DOWN, PLEASE?
Oshita-kun
Sorry!
OKAY...
PEEK

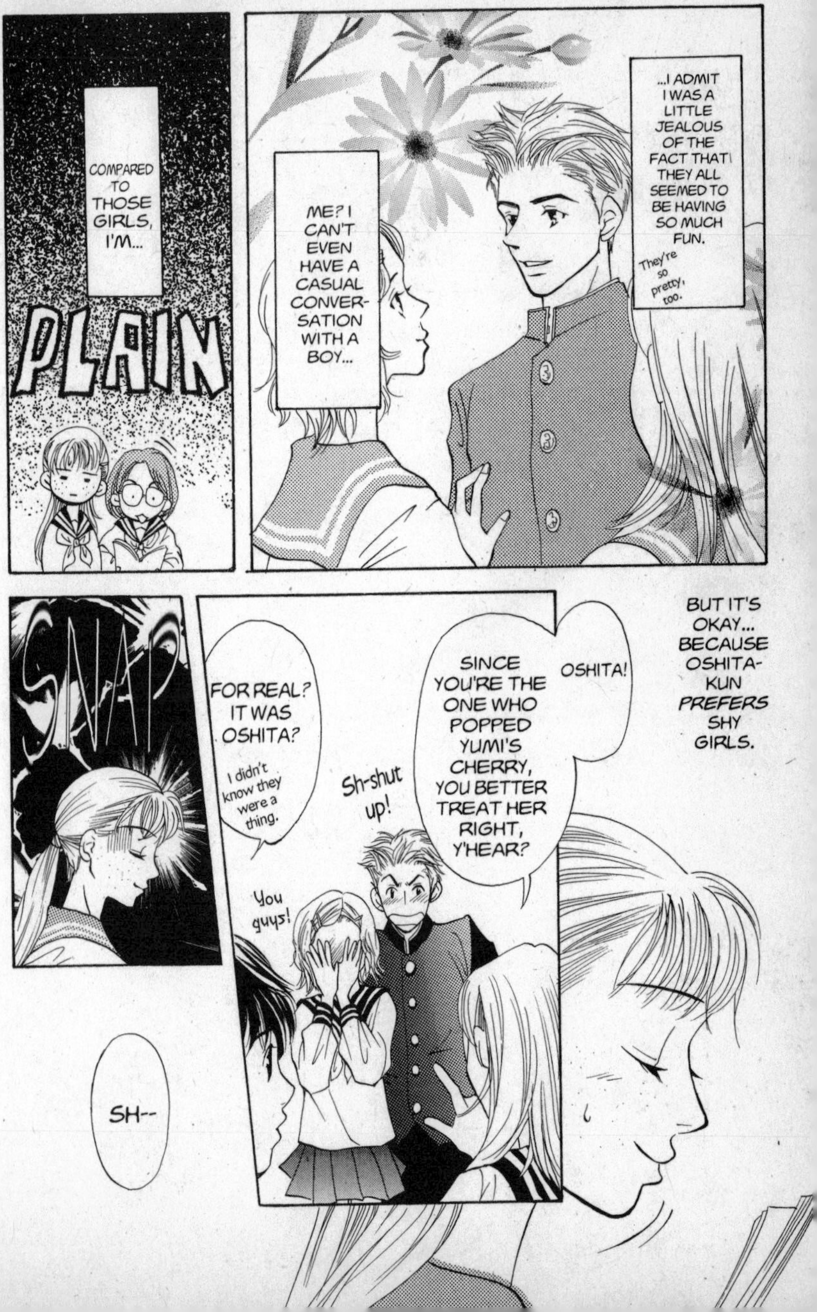
...I ADMIT I WAS A LITTLE JEALOUS OF THE FACT THAT THEY ALL SEEMED TO BE HAVING SO MUCH FUN.
They're so pretty, too.
ME? I CAN'T EVEN HAVE A CASUAL CONVER-SATION WITH A BOY...
COMPARED TO THOSE GIRLS, I'M...
PLAIN
BUT IT'S OKAY... BECAUSE OSHITA-KUN *PREFERS* SHY GIRLS.
OSHITA!
SINCE YOU'RE THE ONE WHO POPPED YUMI'S CHERRY, YOU BETTER TREAT HER RIGHT, Y'HEAR?
Sh-shut up!
FOR REAL? IT WAS OSHITA?
I didn't know they were a thing.
You guys!
SNAP
SH--

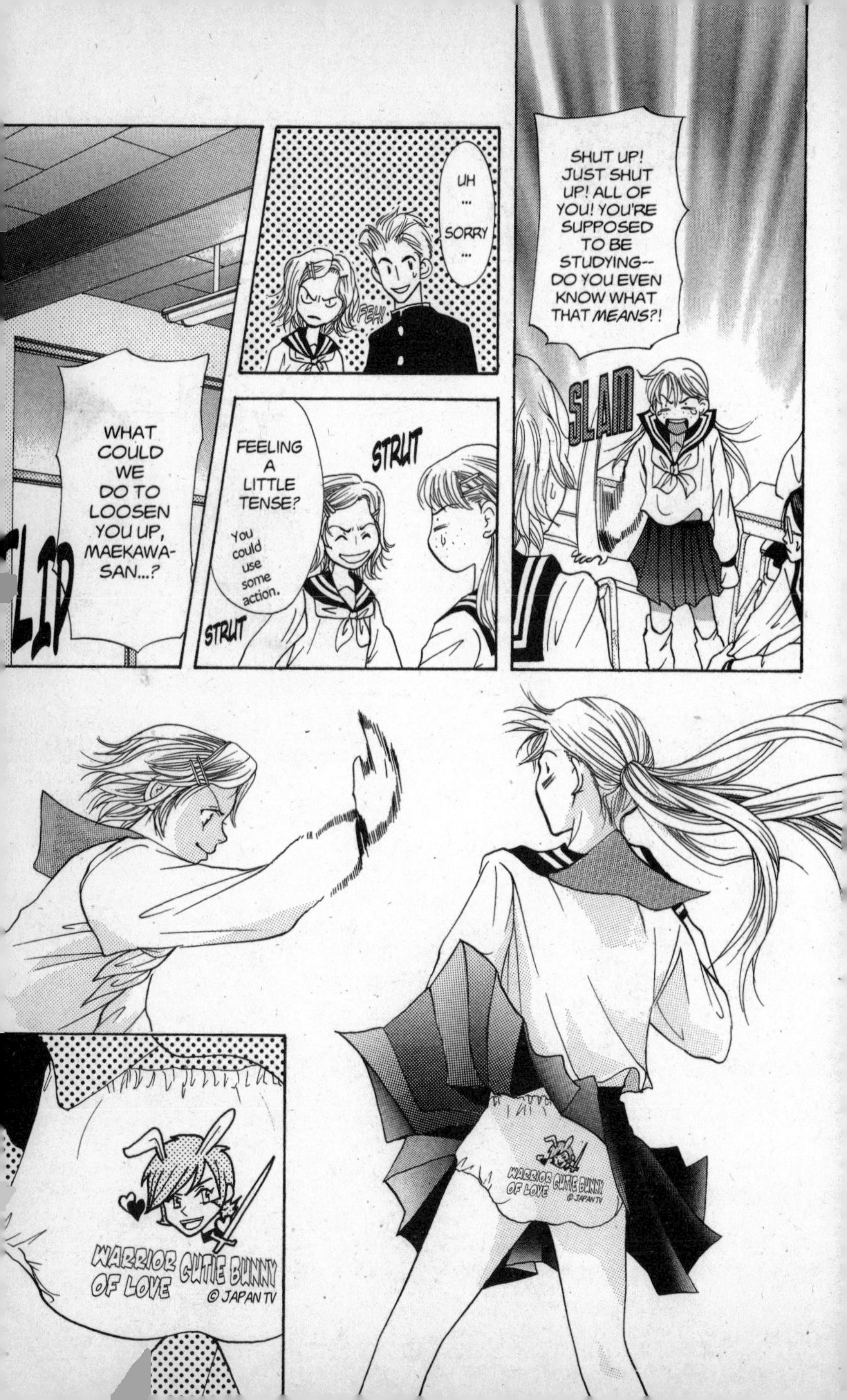

SHUT UP! JUST SHUT UP! ALL OF YOU! YOU'RE SUPPOSED TO BE STUDYING-- DO YOU EVEN KNOW WHAT THAT *MEANS*?!
SLAM
UH ... SORRY ...
FEH!
FEELING A LITTLE TENSE?
You could use some action.
STRUT
STRUT
WHAT COULD WE DO TO LOOSEN YOU UP, MAEKAWA-SAN...?
FLIP
WARRIOR OF LOVE CUTIE BUNNY
© JAPAN TV
WARRIOR OF LOVE CUTIE BUNNY
© JAPAN TV

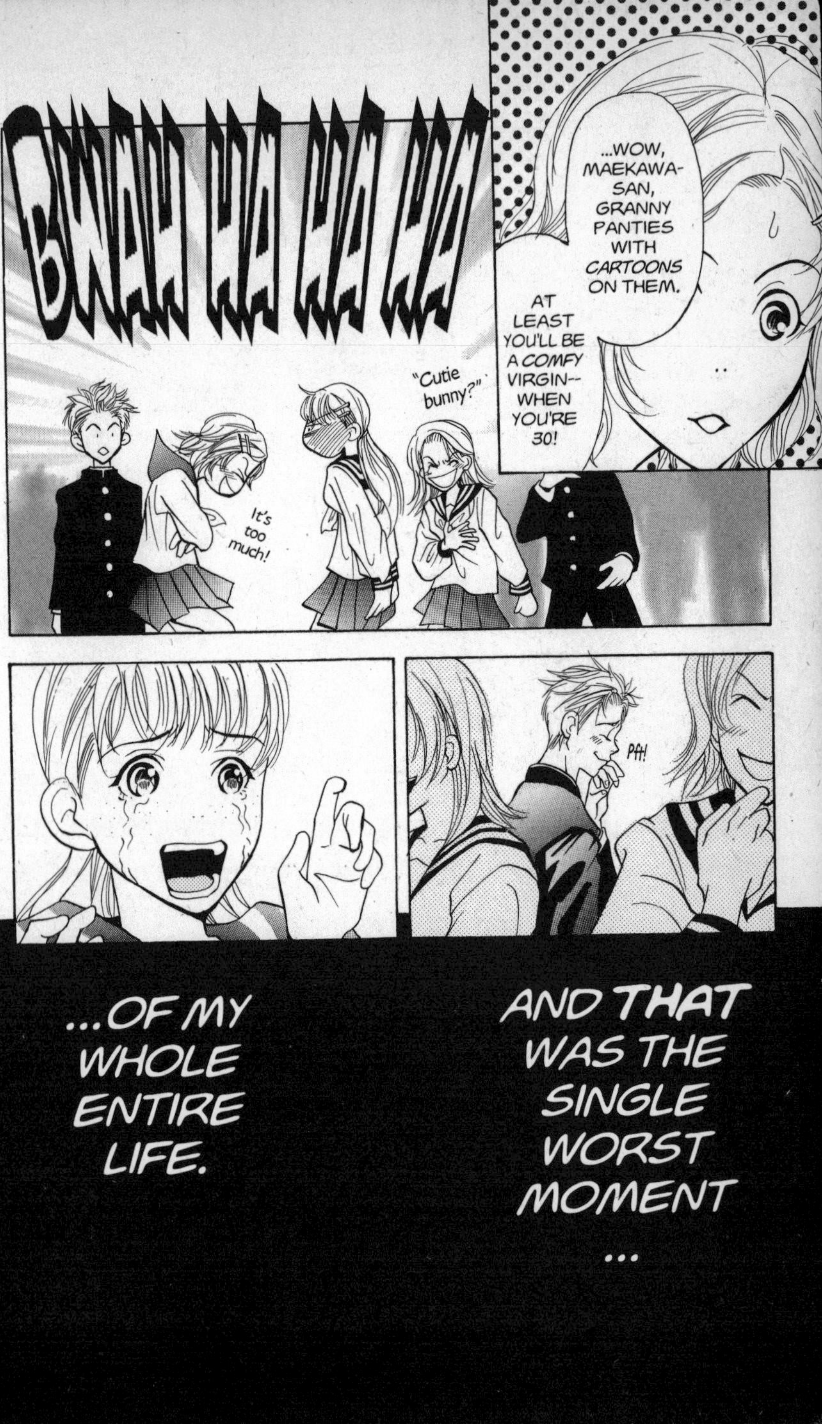
...WOW, MAEKAWA-SAN, GRANNY PANTIES WITH CARTOONS ON THEM.
AT LEAST YOU'LL BE A COMFY VIRGIN-- WHEN YOU'RE 30!
"Cutie bunny?"
It's too much!
Pft!
AND THAT WAS THE SINGLE WORST MOMENT ...
...OF MY WHOLE ENTIRE LIFE.

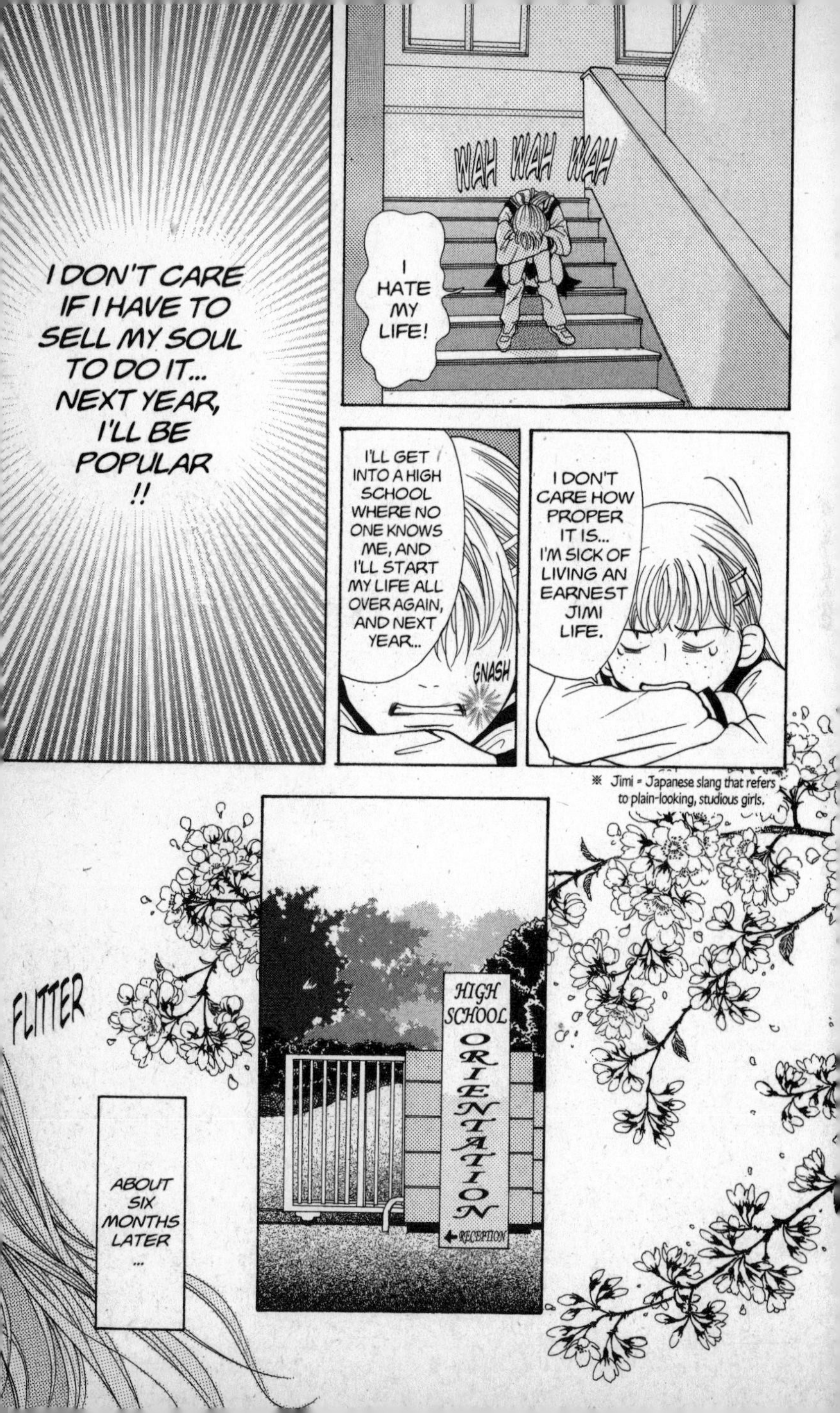

WAH WAH WAH
I HATE MY LIFE!
I DON'T CARE HOW PROPER IT IS... I'M SICK OF LIVING AN EARNEST JIMI LIFE.
I'LL GET INTO A HIGH SCHOOL WHERE NO ONE KNOWS ME, AND I'LL START MY LIFE ALL OVER AGAIN, AND NEXT YEAR...
GNASH
I DON'T CARE IF I HAVE TO SELL MY SOUL TO DO IT... NEXT YEAR, I'LL BE POPULAR!!
※ Jimi = Japanese slang that refers to plain-looking, studious girls.
HIGH SCHOOL ORIENTATION
← RECEPTION
FLITTER
ABOUT SIX MONTHS LATER ...

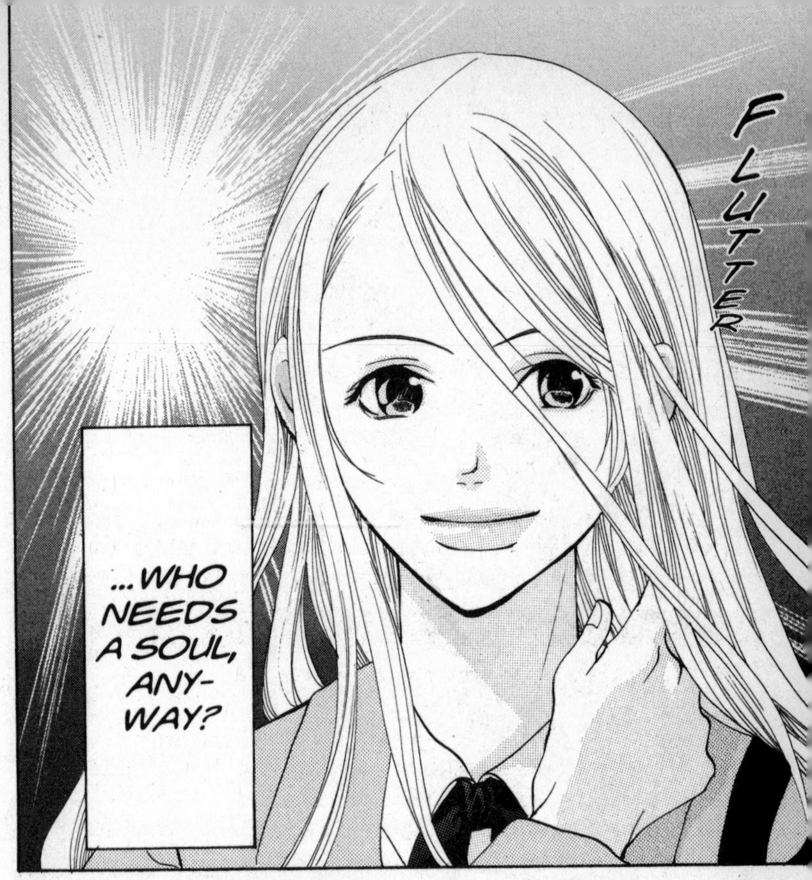
FLUTTER
...WHO NEEDS A SOUL, ANY-WAY?

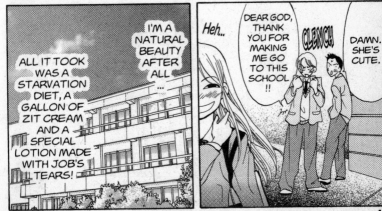

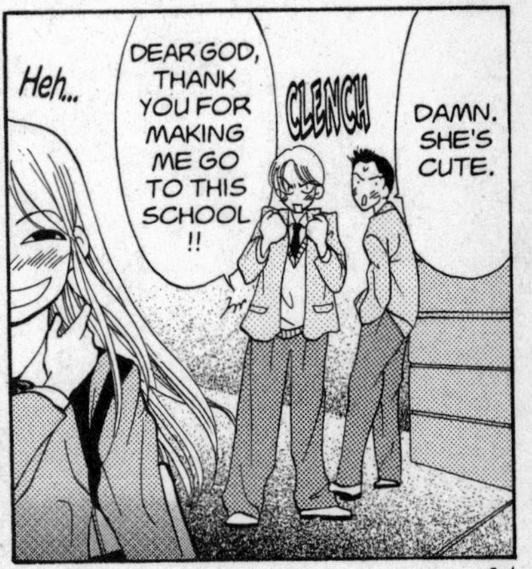
DAMN. SHE'S CUTE.
CLENCH
DEAR GOD, THANK YOU FOR MAKING ME GO TO THIS SCHOOL !!
Heh...

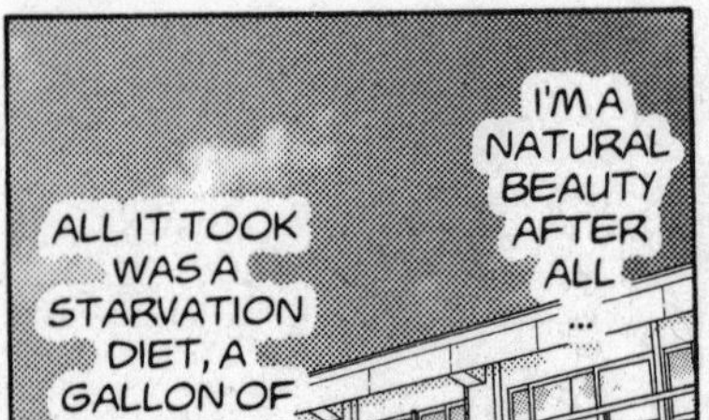
I'M A NATURAL BEAUTY AFTER ALL ...
ALL IT TOOK WAS A STARVATION DIET, A GALLON OF ZIT CREAM AND A SPECIAL LOTION MADE WITH JOB'S TEARS!

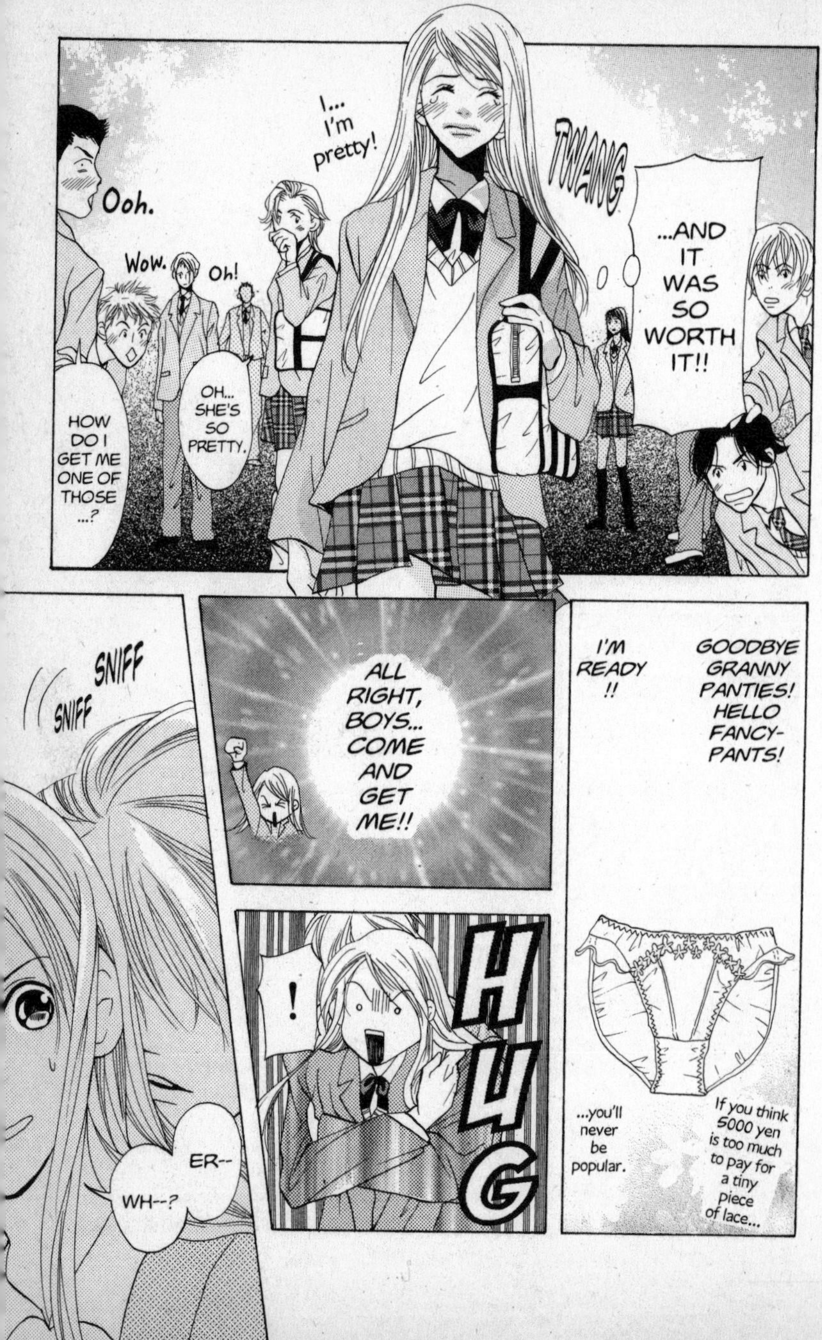
TWANG
...AND IT WAS SO WORTH IT!!
I... I'm pretty!
Ooh.
Oh!
Wow.
OH... SHE'S SO PRETTY.
HOW DO I GET ME ONE OF THOSE ...?
GOODBYE GRANNY PANTIES! HELLO FANCY-PANTS!
I'M READY!!
If you think 5000 yen is too much to pay for a tiny piece of lace...
...you'll never be popular.
ALL RIGHT, BOYS... COME AND GET ME!!
HUG
!
SNIFF
SNIFF
ER--
WH--?

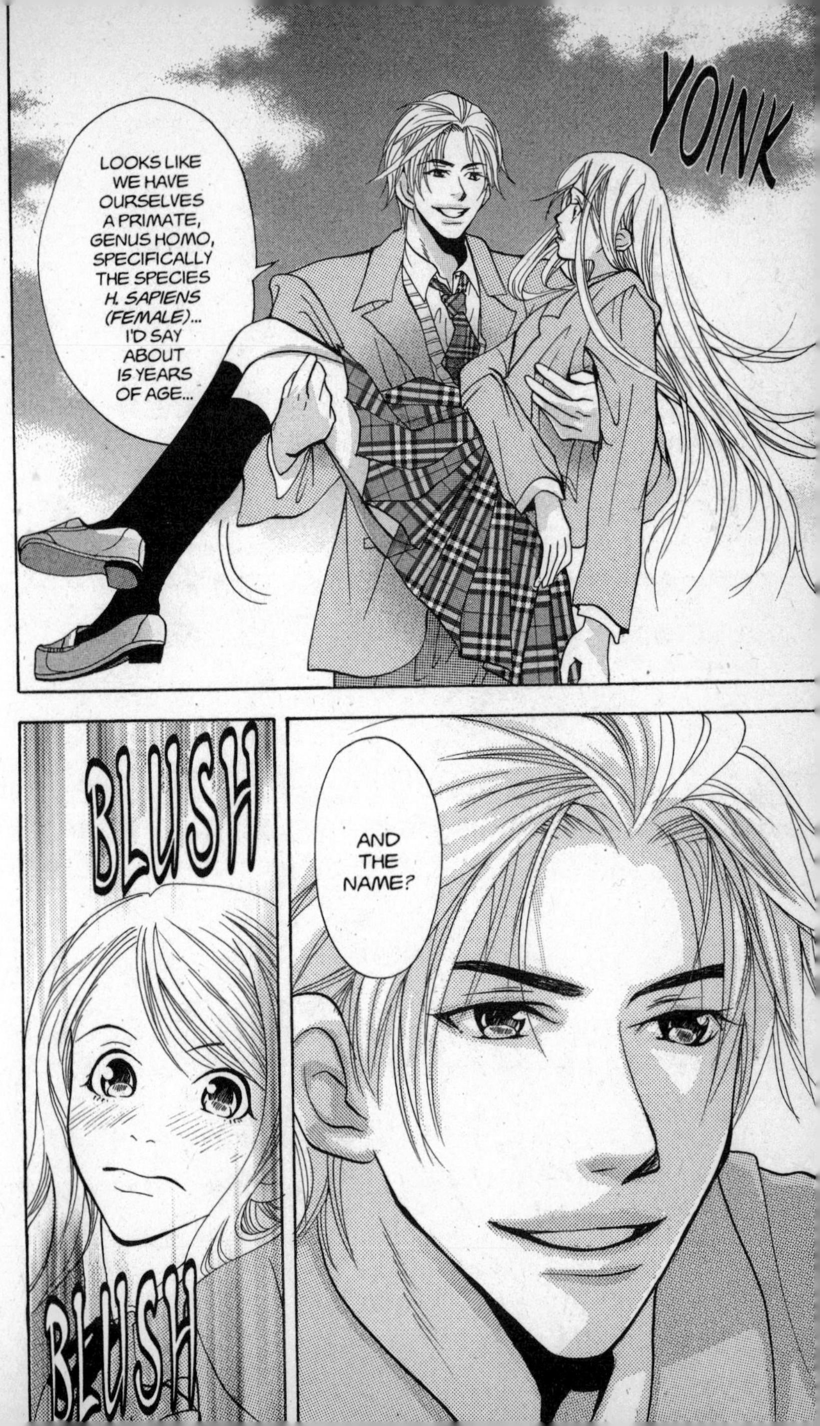
YOINK
LOOKS LIKE WE HAVE OURSELVES A PRIMATE, GENUS HOMO, SPECIFICALLY THE SPECIES H. SAPIENS (FEMALE)... I'D SAY ABOUT 15 YEARS OF AGE...
AND THE NAME?
BLUSH
BLUSH

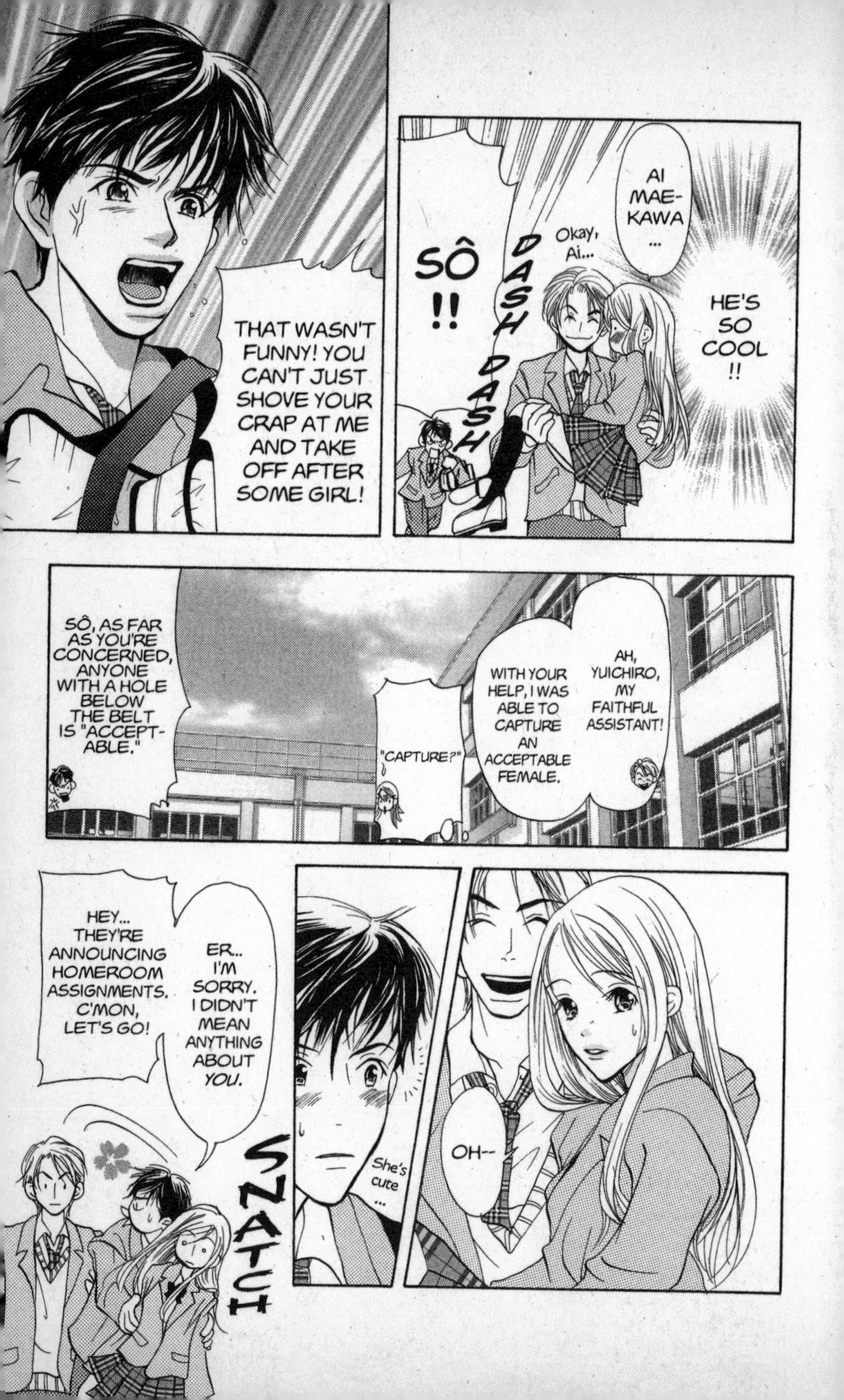
AI MAE-KAWA ...
HE'S SO COOL !!
Okay, Ai...
DASH DASH
SÔ !!
THAT WASN'T FUNNY! YOU CAN'T JUST SHOVE YOUR CRAP AT ME AND TAKE OFF AFTER SOME GIRL!
AH, YUICHIRO, MY FAITHFUL ASSISTANT!
WITH YOUR HELP, I WAS ABLE TO CAPTURE AN ACCEPTABLE FEMALE.
"CAPTURE?"
SÔ, AS FAR AS YOU'RE CONCERNED, ANYONE WITH A HOLE BELOW THE BELT IS "ACCEPT-ABLE."
OH--
She's cute ...
ER.. I'M SORRY. I DIDN'T MEAN ANYTHING ABOUT YOU.
HEY... THEY'RE ANNOUNCING HOMEROOM ASSIGNMENTS. C'MON, LET'S GO!
SNATCH

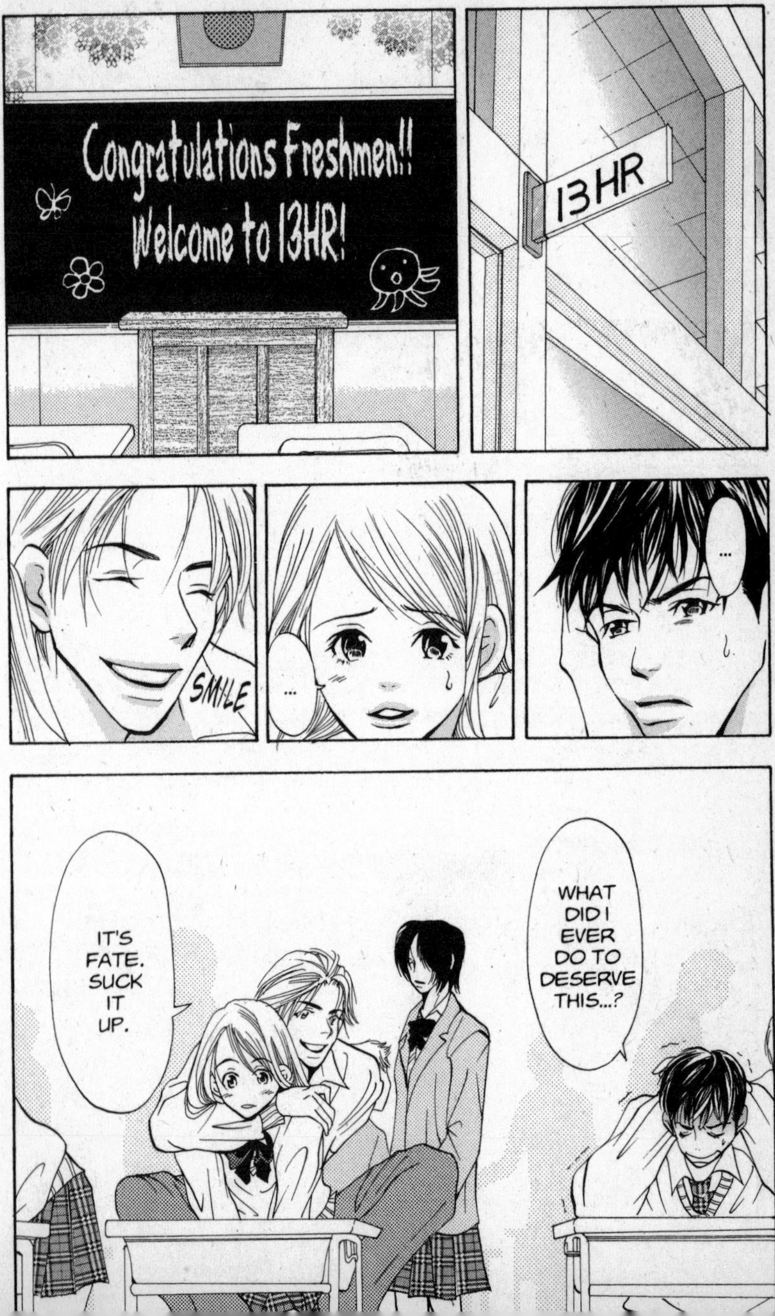
13HR
Congratulations Freshmen!!
Welcome to 13HR!
...
...
SMILE
WHAT DID I EVER DO TO DESERVE THIS...?
IT'S FATE. SUCK IT UP.

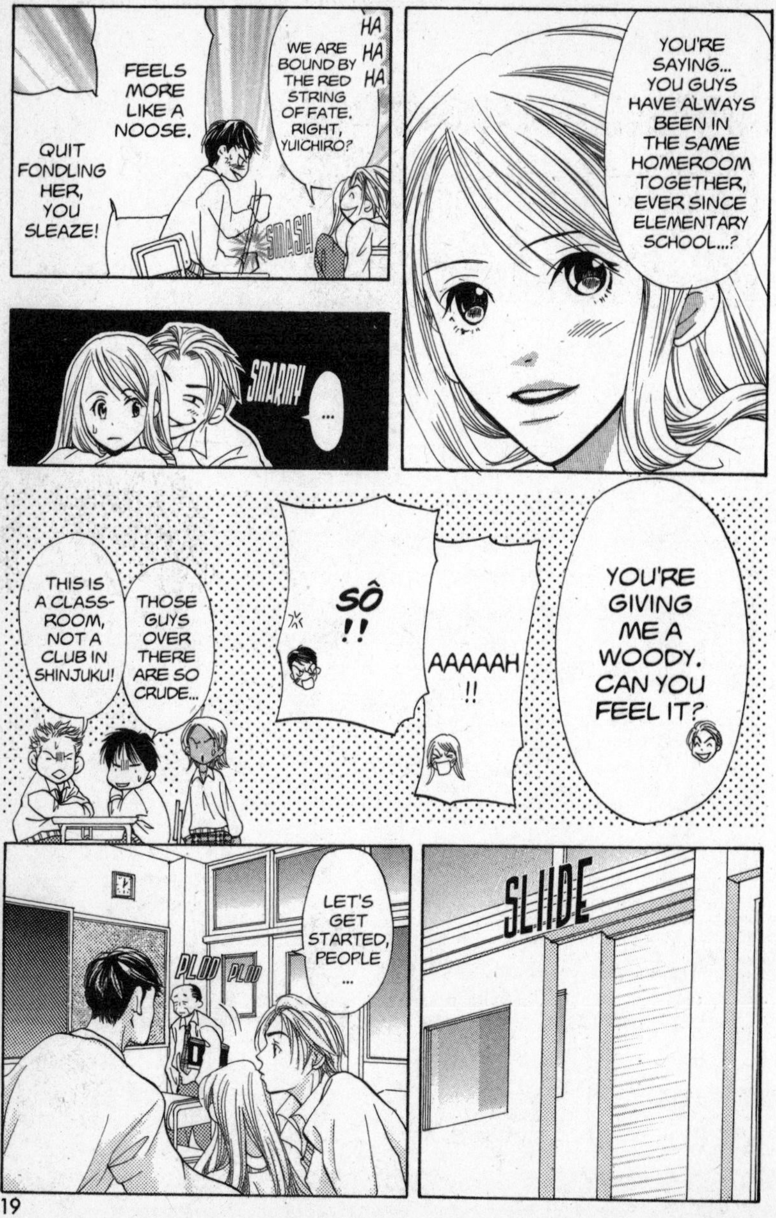
YOU'RE SAYING... YOU GUYS HAVE ALWAYS BEEN IN THE SAME HOMEROOM TOGETHER, EVER SINCE ELEMENTARY SCHOOL...?
HA HA HA
WE ARE BOUND BY THE RED STRING OF FATE. RIGHT, YUICHIRO?
FEELS MORE LIKE A NOOSE.
QUIT FONDLING HER, YOU SLEAZE!
SMASH
...
SMARMY
YOU'RE GIVING ME A WOODY. CAN YOU FEEL IT?
AAAAAH !!
SÔ !!
THOSE GUYS OVER THERE ARE SO CRUDE...
THIS IS A CLASS-ROOM, NOT A CLUB IN SHINJUKU!
SLIIDE
LET'S GET STARTED, PEOPLE ...
PLOD
PLOD

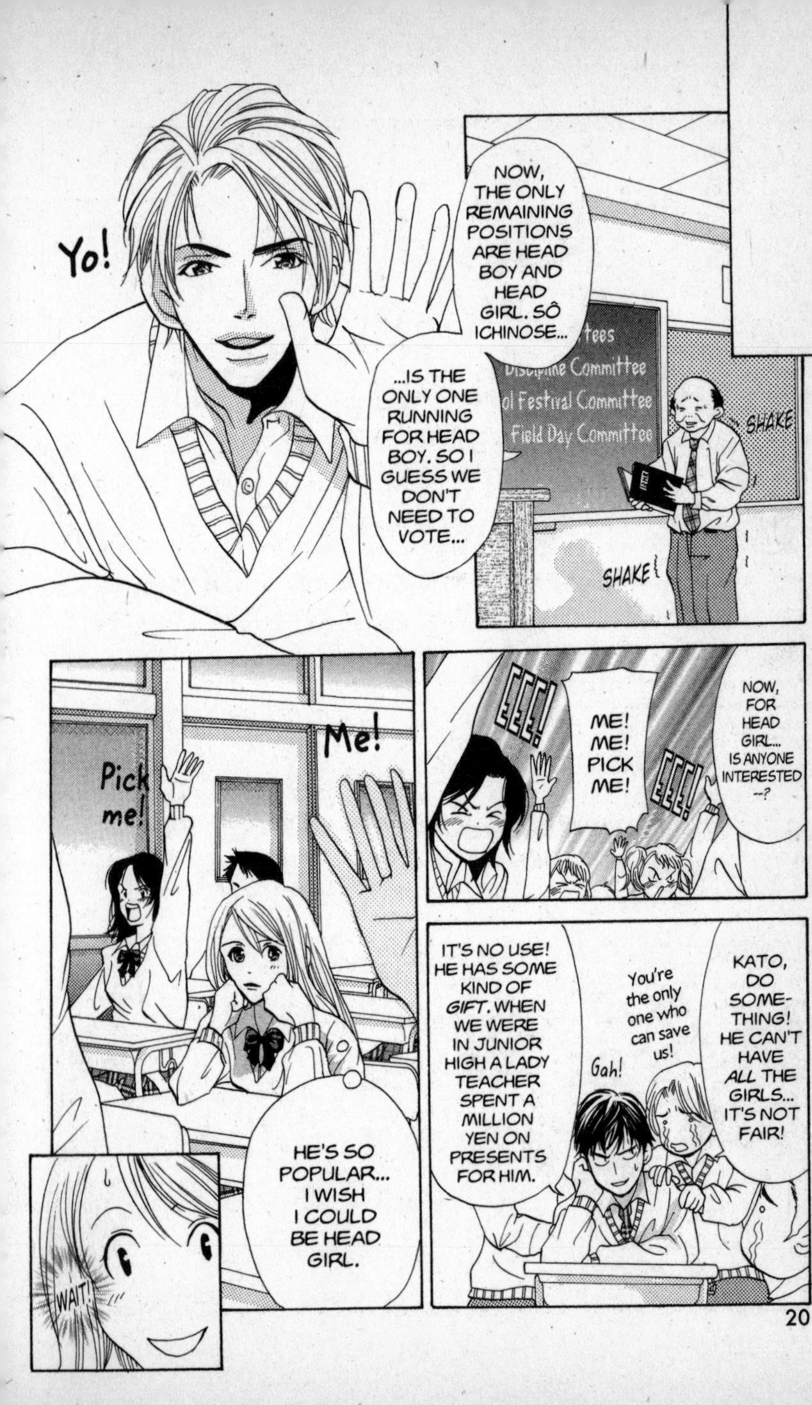
NOW, THE ONLY REMAINING POSITIONS ARE HEAD BOY AND HEAD GIRL. SÔ ICHINOSE...
...IS THE ONLY ONE RUNNING FOR HEAD BOY. SO I GUESS WE DON'T NEED TO VOTE...
SHAKE
SHAKE
Discipline Committee
ol Festival Committee
Field Day Committee
Yo!
NOW, FOR HEAD GIRL... IS ANYONE INTERESTED --?
EEE!
ME! ME! PICK ME!
EEE!
Me!
Pick me!
KATO, DO SOME-THING! HE CAN'T HAVE ALL THE GIRLS... IT'S NOT FAIR!
You're the only one who can save us!
Gah!
IT'S NO USE! HE HAS SOME KIND OF GIFT. WHEN WE WERE IN JUNIOR HIGH A LADY TEACHER SPENT A MILLION YEN ON PRESENTS FOR HIM.
HE'S SO POPULAR... I WISH I COULD BE HEAD GIRL.
WAIT!

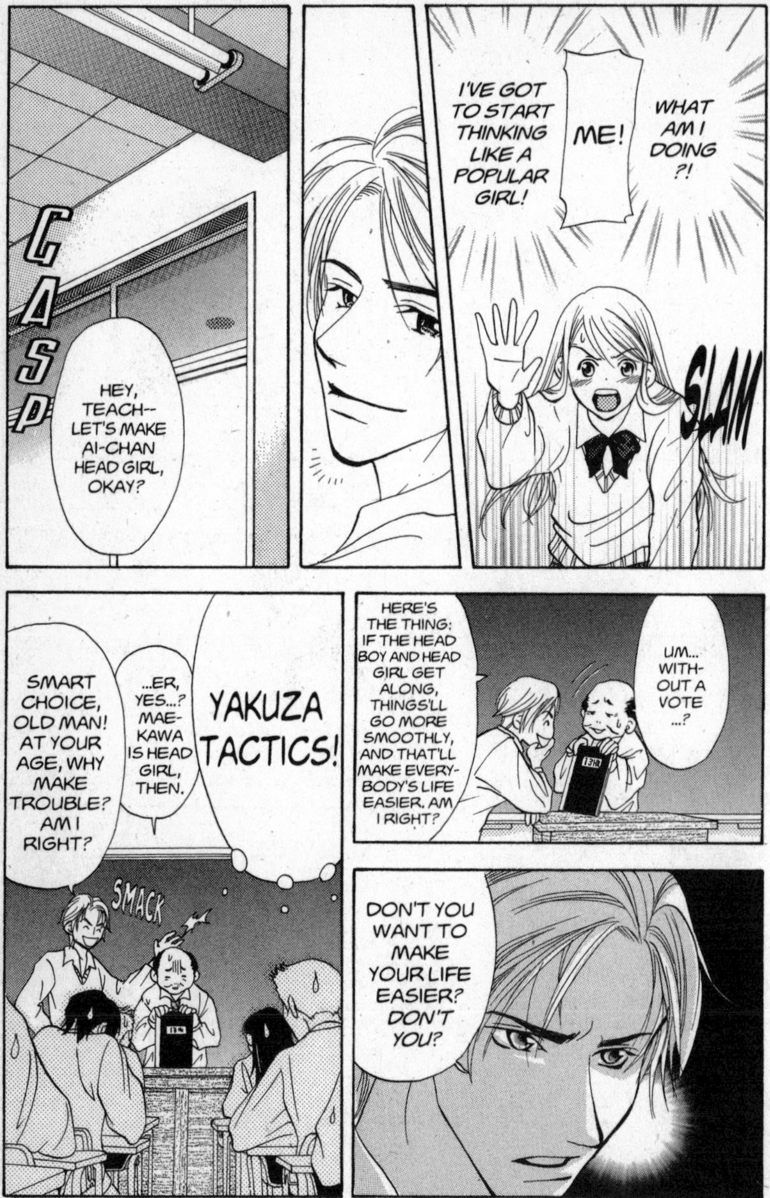
WHAT AM I DOING?!
ME!
I'VE GOT TO START THINKING LIKE A POPULAR GIRL!
SLAM
GASP
HEY, TEACH-- LET'S MAKE AI-CHAN HEAD GIRL, OKAY?
UM... WITH-OUT A VOTE ...?
HERE'S THE THING: IF THE HEAD BOY AND HEAD GIRL GET ALONG, THINGS'LL GO MORE SMOOTHLY, AND THAT'LL MAKE EVERY-BODY'S LIFE EASIER. AM I RIGHT?
DON'T YOU WANT TO MAKE YOUR LIFE EASIER? DON'T YOU?
YAKUZA TACTICS!
...ER, YES...? MAE-KAWA IS HEAD GIRL, THEN.
SMART CHOICE, OLD MAN! AT YOUR AGE, WHY MAKE TROUBLE? AM I RIGHT?
SMACK

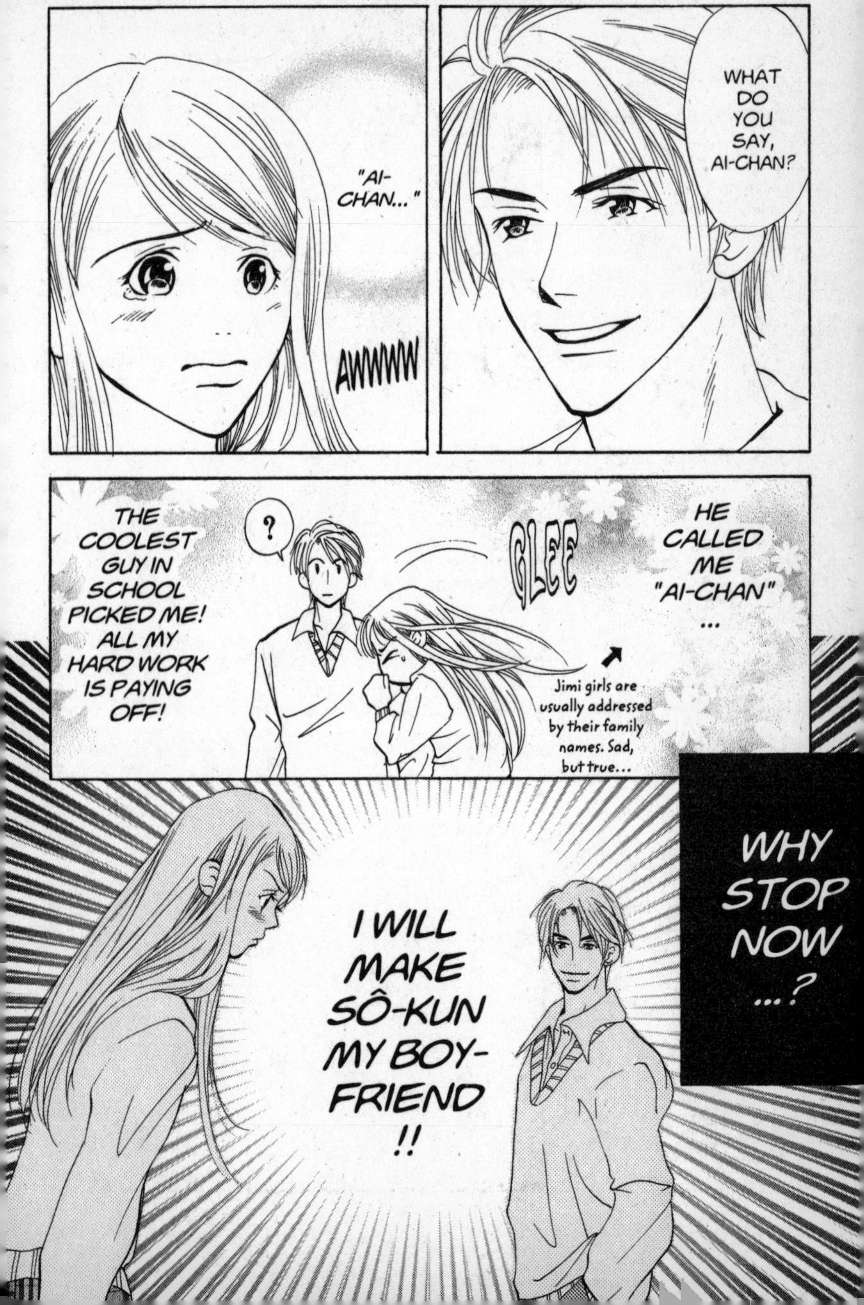
WHAT DO YOU SAY, AI-CHAN?
"AI-CHAN..."
AWWWW
HE CALLED ME "AI-CHAN"...
Jimi girls are usually addressed by their family names. Sad, but true...
GLEE
?
THE COOLEST GUY IN SCHOOL PICKED ME! ALL MY HARD WORK IS PAYING OFF!
WHY STOP NOW...?
I WILL MAKE SÔ-KUN MY BOY-FRIEND!!

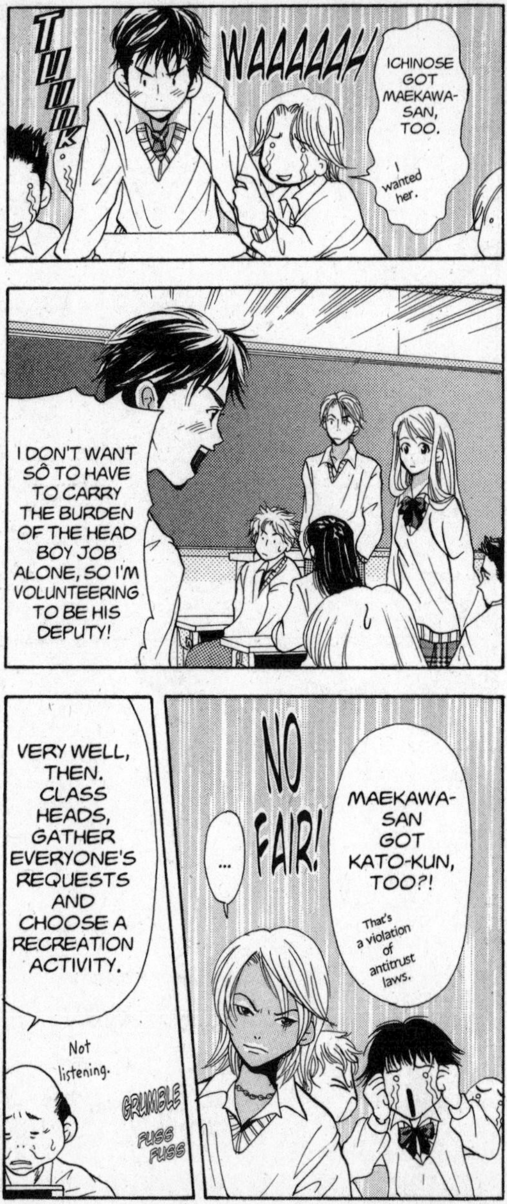
THUNK
WAAAAAH
ICHINOSE GOT MAEKAWA-SAN, TOO.
I wanted her.
I DON'T WANT SÔ TO HAVE TO CARRY THE BURDEN OF THE HEAD BOY JOB ALONE, SO I'M VOLUNTEERING TO BE HIS DEPUTY!
MAEKAWA-SAN GOT KATO-KUN, TOO?!
That's a violation of antitrust laws.
NO FAIR!
...
VERY WELL, THEN. CLASS HEADS, GATHER EVERYONE'S REQUESTS AND CHOOSE A RECREATION ACTIVITY.
Not listening.
GRUMBLE
FUSS FUSS

Special Event!
Exciting Encounters!
An Encyclopedia of Creatures

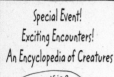

Put yourself in a mudskipper's frame of mind, and let's go!!

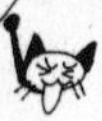

Part 1

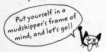

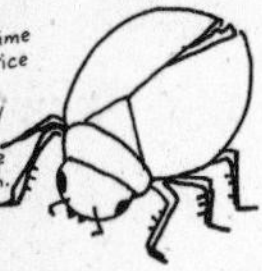
By the time you notice it, it's already dead on the porch.

Beetle (insect)

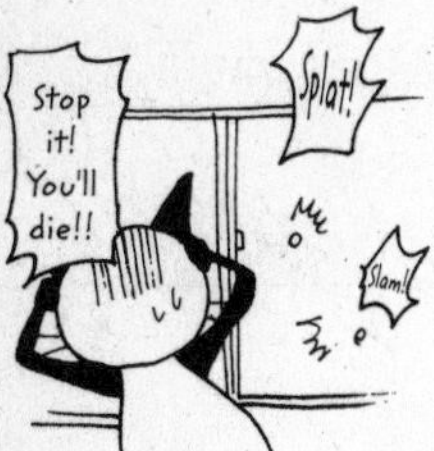
Stop it! You'll die!!
Splat!
Slam!

If you leave your porch light on at night during the summer, you'll see these insects launching **desperate attacks.** I suppose I could learn from their **commando spirits.**

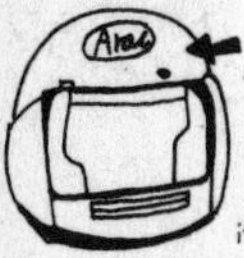

The brave one who attacked my helmet is still splattered where it hit. Too bad... it was an expensive helmet...

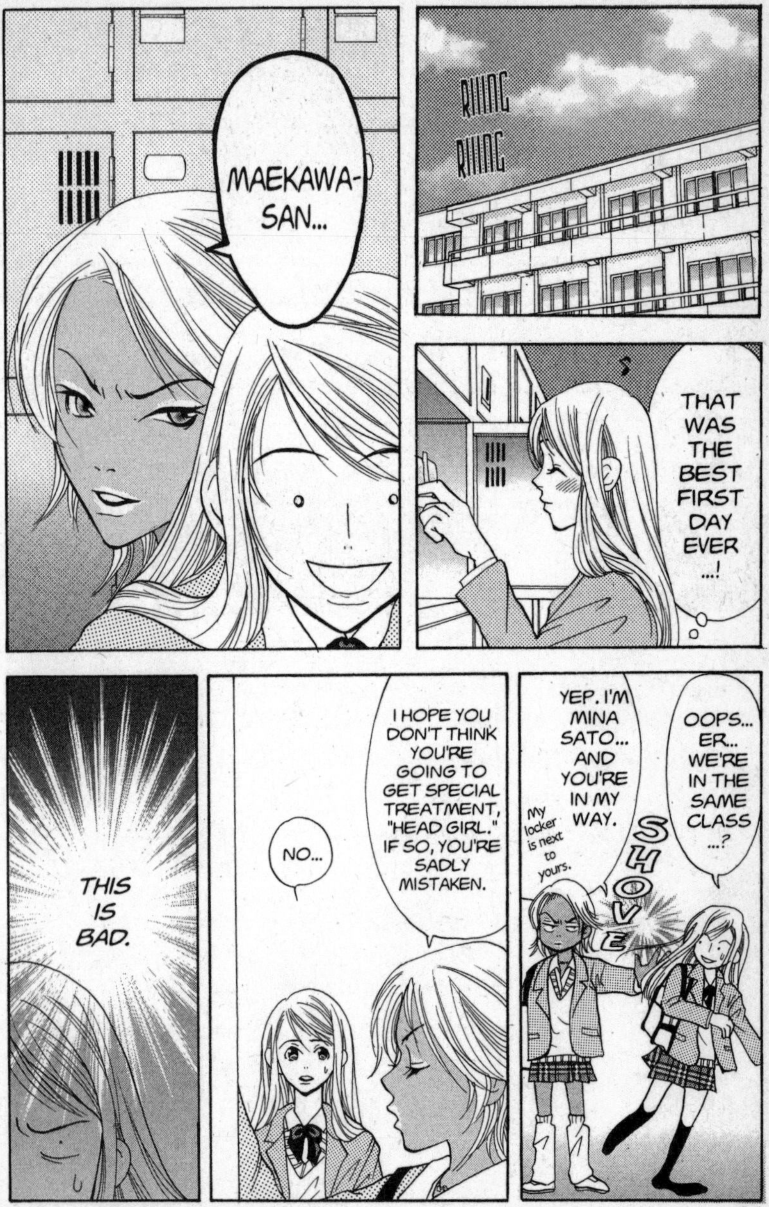
RIIING
RIIING
THAT WAS THE BEST FIRST DAY EVER ...!
MAEKAWA-SAN...
OOPS... ER... WE'RE IN THE SAME CLASS ...?
YEP. I'M MINA SATO... AND YOU'RE IN MY WAY.
My locker is next to yours.
SHOVE
I HOPE YOU DON'T THINK YOU'RE GOING TO GET SPECIAL TREATMENT, "HEAD GIRL." IF SO, YOU'RE SADLY MISTAKEN.
NO...
THIS IS BAD.

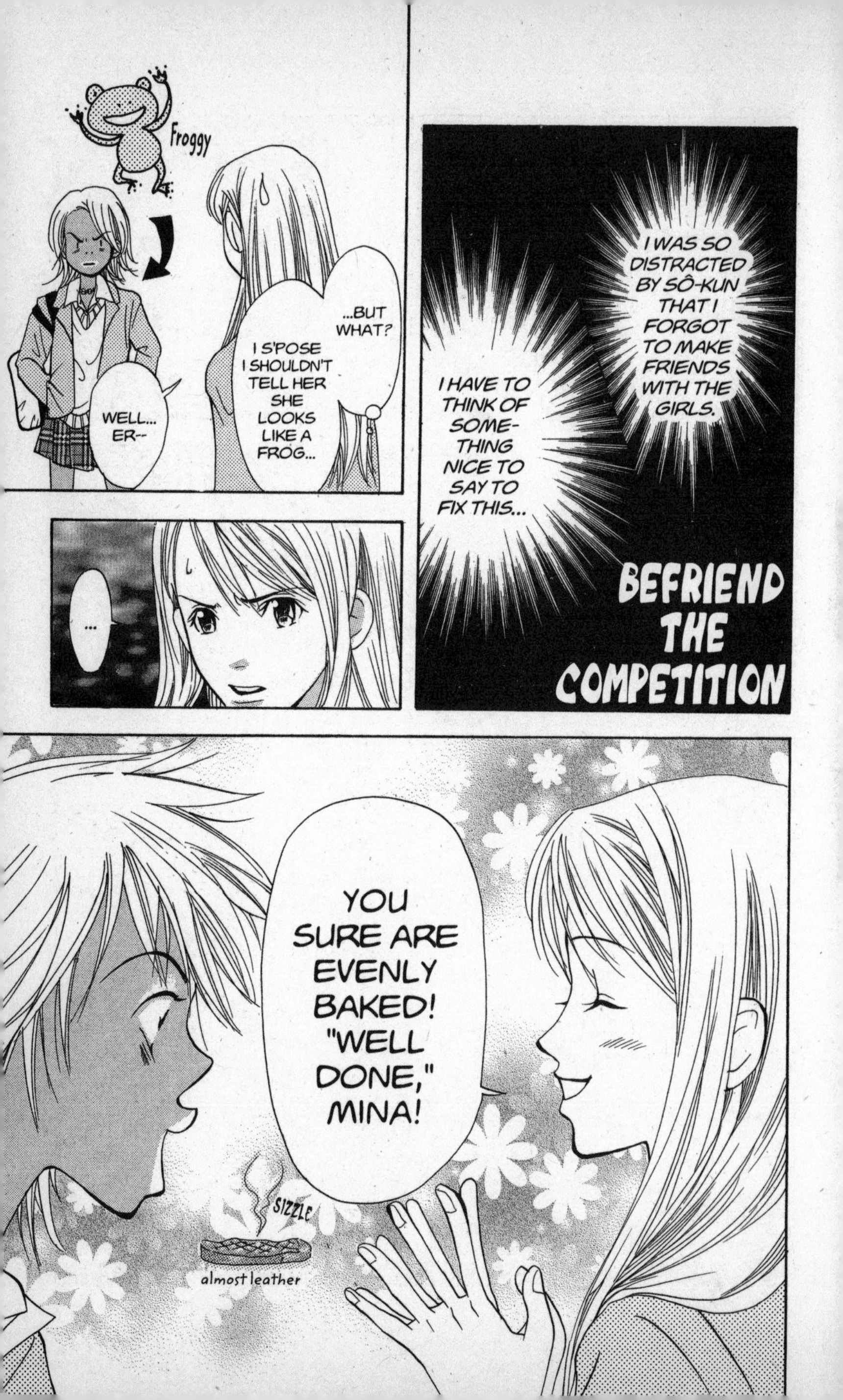
I WAS SO DISTRACTED BY SÔ-KUN THAT I FORGOT TO MAKE FRIENDS WITH THE GIRLS.
I HAVE TO THINK OF SOME-THING NICE TO SAY TO FIX THIS...
BEFRIEND THE COMPETITION
...BUT WHAT?
I S'POSE I SHOULDN'T TELL HER SHE LOOKS LIKE A FROG...
Froggy
WELL... ER--
...
YOU SURE ARE EVENLY BAKED! "WELL DONE," MINA!
SIZZLE
almost leather

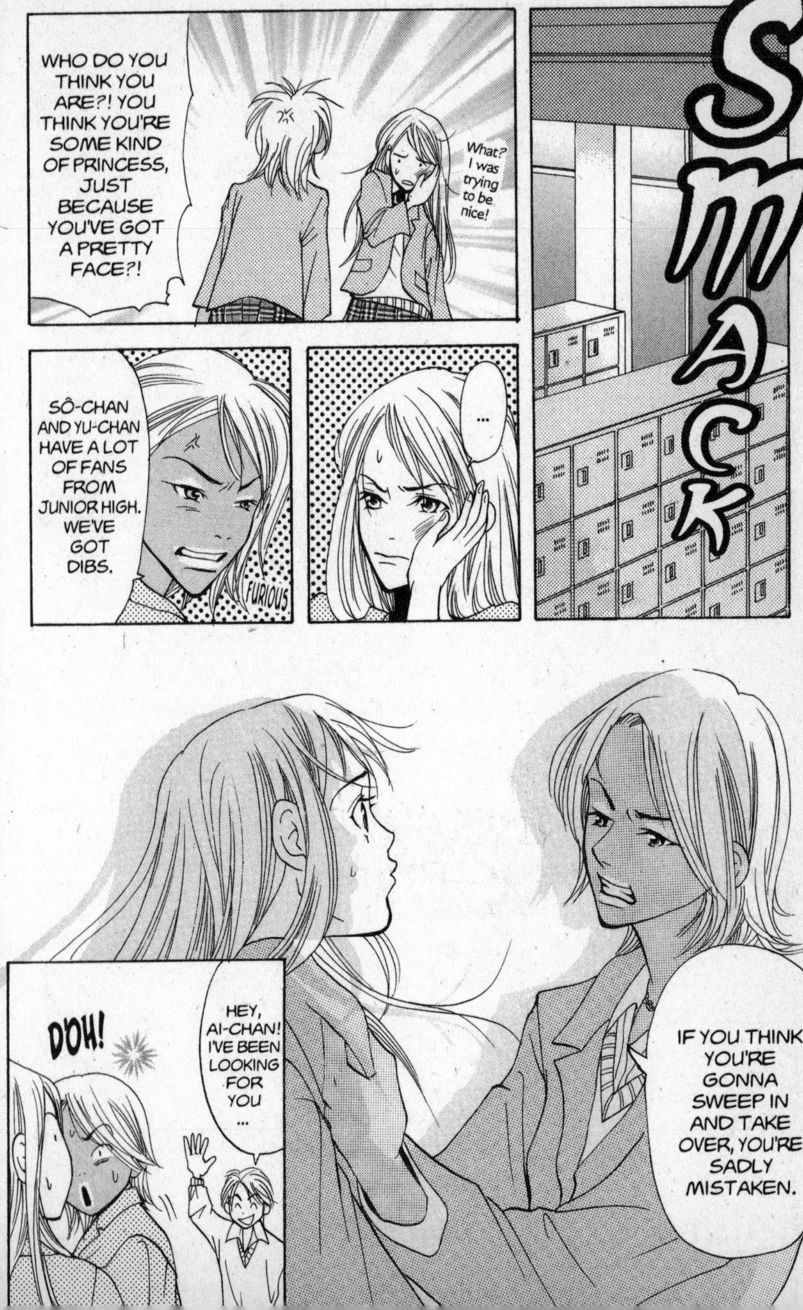
SMACK
What? I was trying to be nice!
WHO DO YOU THINK YOU ARE?! YOU THINK YOU'RE SOME KIND OF PRINCESS, JUST BECAUSE YOU'VE GOT A PRETTY FACE?!
...
SÔ-CHAN AND YU-CHAN HAVE A LOT OF FANS FROM JUNIOR HIGH. WE'VE GOT DIBS.
FURIOUS
IF YOU THINK YOU'RE GONNA SWEEP IN AND TAKE OVER, YOU'RE SADLY MISTAKEN.
HEY, AI-CHAN! I'VE BEEN LOOKING FOR YOU ...
D'OH!

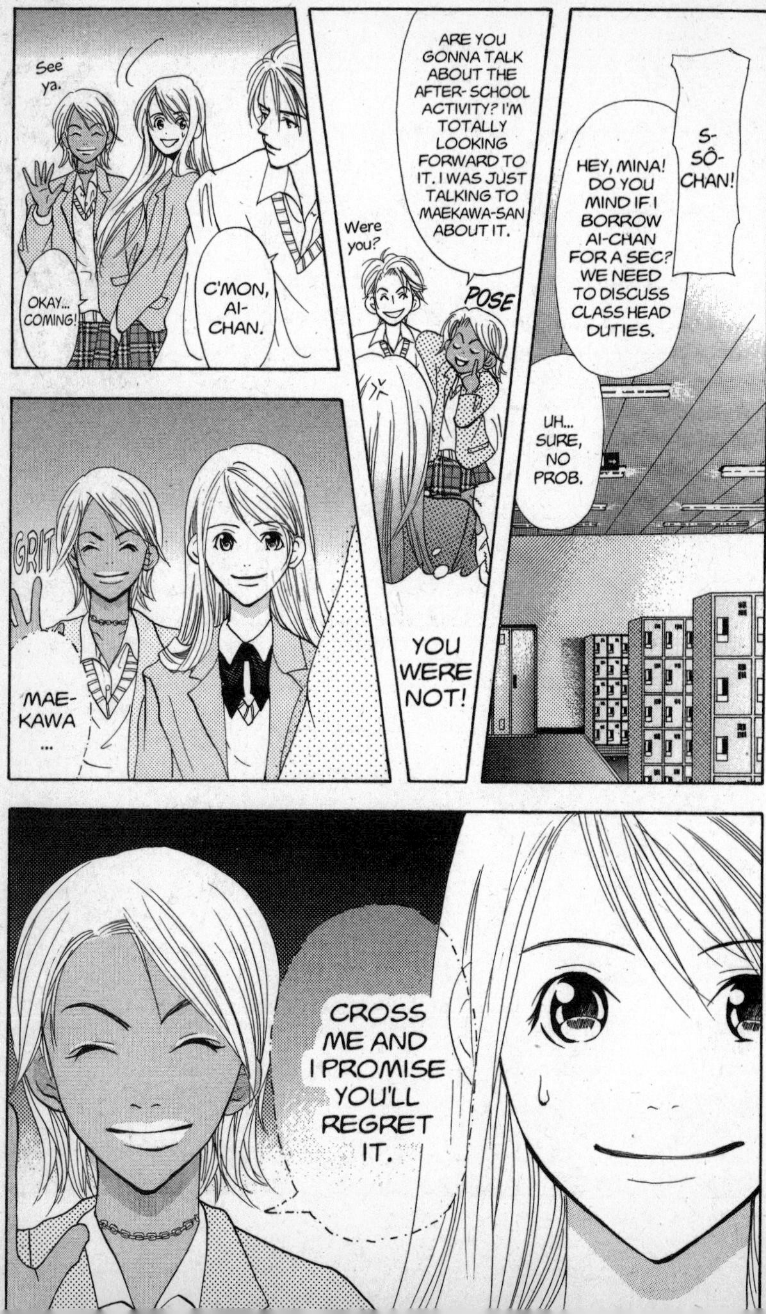
S-SÔ-CHAN!
HEY, MINA! DO YOU MIND IF I BORROW AI-CHAN FOR A SEC? WE NEED TO DISCUSS CLASS HEAD DUTIES.
UH... SURE, NO PROB.
ARE YOU GONNA TALK ABOUT THE AFTER-SCHOOL ACTIVITY? I'M TOTALLY LOOKING FORWARD TO IT. I WAS JUST TALKING TO MAEKAWA-SAN ABOUT IT.
POSE
Were you?
YOU WERE NOT!
See ya.
C'MON, AI-CHAN.
OKAY... COMING!
GRIT
MAE-KAWA ...
CROSS ME AND I PROMISE YOU'LL REGRET IT.

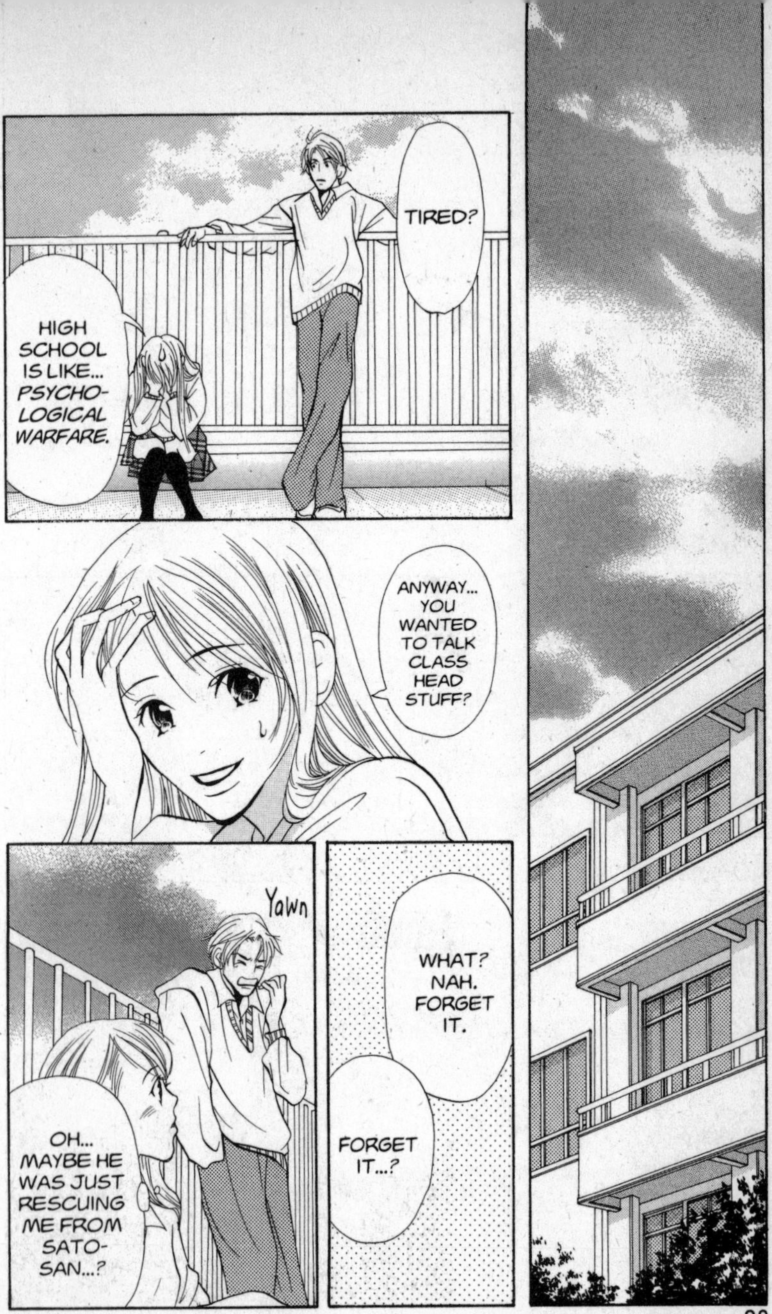
TIRED?
HIGH SCHOOL IS LIKE... PSYCHOLOGICAL WARFARE.
ANYWAY... YOU WANTED TO TALK CLASS HEAD STUFF?
WHAT? NAH. FORGET IT.
FORGET IT...?
Yawn
OH... MAYBE HE WAS JUST RESCUING ME FROM SATO-SAN...?

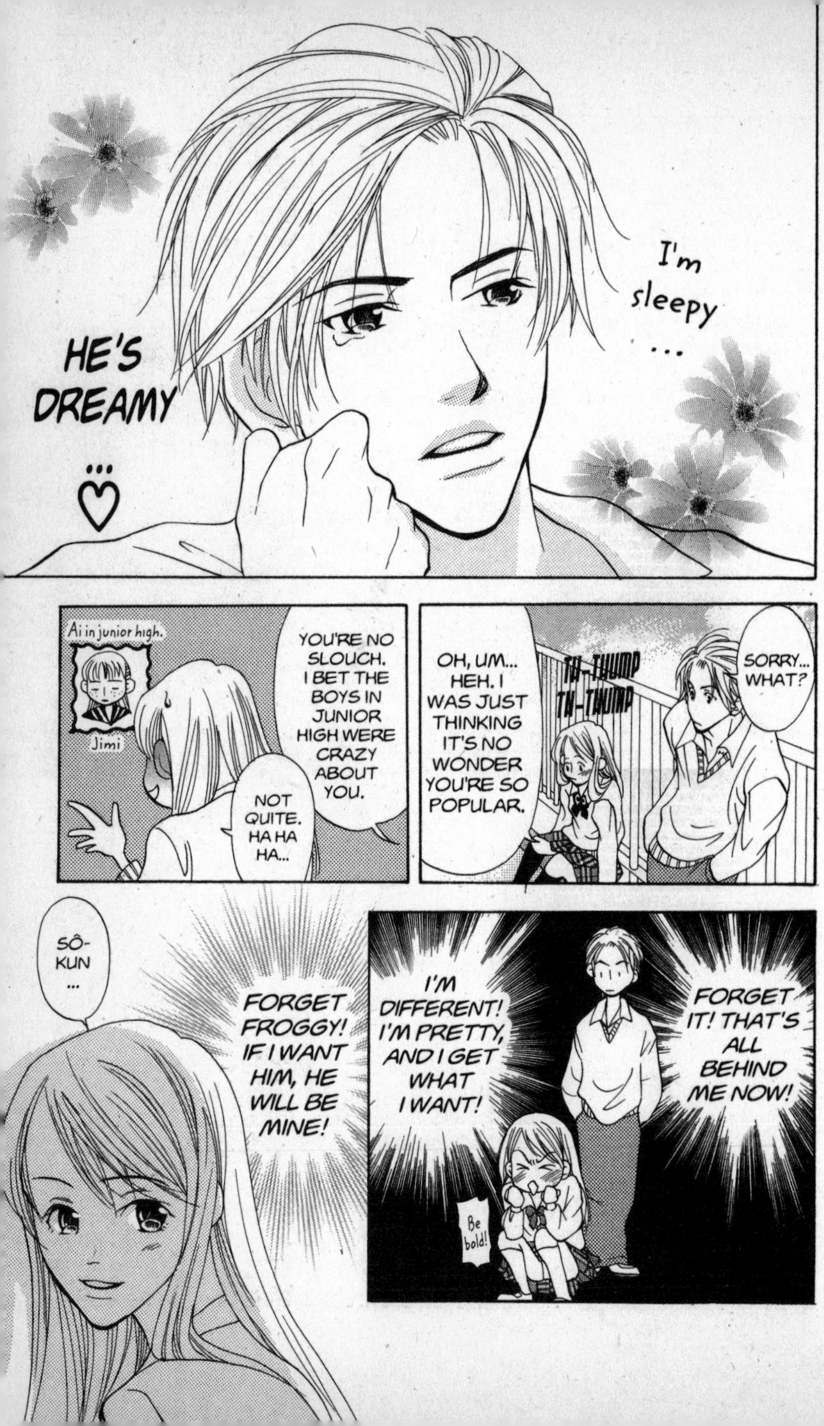
I'm sleepy ...
HE'S DREAMY ... ♡
SORRY... WHAT?
TH-THUMP TH-THUMP
OH, UM... HEH. I WAS JUST THINKING IT'S NO WONDER YOU'RE SO POPULAR.
YOU'RE NO SLOUCH. I BET THE BOYS IN JUNIOR HIGH WERE CRAZY ABOUT YOU.
Ai in junior high.
Jimi
NOT QUITE. HA HA HA...
FORGET IT! THAT'S ALL BEHIND ME NOW!
I'M DIFFERENT! I'M PRETTY, AND I GET WHAT I WANT!
Be bold!
FORGET FROGGY! IF I WANT HIM, HE WILL BE MINE!
SÔ-KUN ...

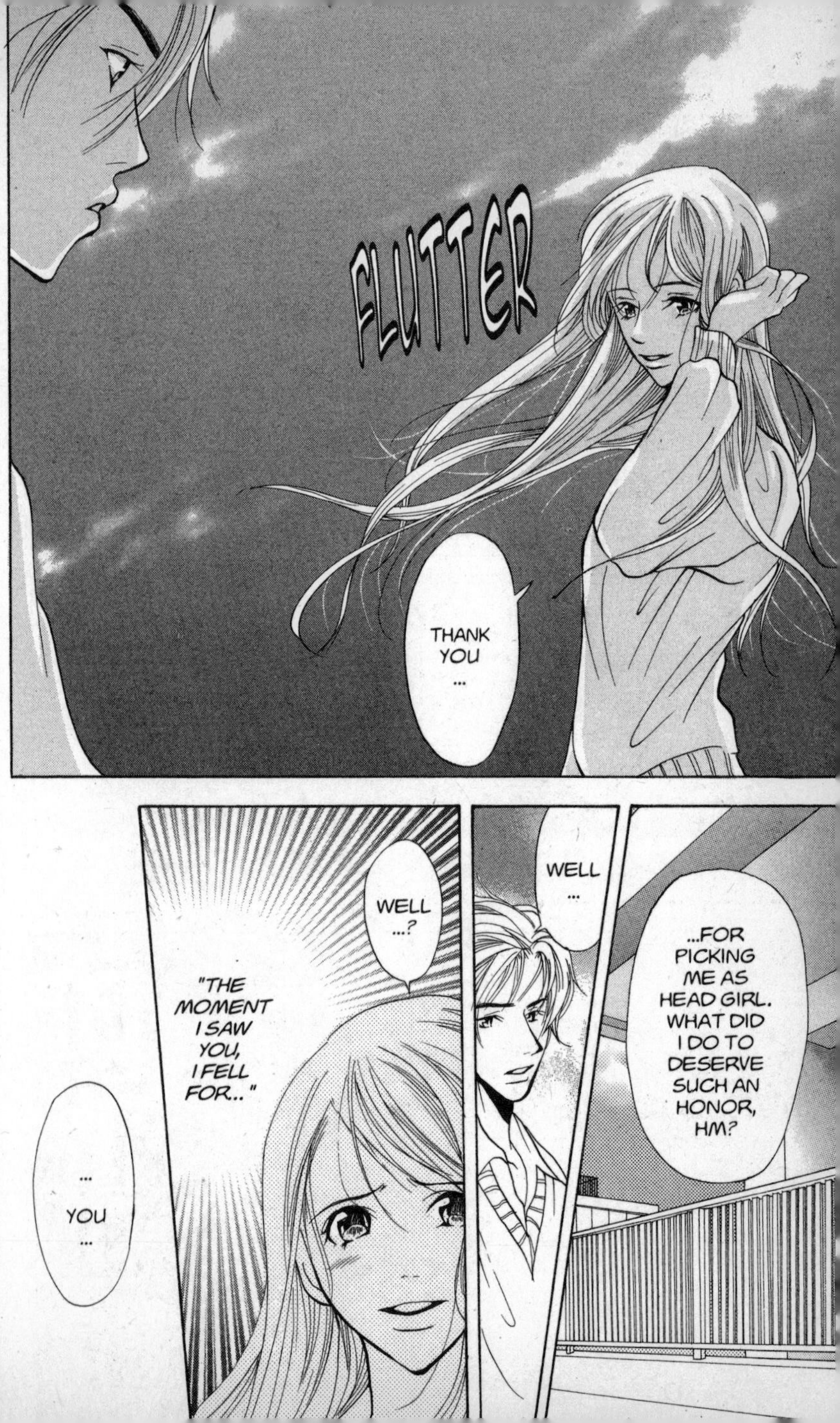
FLUTTER
THANK YOU ...
...FOR PICKING ME AS HEAD GIRL. WHAT DID I DO TO DESERVE SUCH AN HONOR, HM?
WELL ...
WELL ...?
"THE MOMENT I SAW YOU, I FELL FOR..."
... YOU ...

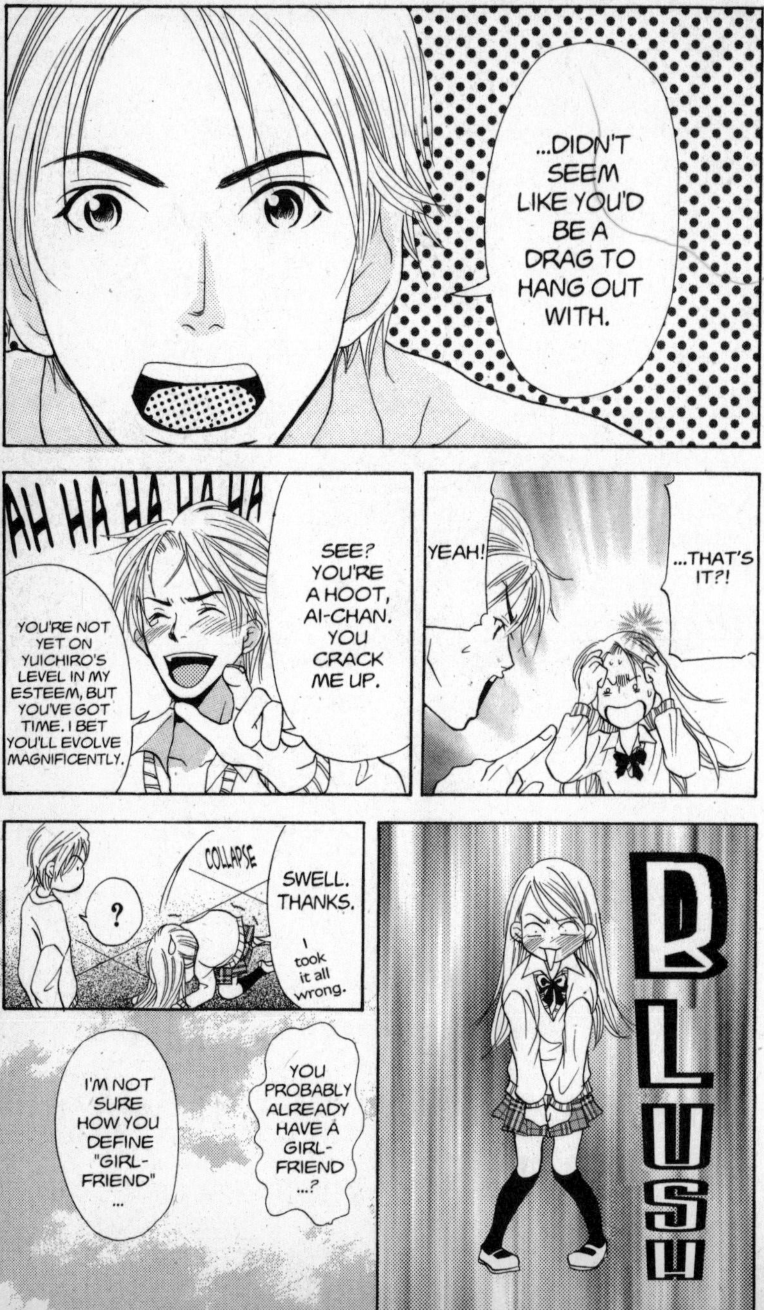

...DIDN'T SEEM LIKE YOU'D BE A DRAG TO HANG OUT WITH.
...THAT'S IT?!
YEAH!
AH HA HA HA HA
SEE? YOU'RE A HOOT, AI-CHAN. YOU CRACK ME UP.
YOU'RE NOT YET ON YUICHIRO'S LEVEL IN MY ESTEEM, BUT YOU'VE GOT TIME. I BET YOU'LL EVOLVE MAGNIFICENTLY.
BLUSH
SWELL. THANKS.
I took it all wrong.
COLLAPSE
?
YOU PROBABLY ALREADY HAVE A GIRL-FRIEND ...?
I'M NOT SURE HOW YOU DEFINE "GIRL-FRIEND" ...

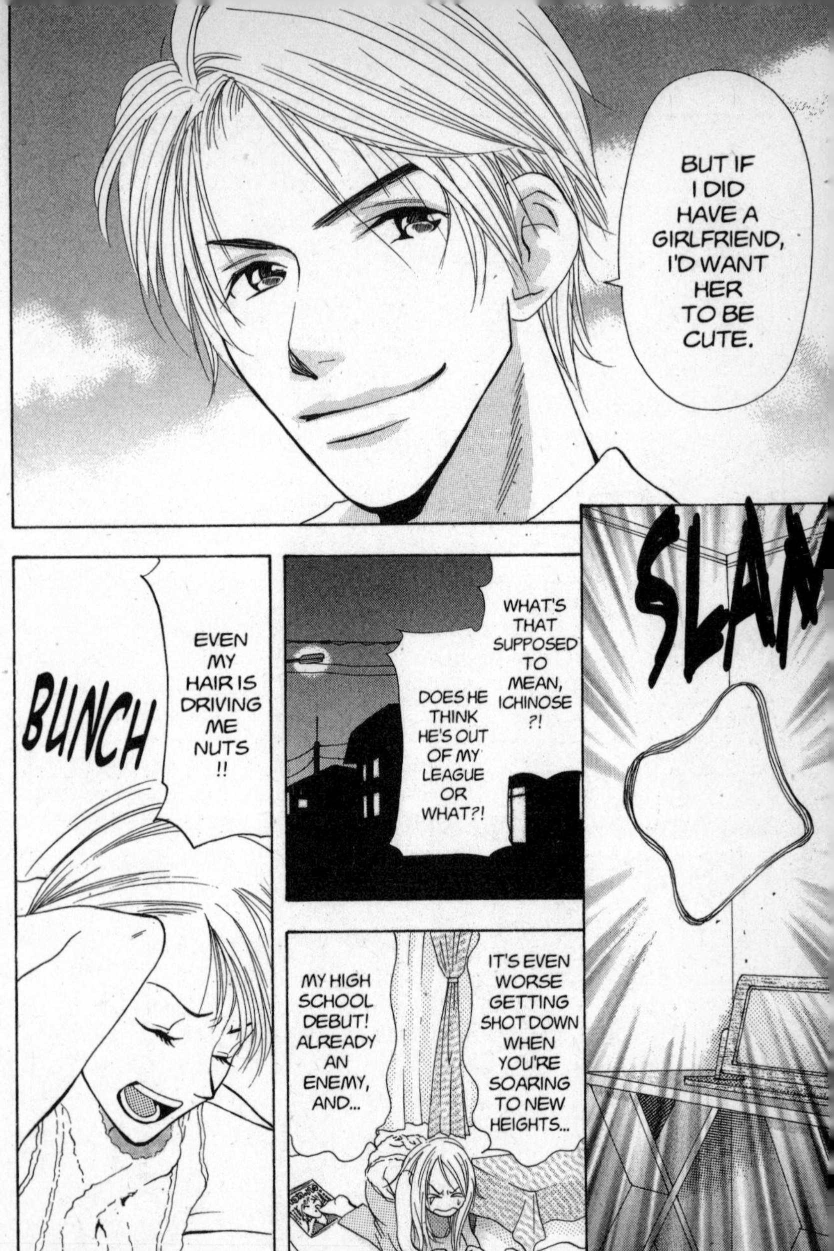
BUT IF I DID HAVE A GIRLFRIEND, I'D WANT HER TO BE CUTE.
SLAM
WHAT'S THAT SUPPOSED TO MEAN, ICHINOSE ?!
DOES HE THINK HE'S OUT OF MY LEAGUE OR WHAT?!
IT'S EVEN WORSE GETTING SHOT DOWN WHEN YOU'RE SOARING TO NEW HEIGHTS...
MY HIGH SCHOOL DEBUT! ALREADY AN ENEMY, AND...
BUNCH
EVEN MY HAIR IS DRIVING ME NUTS !!

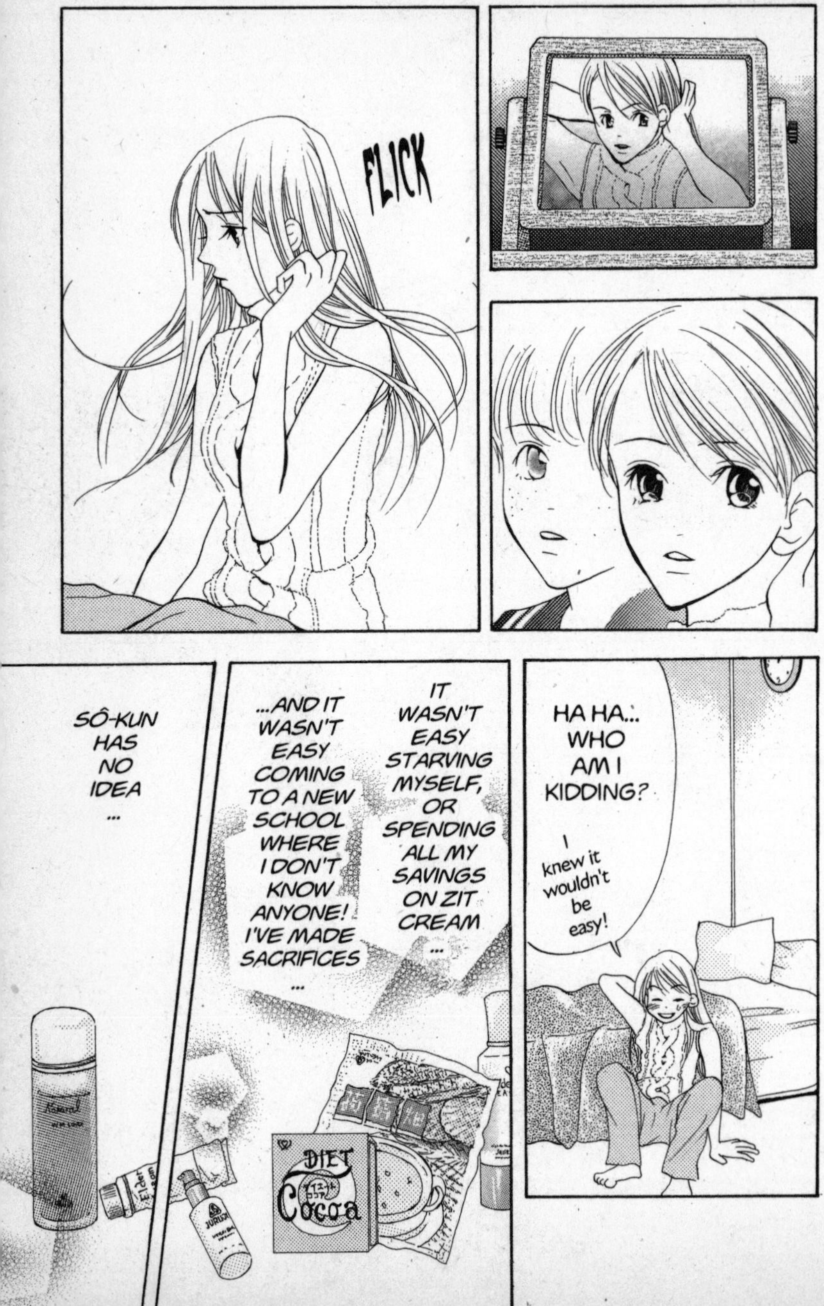
FLICK
HA HA... WHO AM I KIDDING?
I knew it wouldn't be easy!
IT WASN'T EASY STARVING MYSELF, OR SPENDING ALL MY SAVINGS ON ZIT CREAM...
...AND IT WASN'T EASY COMING TO A NEW SCHOOL WHERE I DON'T KNOW ANYONE! I'VE MADE SACRIFICES...
DIET Cocoa
SÔ-KUN HAS NO IDEA...

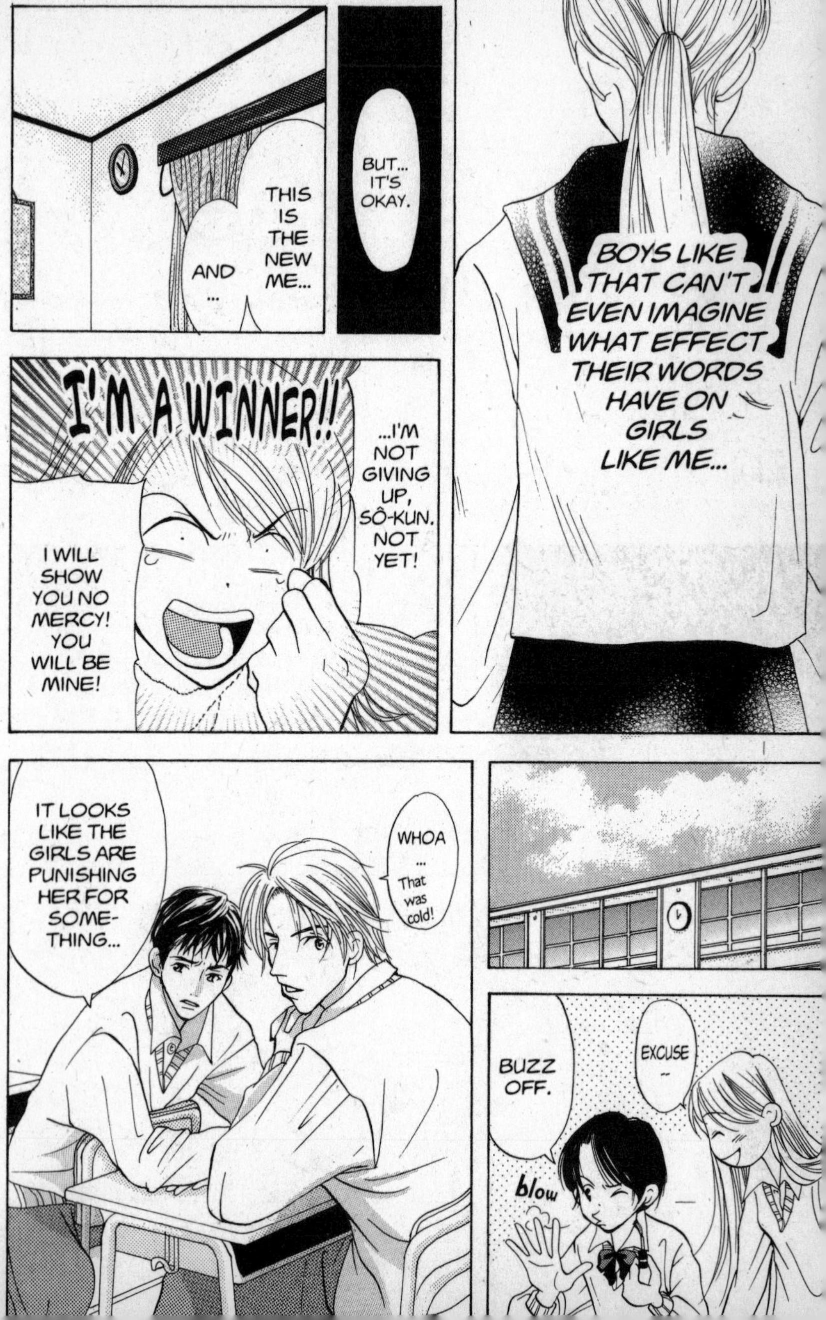
BOYS LIKE THAT CAN'T EVEN IMAGINE WHAT EFFECT THEIR WORDS HAVE ON GIRLS LIKE ME...
BUT... IT'S OKAY.
THIS IS THE NEW ME...
AND ...
...I'M NOT GIVING UP, SÔ-KUN. NOT YET!
I'M A WINNER!!
I WILL SHOW YOU NO MERCY! YOU WILL BE MINE!
EXCUSE --
BUZZ OFF.
blow
WHOA ... That was cold!
IT LOOKS LIKE THE GIRLS ARE PUNISHING HER FOR SOME-THING...

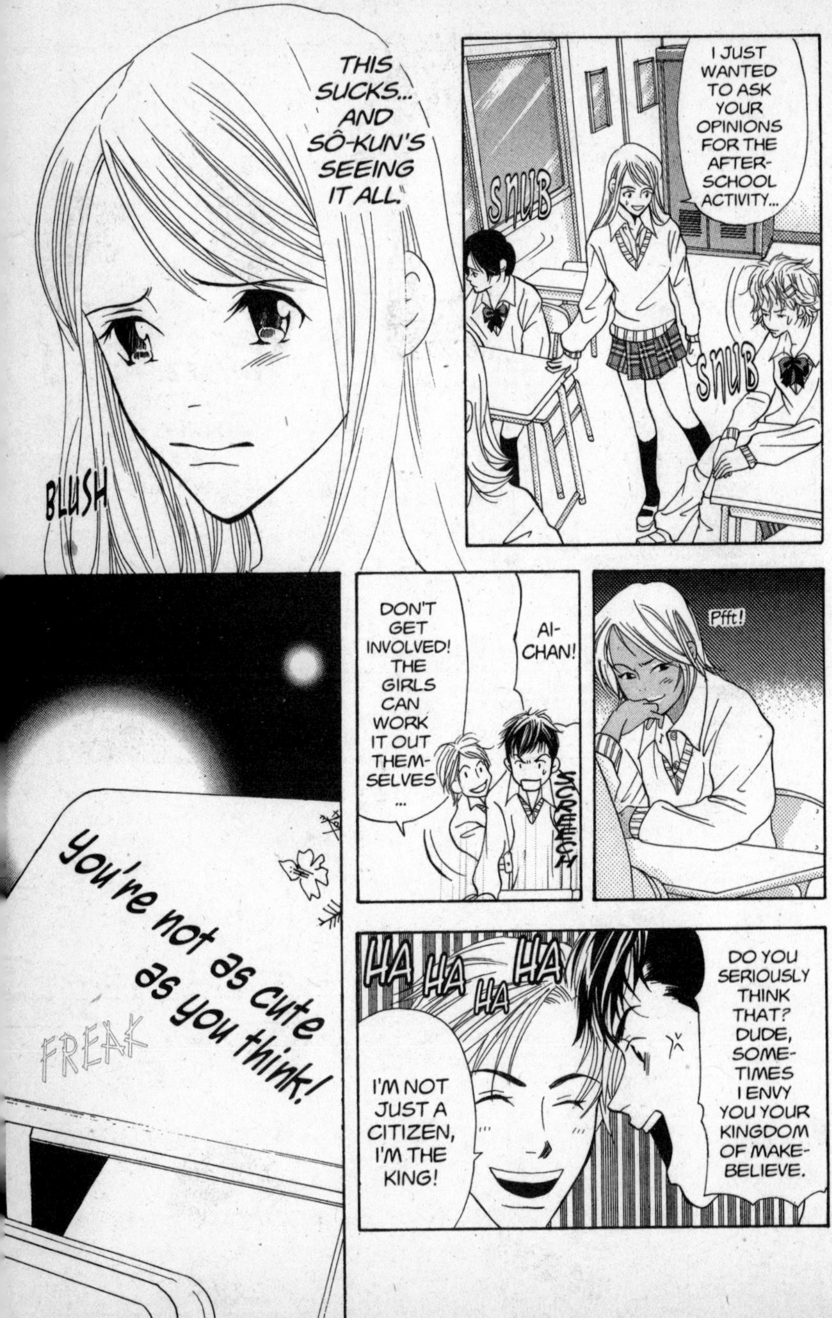

I JUST WANTED TO ASK YOUR OPINIONS FOR THE AFTER-SCHOOL ACTIVITY...
SNUB
SNUB
THIS SUCKS... AND SÔ-KUN'S SEEING IT ALL.
BLUSH
Pfft!
AI-CHAN!
DON'T GET INVOLVED! THE GIRLS CAN WORK IT OUT THEMSELVES ...
SCREECH
HA HA HA HA
DO YOU SERIOUSLY THINK THAT? DUDE, SOMETIMES I ENVY YOU YOUR KINGDOM OF MAKE-BELIEVE.
I'M NOT JUST A CITIZEN, I'M THE KING!
You're not as cute as you think!
FREAK

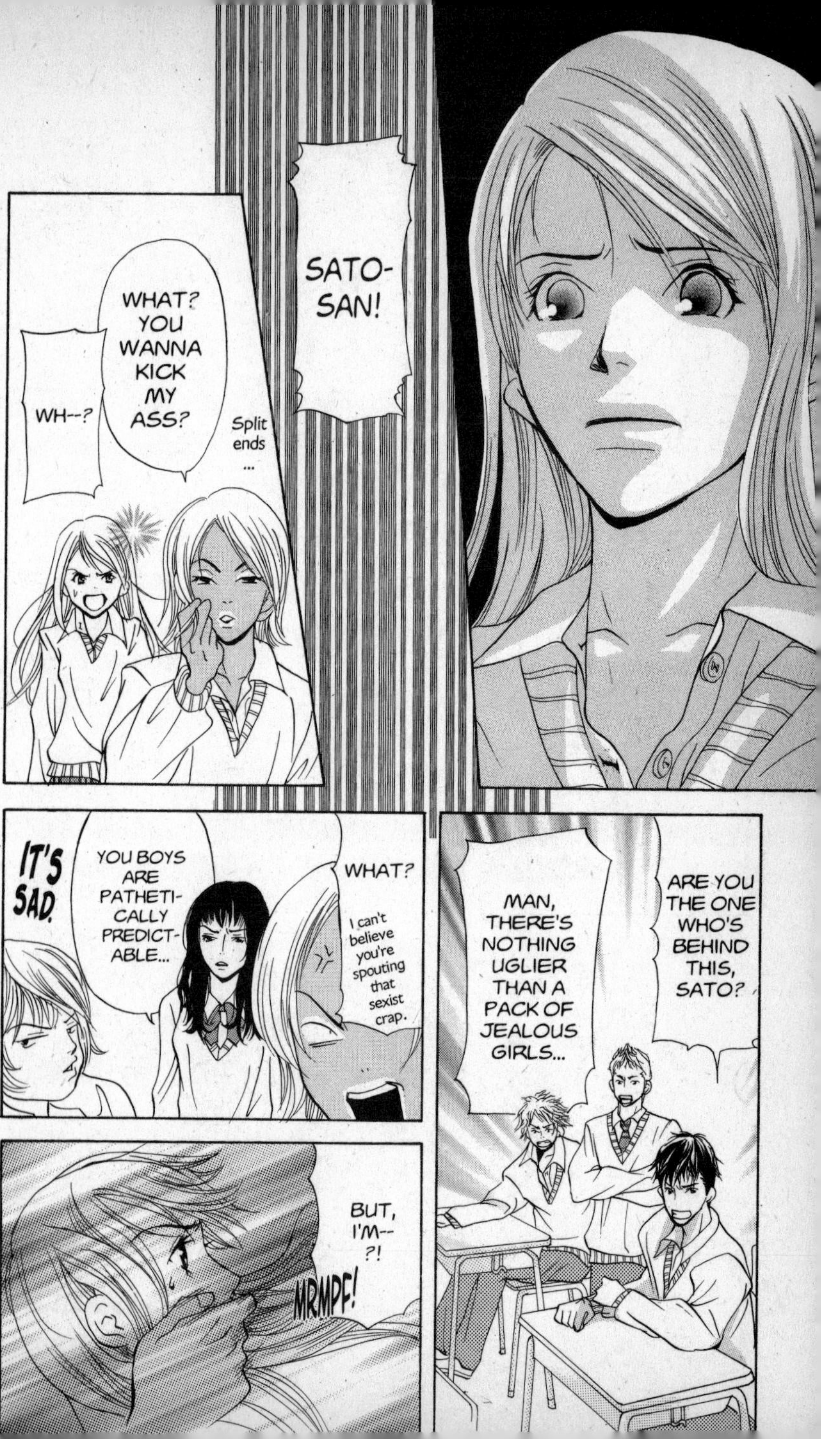
SATO-SAN!
WHAT? YOU WANNA KICK MY ASS?
Split ends ...
WH--?
ARE YOU THE ONE WHO'S BEHIND THIS, SATO?
MAN, THERE'S NOTHING UGLIER THAN A PACK OF JEALOUS GIRLS...
WHAT?
I can't believe you're spouting that sexist crap.
YOU BOYS ARE PATHETICALLY PREDICTABLE...
IT'S SAD.
BUT, I'M-- ?!
MRMPF!

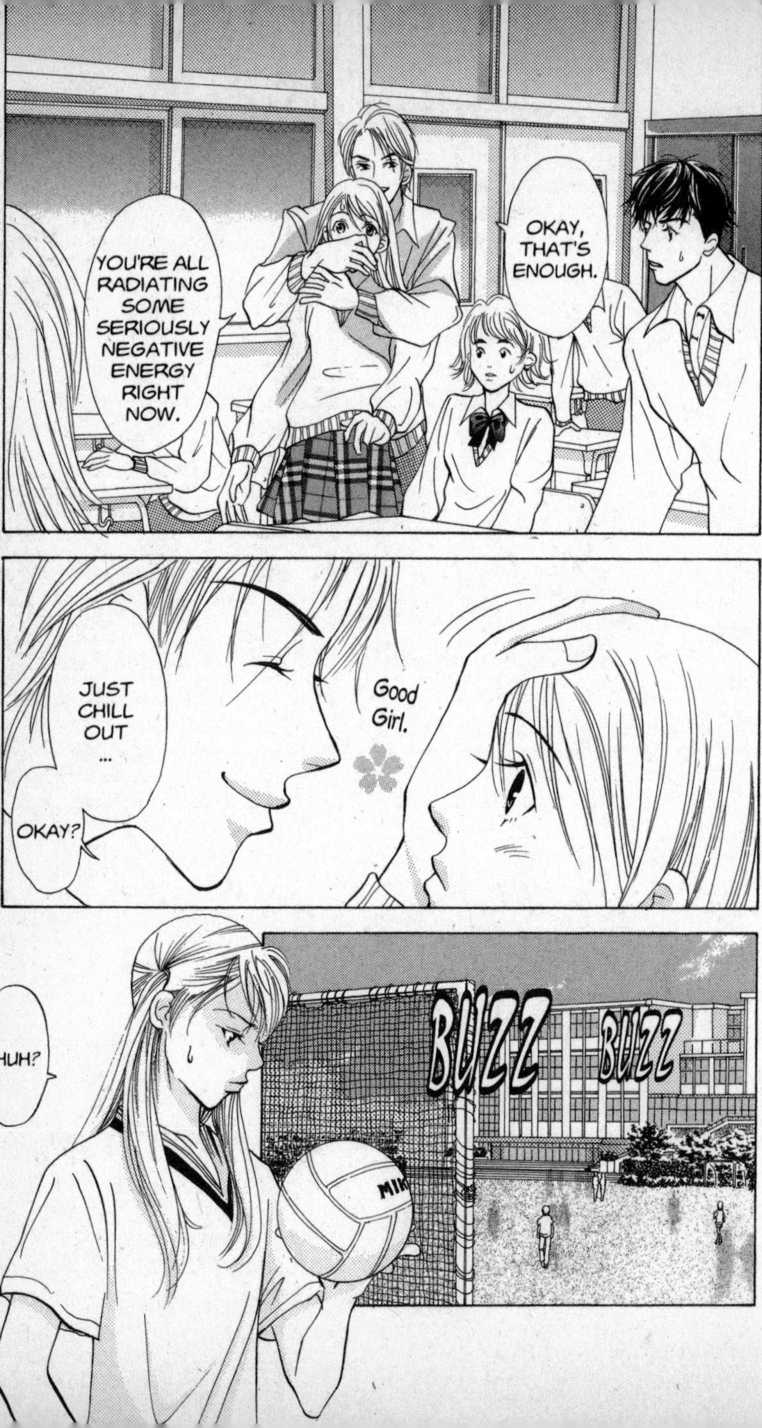
OKAY, THAT'S ENOUGH.
YOU'RE ALL RADIATING SOME SERIOUSLY NEGATIVE ENERGY RIGHT NOW.
Good Girl.
JUST CHILL OUT ...
OKAY?
BUZZ
BUZZ
...HUH?

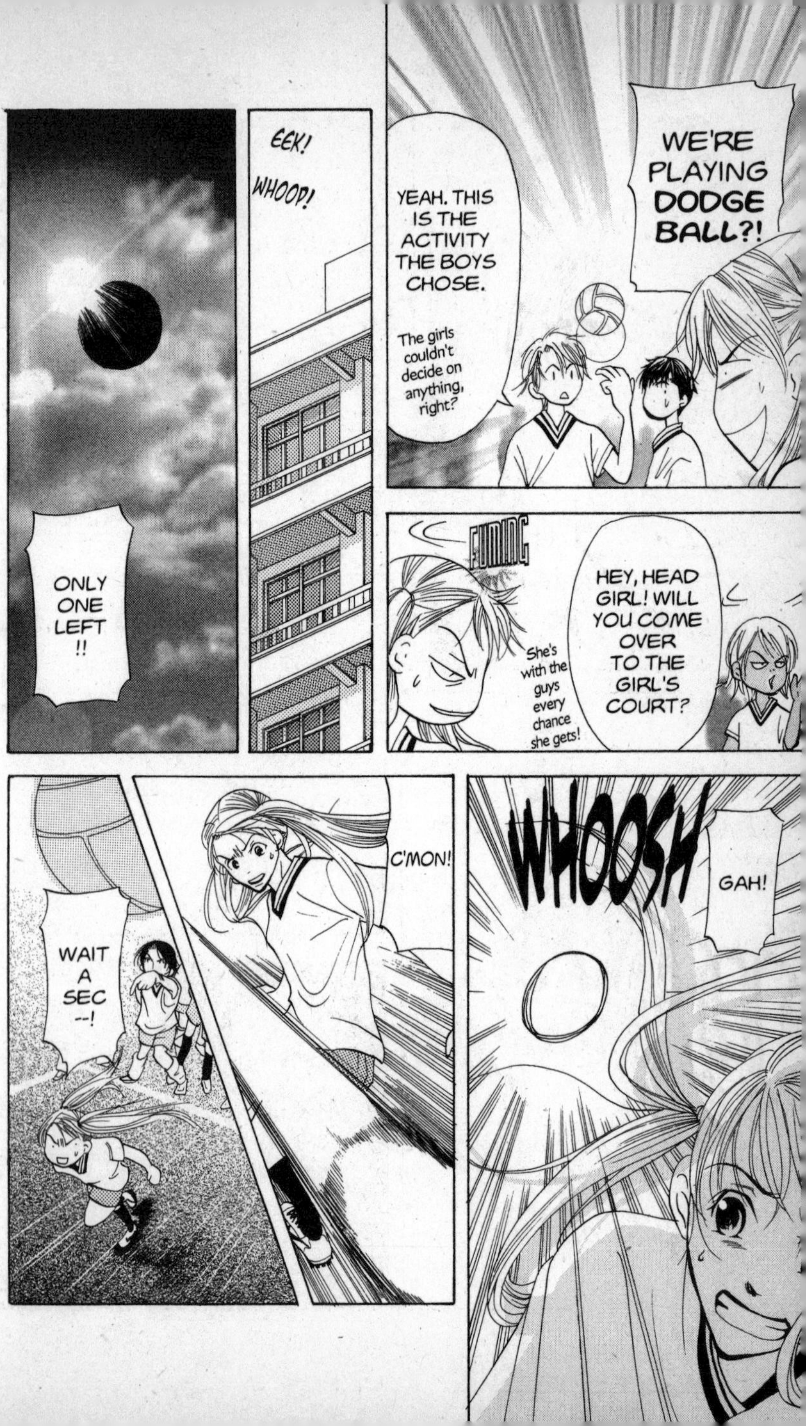
WE'RE PLAYING DODGE BALL?!
YEAH. THIS IS THE ACTIVITY THE BOYS CHOSE.
The girls couldn't decide on anything, right?
HEY, HEAD GIRL! WILL YOU COME OVER TO THE GIRL'S COURT?
FUMING
She's with the guys every chance she gets!
EEK!
WHOOP!
ONLY ONE LEFT !!
GAH!
WHOOSH
C'MON!
WAIT A SEC --!

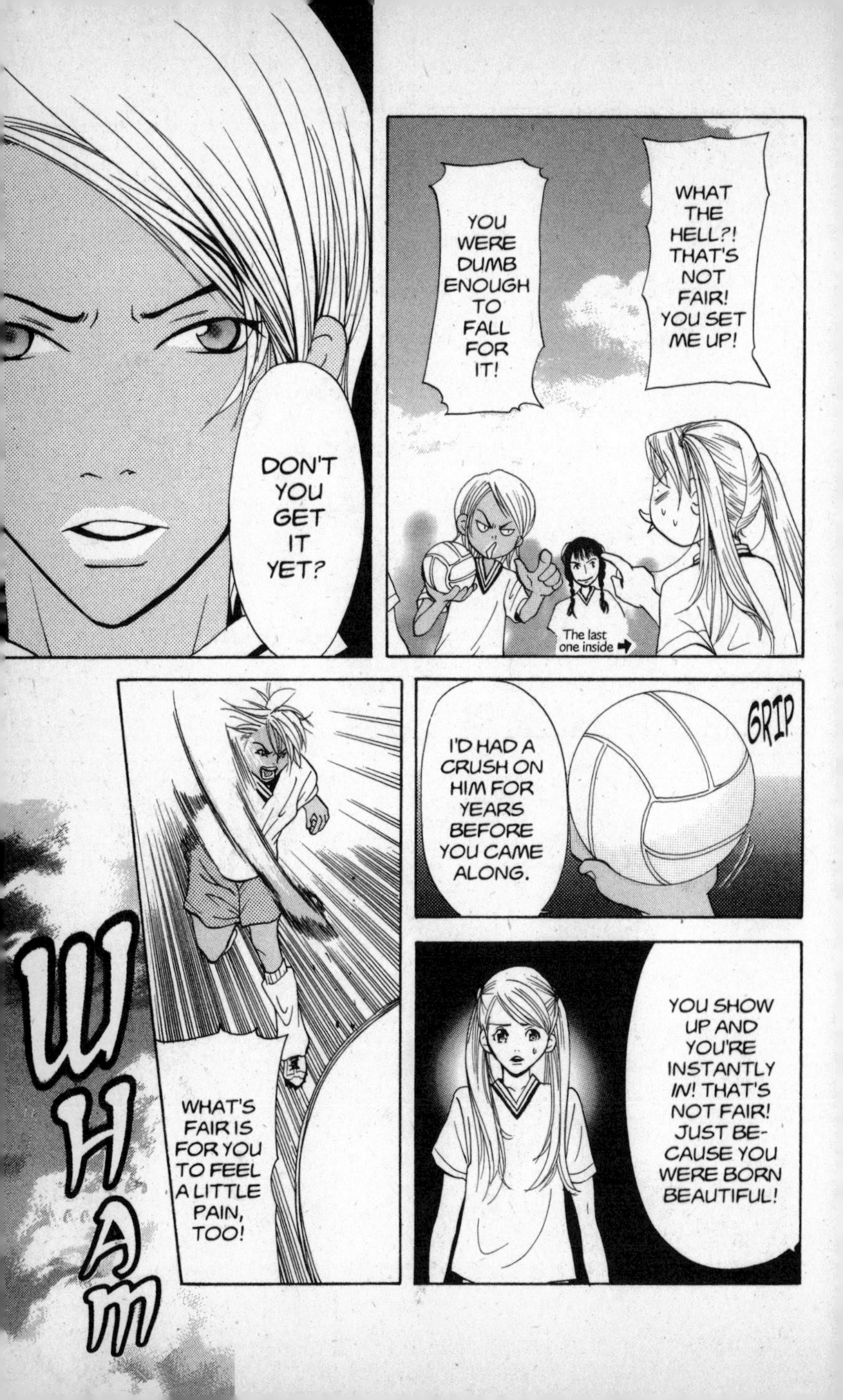
WHAT THE HELL?! THAT'S NOT FAIR! YOU SET ME UP!
YOU WERE DUMB ENOUGH TO FALL FOR IT!
The last one inside
DON'T YOU GET IT YET?
GRIP
I'D HAD A CRUSH ON HIM FOR YEARS BEFORE YOU CAME ALONG.
YOU SHOW UP AND YOU'RE INSTANTLY *IN*! THAT'S NOT FAIR! JUST BECAUSE YOU WERE BORN BEAUTIFUL!
WHAT'S FAIR IS FOR YOU TO FEEL A LITTLE PAIN, TOO!
WHAM

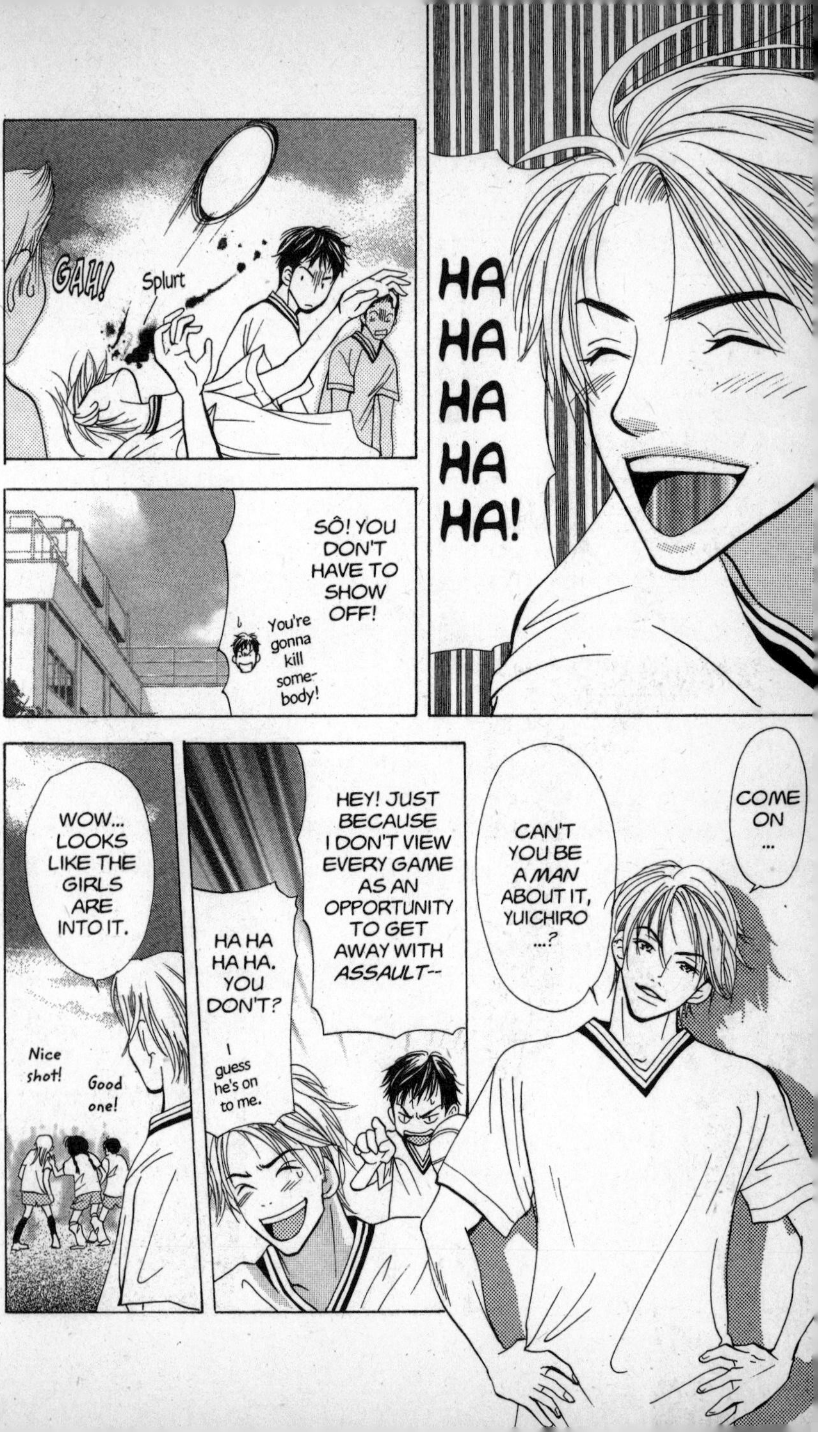
HA HA HA HA HA!
GAH!
Splurt
SÔ! YOU DON'T HAVE TO SHOW OFF!
You're gonna kill some-body!
COME ON ...
CAN'T YOU BE A *MAN* ABOUT IT, YUICHIRO ...?
HEY! JUST BECAUSE I DON'T VIEW EVERY GAME AS AN OPPORTUNITY TO GET AWAY WITH *ASSAULT*--
HA HA HA HA. YOU DON'T?
I guess he's on to me.
WOW... LOOKS LIKE THE GIRLS ARE INTO IT.
Nice shot!
Good one!

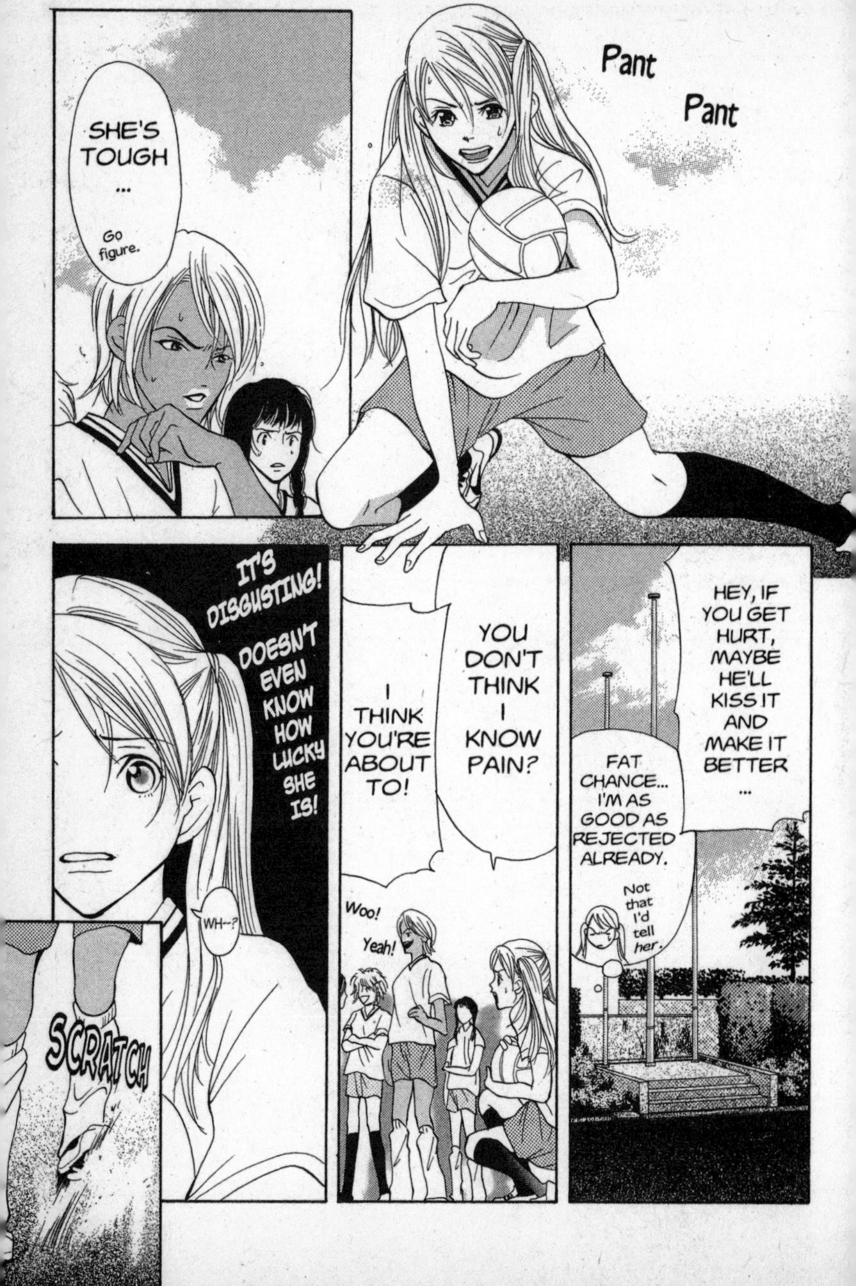
Pant
Pant
SHE'S TOUGH ...
Go figure.
HEY, IF YOU GET HURT, MAYBE HE'LL KISS IT AND MAKE IT BETTER ...
FAT CHANCE... I'M AS GOOD AS REJECTED ALREADY.
Not that I'd tell her.
YOU DON'T THINK I KNOW PAIN?
I THINK YOU'RE ABOUT TO!
Woo!
Yeah!
IT'S DISGUSTING!
DOESN'T EVEN KNOW HOW LUCKY SHE IS!
WH--?
SCRATCH

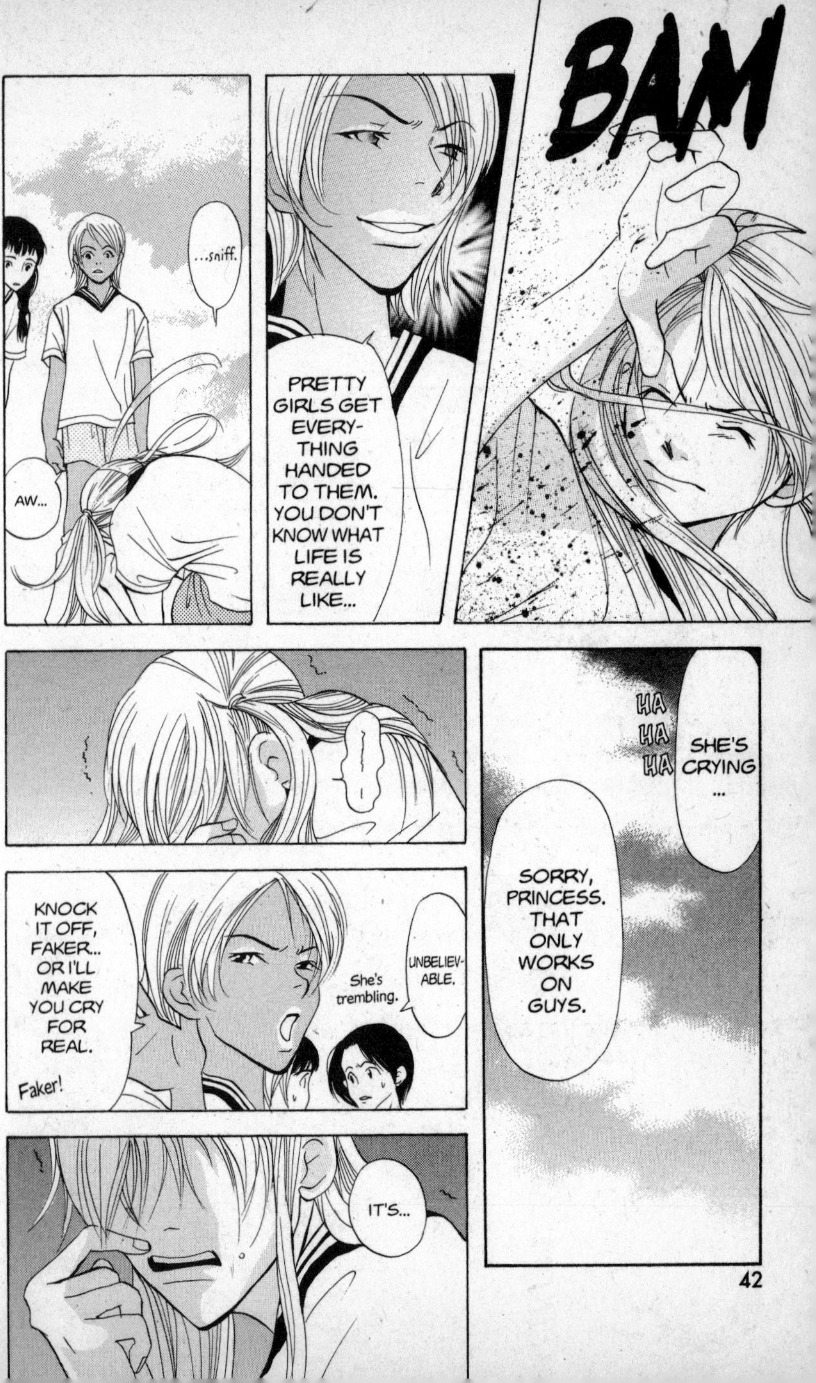
BAM
PRETTY GIRLS GET EVERY-THING HANDED TO THEM. YOU DON'T KNOW WHAT LIFE IS REALLY LIKE...
...sniff.
AW...
SHE'S CRYING ...
HA HA HA
SORRY, PRINCESS. THAT ONLY WORKS ON GUYS.
UNBELIEV-ABLE.
She's trembling.
KNOCK IT OFF, FAKER... OR I'LL MAKE YOU CRY FOR REAL.
Faker!
IT'S...

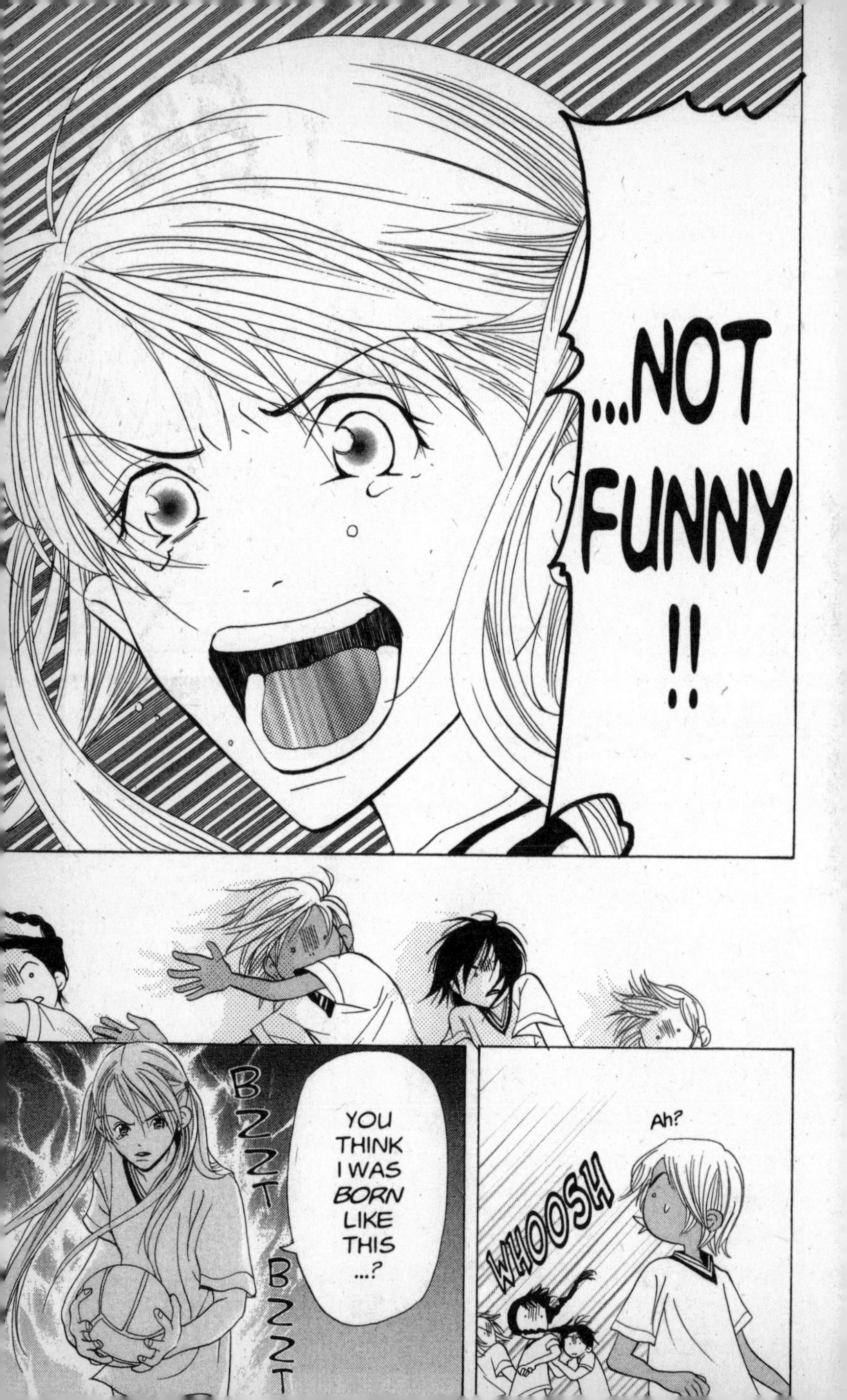
...NOT FUNNY !!
Ah?
WHOOSH
YOU THINK I WAS *BORN* LIKE THIS ...?
BZZT BZZT

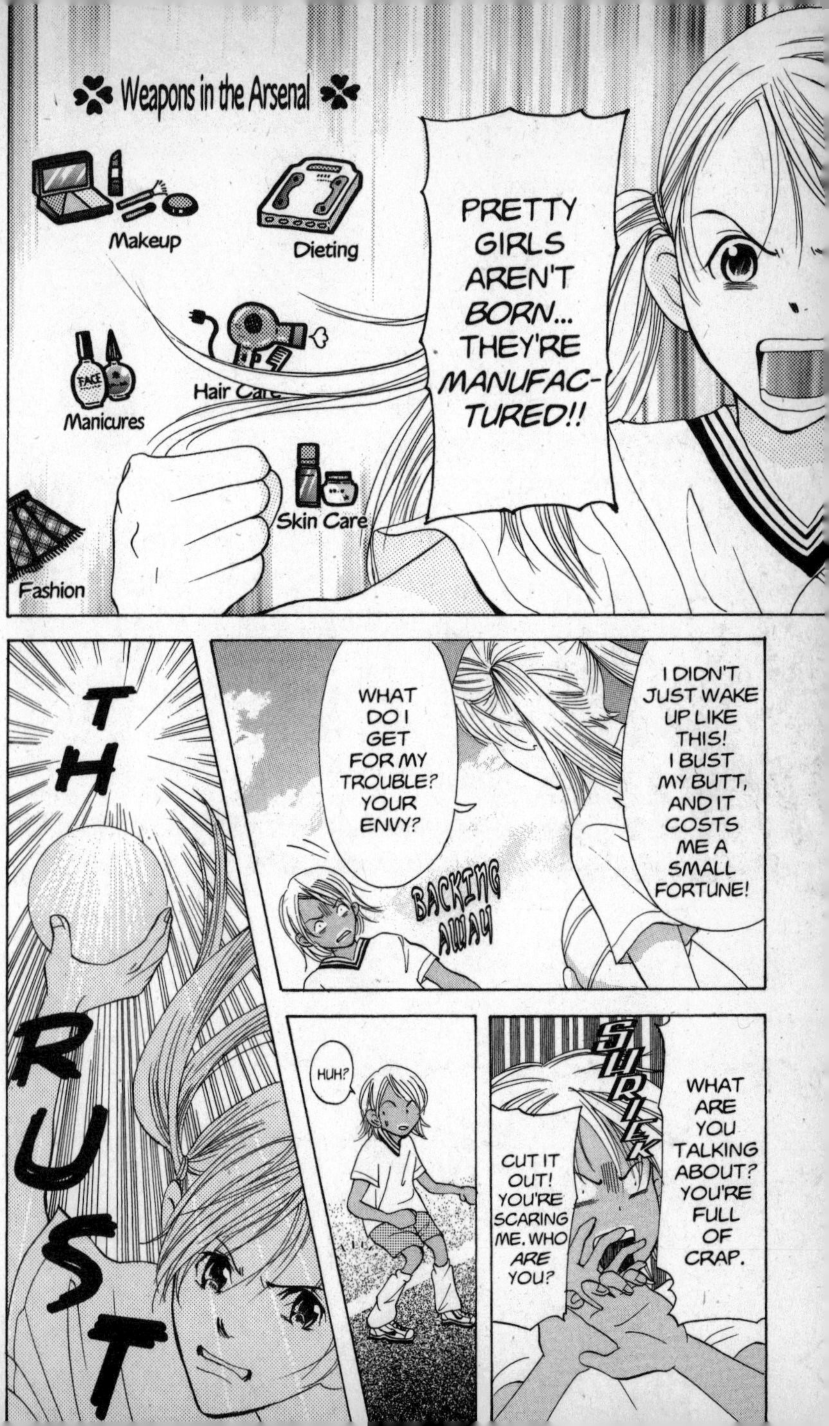
PRETTY GIRLS AREN'T BORN... THEY'RE MANUFACTURED!!
Weapons in the Arsenal
Makeup
Dieting
Hair Care
Manicures
Skin Care
Fashion
I DIDN'T JUST WAKE UP LIKE THIS! I BUST MY BUTT, AND IT COSTS ME A SMALL FORTUNE!
WHAT DO I GET FOR MY TROUBLE? YOUR ENVY?
BACKING AWAY
SHRIEK
WHAT ARE YOU TALKING ABOUT? YOU'RE FULL OF CRAP.
CUT IT OUT! YOU'RE SCARING ME. WHO ARE YOU?
HUH?
THRUST

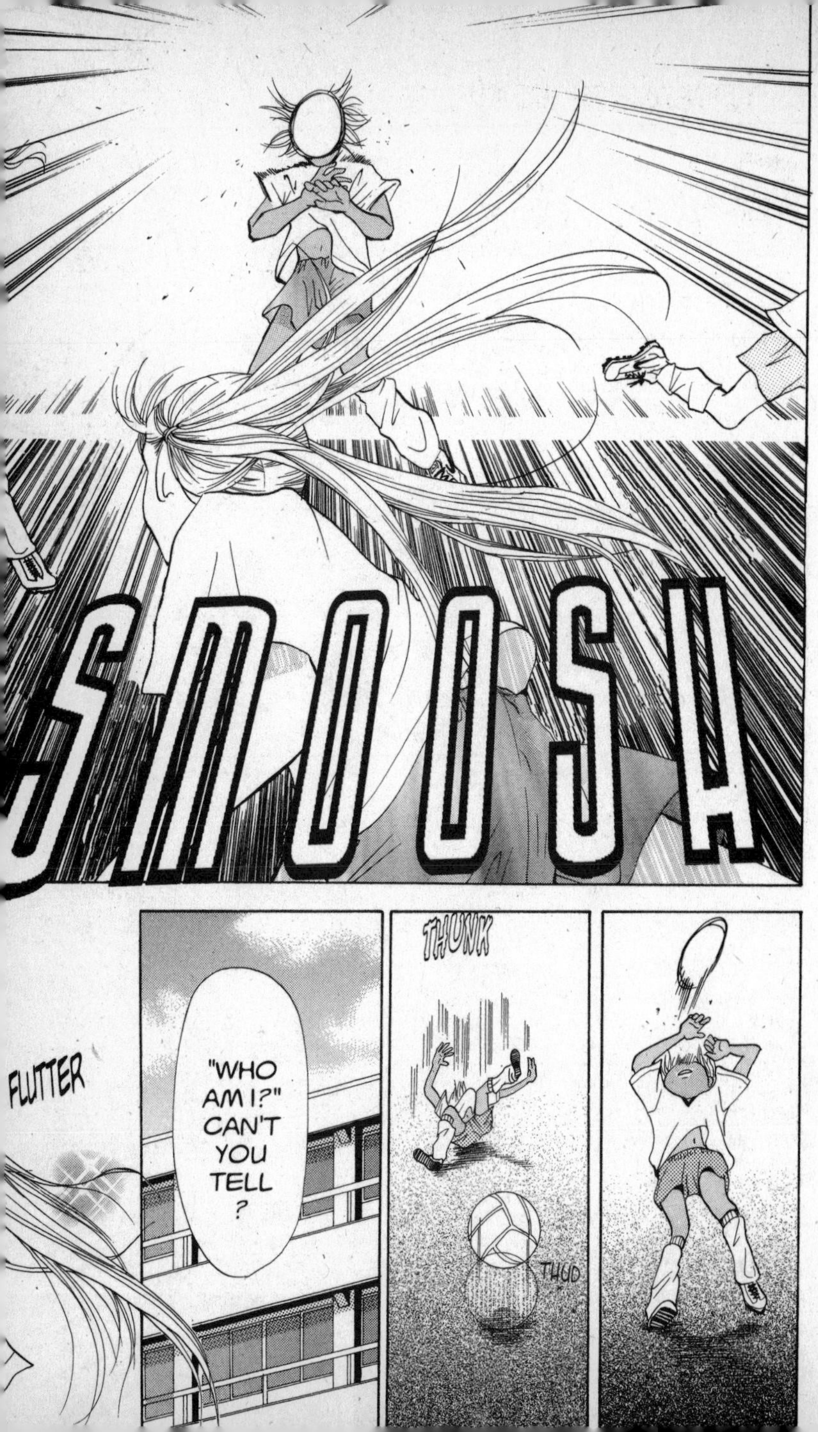
SWOOSH
THUNK
THUD
"WHO AM I?" CAN'T YOU TELL?
FLUTTER

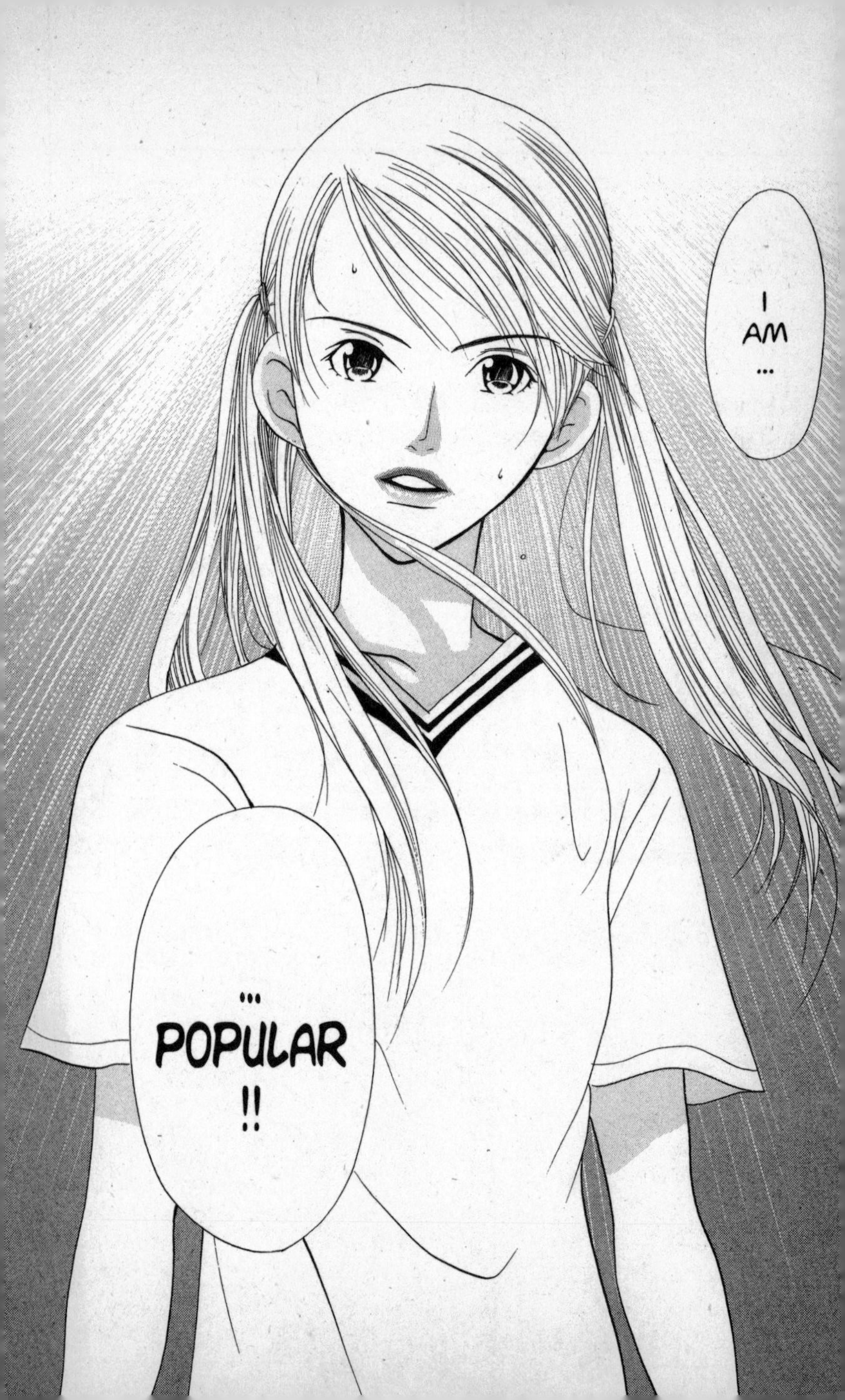
I AM ...
... POPULAR !!

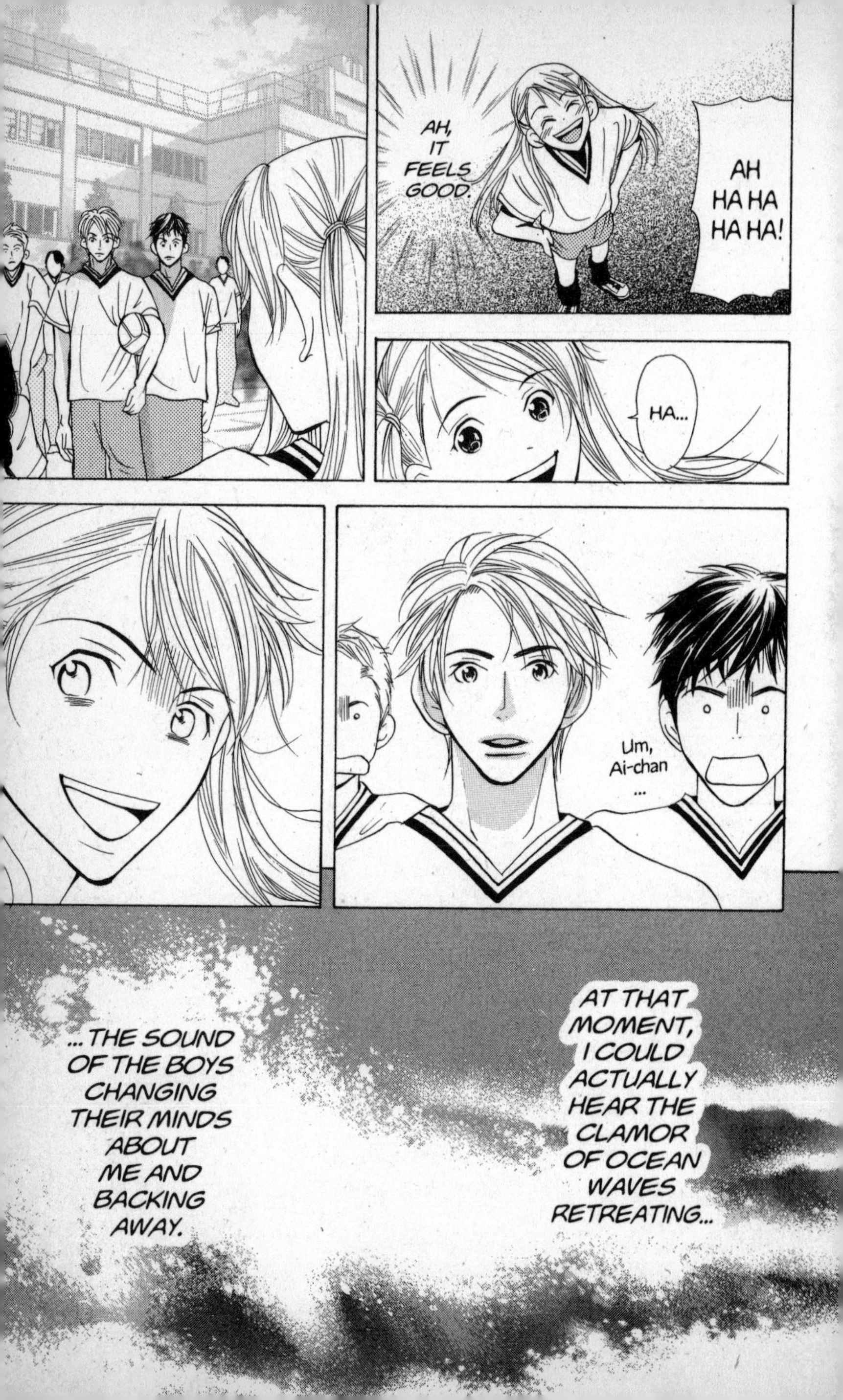
AH HA HA HA HA!
AH, IT FEELS GOOD.
HA...
Um, Ai-chan ...
AT THAT MOMENT, I COULD ACTUALLY HEAR THE CLAMOR OF OCEAN WAVES RETREATING...
...THE SOUND OF THE BOYS CHANGING THEIR MINDS ABOUT ME AND BACKING AWAY.

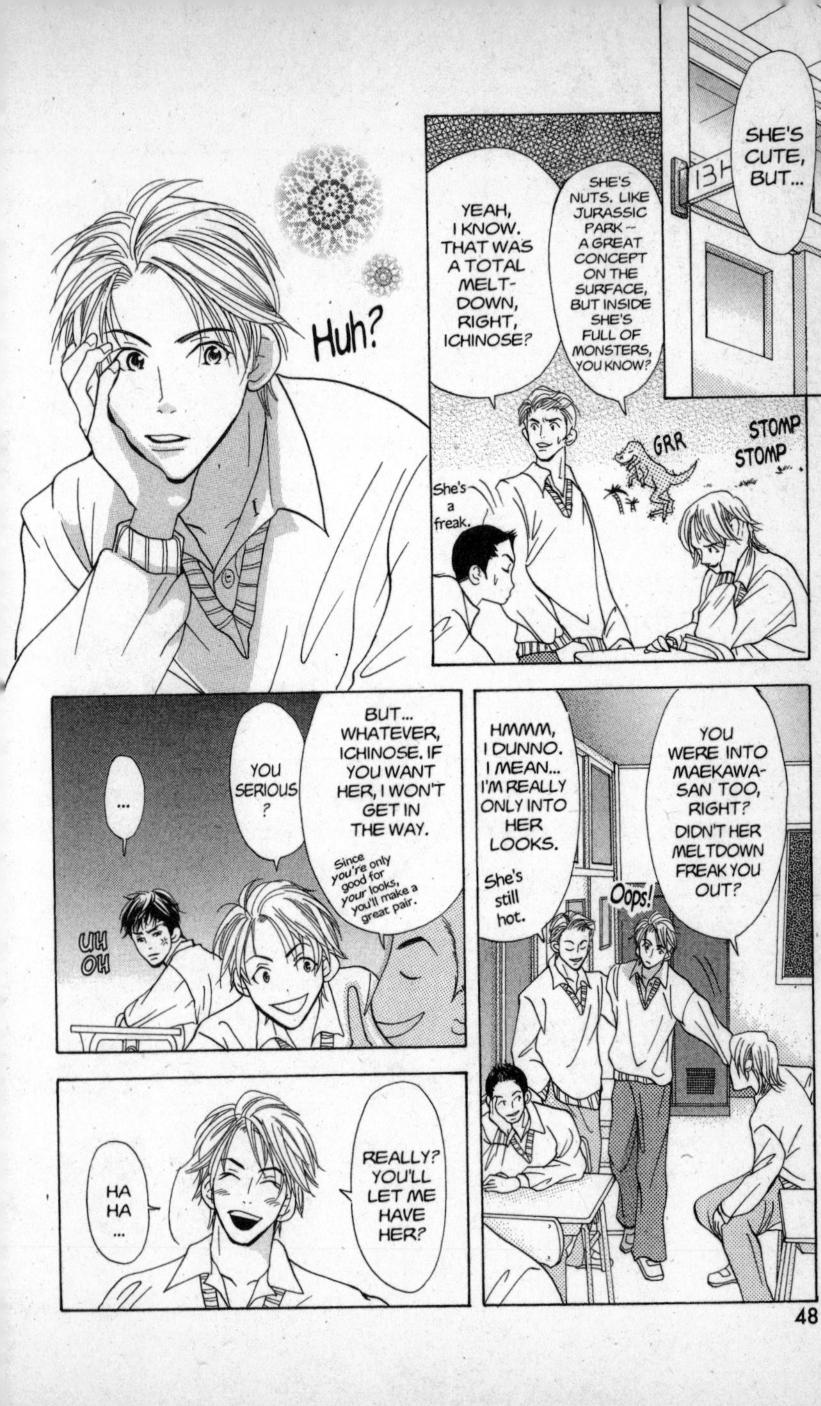

SHE'S CUTE, BUT...
13H
SHE'S NUTS. LIKE JURASSIC PARK -- A GREAT CONCEPT ON THE SURFACE, BUT INSIDE SHE'S FULL OF MONSTERS, YOU KNOW?
YEAH, I KNOW. THAT WAS A TOTAL MELT-DOWN, RIGHT, ICHINOSE?
GRR
STOMP STOMP
She's a freak.
Huh?
YOU WERE INTO MAEKAWA-SAN TOO, RIGHT? DIDN'T HER MELTDOWN FREAK YOU OUT?
HMMM, I DUNNO. I MEAN... I'M REALLY ONLY INTO HER LOOKS.
She's still hot.
Oops!
BUT... WHATEVER, ICHINOSE. IF YOU WANT HER, I WON'T GET IN THE WAY.
Since you're only good for your looks, you'll make a great pair.
YOU SERIOUS?
...
UH OH
REALLY? YOU'LL LET ME HAVE HER?
HA HA ...

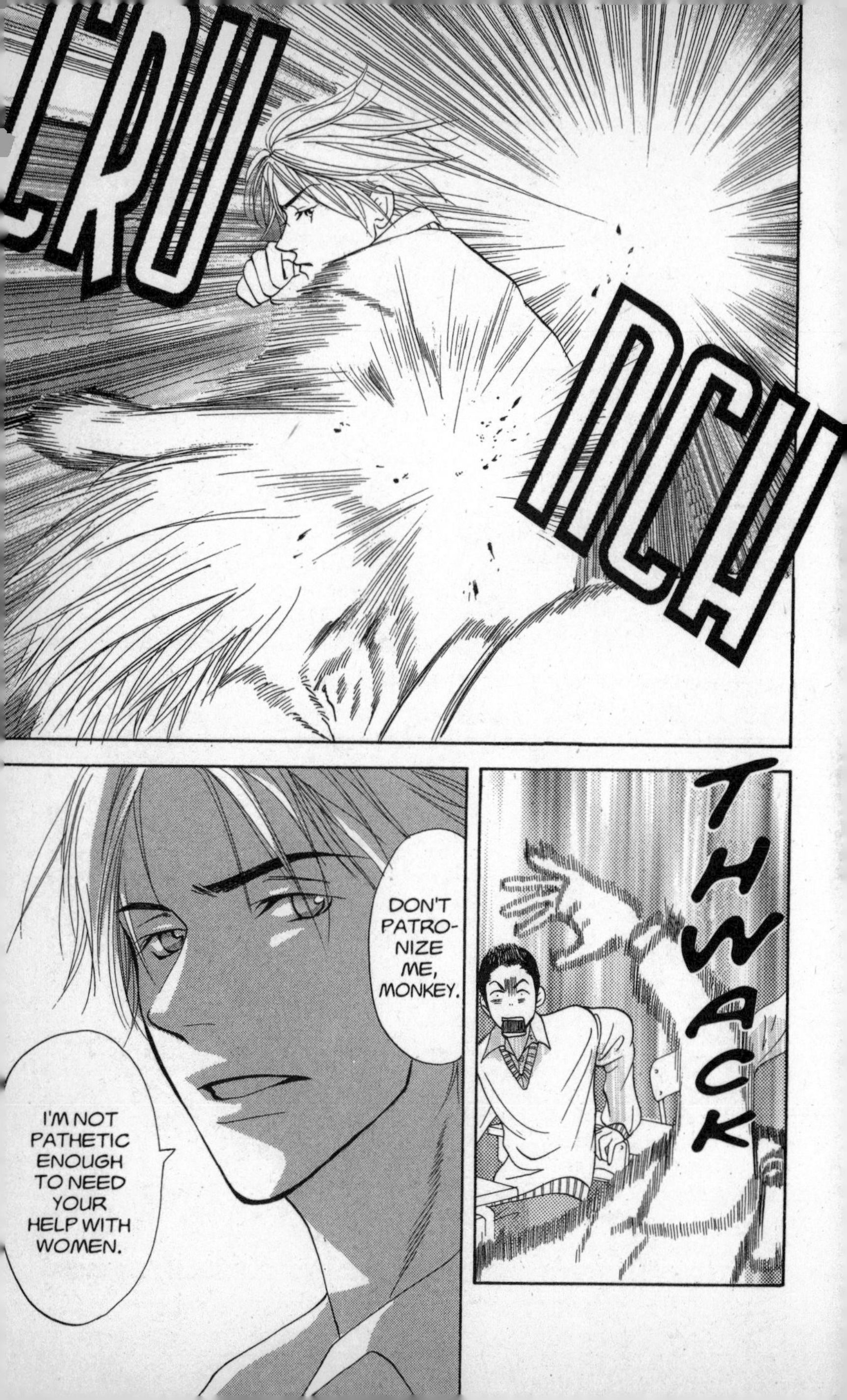
CRU
NCH
THWACK
DON'T PATRONIZE ME, MONKEY.
I'M NOT PATHETIC ENOUGH TO NEED YOUR HELP WITH WOMEN.

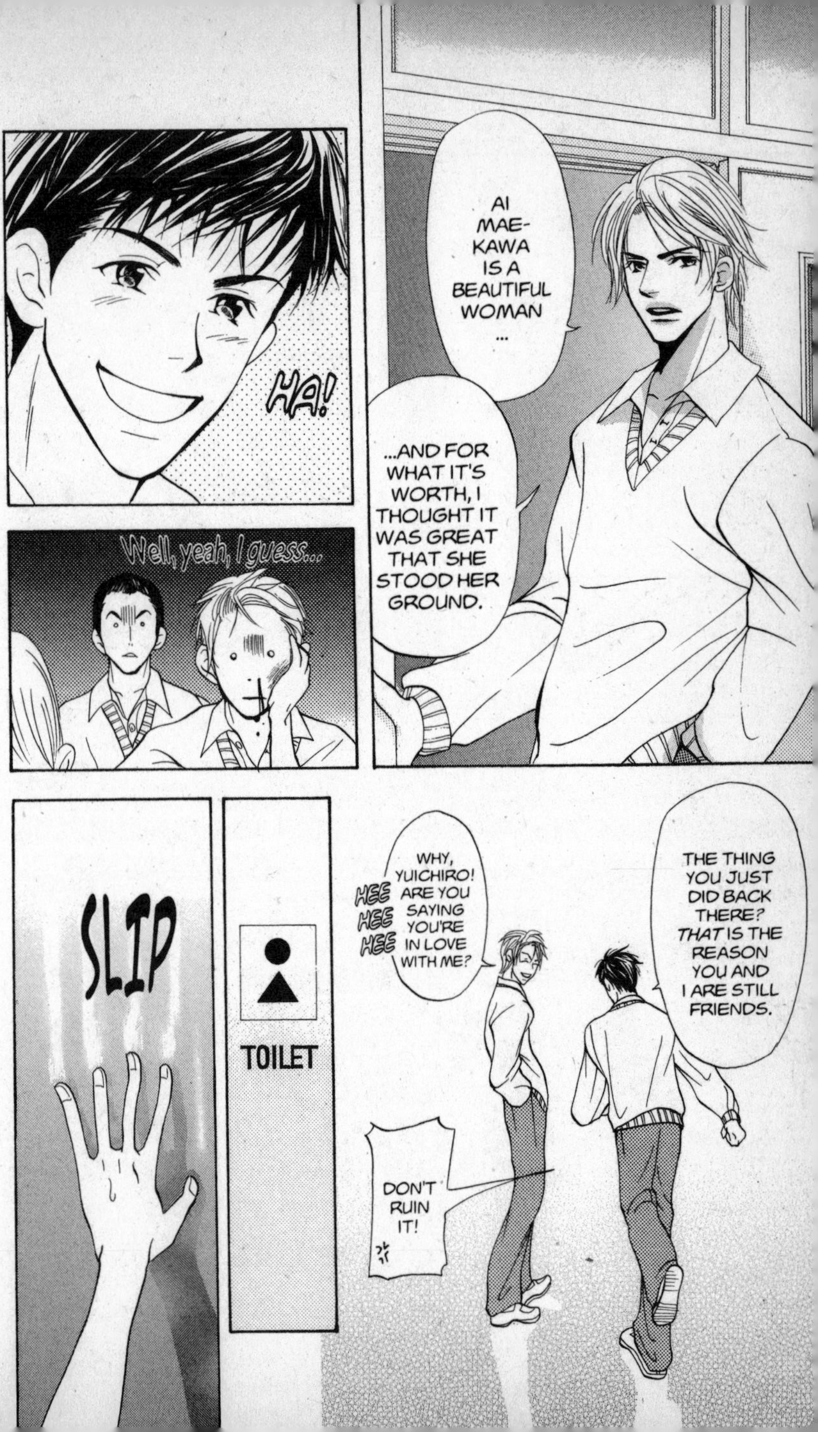
AI MAE-KAWA IS A BEAUTIFUL WOMAN ...
...AND FOR WHAT IT'S WORTH, I THOUGHT IT WAS GREAT THAT SHE STOOD HER GROUND.
HA!
Well, yeah, I guess...
THE THING YOU JUST DID BACK THERE? *THAT* IS THE REASON YOU AND I ARE STILL FRIENDS.
WHY, YUICHIRO! ARE YOU SAYING YOU'RE IN LOVE WITH ME?
HEE HEE HEE
DON'T RUIN IT!
TOILET
SLIP

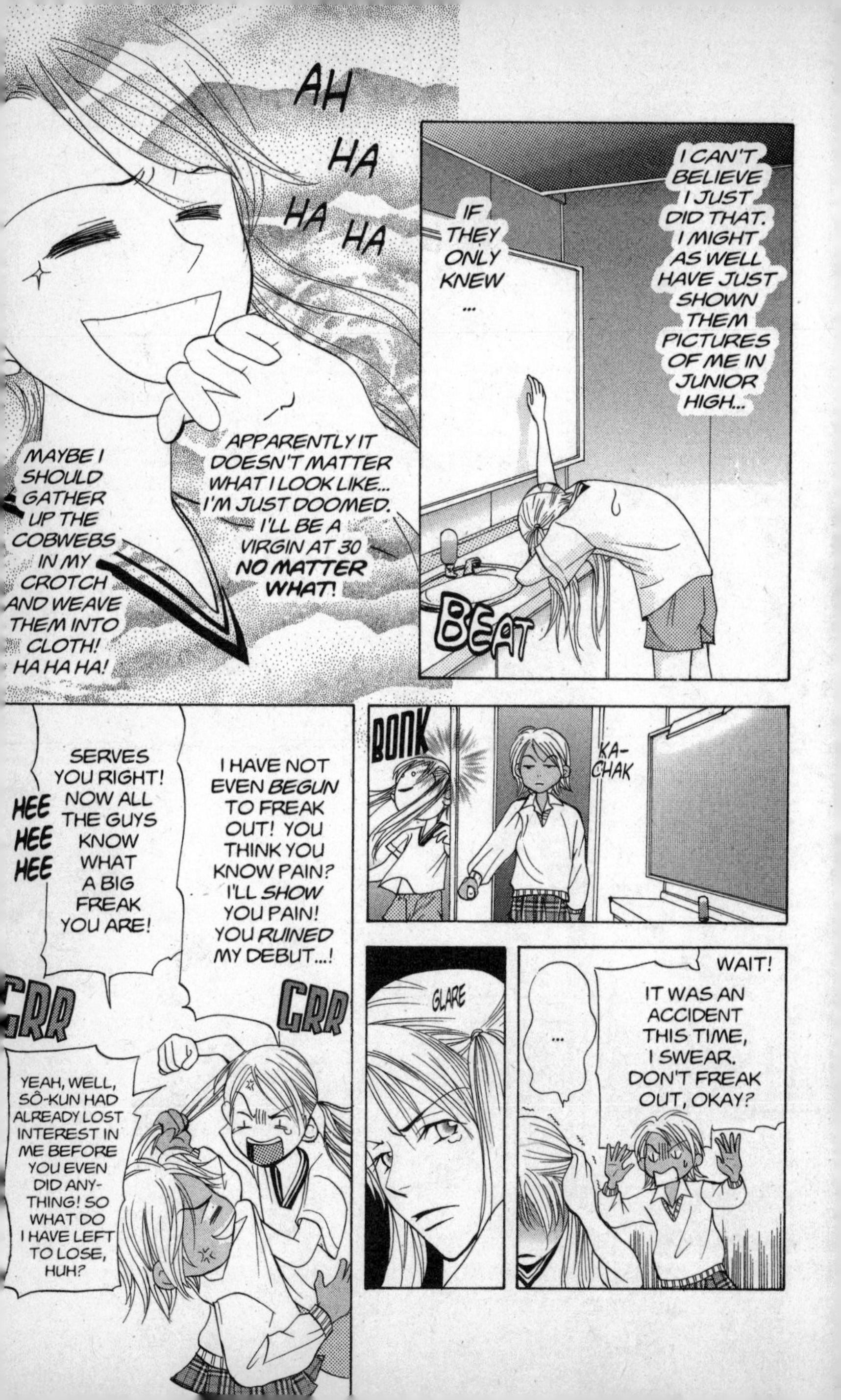
I CAN'T BELIEVE I JUST DID THAT. I MIGHT AS WELL HAVE JUST SHOWN THEM PICTURES OF ME IN JUNIOR HIGH...
IF THEY ONLY KNEW ...
BEAT
AH HA HA HA
APPARENTLY IT DOESN'T MATTER WHAT I LOOK LIKE... I'M JUST DOOMED. I'LL BE A VIRGIN AT 30 NO MATTER WHAT!
MAYBE I SHOULD GATHER UP THE COBWEBS IN MY CROTCH AND WEAVE THEM INTO CLOTH! HA HA HA!
KA-CHAK
BONK
WAIT! IT WAS AN ACCIDENT THIS TIME, I SWEAR. DON'T FREAK OUT, OKAY?
...
GLARE
I HAVE NOT EVEN BEGUN TO FREAK OUT! YOU THINK YOU KNOW PAIN? I'LL SHOW YOU PAIN! YOU RUINED MY DEBUT...!
SERVES YOU RIGHT! NOW ALL THE GUYS KNOW WHAT A BIG FREAK YOU ARE!
HEE HEE HEE
GRR
GRR
YEAH, WELL, SÔ-KUN HAD ALREADY LOST INTEREST IN ME BEFORE YOU EVEN DID ANY-THING! SO WHAT DO I HAVE LEFT TO LOSE, HUH?

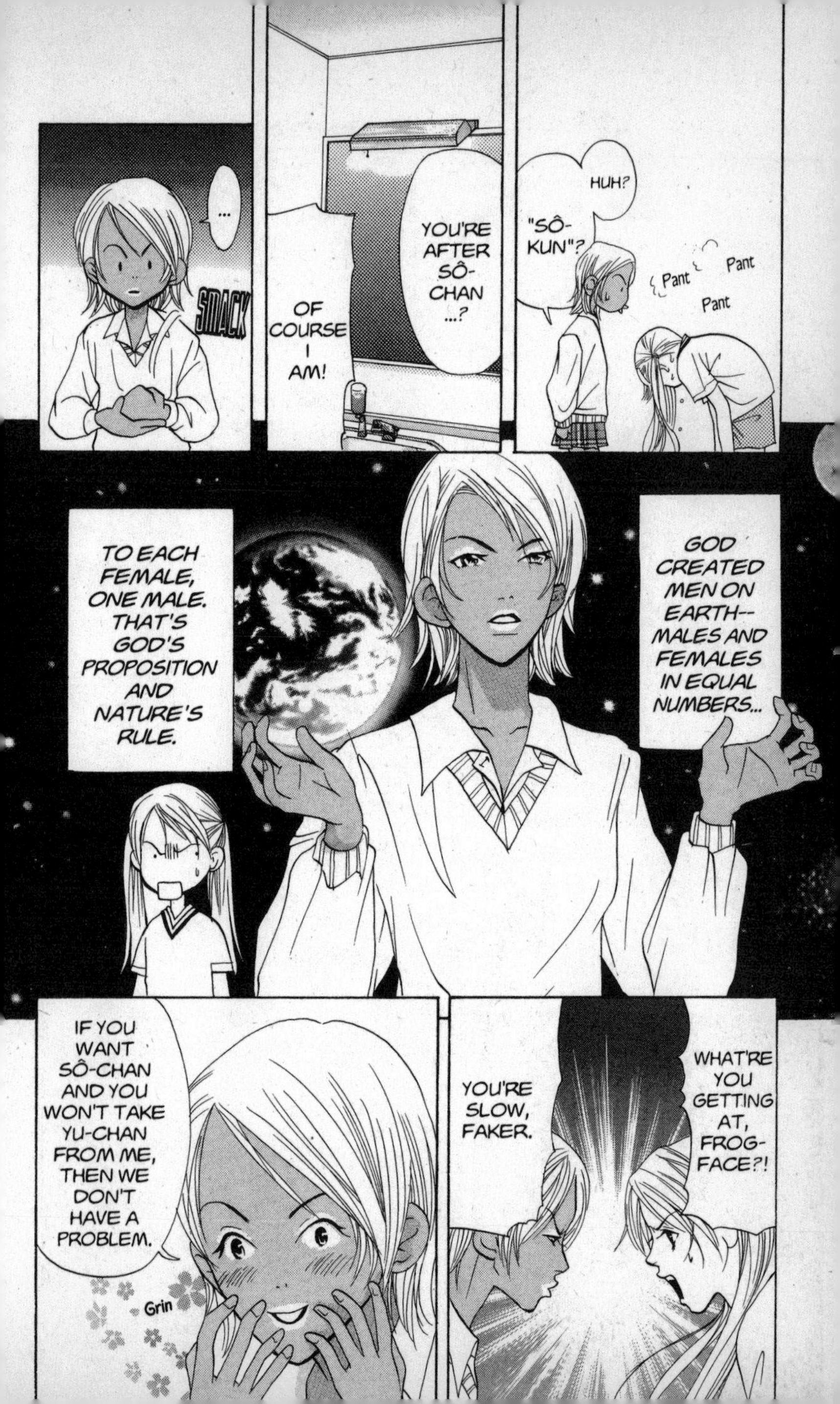
HUH?
"SÔ-KUN"?
Pant
Pant
Pant
YOU'RE AFTER SÔ-CHAN ...?
OF COURSE I AM!
...
SMACK
GOD CREATED MEN ON EARTH-- MALES AND FEMALES IN EQUAL NUMBERS...
TO EACH FEMALE, ONE MALE. THAT'S GOD'S PROPOSITION AND NATURE'S RULE.
WHAT'RE YOU GETTING AT, FROG-FACE?!
YOU'RE SLOW, FAKER.
IF YOU WANT SÔ-CHAN AND YOU WON'T TAKE YU-CHAN FROM ME, THEN WE DON'T HAVE A PROBLEM.
Grin

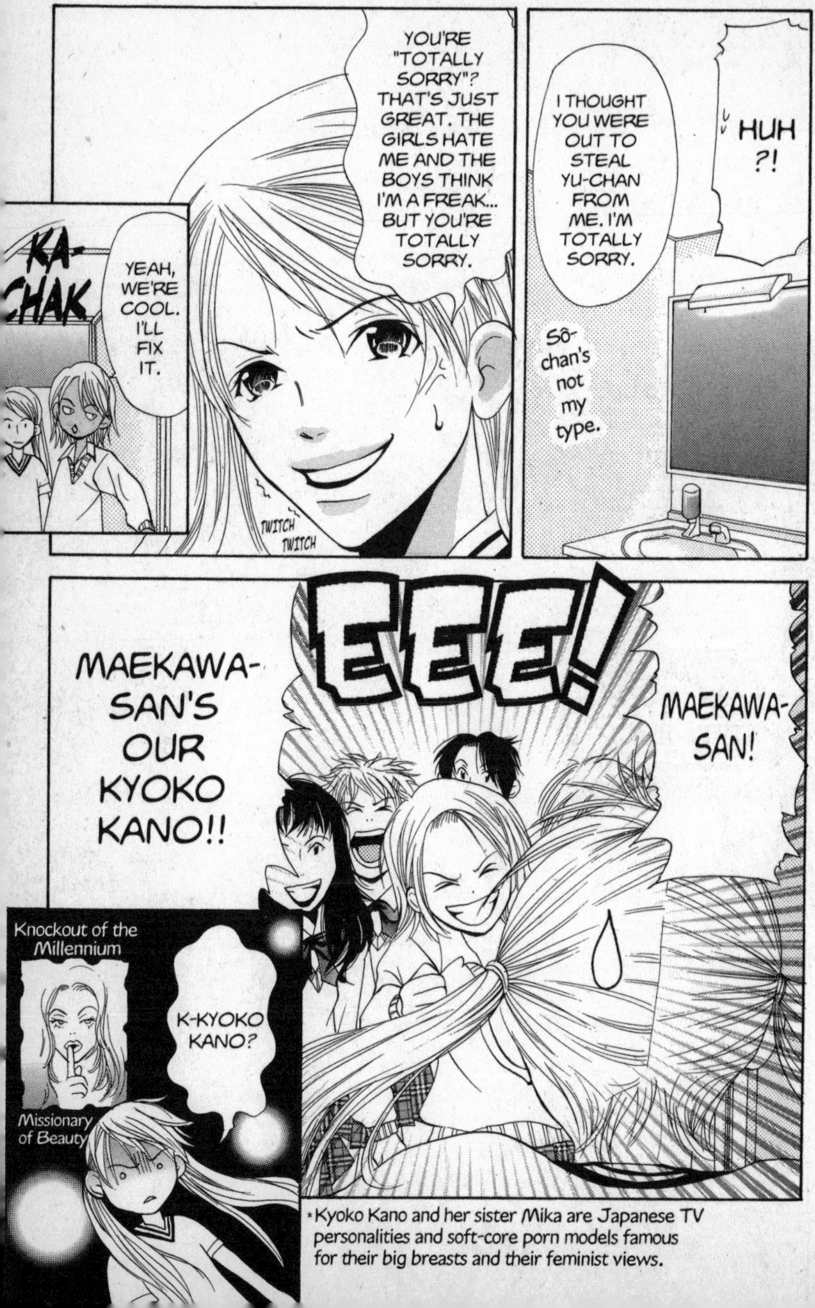
HUH ?!
I THOUGHT YOU WERE OUT TO STEAL YU-CHAN FROM ME. I'M TOTALLY SORRY.
Sô-chan's not my type.
YOU'RE "TOTALLY SORRY"? THAT'S JUST GREAT. THE GIRLS HATE ME AND THE BOYS THINK I'M A FREAK... BUT YOU'RE TOTALLY SORRY.
TWITCH TWITCH
YEAH, WE'RE COOL. I'LL FIX IT.
KA-CHAK
EEE!
MAEKAWA-SAN!
MAEKAWA-SAN'S OUR KYOKO KANO!!
Knockout of the Millennium
K-KYOKO KANO?
Missionary of Beauty

*Kyoko Kano and her sister Mika are Japanese TV personalities and soft-core porn models famous for their big breasts and their feminist views.

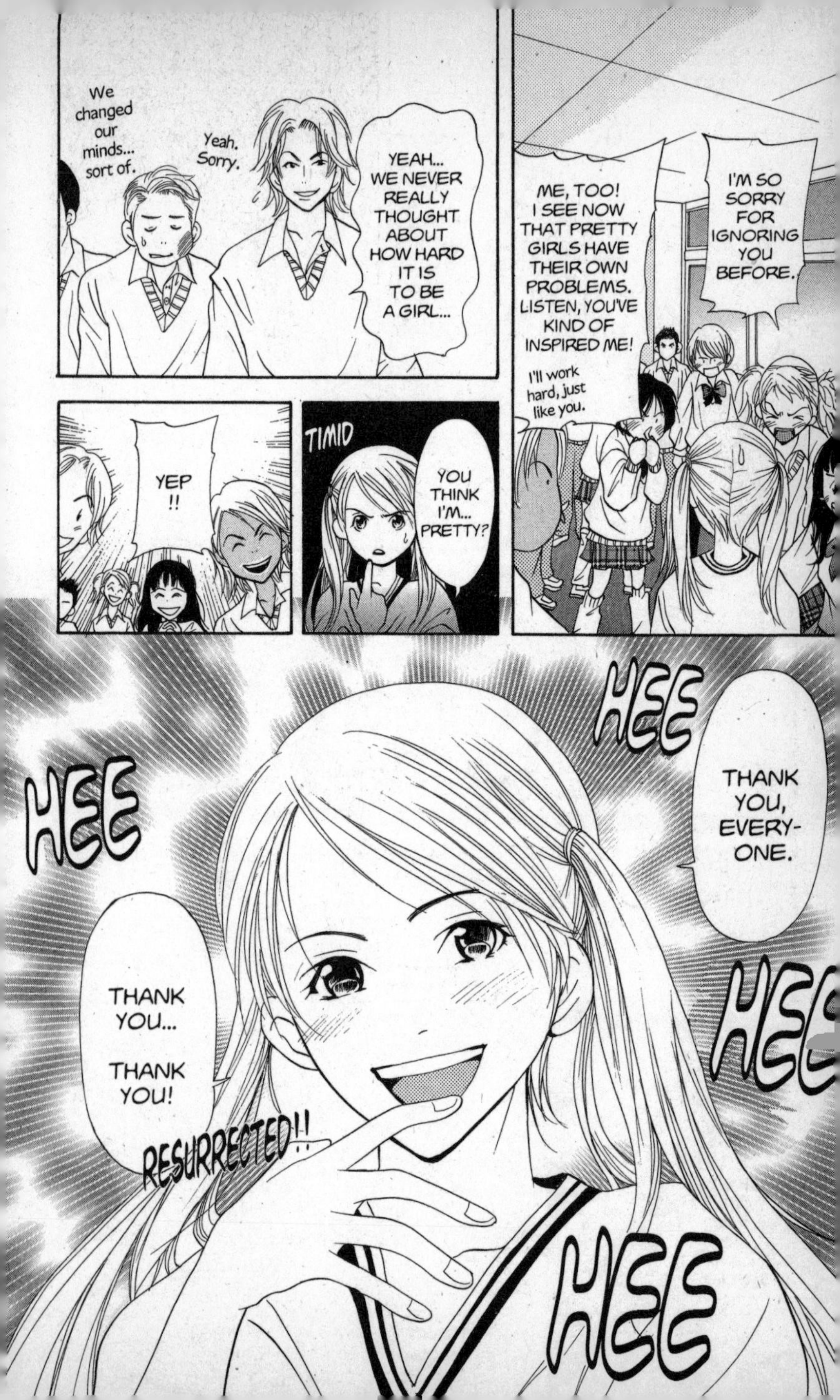

I'M SO SORRY FOR IGNORING YOU BEFORE.
ME, TOO! I SEE NOW THAT PRETTY GIRLS HAVE THEIR OWN PROBLEMS. LISTEN, YOU'VE KIND OF INSPIRED ME!
I'll work hard, just like you.
YEAH... WE NEVER REALLY THOUGHT ABOUT HOW HARD IT IS TO BE A GIRL...
Yeah. Sorry.
We changed our minds... sort of.
TIMID
YOU THINK I'M... PRETTY?
YEP !!
HEE
THANK YOU, EVERY-ONE.
HEE
HEE
THANK YOU...
THANK YOU!
RESURRECTED!!
HEE

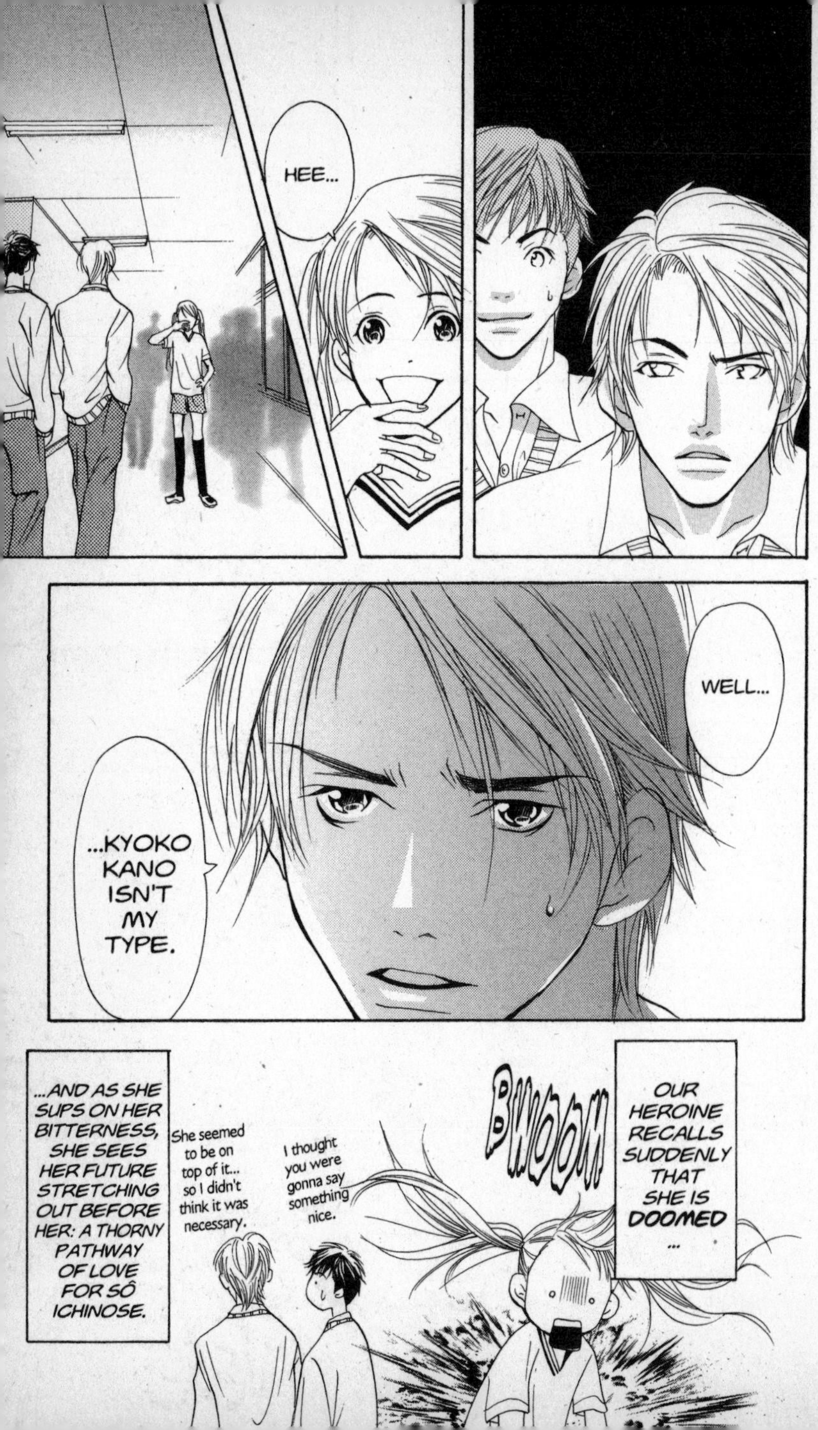
HEE...
WELL...
...KYOKO KANO ISN'T MY TYPE.
OUR HEROINE RECALLS SUDDENLY THAT SHE IS DOOMED ...
BWOOM
I thought you were gonna say something nice.
She seemed to be on top of it... so I didn't think it was necessary.
...AND AS SHE SUPS ON HER BITTERNESS, SHE SEES HER FUTURE STRETCHING OUT BEFORE HER: A THORNY PATHWAY OF LOVE FOR SÔ ICHINOSE.

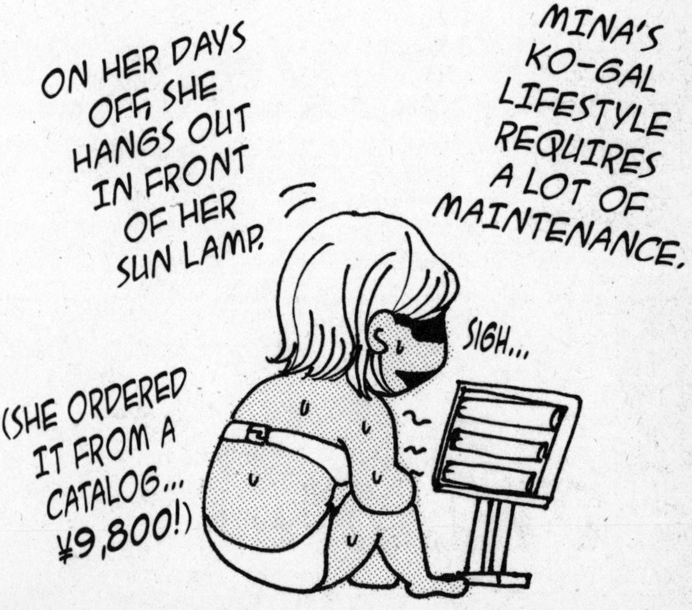
MINA'S KO-GAL LIFESTYLE REQUIRES A LOT OF MAINTENANCE.
ON HER DAYS OFF, SHE HANGS OUT IN FRONT OF HER SUN LAMP.
SIGH...
(SHE ORDERED IT FROM A CATALOG... ¥9,800!)

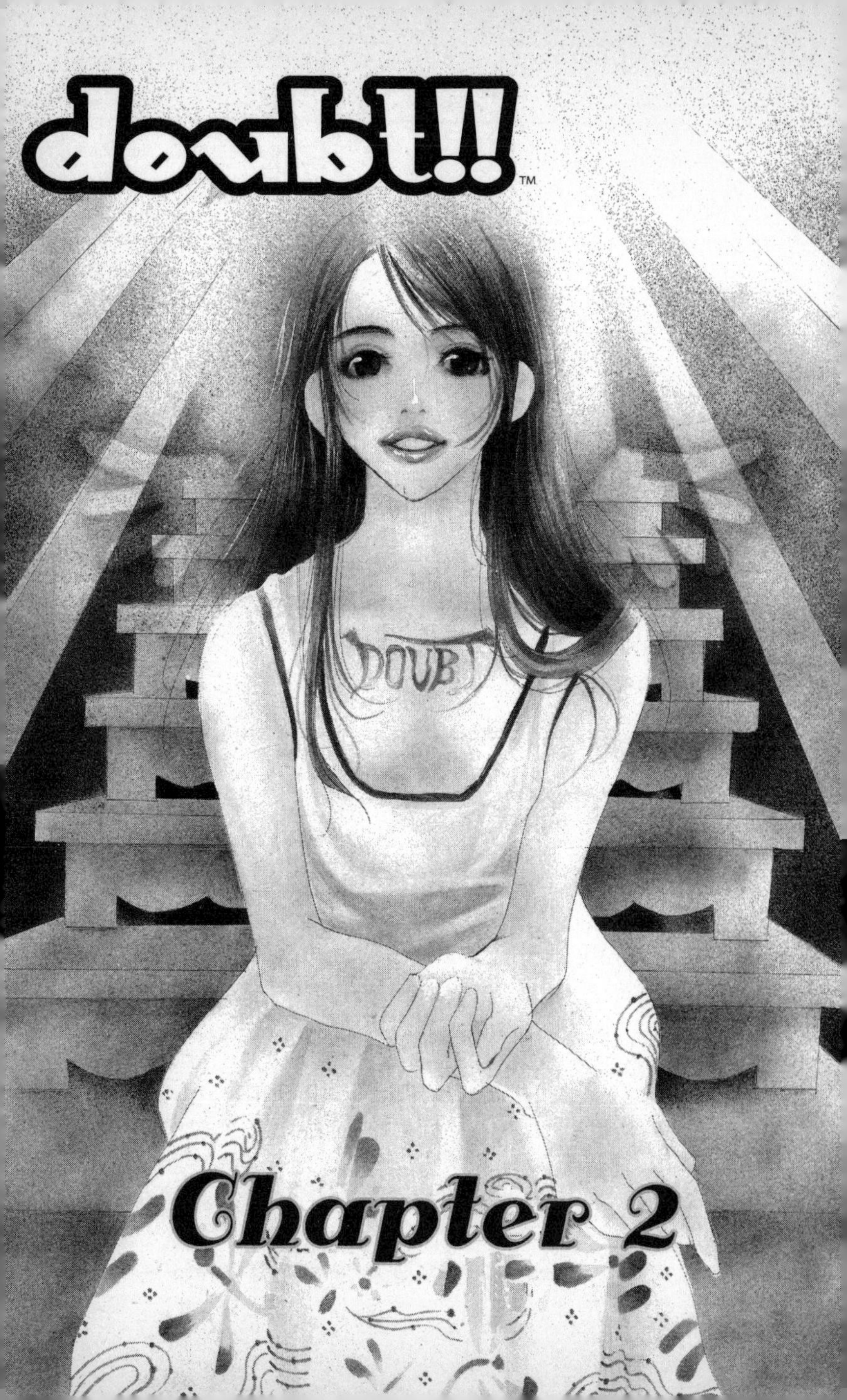
doubt!!™
DOUB
Chapter 2

I DRESSED UP TO MAKE MY DEBUT AT SCHOOL, BUT AT HOME I USUALLY JUST WEAR SWEAT PANTS...
I WEAR 'EM UNTIL THEY TURN INTO RAGS.

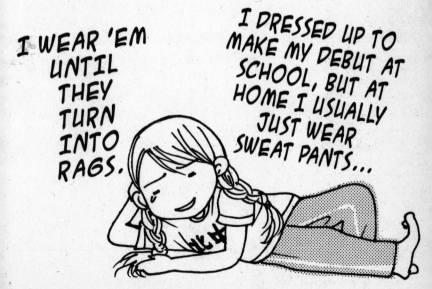

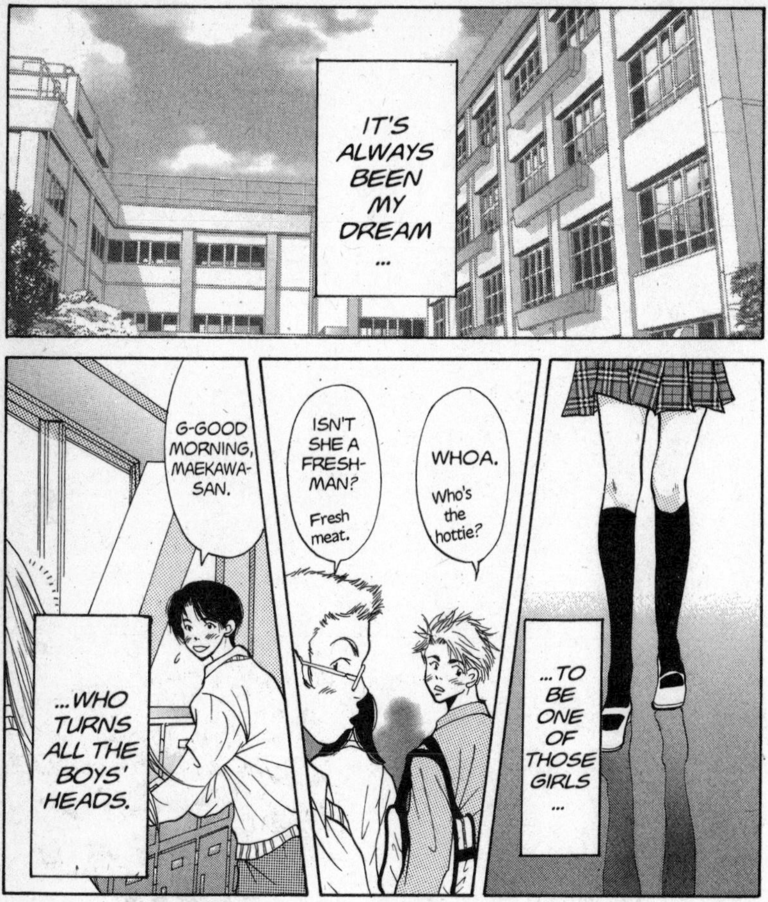
IT'S ALWAYS BEEN MY DREAM ...
...TO BE ONE OF THOSE GIRLS ...
WHOA.
Who's the hottie?
ISN'T SHE A FRESHMAN?
Fresh meat.
G-GOOD MORNING, MAEKAWA-SAN.
...WHO TURNS ALL THE BOYS' HEADS.

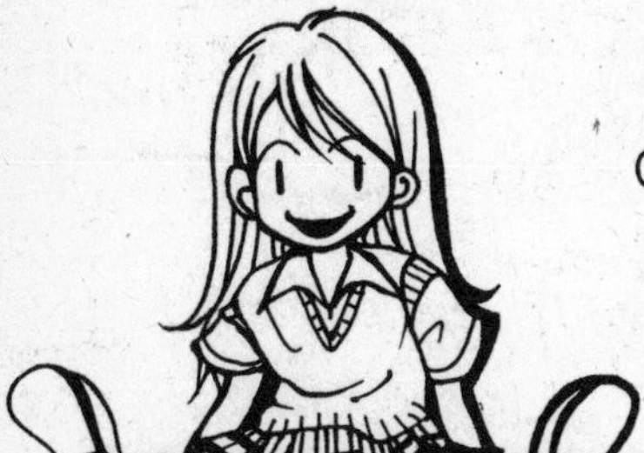

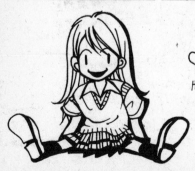

♡ AI MAEKAWA

Her personality hasn't really presented itself yet -- I think I set her up to be a kind of blank slate. How will she transform? Even I don't know. (Maybe I haven't figured it out yet...) Anyhow, I hope you'll continue to enjoy the story.

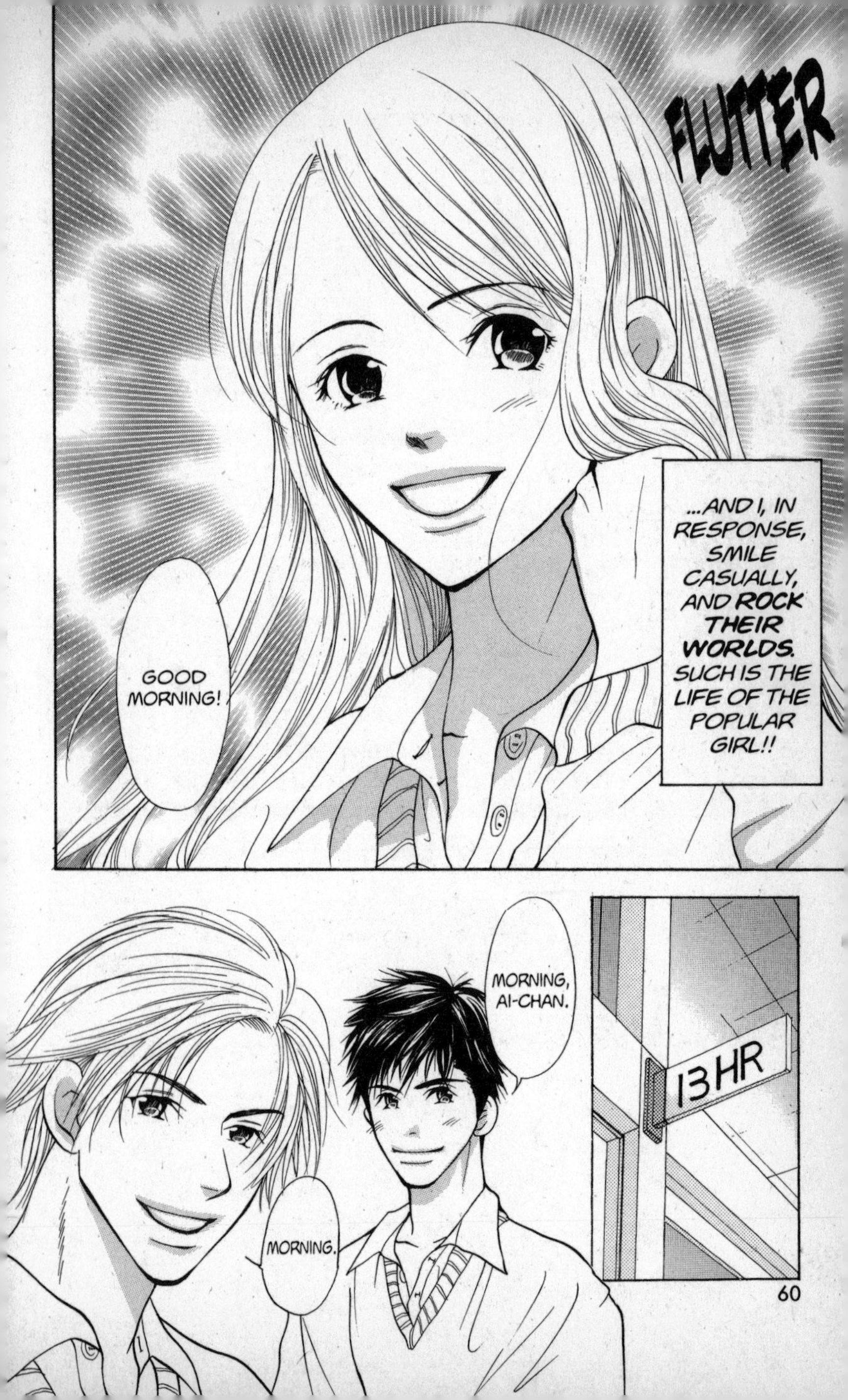
FLUTTER
...AND I, IN RESPONSE, SMILE CASUALLY, AND **ROCK THEIR WORLDS.** SUCH IS THE LIFE OF THE POPULAR GIRL!!
GOOD MORNING!
13 HR
MORNING, AI-CHAN.
MORNING.

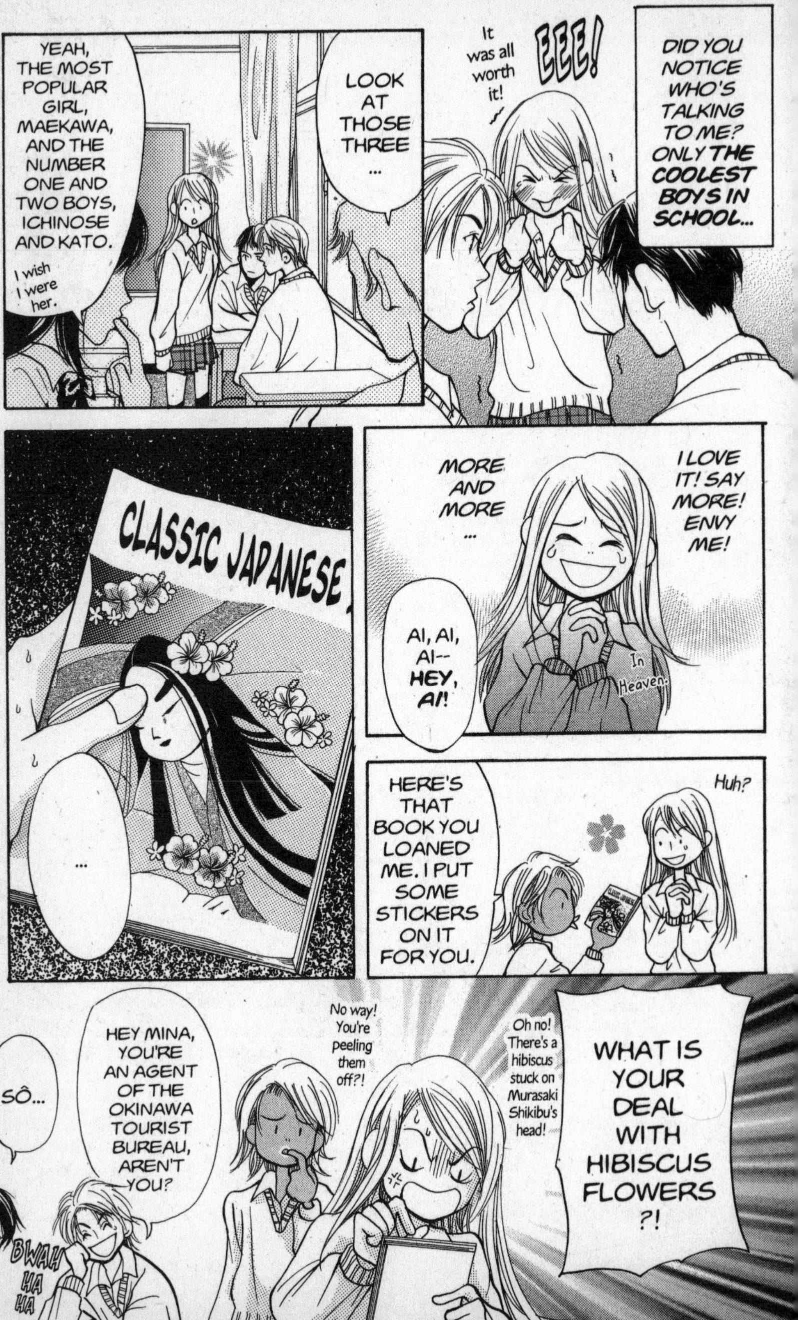
DID YOU NOTICE WHO'S TALKING TO ME? ONLY THE COOLEST BOYS IN SCHOOL...
EEE!
It was all worth it!
LOOK AT THOSE THREE ...
YEAH, THE MOST POPULAR GIRL, MAEKAWA, AND THE NUMBER ONE AND TWO BOYS, ICHINOSE AND KATO.
I wish I were her.
I LOVE IT! SAY MORE! ENVY ME!
MORE AND MORE ...
In Heaven.
AI, AI, AI-- HEY, AI!
Huh?
HERE'S THAT BOOK YOU LOANED ME. I PUT SOME STICKERS ON IT FOR YOU.
CLASSIC JAPANESE
...
WHAT IS YOUR DEAL WITH HIBISCUS FLOWERS ?!
Oh no! There's a hibiscus stuck on Murasaki Shikibu's head!
No way! You're peeling them off?!
HEY MINA, YOU'RE AN AGENT OF THE OKINAWA TOURIST BUREAU, AREN'T YOU?
SÔ...
BWAH HA HA

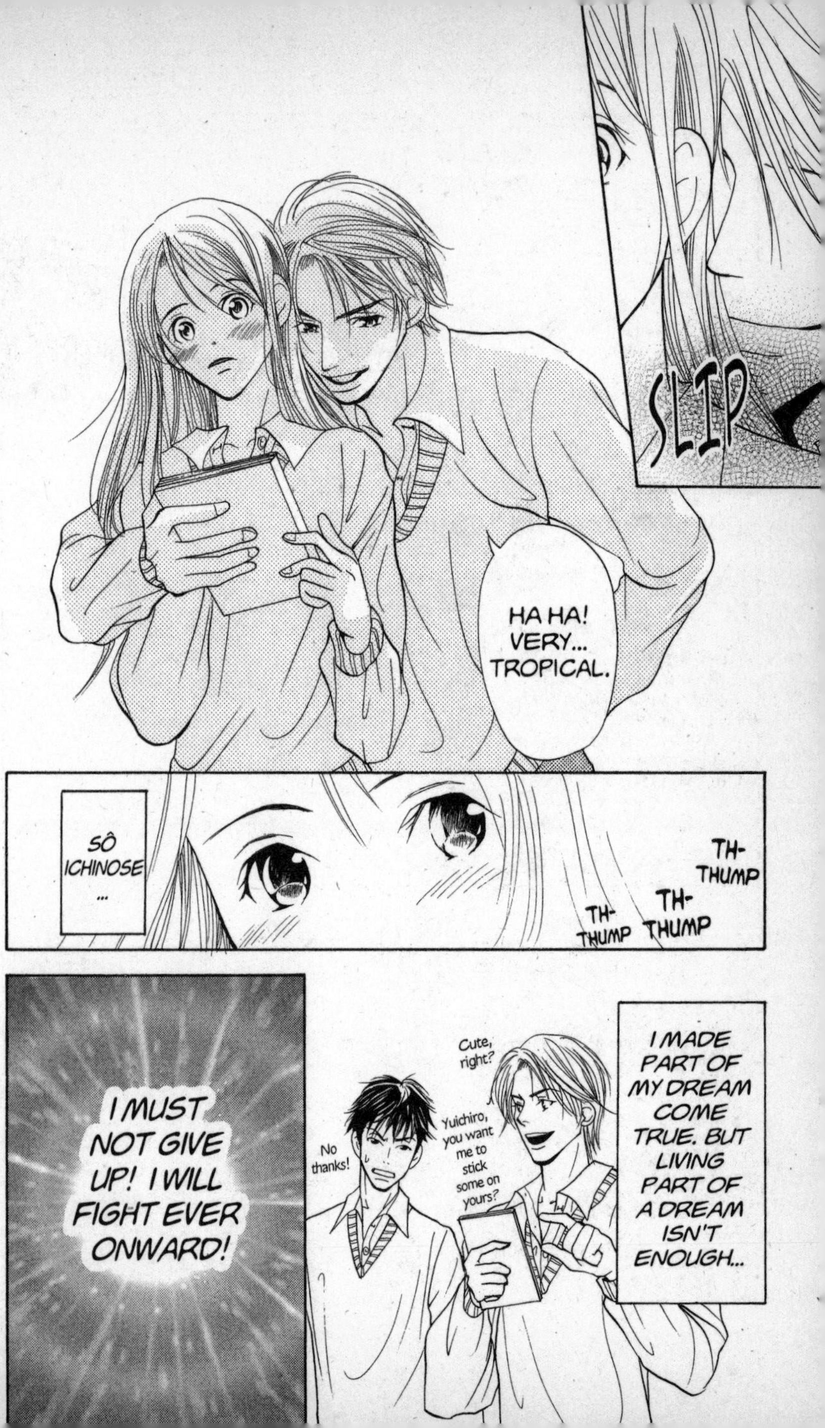
SLIP
HA HA! VERY... TROPICAL.
TH-THUMP
TH-THUMP
TH-THUMP
SÔ ICHINOSE ...
I MADE PART OF MY DREAM COME TRUE. BUT LIVING PART OF A DREAM ISN'T ENOUGH...
Cute, right?
Yuichiro, you want me to stick some on yours?
No thanks!
I MUST NOT GIVE UP! I WILL FIGHT EVER ONWARD!

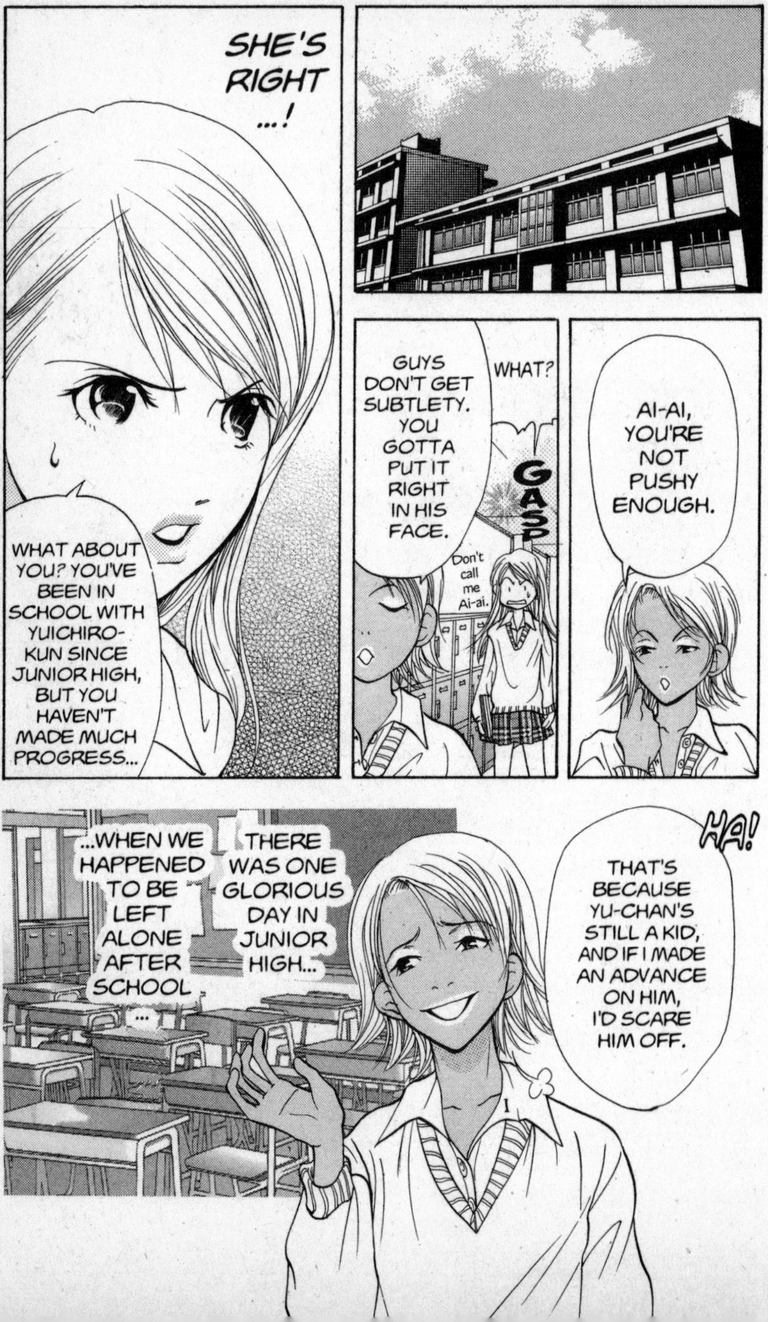
AI-AI, YOU'RE NOT PUSHY ENOUGH.
GUYS DON'T GET SUBTLETY. YOU GOTTA PUT IT RIGHT IN HIS FACE.
WHAT?
GASP
Don't call me Ai-ai.
SHE'S RIGHT ...!
WHAT ABOUT YOU? YOU'VE BEEN IN SCHOOL WITH YUICHIRO-KUN SINCE JUNIOR HIGH, BUT YOU HAVEN'T MADE MUCH PROGRESS...
HA!
THAT'S BECAUSE YU-CHAN'S STILL A KID, AND IF I MADE AN ADVANCE ON HIM, I'D SCARE HIM OFF.
THERE WAS ONE GLORIOUS DAY IN JUNIOR HIGH...
...WHEN WE HAPPENED TO BE LEFT ALONE AFTER SCHOOL
...

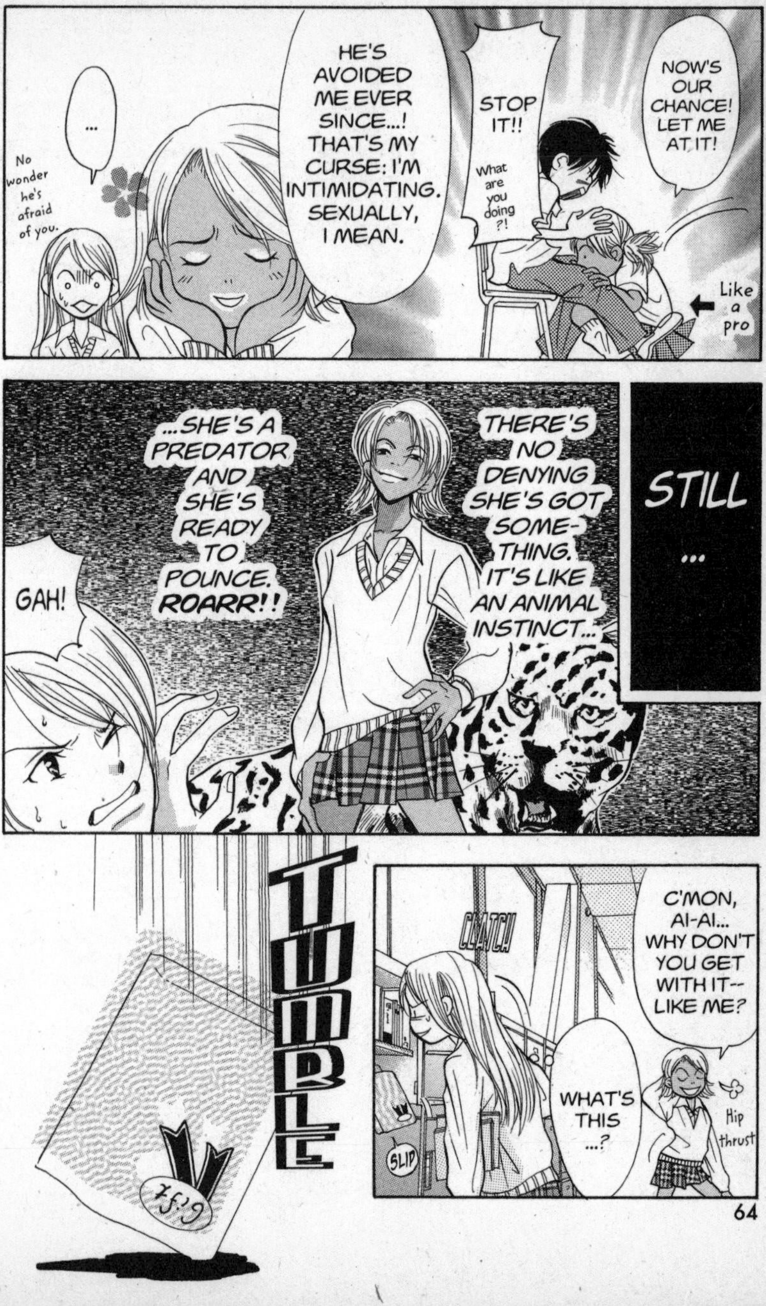
Like a pro
NOW'S OUR CHANCE! LET ME AT IT!
STOP IT!!
What are you doing?!
HE'S AVOIDED ME EVER SINCE...! THAT'S MY CURSE: I'M INTIMIDATING. SEXUALLY, I MEAN.
...
No wonder he's afraid of you.
STILL ...
THERE'S NO DENYING SHE'S GOT SOME-THING. IT'S LIKE AN ANIMAL INSTINCT...
...SHE'S A PREDATOR AND SHE'S READY TO POUNCE. ROARR!!
GAH!
C'MON, AI-AI... WHY DON'T YOU GET WITH IT--LIKE ME?
Hip thrust
WHAT'S THIS ...?
CLATCH
SLIP
TUMBLE

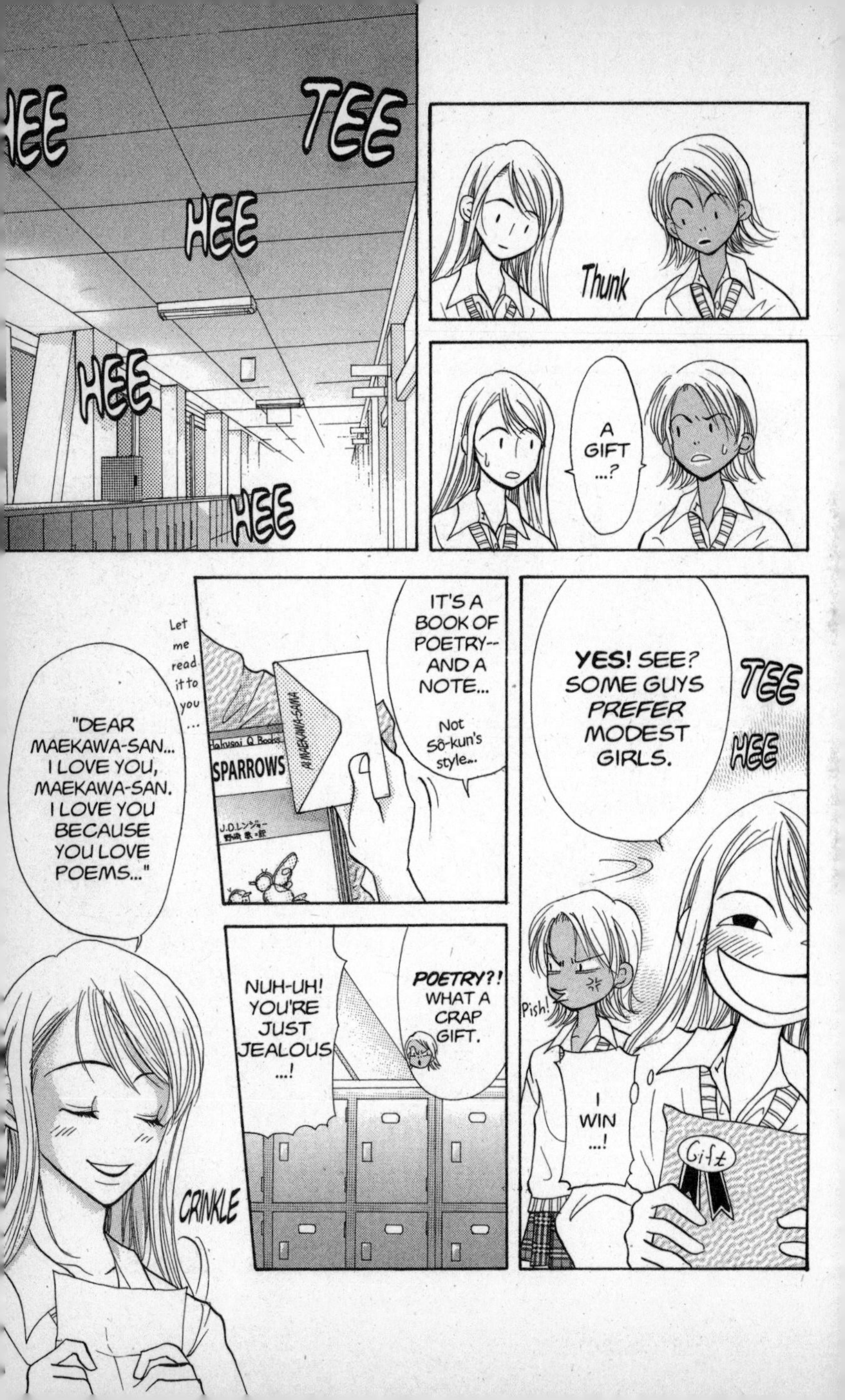
Thunk
A GIFT ...?
TEE
HEE
HEE
HEE
HEE
YES! SEE? SOME GUYS PREFER MODEST GIRLS.
TEE HEE
Pish!
I WIN ...!
Gift
IT'S A BOOK OF POETRY-- AND A NOTE...
Not Sō-kun's style...
AI MAEKAWA-SAMA
Hakusui Q Books
SPARROWS
POETRY?! WHAT A CRAP GIFT.
NUH-UH! YOU'RE JUST JEALOUS ...!
Let me read it to you ...
"DEAR MAEKAWA-SAN... I LOVE YOU, MAEKAWA-SAN. I LOVE YOU BECAUSE YOU LOVE POEMS..."
CRINKLE

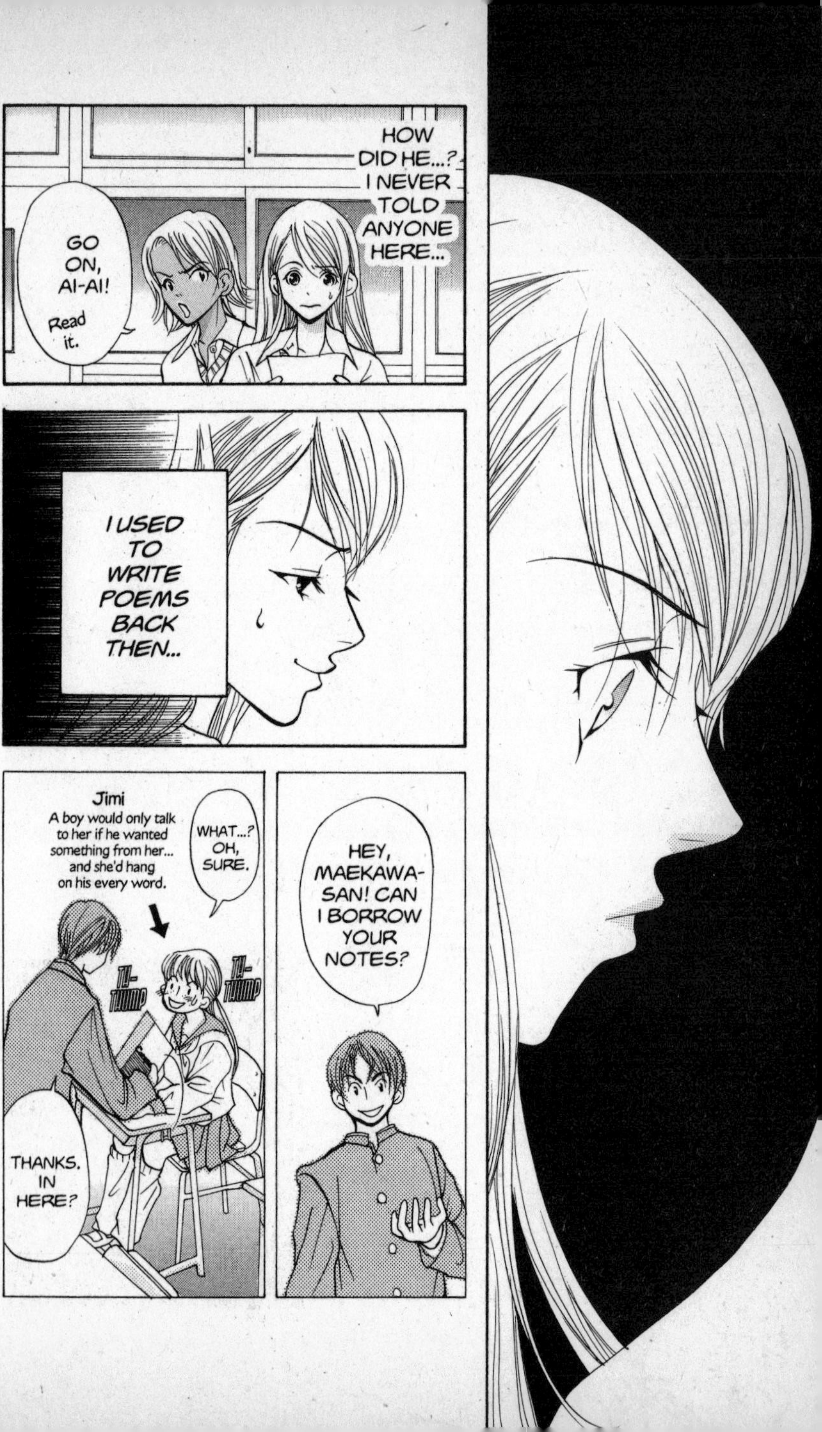
HOW DID HE...? I NEVER TOLD ANYONE HERE...
GO ON, AI-AI!
Read it.
I USED TO WRITE POEMS BACK THEN...
HEY, MAEKAWA-SAN! CAN I BORROW YOUR NOTES?
Jimi
A boy would only talk to her if he wanted something from her... and she'd hang on his every word.
WHAT...? OH, SURE.
THANKS. IN HERE?

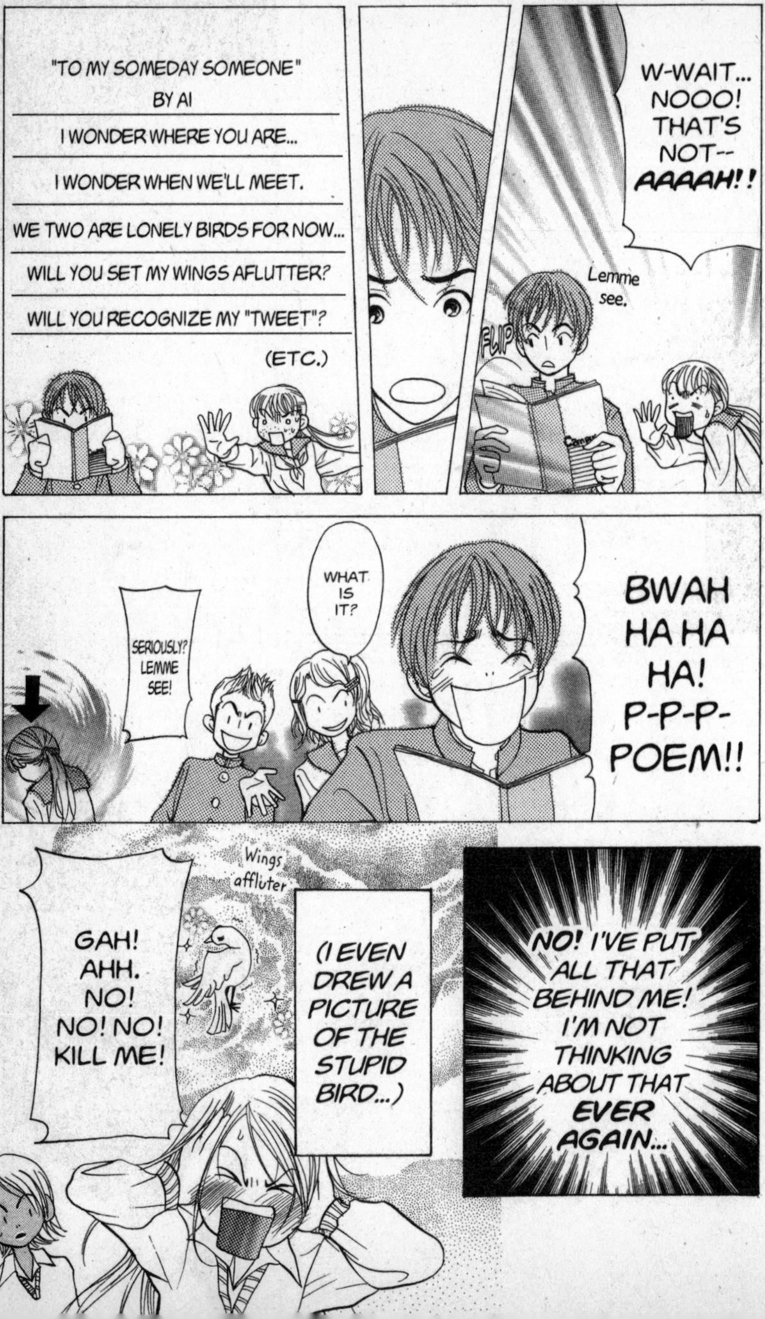

W-WAIT... NOOO! THAT'S NOT-- AAAAH!!
Lemme see.
FLIP
"TO MY SOMEDAY SOMEONE"
BY AI
I WONDER WHERE YOU ARE...
I WONDER WHEN WE'LL MEET.
WE TWO ARE LONELY BIRDS FOR NOW...
WILL YOU SET MY WINGS AFLUTTER?
WILL YOU RECOGNIZE MY "TWEET"?
(ETC.)
BWAH HA HA HA! P-P-P-POEM!!
WHAT IS IT?
SERIOUSLY? LEMME SEE!
NO! I'VE PUT ALL THAT BEHIND ME! I'M NOT THINKING ABOUT THAT EVER AGAIN...
(I EVEN DREW A PICTURE OF THE STUPID BIRD...)
Wings afflutter
GAH! AHH. NO! NO! NO! KILL ME!
Ai-ai ...?

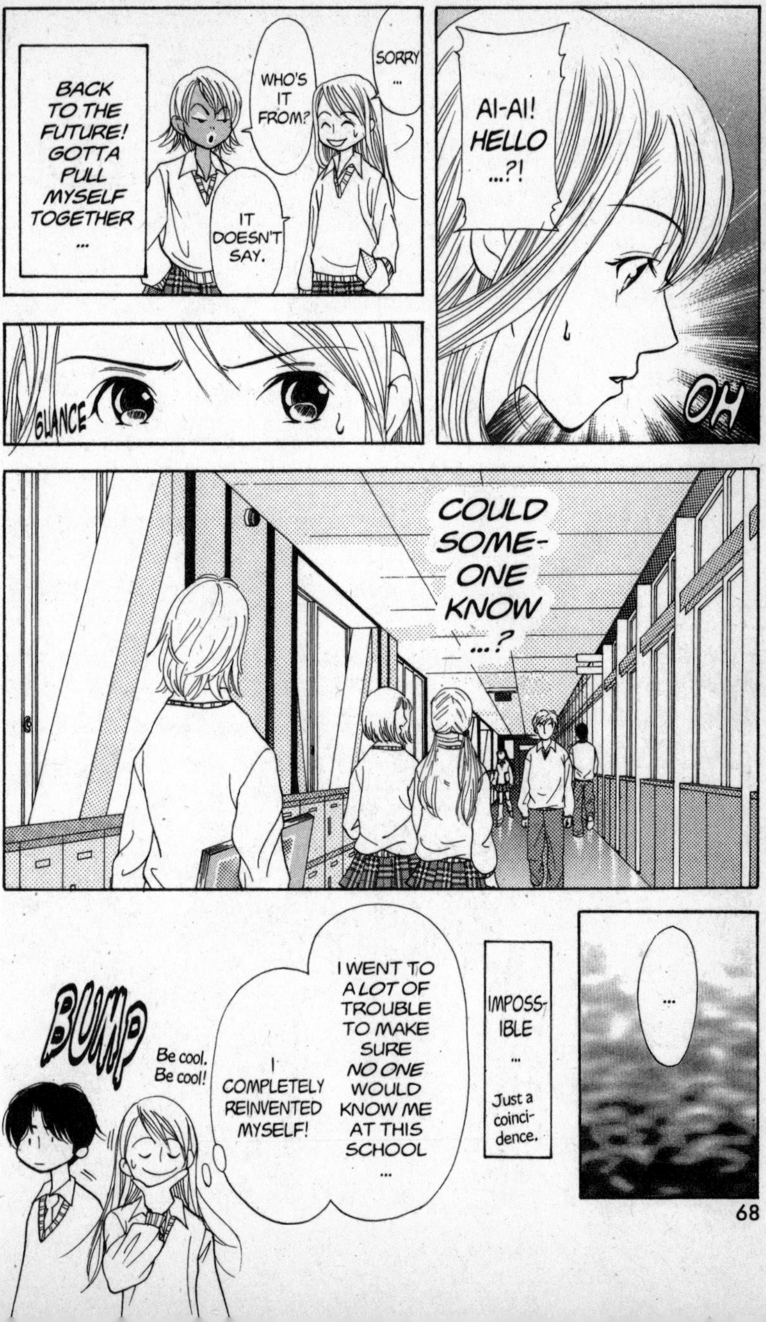
AI-AI! HELLO ...?!
OH
SORRY ...
WHO'S IT FROM?
IT DOESN'T SAY.
BACK TO THE FUTURE! GOTTA PULL MYSELF TOGETHER ...
GLANCE
COULD SOME-ONE KNOW ...?
...
IMPOSS-IBLE ...
Just a coinci-dence.
I WENT TO A LOT OF TROUBLE TO MAKE SURE *NO ONE* WOULD KNOW ME AT THIS SCHOOL ...
I COMPLETELY REINVENTED MYSELF!
Be cool. Be cool!
BUMP

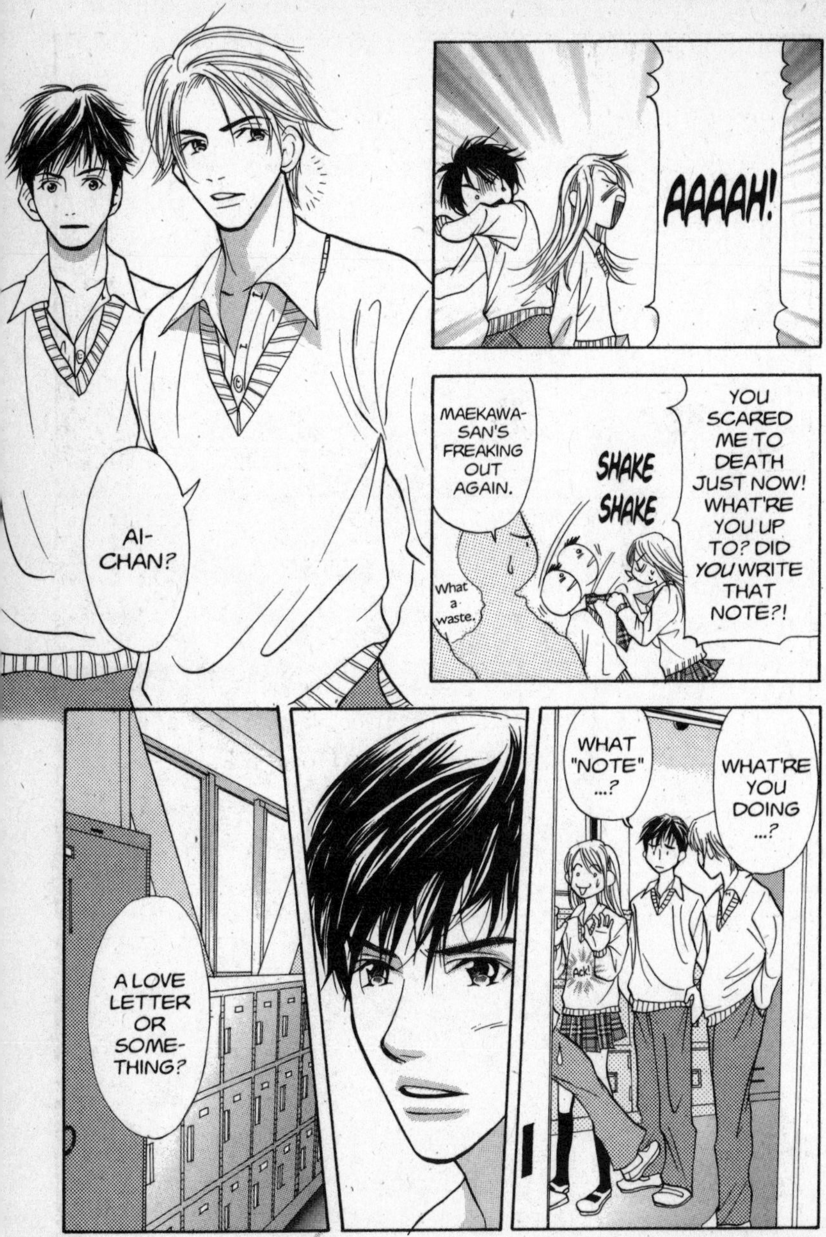
AAAAH!
YOU SCARED ME TO DEATH JUST NOW! WHAT'RE YOU UP TO? DID *YOU* WRITE THAT NOTE?!
MAEKAWA-SAN'S FREAKING OUT AGAIN.
SHAKE SHAKE
What a waste.
AI-CHAN?
WHAT'RE YOU DOING ...?
WHAT "NOTE" ...?
Ack!
A LOVE LETTER OR SOME-THING?

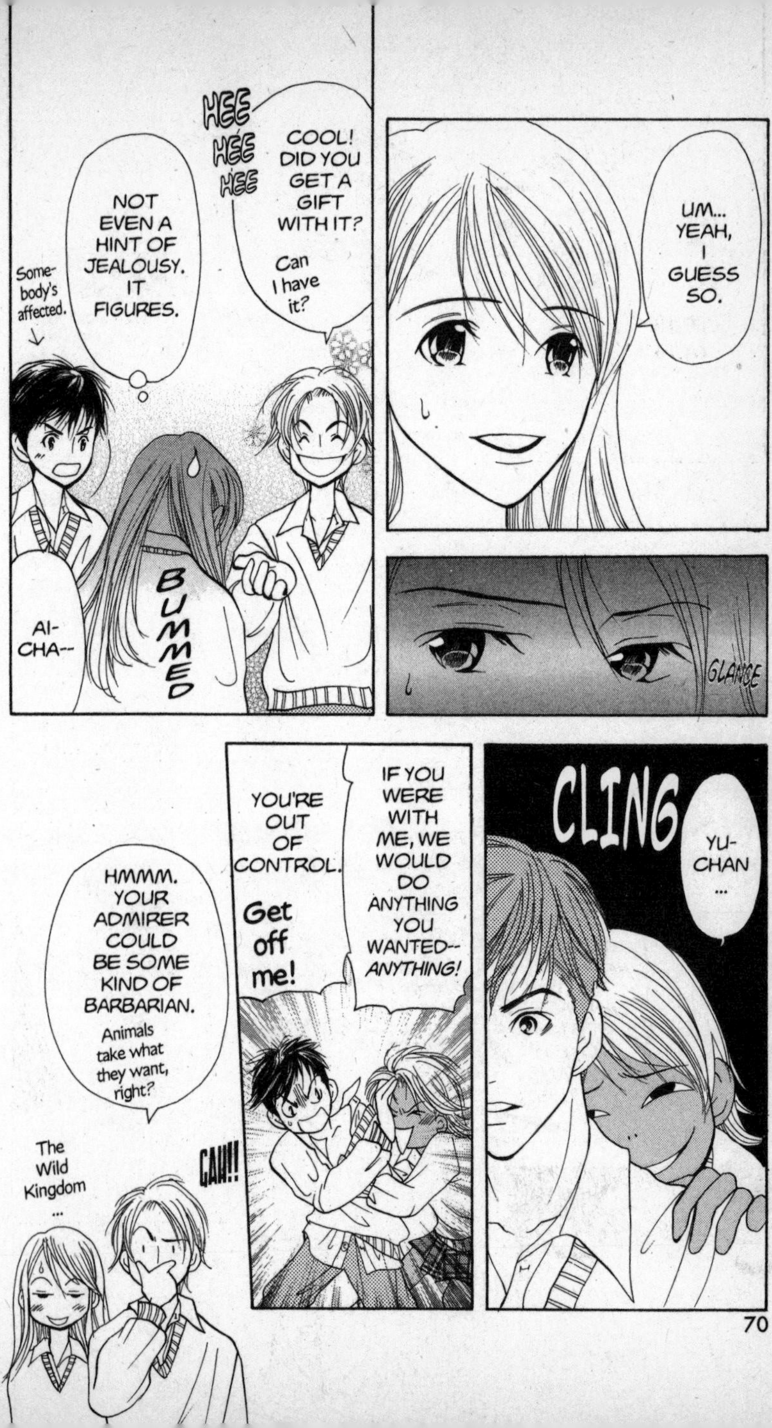
UM... YEAH, I GUESS SO.
GLANCE
HEE HEE HEE
COOL! DID YOU GET A GIFT WITH IT?
Can I have it?
NOT EVEN A HINT OF JEALOUSY. IT FIGURES.
Some-body's affected.
BUMMED
AI-CHA--
CLING
YU-CHAN ...
IF YOU WERE WITH ME, WE WOULD DO ANYTHING YOU WANTED-- ANYTHING!
YOU'RE OUT OF CONTROL.
Get off me!
GAH!!
HMMM. YOUR ADMIRER COULD BE SOME KIND OF BARBARIAN.
Animals take what they want, right?
The Wild Kingdom ...

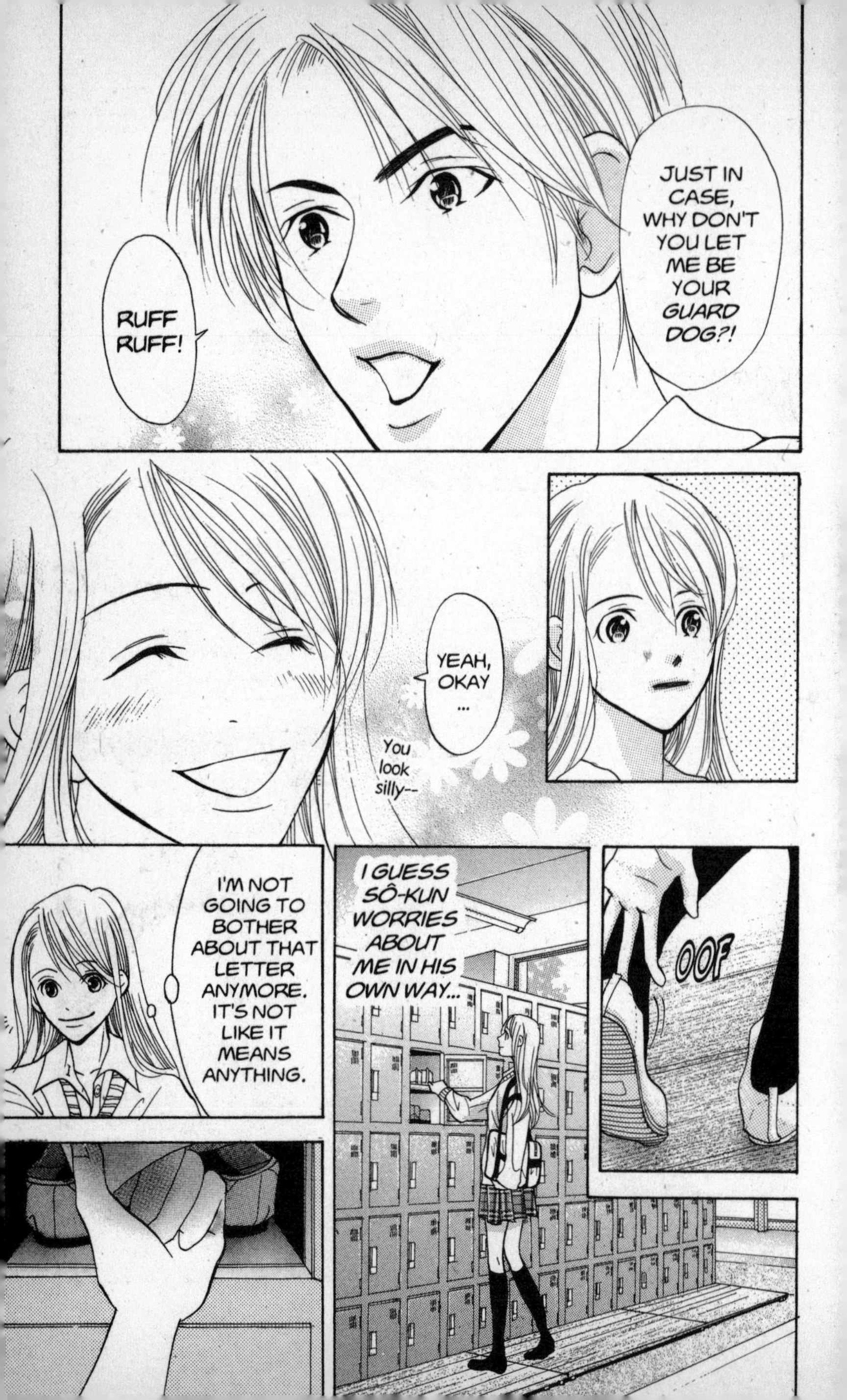
JUST IN CASE, WHY DON'T YOU LET ME BE YOUR GUARD DOG?!
RUFF RUFF!
YEAH, OKAY ...
You look silly--
OOF
I GUESS SÔ-KUN WORRIES ABOUT ME IN HIS OWN WAY...
I'M NOT GOING TO BOTHER ABOUT THAT LETTER ANYMORE. IT'S NOT LIKE IT MEANS ANYTHING.

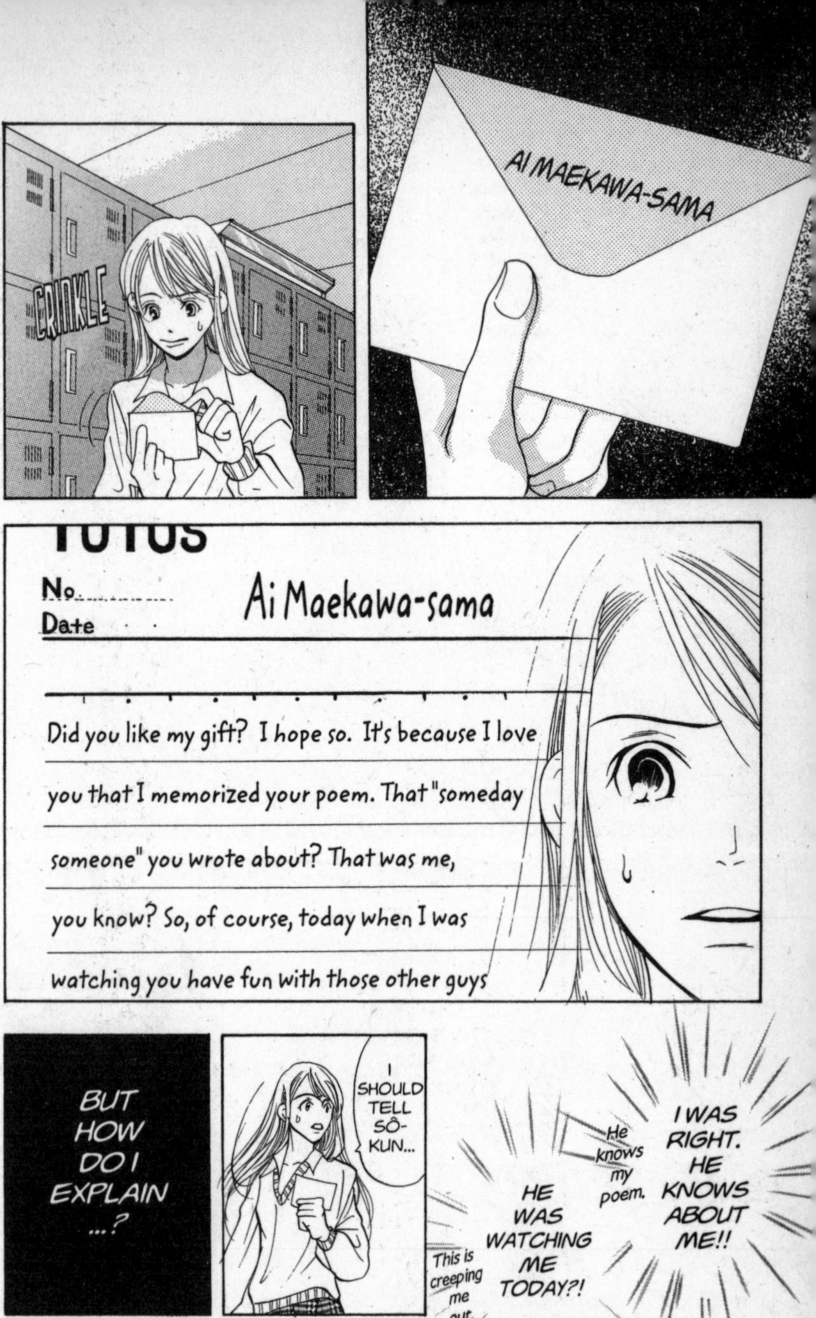
AI MAEKAWA-SAMA
CRINKLE
No.
Date
Ai Maekawa-sama
Did you like my gift? I hope so. It's because I love you that I memorized your poem. That "someday someone" you wrote about? That was me, you know? So, of course, today when I was watching you have fun with those other guys
I WAS RIGHT. HE KNOWS ABOUT ME!!
He knows my poem.
HE WAS WATCHING ME TODAY?!
This is creeping me out.
I SHOULD TELL SÔ-KUN...
BUT HOW DO I EXPLAIN ...?

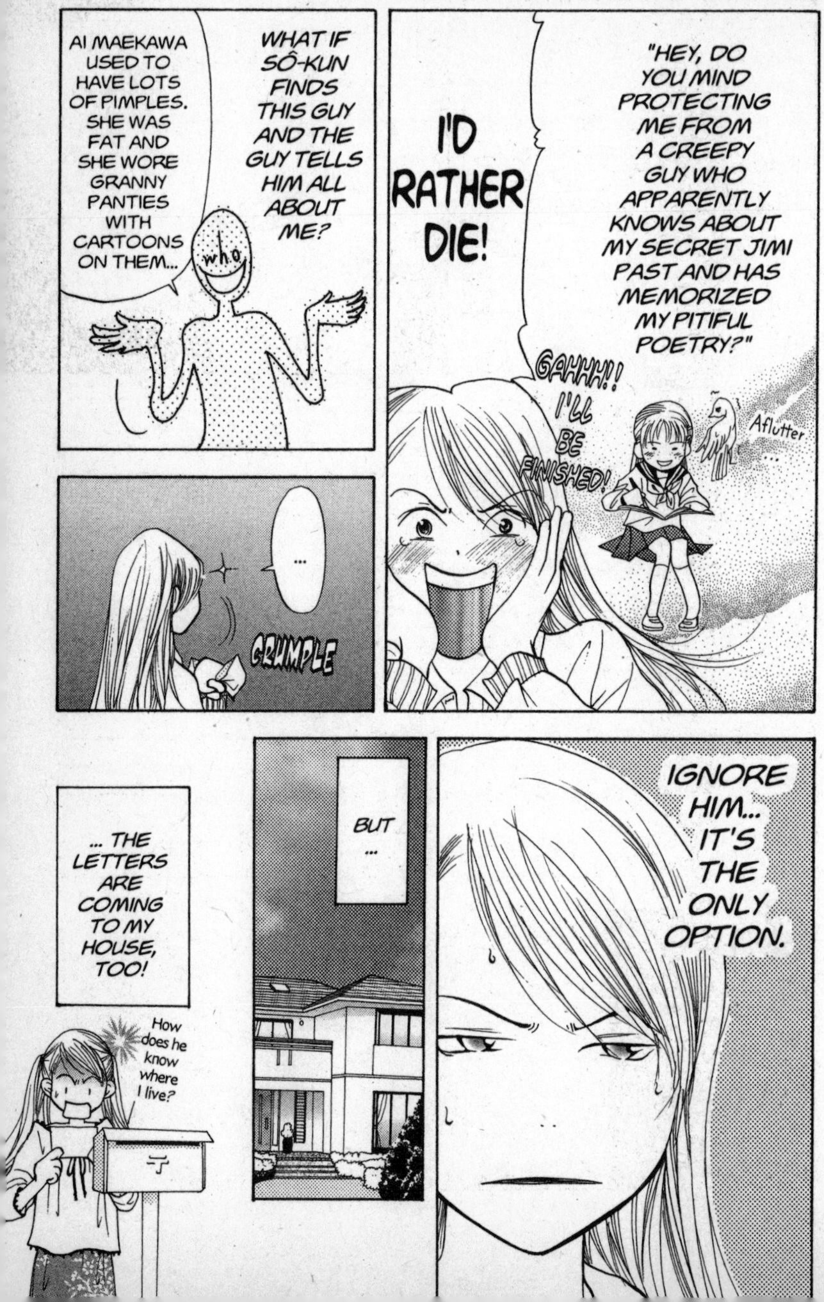
"HEY, DO YOU MIND PROTECTING ME FROM A CREEPY GUY WHO APPARENTLY KNOWS ABOUT MY SECRET JIMI PAST AND HAS MEMORIZED MY PITIFUL POETRY?"
I'D RATHER DIE!
GAHHH!! I'LL BE FINISHED!
Aflutter ...
WHAT IF SÔ-KUN FINDS THIS GUY AND THE GUY TELLS HIM ALL ABOUT ME?
AI MAEKAWA USED TO HAVE LOTS OF PIMPLES. SHE WAS FAT AND SHE WORE GRANNY PANTIES WITH CARTOONS ON THEM...
who
...
CRUMPLE
IGNORE HIM... IT'S THE ONLY OPTION.
BUT ...
... THE LETTERS ARE COMING TO MY HOUSE, TOO!
How does he know where I live?

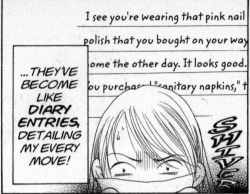

THE LETTERS ...
I see you're wearing that pink nail
polish that you bought on your way
ome the other day. It looks good.
ou purchas "sanitary napkins," t
...THEY'VE BECOME LIKE DIARY ENTRIES, DETAILING MY EVERY MOVE!
SHIVER
SIGH...
...
RIIING
RIIING
ALL RIGHT. CLASS HEADS, COLLECT THE NOTEBOOKS AND BRING THEM TO THE TEACHER'S LOUNGE, PLEASE.
AI-AI...
WILL YOU STOP CALLING ME THAT?! IT SOUNDS LIKE A MONKEY'S NAME.*

*Actually, the aye-aye is a lemur: http://www.lemurs.animalzoo.co.uk/lemurs/aye-aye.htm

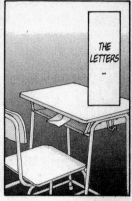

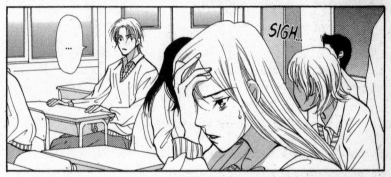

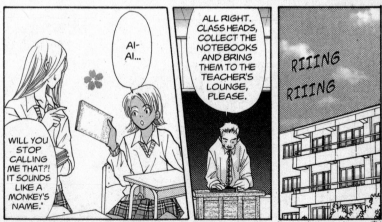

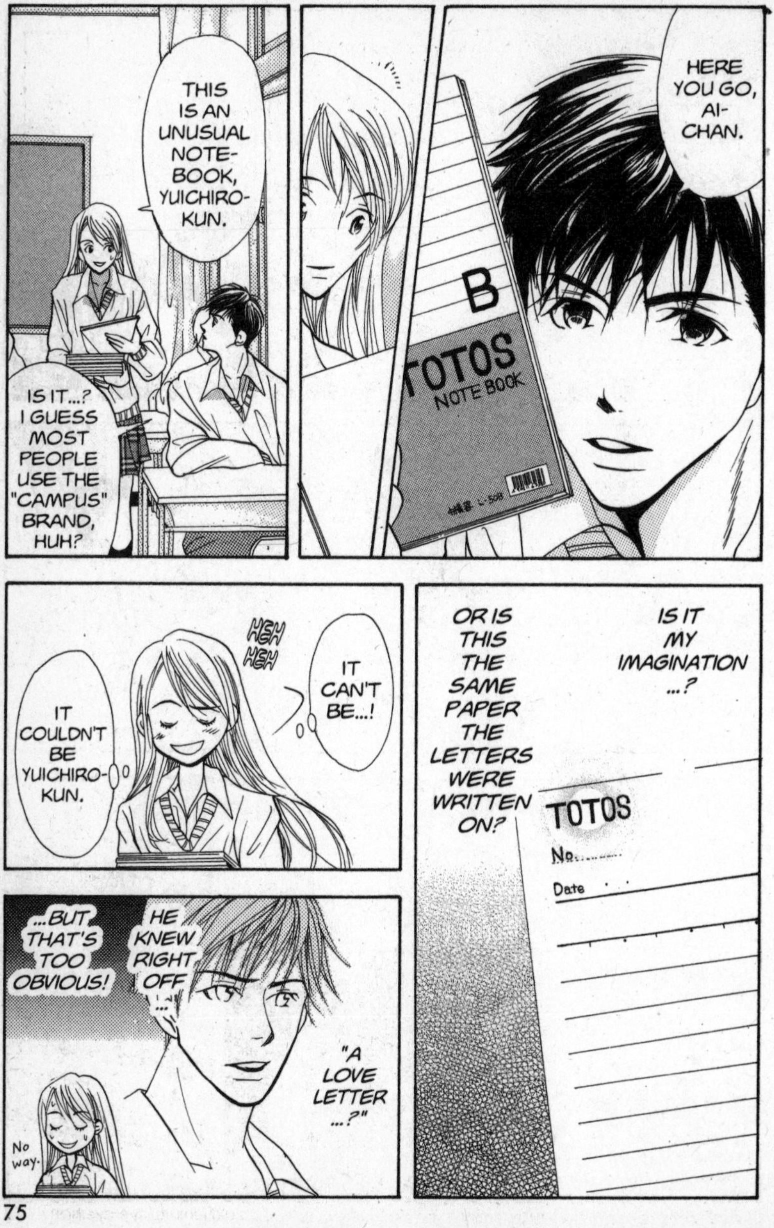
HERE YOU GO, AI-CHAN.
B
TOTOS NOTE BOOK
THIS IS AN UNUSUAL NOTE-BOOK, YUICHIRO-KUN.
IS IT...? I GUESS MOST PEOPLE USE THE "CAMPUS" BRAND, HUH?
IS IT MY IMAGINATION ...?
OR IS THIS THE SAME PAPER THE LETTERS WERE WRITTEN ON?
TOTOS
No.
Date
IT CAN'T BE...!
HEH HEH
IT COULDN'T BE YUICHIRO-KUN.
HE KNEW RIGHT OFF ...
...BUT THAT'S TOO OBVIOUS!
"A LOVE LETTER ...?"
No way.

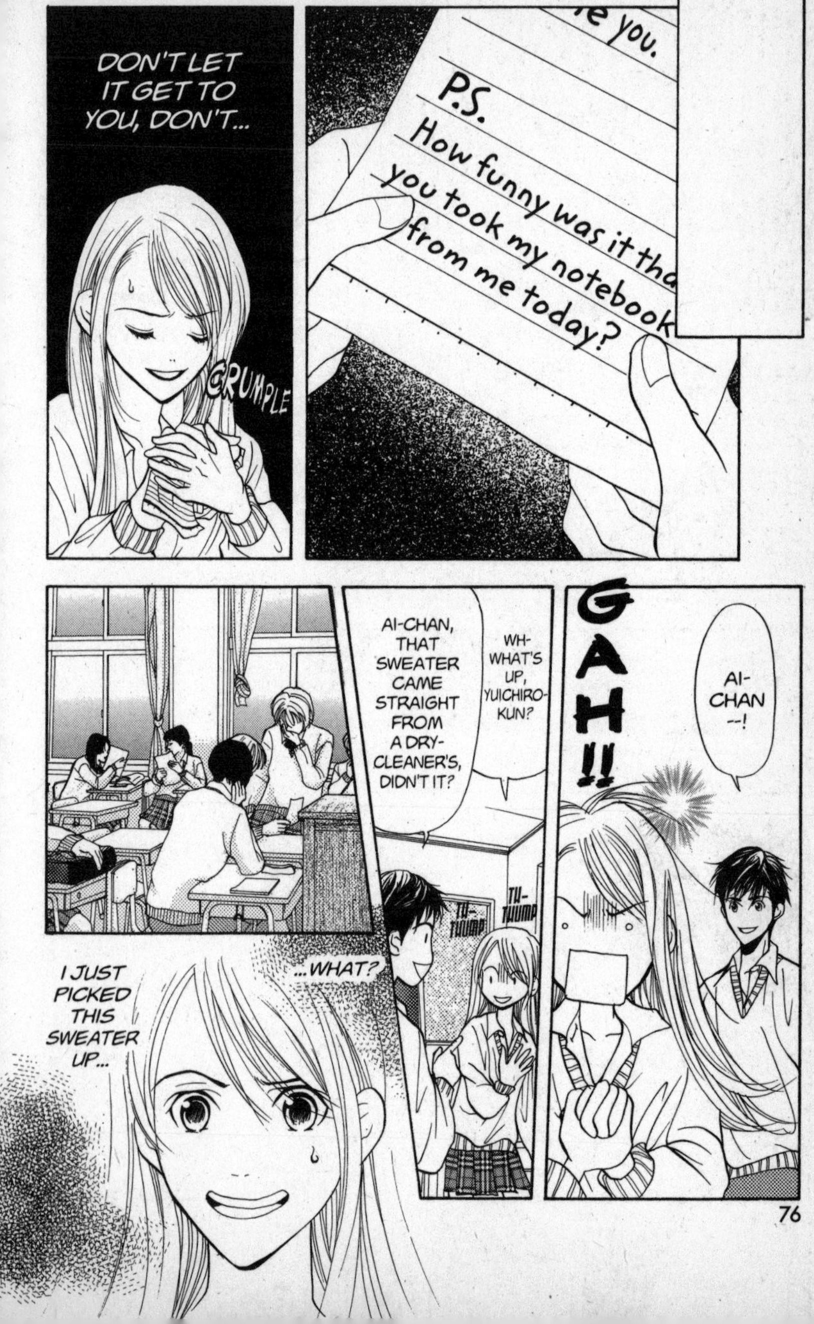

e you.
P.S.
How funny was it tha
you took my notebook
from me today?
DON'T LET IT GET TO YOU, DON'T...
CRUMPLE
AI-CHAN--!
GAH!!
WH-WHAT'S UP, YUICHIRO-KUN?
AI-CHAN, THAT SWEATER CAME STRAIGHT FROM A DRY-CLEANER'S, DIDN'T IT?
TH-THUMP
TH-THUMP
...WHAT?
I JUST PICKED THIS SWEATER UP...

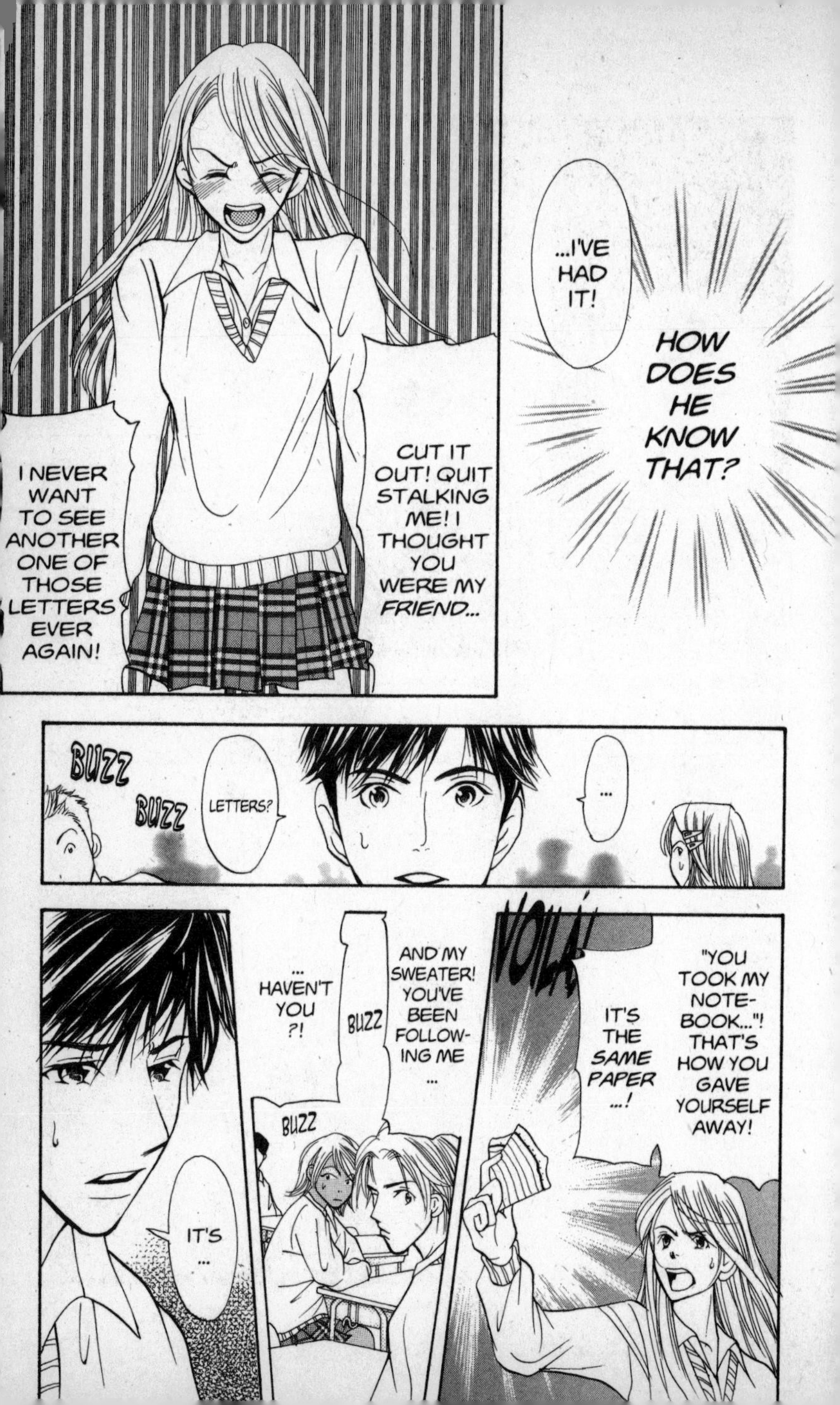

...I'VE HAD IT!
HOW DOES HE KNOW THAT?
CUT IT OUT! QUIT STALKING ME! I THOUGHT YOU WERE MY FRIEND...
I NEVER WANT TO SEE ANOTHER ONE OF THOSE LETTERS EVER AGAIN!
...
LETTERS?
BUZZ
BUZZ
VOILÀ!
"YOU TOOK MY NOTE-BOOK..."! THAT'S HOW YOU GAVE YOURSELF AWAY!
IT'S THE SAME PAPER ...!
AND MY SWEATER! YOU'VE BEEN FOLLOW-ING ME ...
BUZZ
... HAVEN'T YOU ?!
BUZZ
IT'S ...

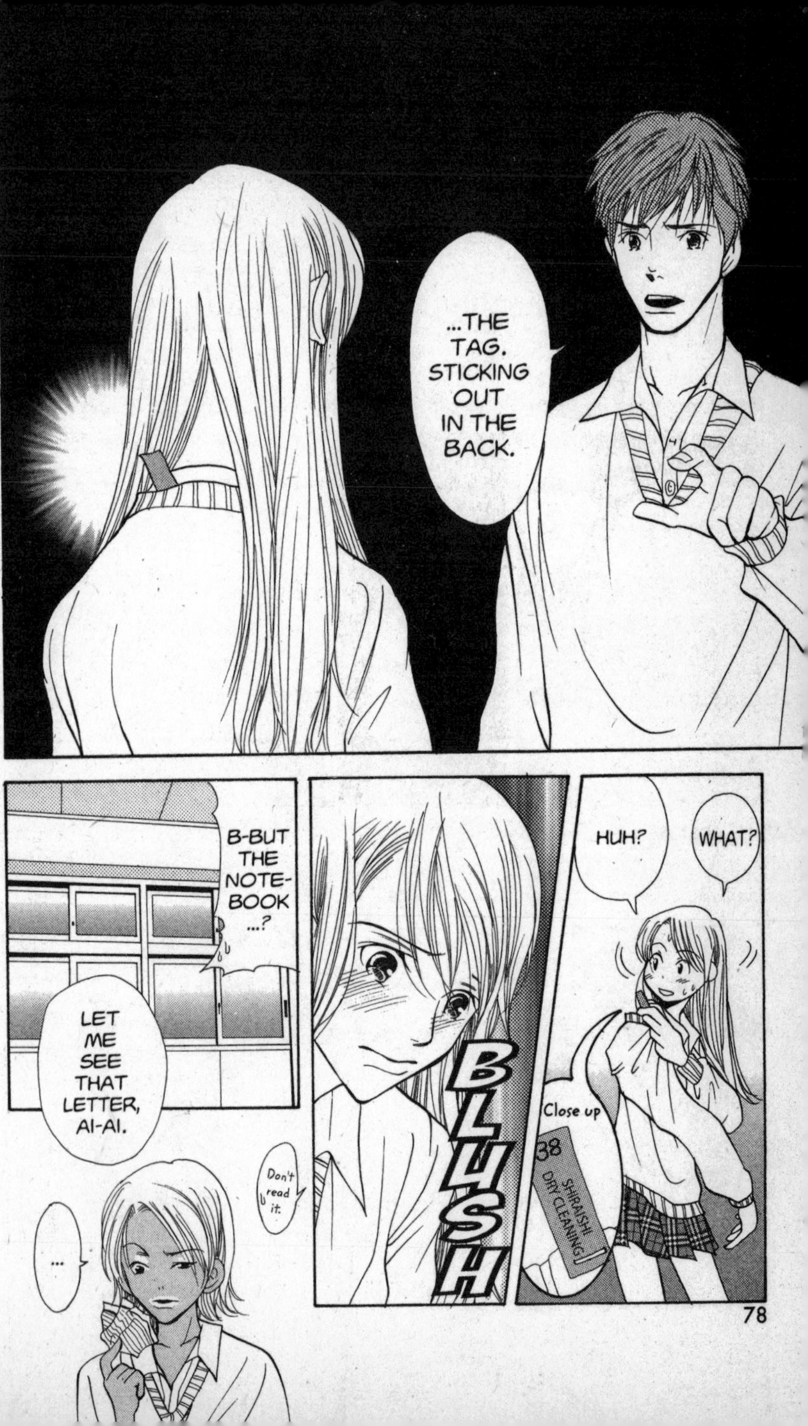
...THE TAG. STICKING OUT IN THE BACK.
WHAT?
HUH?
Close up
38 SHIRAISHI DRY CLEANING
BLUSH
B-BUT THE NOTE-BOOK ...?
LET ME SEE THAT LETTER, AI-AI.
Don't read it.
...

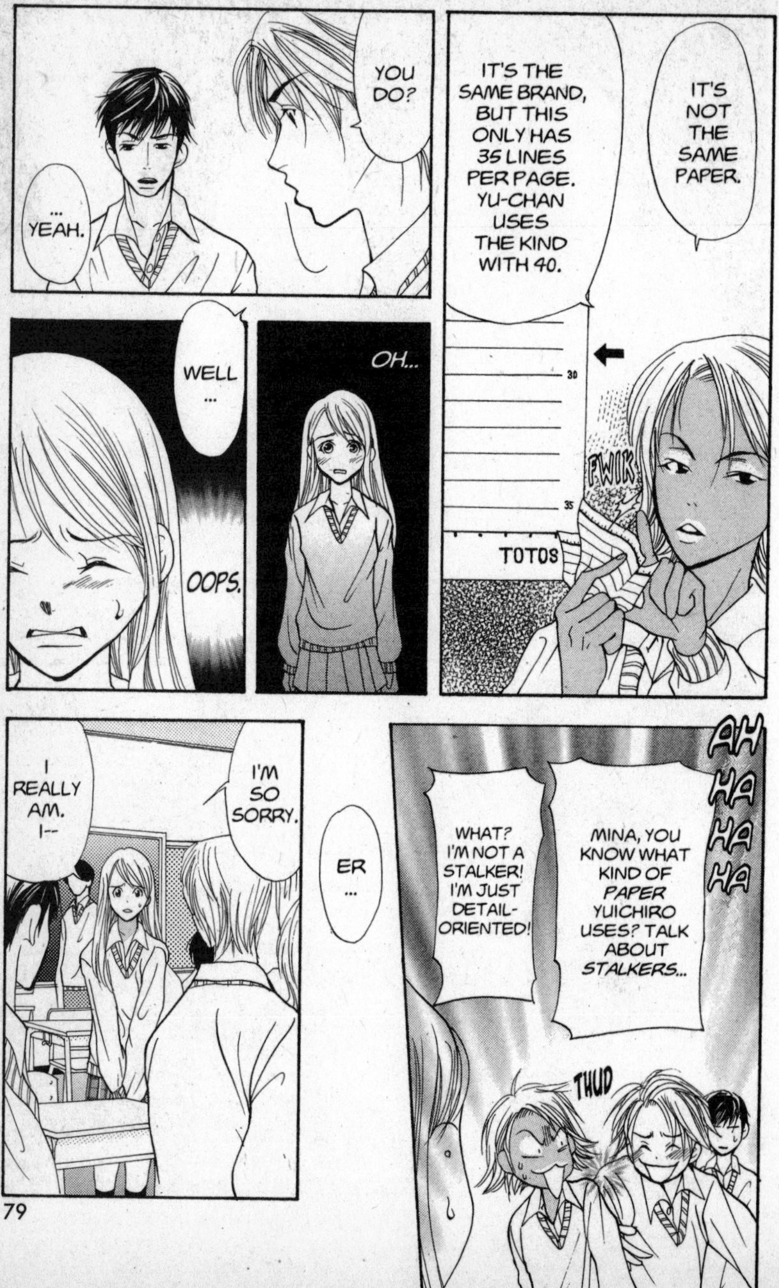
IT'S NOT THE SAME PAPER.
IT'S THE SAME BRAND, BUT THIS ONLY HAS 35 LINES PER PAGE. YU-CHAN USES THE KIND WITH 40.
30
35
TOTOS
FWIK
YOU DO?
... YEAH.
OH...
WELL ...
OOPS.
AH HA HA HA
MINA, YOU KNOW WHAT KIND OF PAPER YUICHIRO USES? TALK ABOUT STALKERS...
WHAT? I'M NOT A STALKER! I'M JUST DETAIL-ORIENTED!
THUD
ER ...
I'M SO SORRY.
I REALLY AM. I--

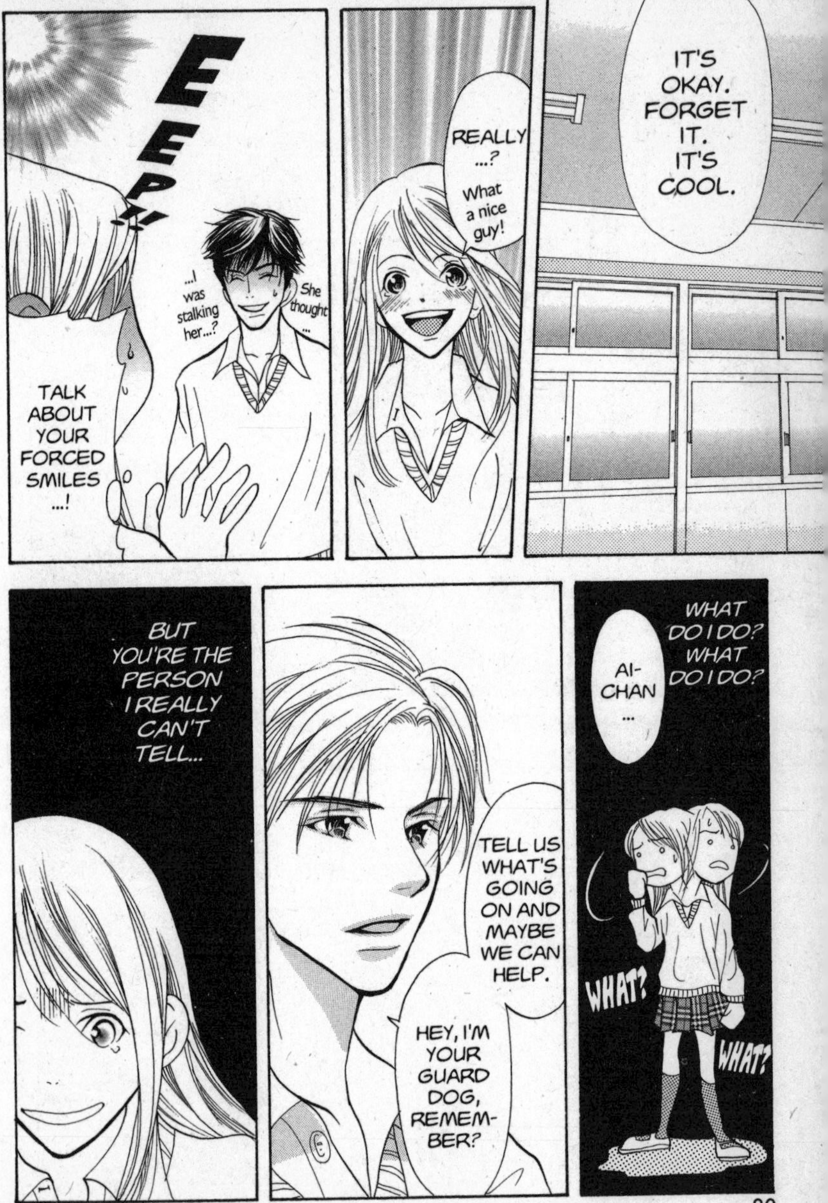

IT'S OKAY. FORGET IT. IT'S COOL.
REALLY ...?
What a nice guy!
EEEP!!
She thought ...
...I was stalking her...?
TALK ABOUT YOUR FORCED SMILES ...!
WHAT DO I DO? WHAT DO I DO?
AI-CHAN ...
WHAT?
WHAT?
TELL US WHAT'S GOING ON AND MAYBE WE CAN HELP.
HEY, I'M YOUR GUARD DOG, REMEMBER?
BUT YOU'RE THE PERSON I REALLY CAN'T TELL...

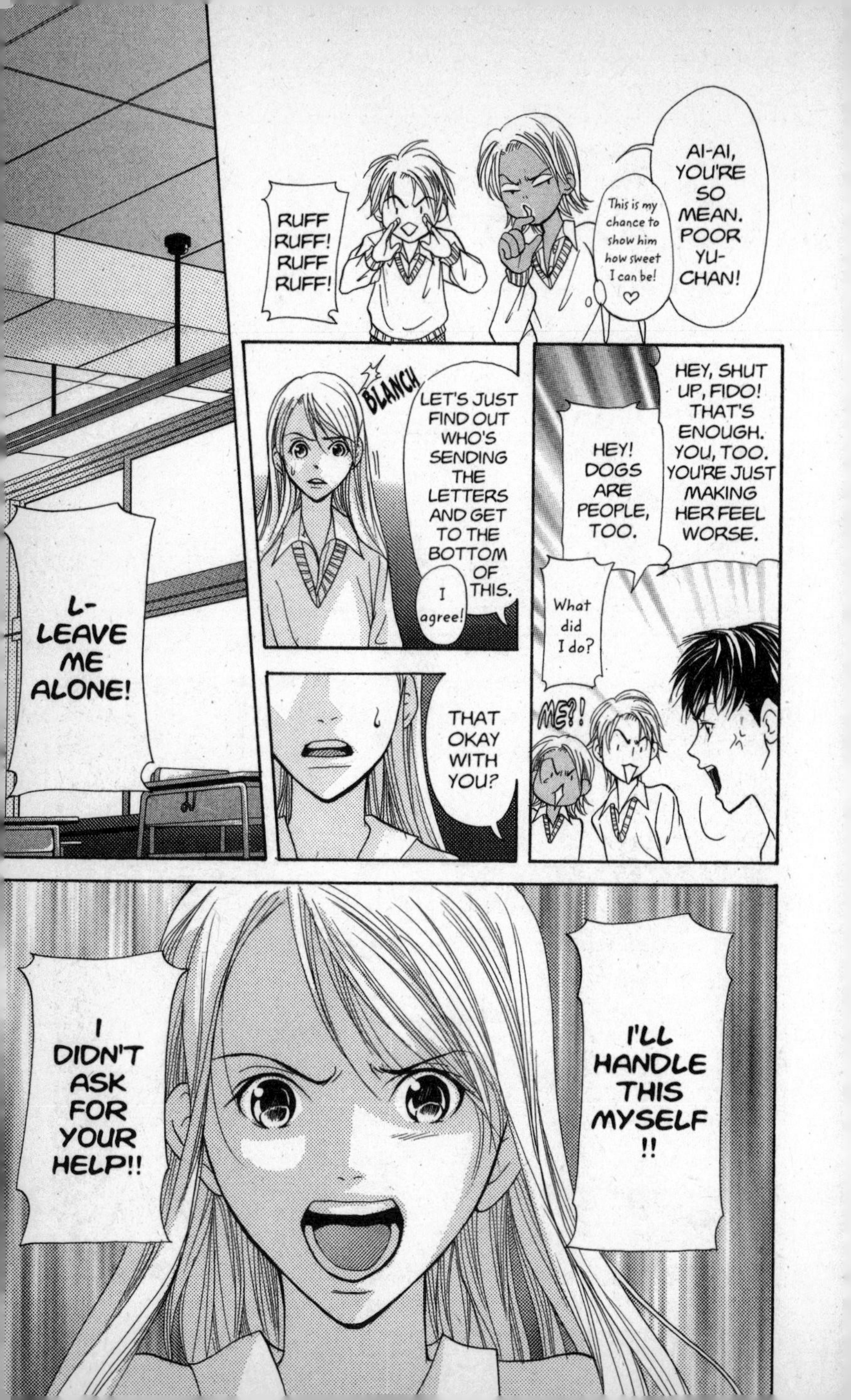
AI-AI, YOU'RE SO MEAN. POOR YU-CHAN!
This is my chance to show him how sweet I can be! ♡
RUFF RUFF! RUFF RUFF!
HEY, SHUT UP, FIDO! THAT'S ENOUGH. YOU, TOO. YOU'RE JUST MAKING HER FEEL WORSE.
HEY! DOGS ARE PEOPLE, TOO.
What did I do?
ME?!
BLANCH
LET'S JUST FIND OUT WHO'S SENDING THE LETTERS AND GET TO THE BOTTOM OF THIS.
I agree!
THAT OKAY WITH YOU?
L-LEAVE ME ALONE!
I'LL HANDLE THIS MYSELF!!
I DIDN'T ASK FOR YOUR HELP!!

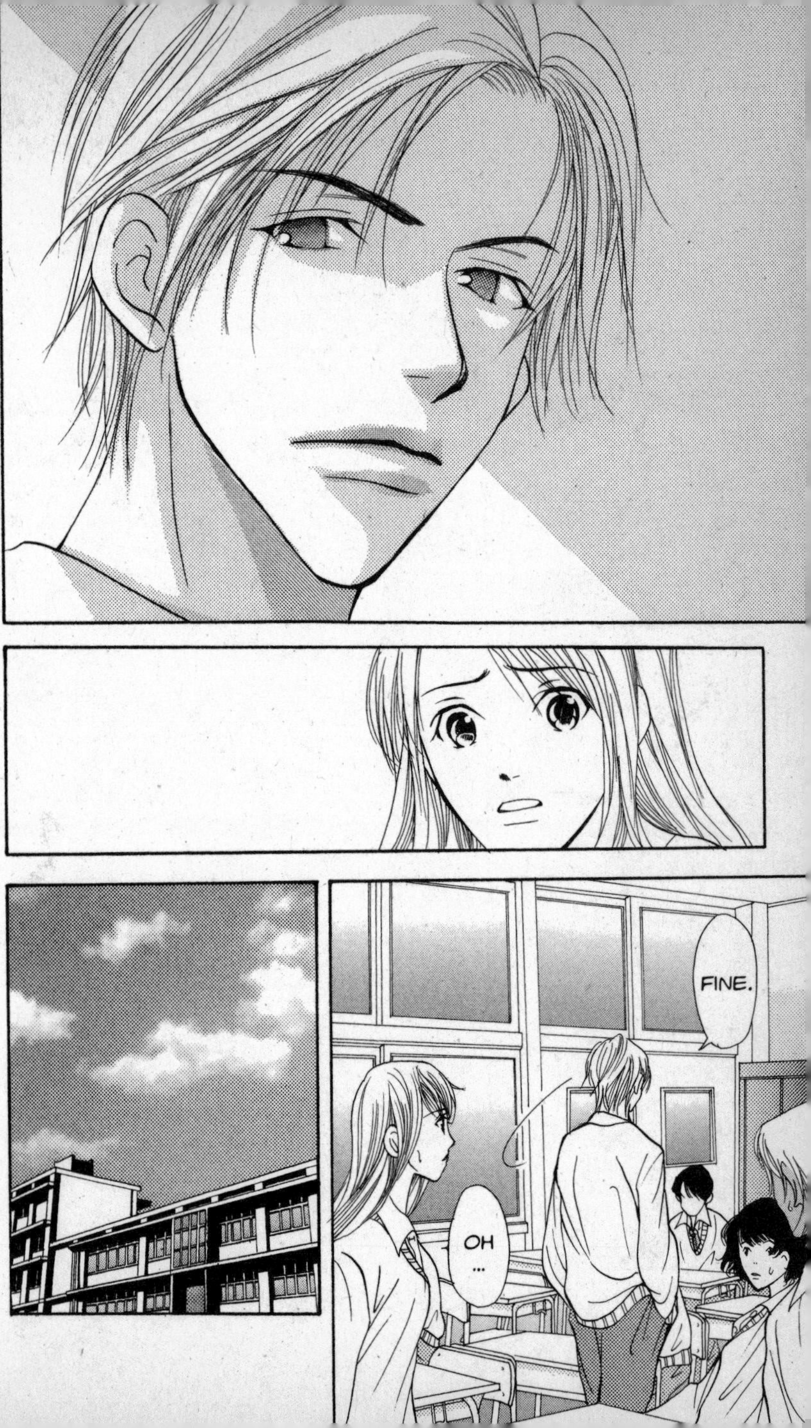
FINE.
OH ...

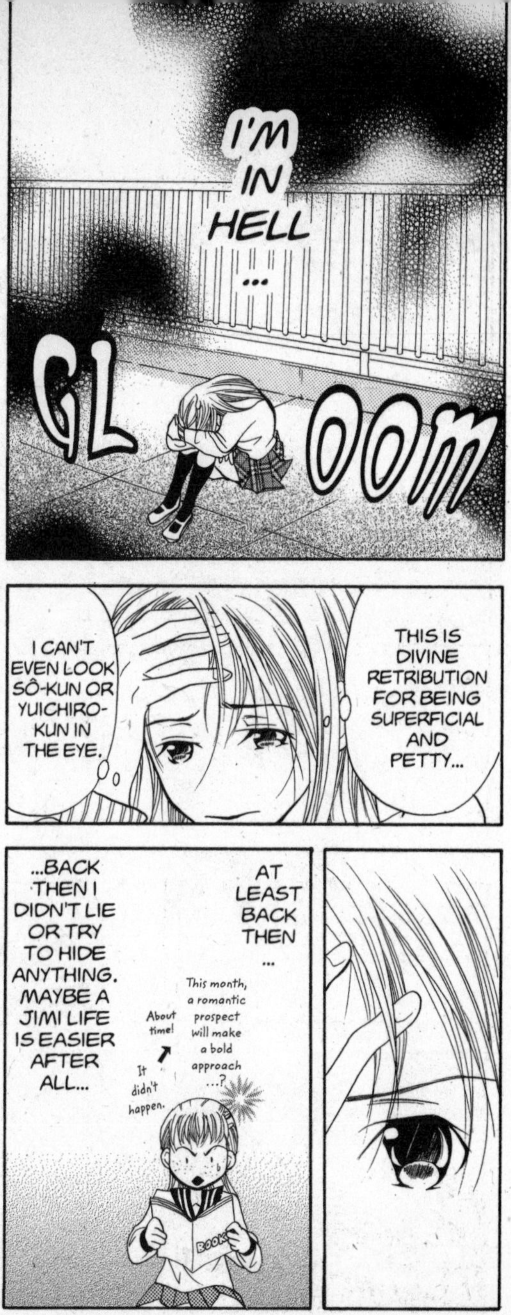
I'M IN HELL ...
GL OOM
THIS IS DIVINE RETRIBUTION FOR BEING SUPERFICIAL AND PETTY...
I CAN'T EVEN LOOK SÔ-KUN OR YUICHIRO-KUN IN THE EYE.
AT LEAST BACK THEN ...
...BACK THEN I DIDN'T LIE OR TRY TO HIDE ANYTHING. MAYBE A JIMI LIFE IS EASIER AFTER ALL...
This month, a romantic prospect will make a bold approach ...?
About time!
It didn't happen.
BOOK

Exciting Encounters!
An Encyclopedia of Creatures

Part 2

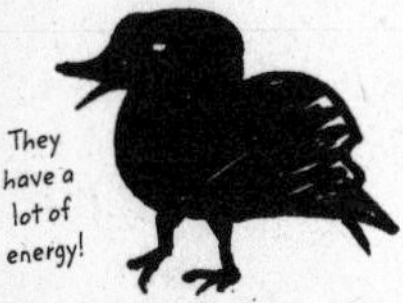
They have a lot of energy!

Crow (Bird)

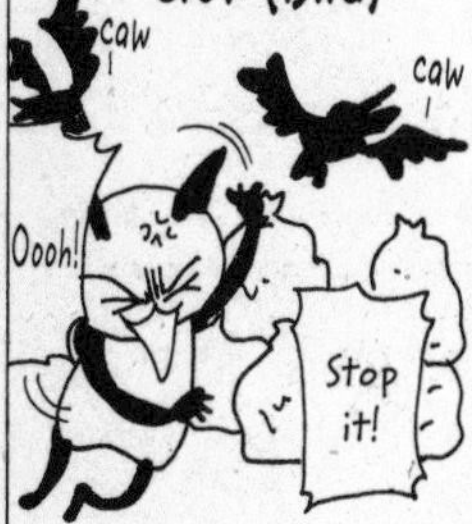
caw
caw
Oooh!
Stop it!

How many times have I had to shoo them away from the garbage...? They're hell-bent on shredding my trash bags so that my embarrassing **first drafts** will spill out for the world to see...

Seriously, please leave me alone, you awful birds! If my neighbors knew how bad my first drafts were, I'd just die...

There was this one particular bird among them...

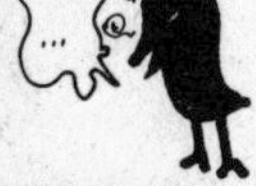
caaaw ...

⇐ weak squawk. Was he sick? I wonder what happened to him...

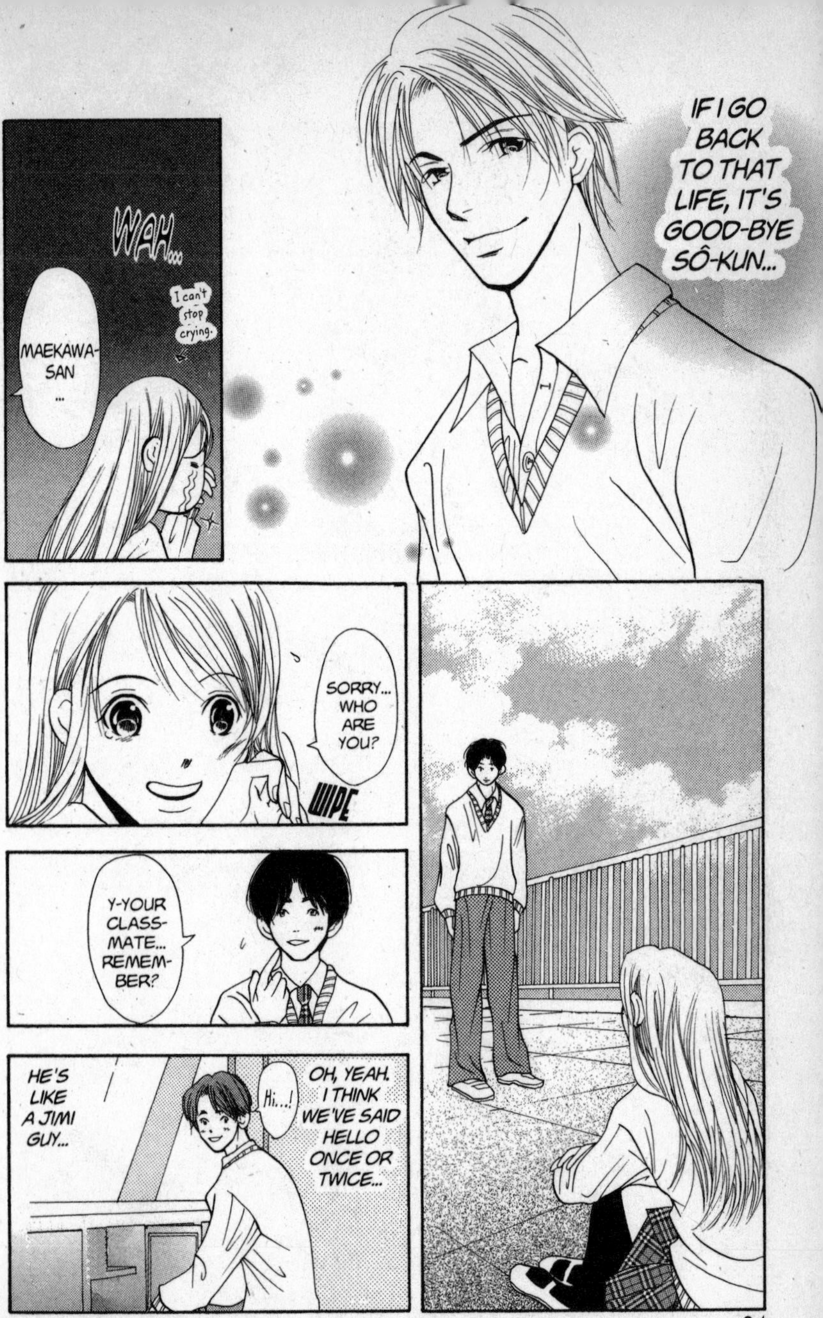
IF I GO BACK TO THAT LIFE, IT'S GOOD-BYE SÔ-KUN...
WAH...
I can't stop crying.
MAEKAWA-SAN ...
SORRY... WHO ARE YOU?
WIPE
Y-YOUR CLASSMATE... REMEMBER?
OH, YEAH. I THINK WE'VE SAID HELLO ONCE OR TWICE...
Hi...!
HE'S LIKE A JIMI GUY...

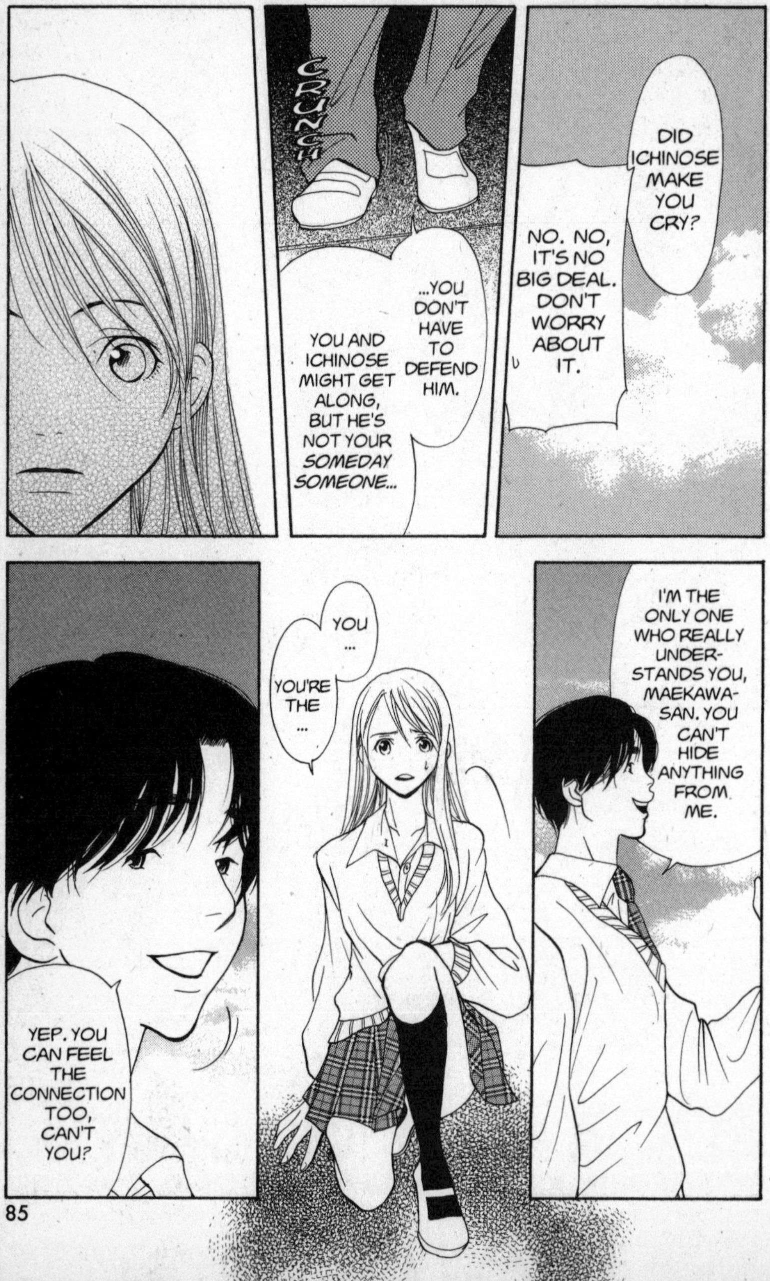
DID ICHINOSE MAKE YOU CRY?
NO. NO, IT'S NO BIG DEAL. DON'T WORRY ABOUT IT.
CRUNCH
...YOU DON'T HAVE TO DEFEND HIM.
YOU AND ICHINOSE MIGHT GET ALONG, BUT HE'S NOT YOUR *SOMEDAY SOMEONE*...
I'M THE ONLY ONE WHO REALLY UNDERSTANDS YOU, MAEKAWA-SAN. YOU CAN'T HIDE ANYTHING FROM ME.
YOU ... YOU'RE THE ...
YEP. YOU CAN FEEL THE CONNECTION TOO, CAN'T YOU?

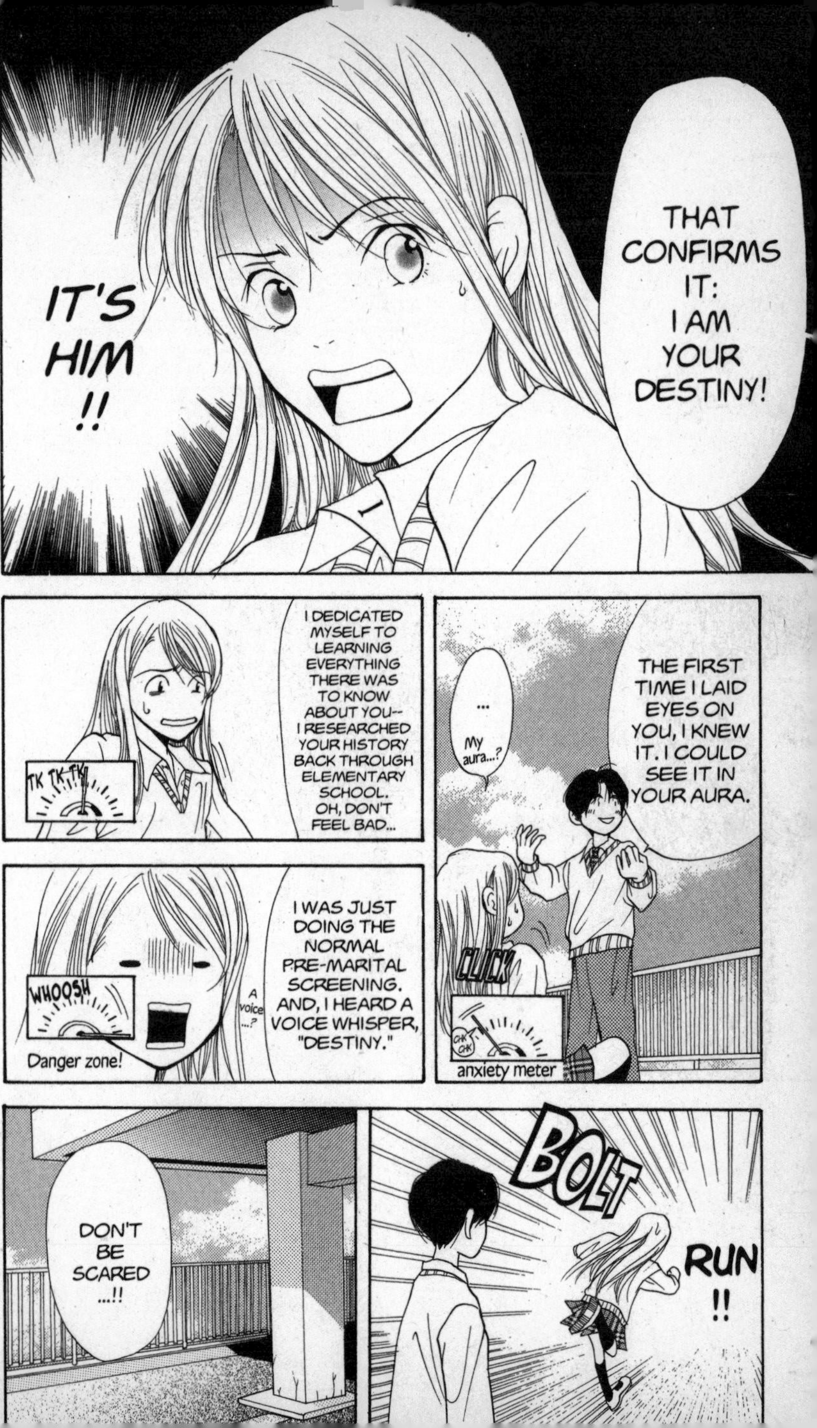
THAT CONFIRMS IT: I AM YOUR DESTINY!
IT'S HIM !!
THE FIRST TIME I LAID EYES ON YOU, I KNEW IT. I COULD SEE IT IN YOUR AURA.
...
My aura...?
CLICK
CHK CHK
anxiety meter
I DEDICATED MYSELF TO LEARNING EVERYTHING THERE WAS TO KNOW ABOUT YOU-- I RESEARCHED YOUR HISTORY BACK THROUGH ELEMENTARY SCHOOL. OH, DON'T FEEL BAD...
TK TK TK
I WAS JUST DOING THE NORMAL PRE-MARITAL SCREENING. AND, I HEARD A VOICE WHISPER, "DESTINY."
A voice ...?
WHOOSH
Danger zone!
BOLT
RUN !!
DON'T BE SCARED ...!!

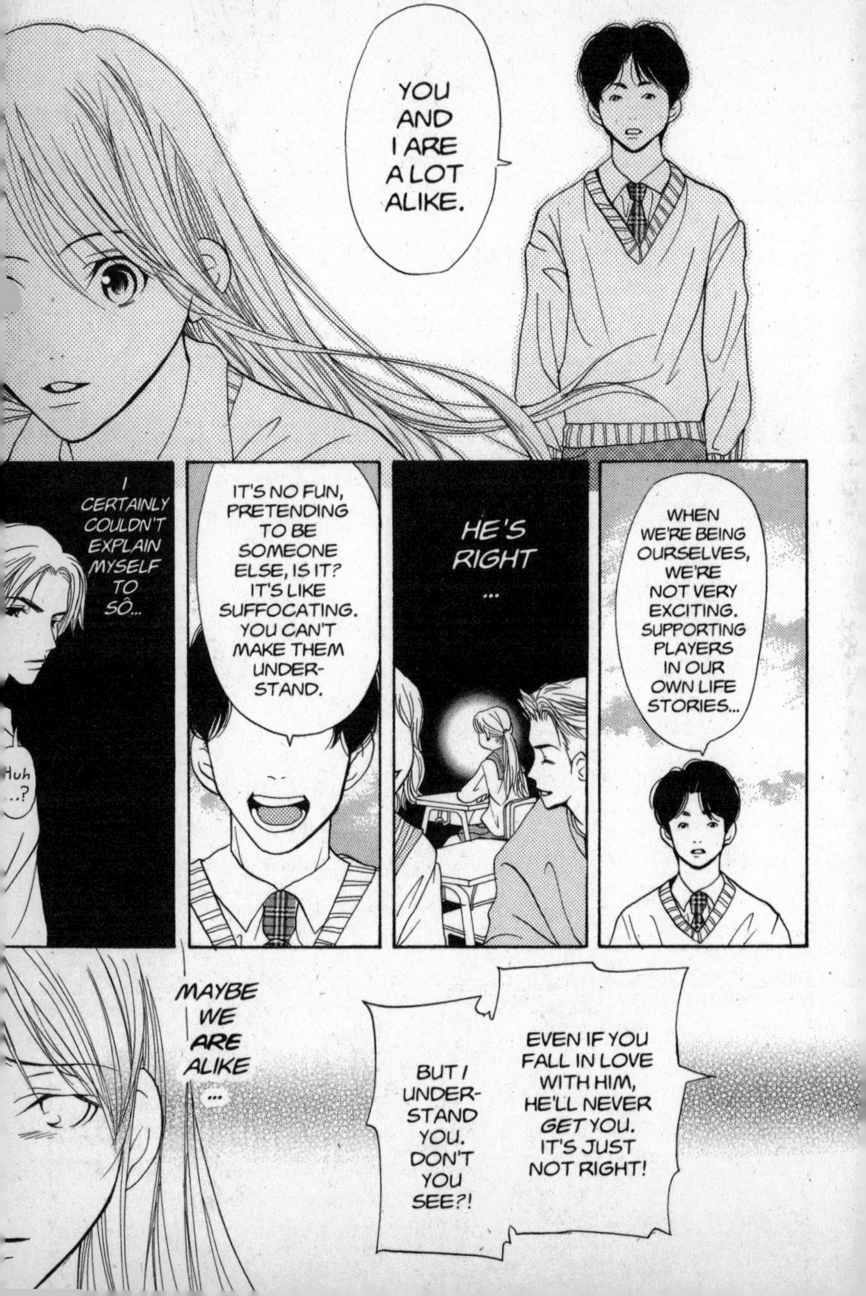
YOU AND I ARE A LOT ALIKE.
WHEN WE'RE BEING OURSELVES, WE'RE NOT VERY EXCITING. SUPPORTING PLAYERS IN OUR OWN LIFE STORIES...
HE'S RIGHT ...
IT'S NO FUN, PRETENDING TO BE SOMEONE ELSE, IS IT? IT'S LIKE SUFFOCATING. YOU CAN'T MAKE THEM UNDER-STAND.
I CERTAINLY COULDN'T EXPLAIN MYSELF TO SÔ...
Huh ...?
EVEN IF YOU FALL IN LOVE WITH HIM, HE'LL NEVER GET YOU. IT'S JUST NOT RIGHT!
BUT I UNDER-STAND YOU. DON'T YOU SEE?!
MAYBE WE ARE ALIKE ...

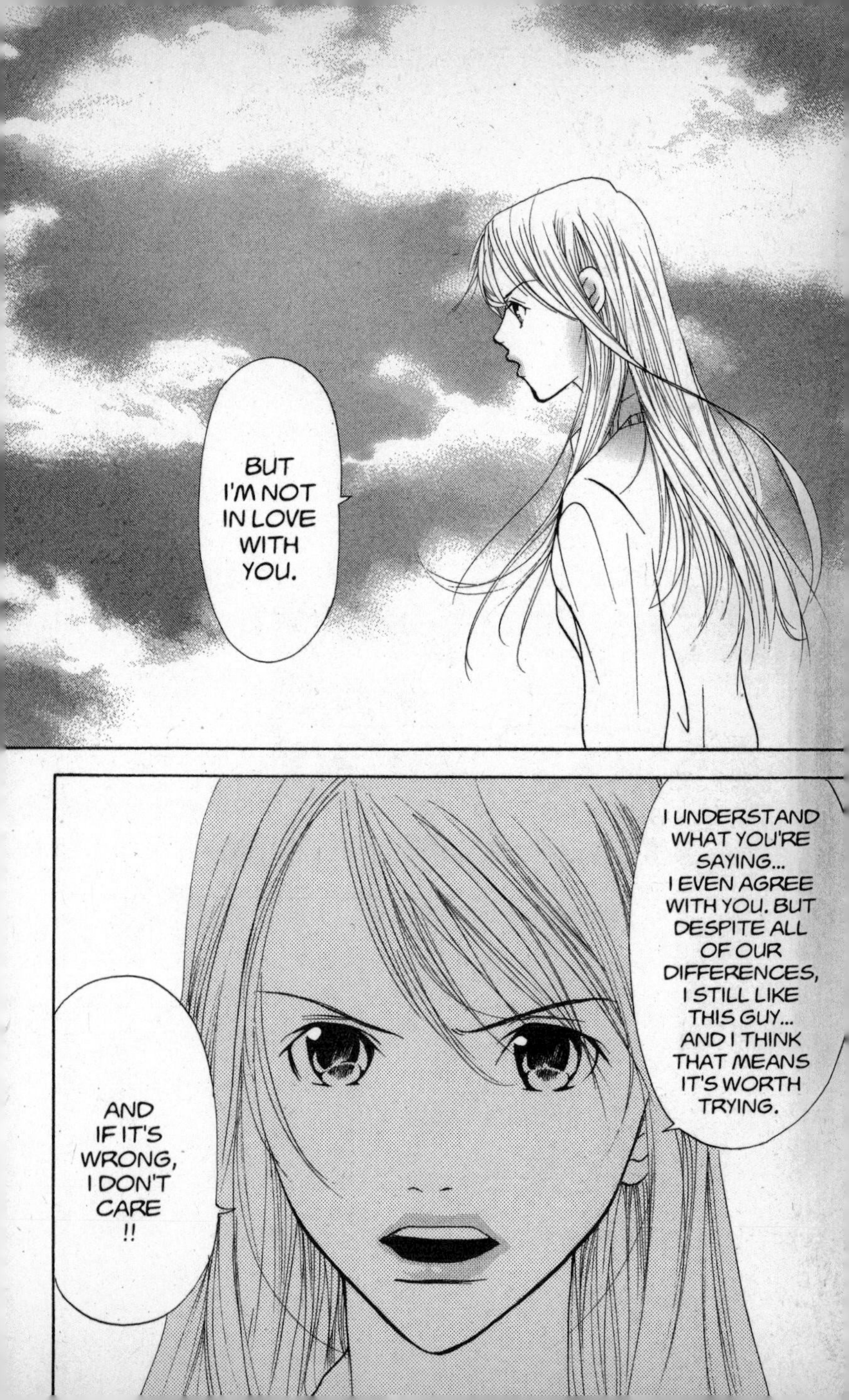
BUT I'M NOT IN LOVE WITH YOU.
I UNDERSTAND WHAT YOU'RE SAYING... I EVEN AGREE WITH YOU. BUT DESPITE ALL OF OUR DIFFERENCES, I STILL LIKE THIS GUY... AND I THINK THAT MEANS IT'S WORTH TRYING.
AND IF IT'S WRONG, I DON'T CARE !!

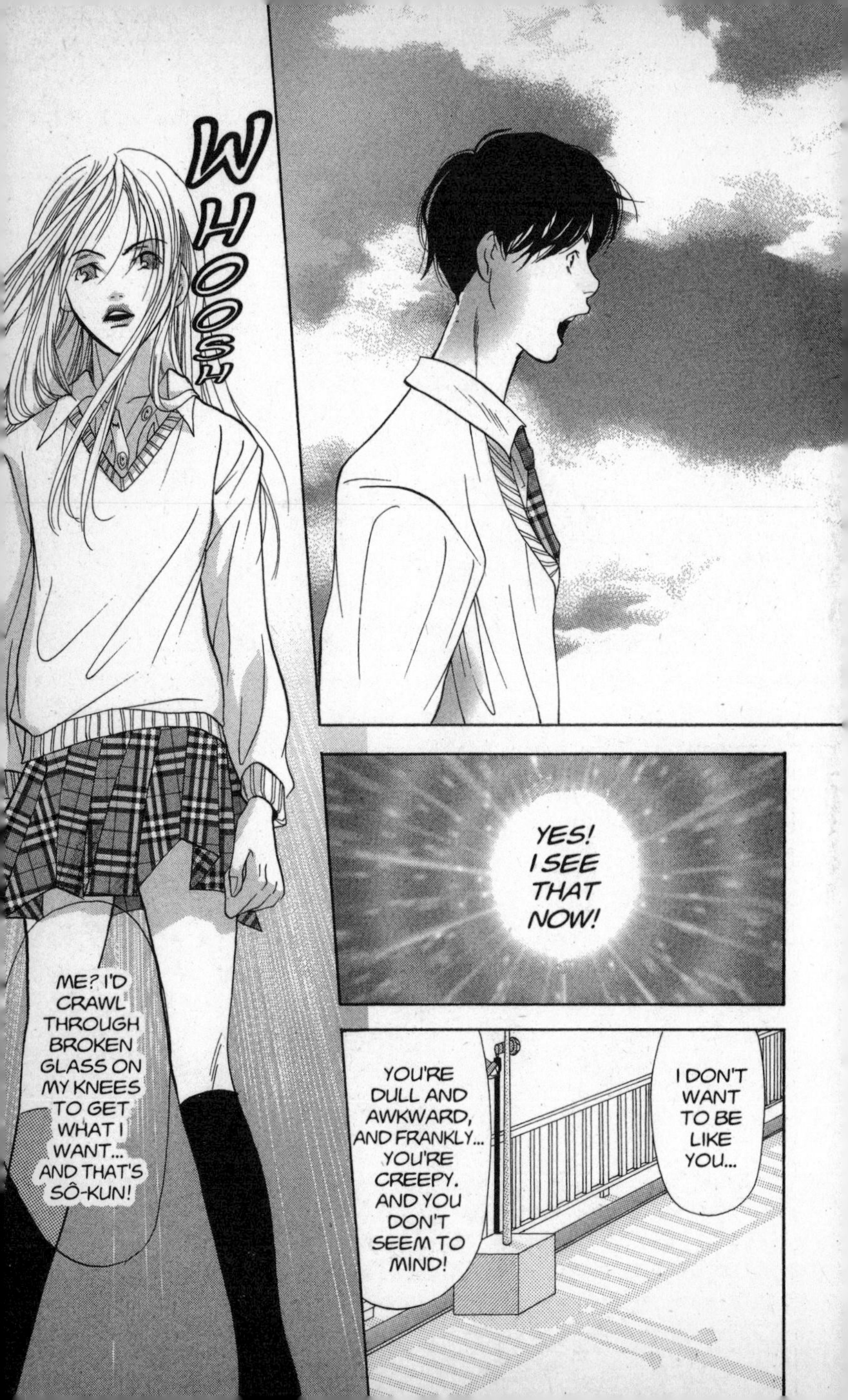
YES! I SEE THAT NOW!
I DON'T WANT TO BE LIKE YOU...
YOU'RE DULL AND AWKWARD, AND FRANKLY... YOU'RE CREEPY. AND YOU DON'T SEEM TO MIND!
WHOOOSH
ME? I'D CRAWL THROUGH BROKEN GLASS ON MY KNEES TO GET WHAT I WANT... AND THAT'S SÔ-KUN!

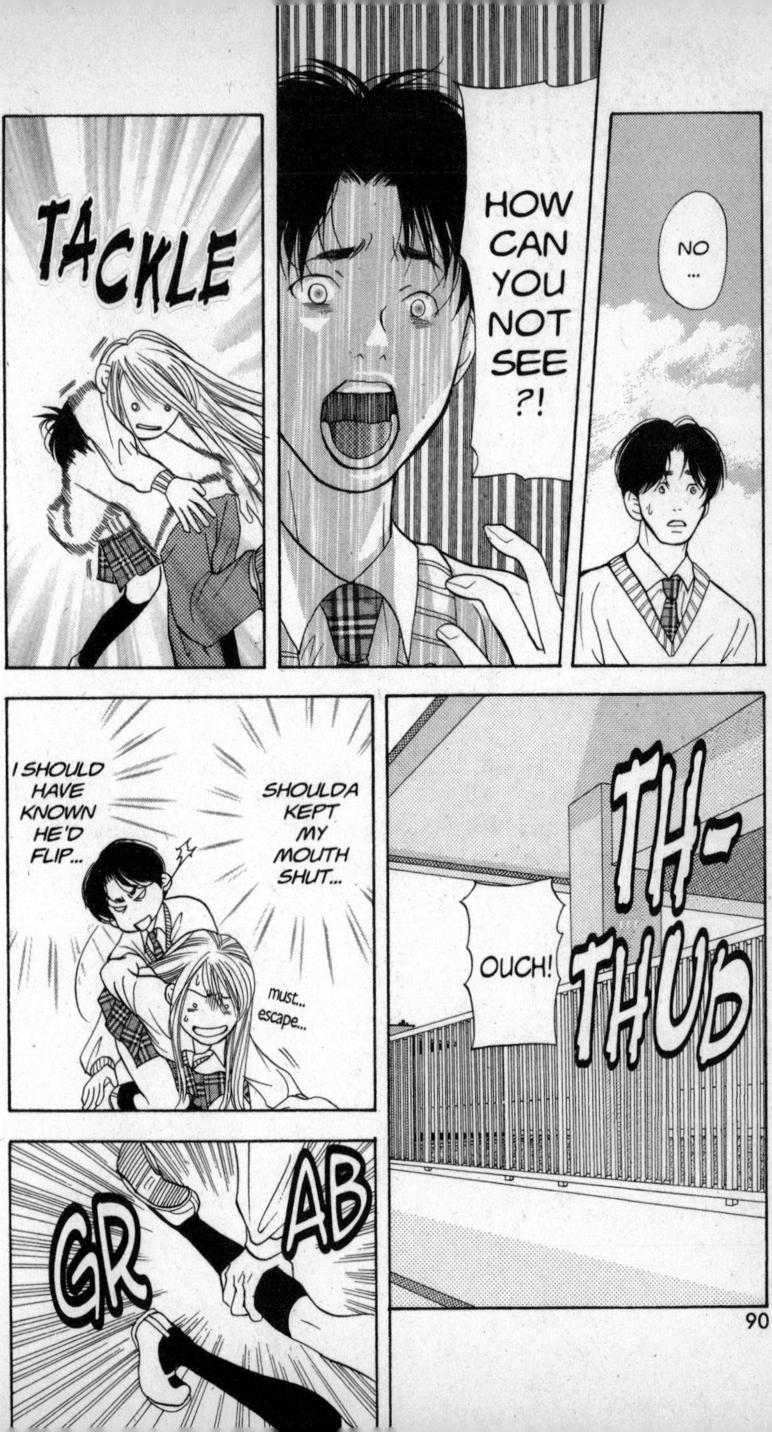
NO ...
HOW CAN YOU NOT SEE ?!
TACKLE
OUCH!
TH-THUD
SHOULDA KEPT MY MOUTH SHUT...
I SHOULD HAVE KNOWN HE'D FLIP...
must... escape...
GR AB

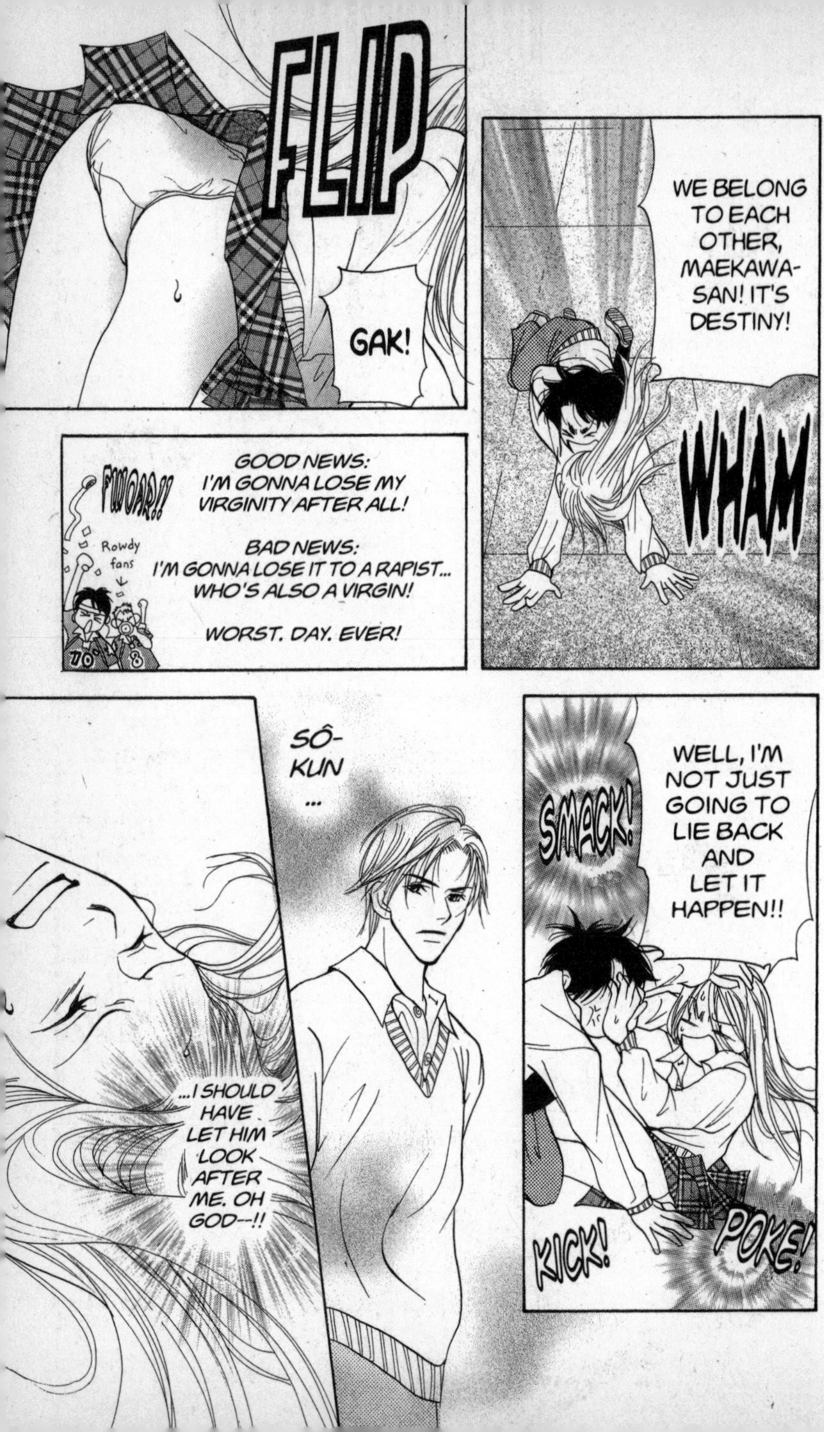
WE BELONG TO EACH OTHER, MAEKAWA-SAN! IT'S DESTINY!
WHAM
FLIP
GAK!
FWOAR!!
Rowdy fans
GOOD NEWS: I'M GONNA LOSE MY VIRGINITY AFTER ALL!
BAD NEWS: I'M GONNA LOSE IT TO A RAPIST... WHO'S ALSO A VIRGIN!
WORST. DAY. EVER!
WELL, I'M NOT JUST GOING TO LIE BACK AND LET IT HAPPEN!!
SMACK!
KICK!
POKE!
SÔ-KUN ...
...I SHOULD HAVE LET HIM LOOK AFTER ME. OH GOD--!!

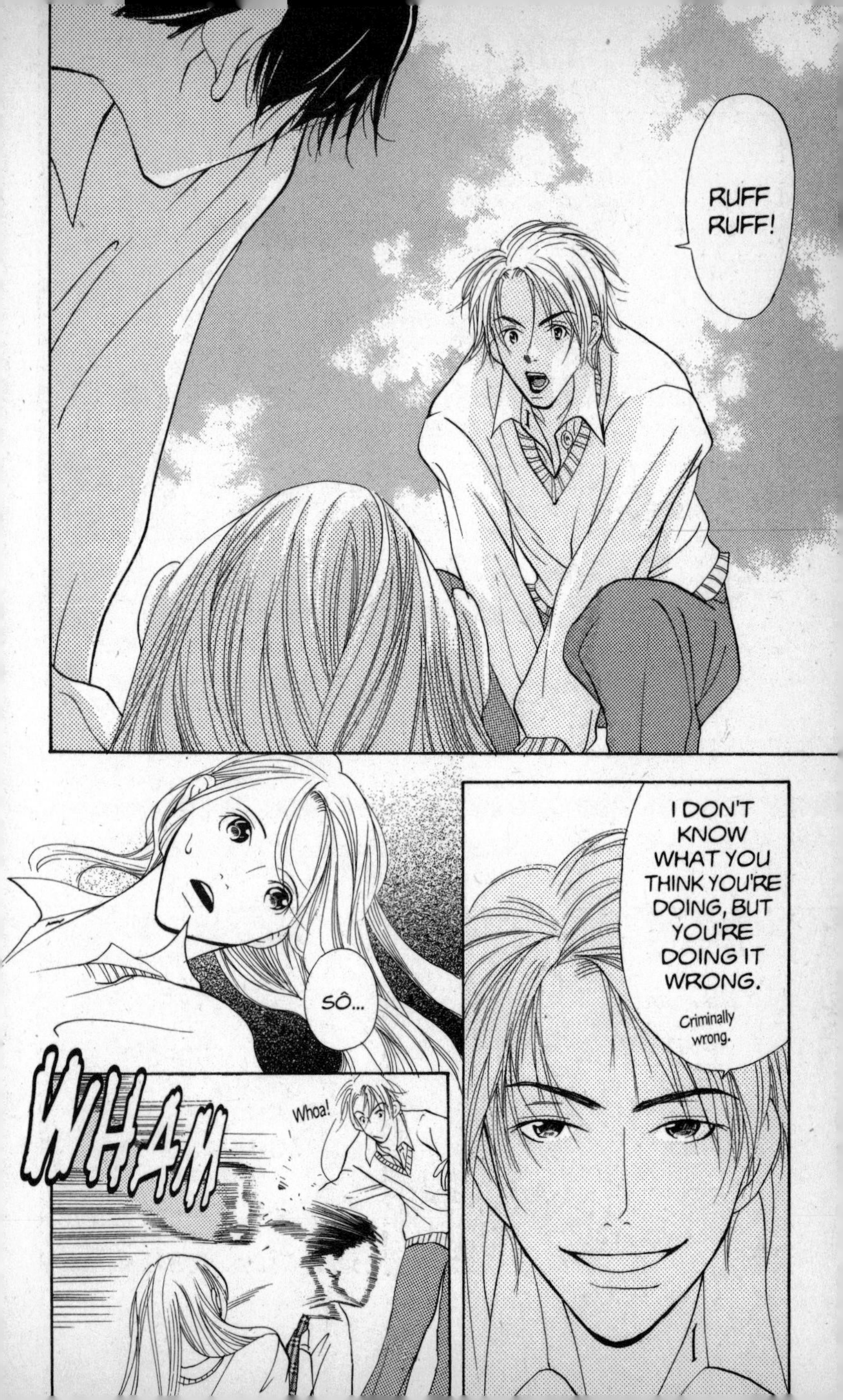

RUFF RUFF!
I DON'T KNOW WHAT YOU THINK YOU'RE DOING, BUT YOU'RE DOING IT WRONG.
Criminally wrong.
SÔ...
Whoa!
WHAM

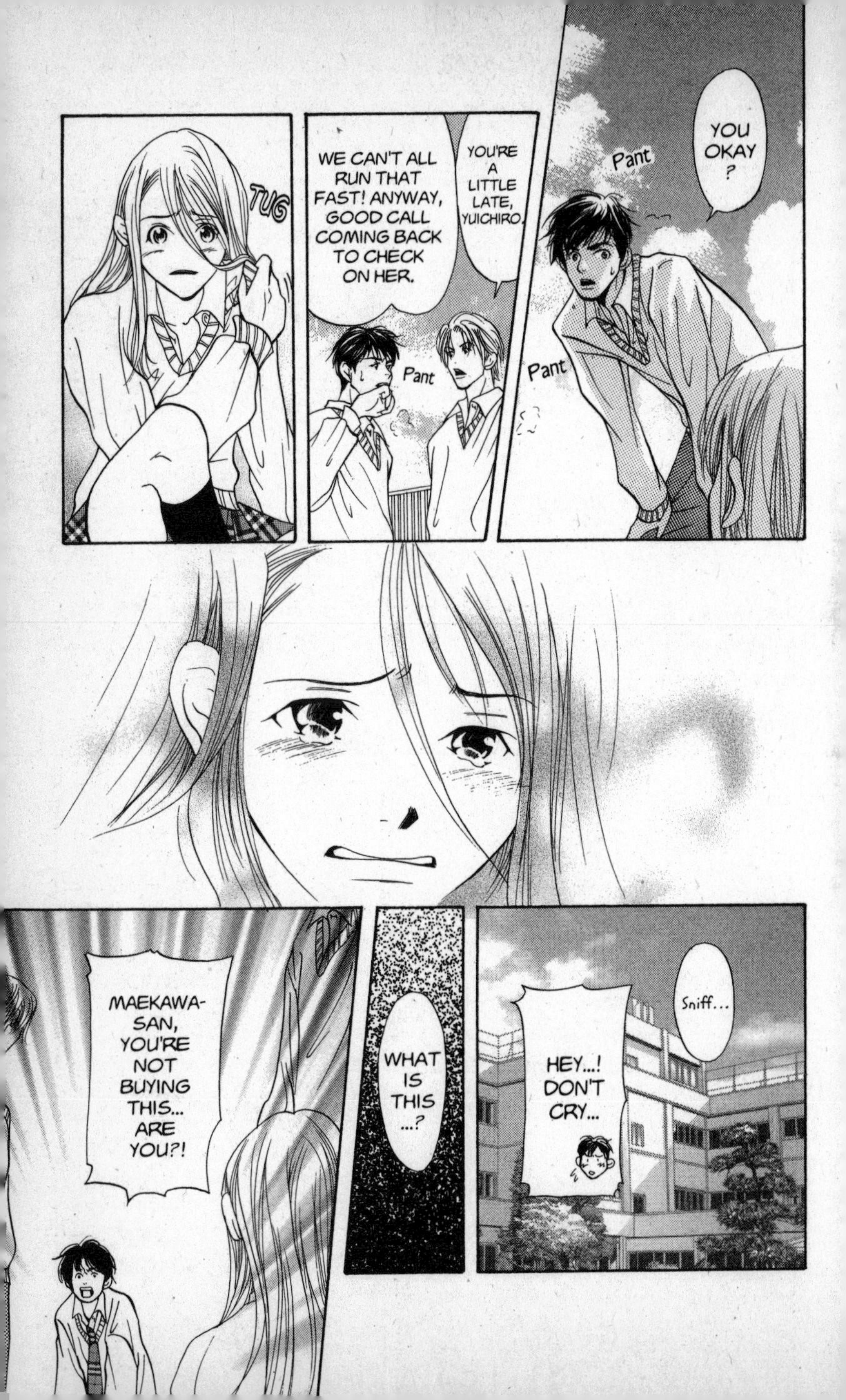

YOU OKAY?
Pant
Pant
YOU'RE A LITTLE LATE, YUICHIRO.
WE CAN'T ALL RUN THAT FAST! ANYWAY, GOOD CALL COMING BACK TO CHECK ON HER.
Pant
TUG
Sniff...
HEY...! DON'T CRY...
WHAT IS THIS ...?
MAEKAWA-SAN, YOU'RE NOT BUYING THIS... ARE YOU?!

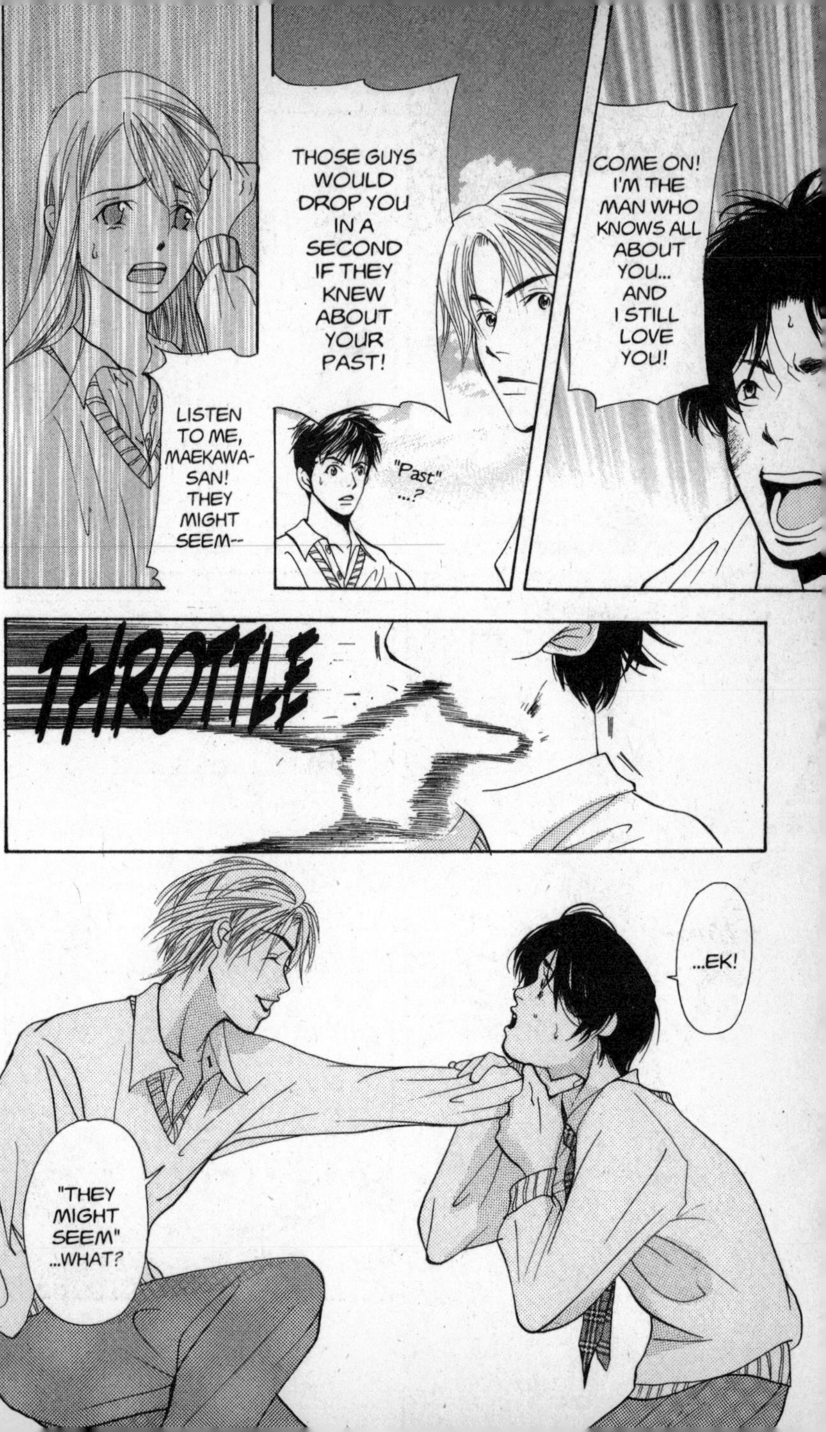
COME ON! I'M THE MAN WHO KNOWS ALL ABOUT YOU... AND I STILL LOVE YOU!
THOSE GUYS WOULD DROP YOU IN A SECOND IF THEY KNEW ABOUT YOUR PAST!
"Past" ...?
LISTEN TO ME, MAEKAWA-SAN! THEY MIGHT SEEM--
THROTTLE
...EK!
"THEY MIGHT SEEM" ...WHAT?

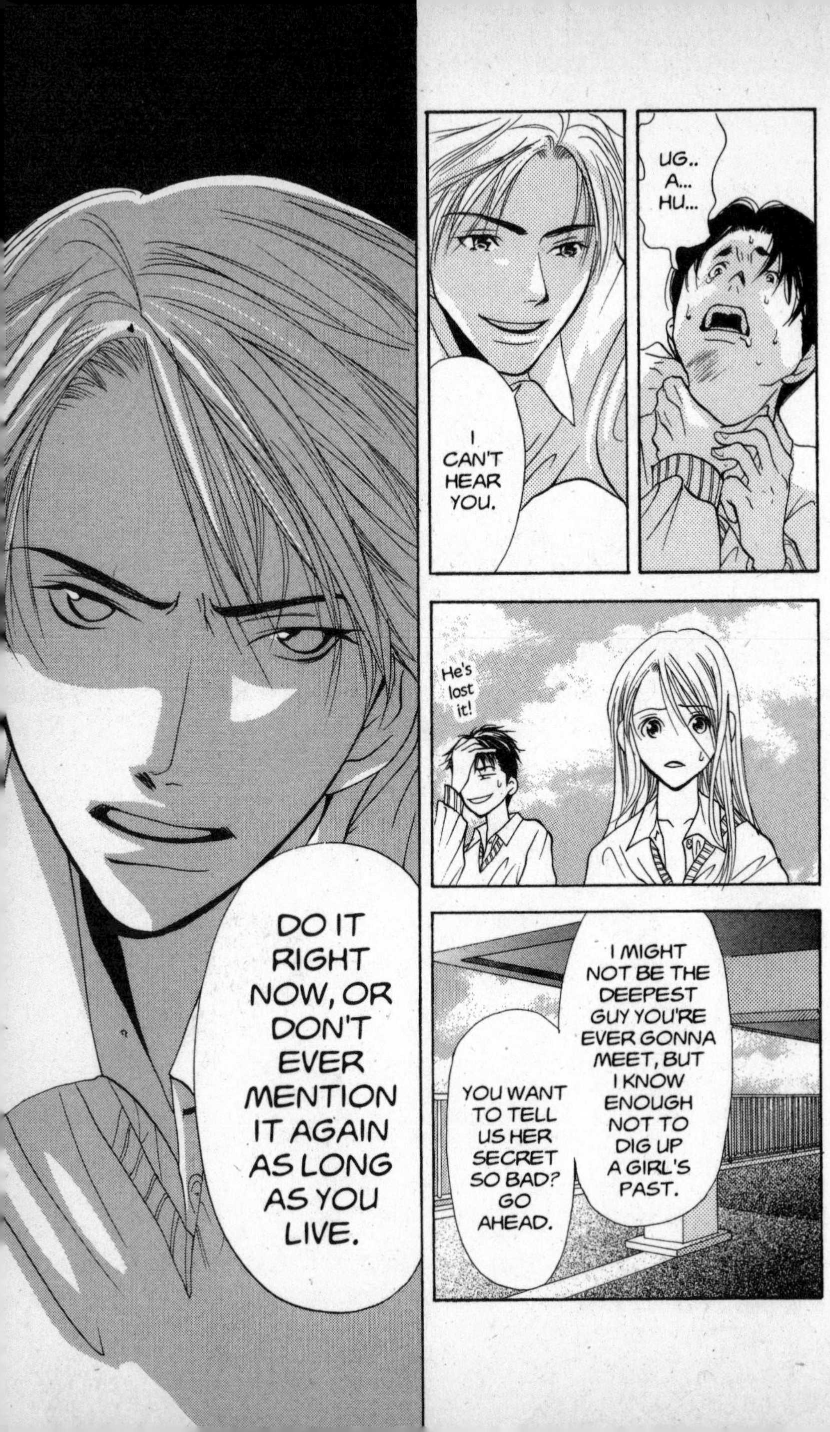
UG.. A... HU...
I CAN'T HEAR YOU.
He's lost it!
I MIGHT NOT BE THE DEEPEST GUY YOU'RE EVER GONNA MEET, BUT I KNOW ENOUGH NOT TO DIG UP A GIRL'S PAST.
YOU WANT TO TELL US HER SECRET SO BAD? GO AHEAD.
DO IT RIGHT NOW, OR DON'T EVER MENTION IT AGAIN AS LONG AS YOU LIVE.

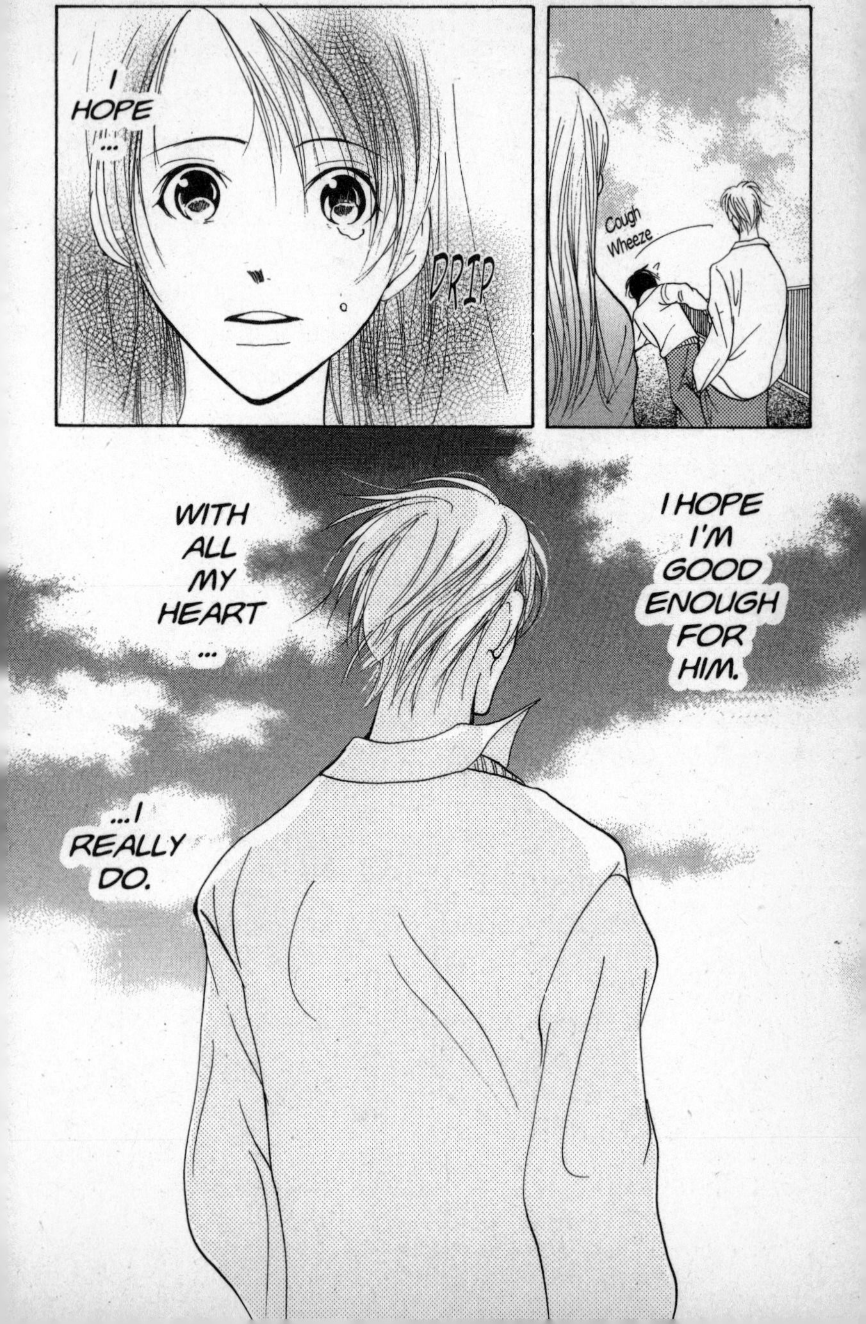
Cough Wheeze
I HOPE ...
DRIP
I HOPE I'M GOOD ENOUGH FOR HIM.
WITH ALL MY HEART ...
...I REALLY DO.

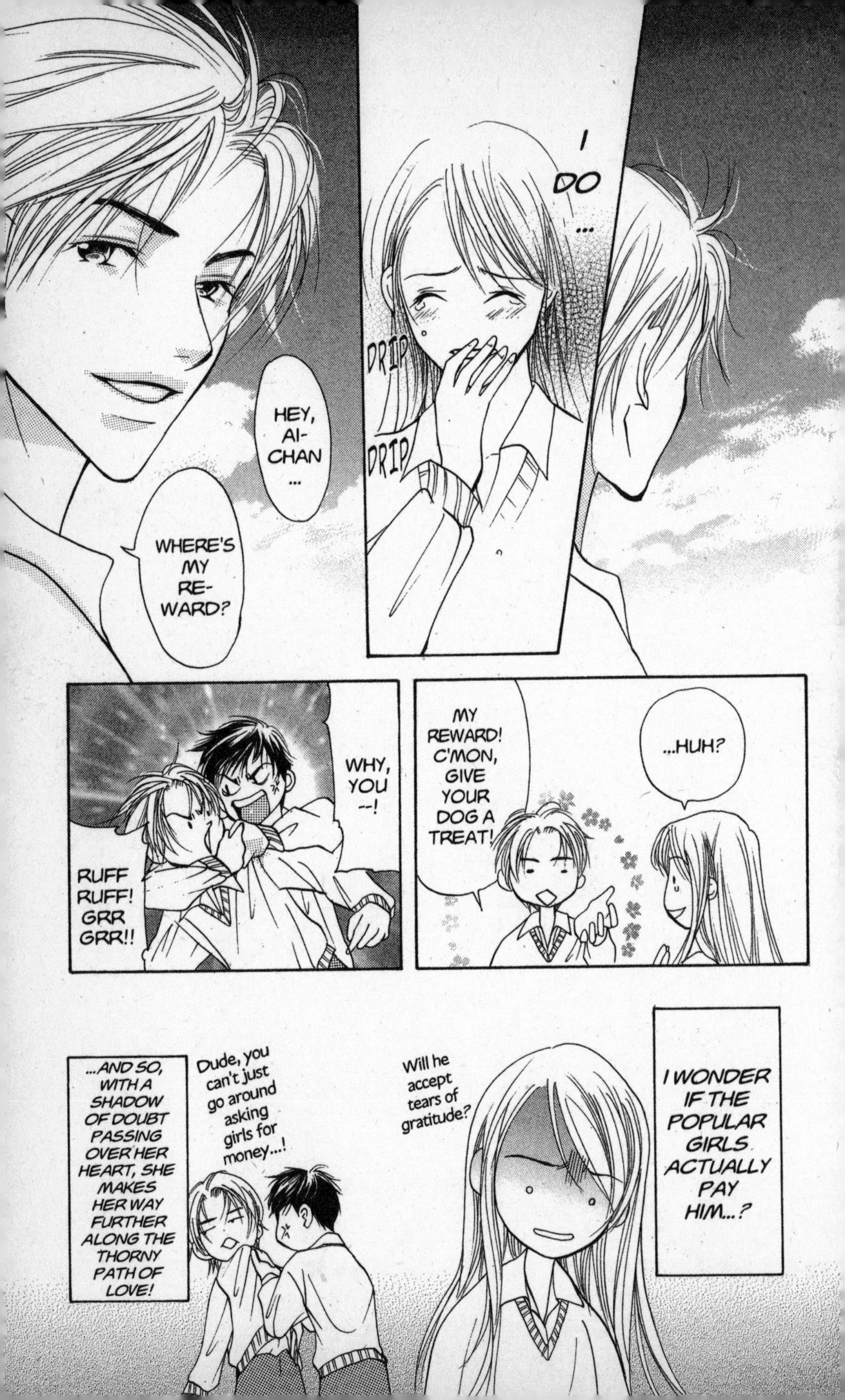
I DO ...
DRIP
DRIP
HEY, AI-CHAN ...
WHERE'S MY RE-WARD?
...HUH?
MY REWARD! C'MON, GIVE YOUR DOG A TREAT!
WHY, YOU --!
RUFF RUFF! GRR GRR!!
I WONDER IF THE POPULAR GIRLS ACTUALLY PAY HIM...?
Will he accept tears of gratitude?
Dude, you can't just go around asking girls for money...!
...AND SO, WITH A SHADOW OF DOUBT PASSING OVER HER HEART, SHE MAKES HER WAY FURTHER ALONG THE THORNY PATH OF LOVE!

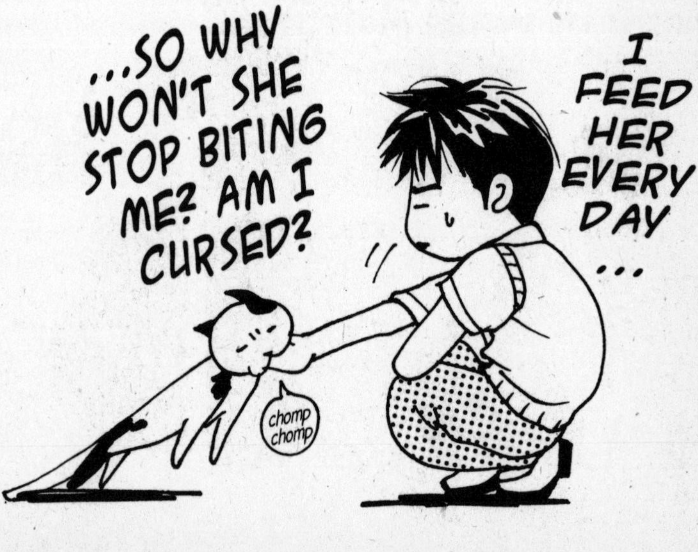
I FEED HER EVERY DAY...
...SO WHY WON'T SHE STOP BITING ME? AM I CURSED?
chomp chomp

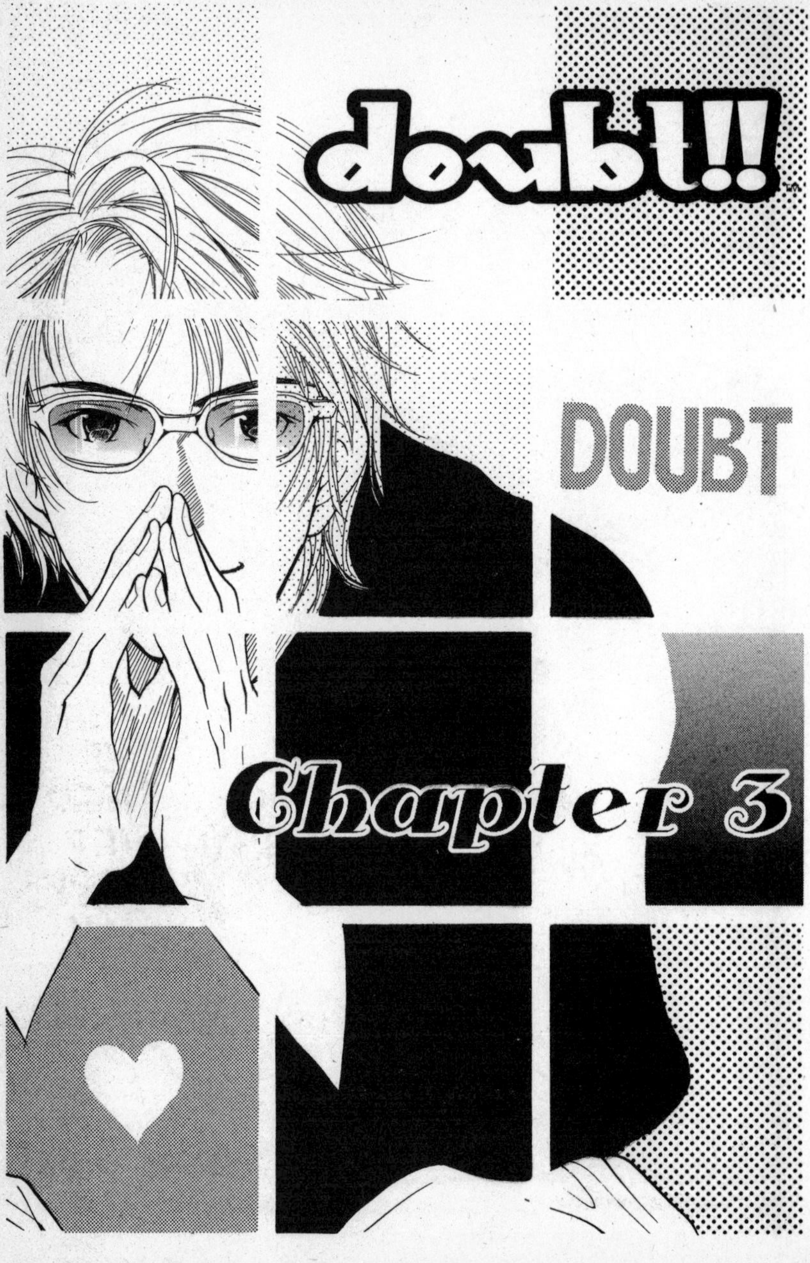
doubt!!™
DOUBT
Chapter 3

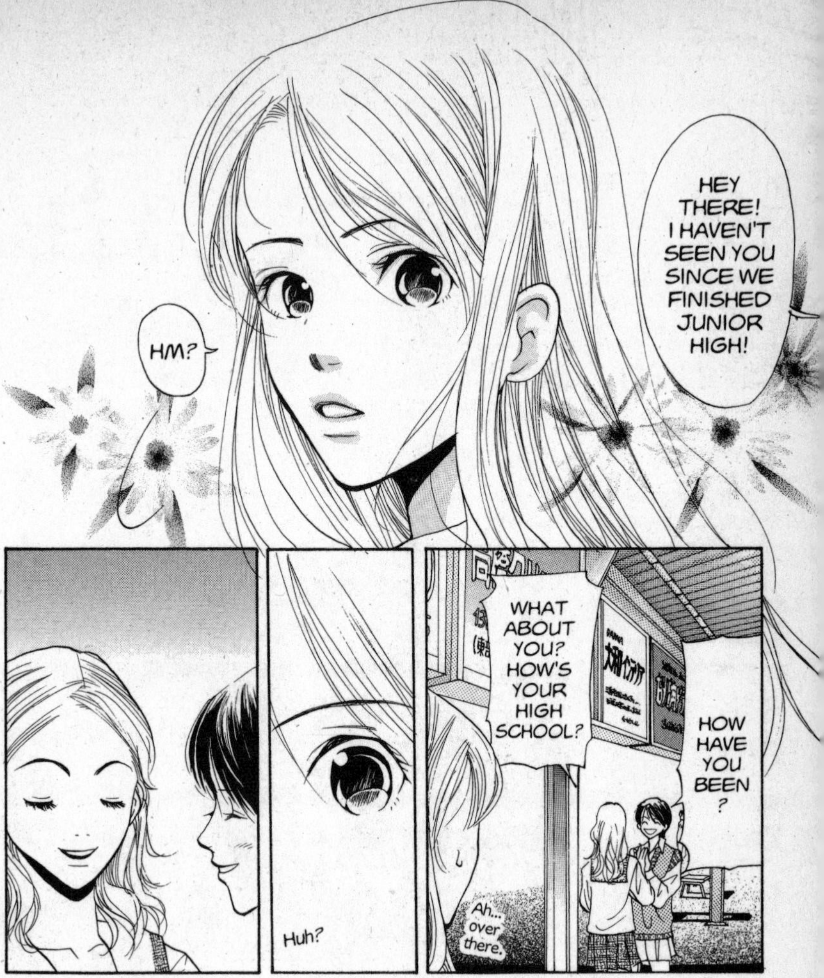
HEY THERE! I HAVEN'T SEEN YOU SINCE WE FINISHED JUNIOR HIGH!
HM?
HOW HAVE YOU BEEN?
WHAT ABOUT YOU? HOW'S YOUR HIGH SCHOOL?
Ah... over there.
Huh?

♡– Sô Ichinose

An extraordinary man with an extraordinary backbone, though that has yet to be revealed in our story. Guess you'll have to wait until I figure out how that's going to happen, huh? He's our heroine's counterpart, so I meant for him to be a princely ideal, but, uh, he had other ideas... oh, well.

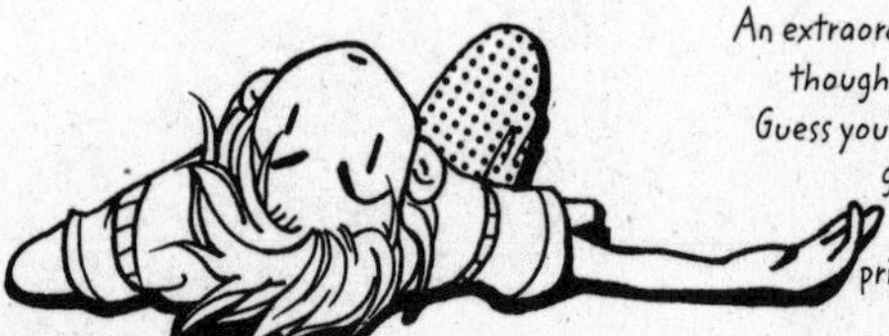

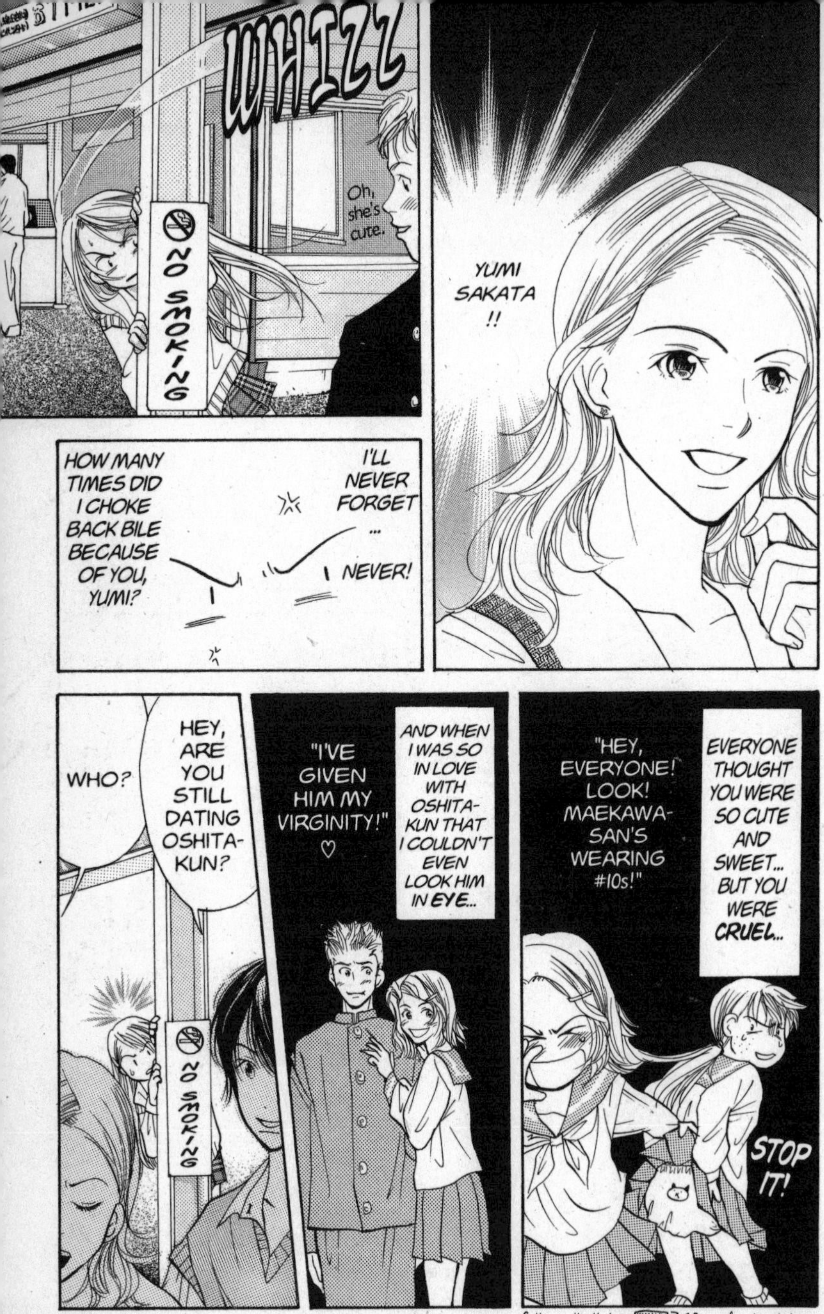
YUMI SAKATA !!
WHIZZ
Oh, she's cute.
NO SMOKING
I'LL NEVER FORGET ... NEVER!
HOW MANY TIMES DID I CHOKE BACK BILE BECAUSE OF YOU, YUMI?
EVERYONE THOUGHT YOU WERE SO CUTE AND SWEET... BUT YOU WERE CRUEL...
"HEY, EVERYONE! LOOK! MAEKAWA-SAN'S WEARING #10s!"
STOP IT!
AND WHEN I WAS SO IN LOVE WITH OSHITA-KUN THAT I COULDN'T EVEN LOOK HIM IN EYE...
"I'VE GIVEN HIM MY VIRGINITY!" ♡
HEY, ARE YOU STILL DATING OSHITA-KUN?
WHO?
NO SMOKING

Cotton panties that are ["ᴥ"] }10 cm from here to here are called #10s.

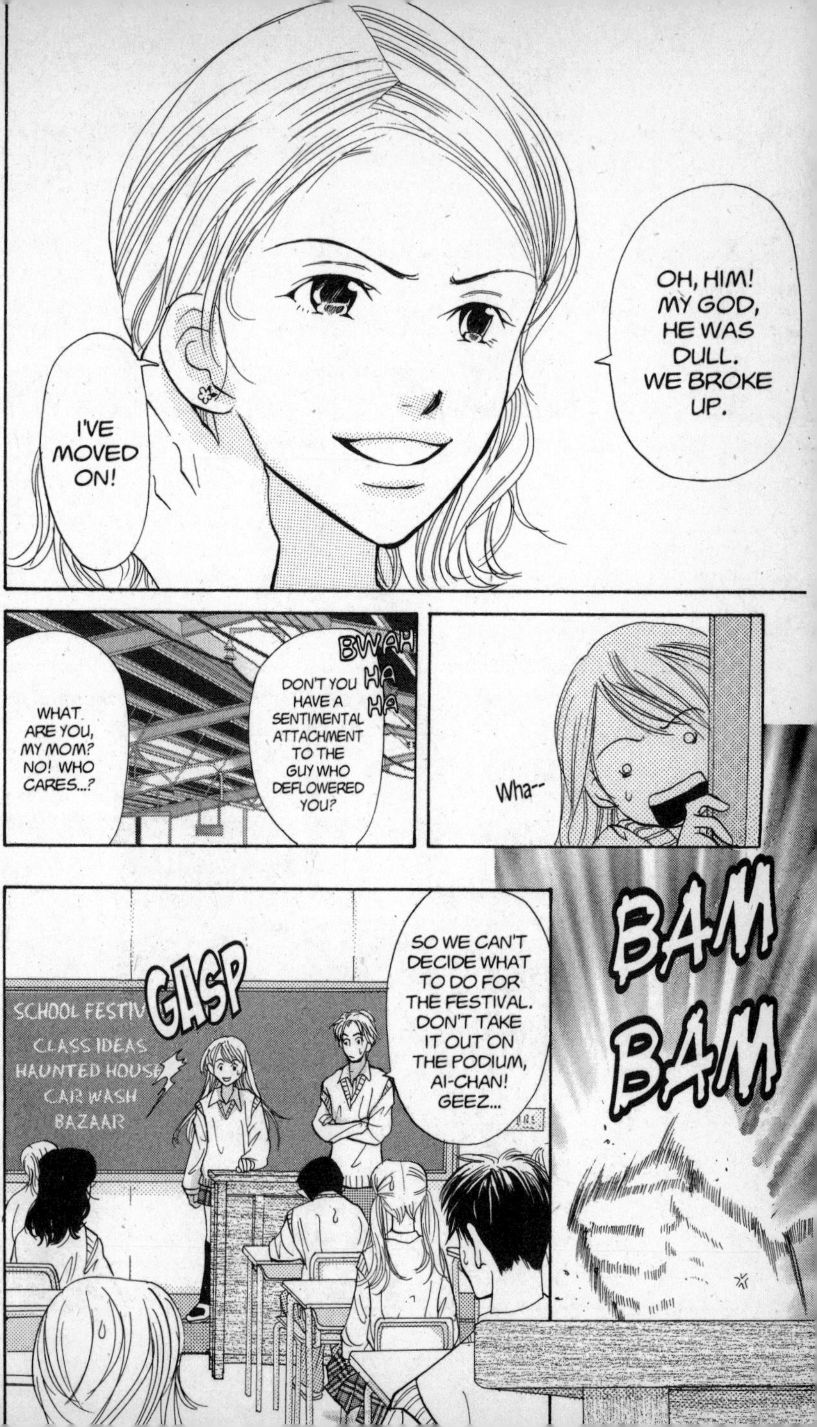
OH, HIM! MY GOD, HE WAS DULL. WE BROKE UP.
I'VE MOVED ON!
Wha--
BWAH HA HA
DON'T YOU HAVE A SENTIMENTAL ATTACHMENT TO THE GUY WHO DEFLOWERED YOU?
WHAT ARE YOU, MY MOM? NO! WHO CARES...?
BAM BAM
SO WE CAN'T DECIDE WHAT TO DO FOR THE FESTIVAL. DON'T TAKE IT OUT ON THE PODIUM, AI-CHAN! GEEZ...
GASP
SCHOOL FESTIV
CLASS IDEAS
HAUNTED HOUSE
CAR WASH
BAZAAR

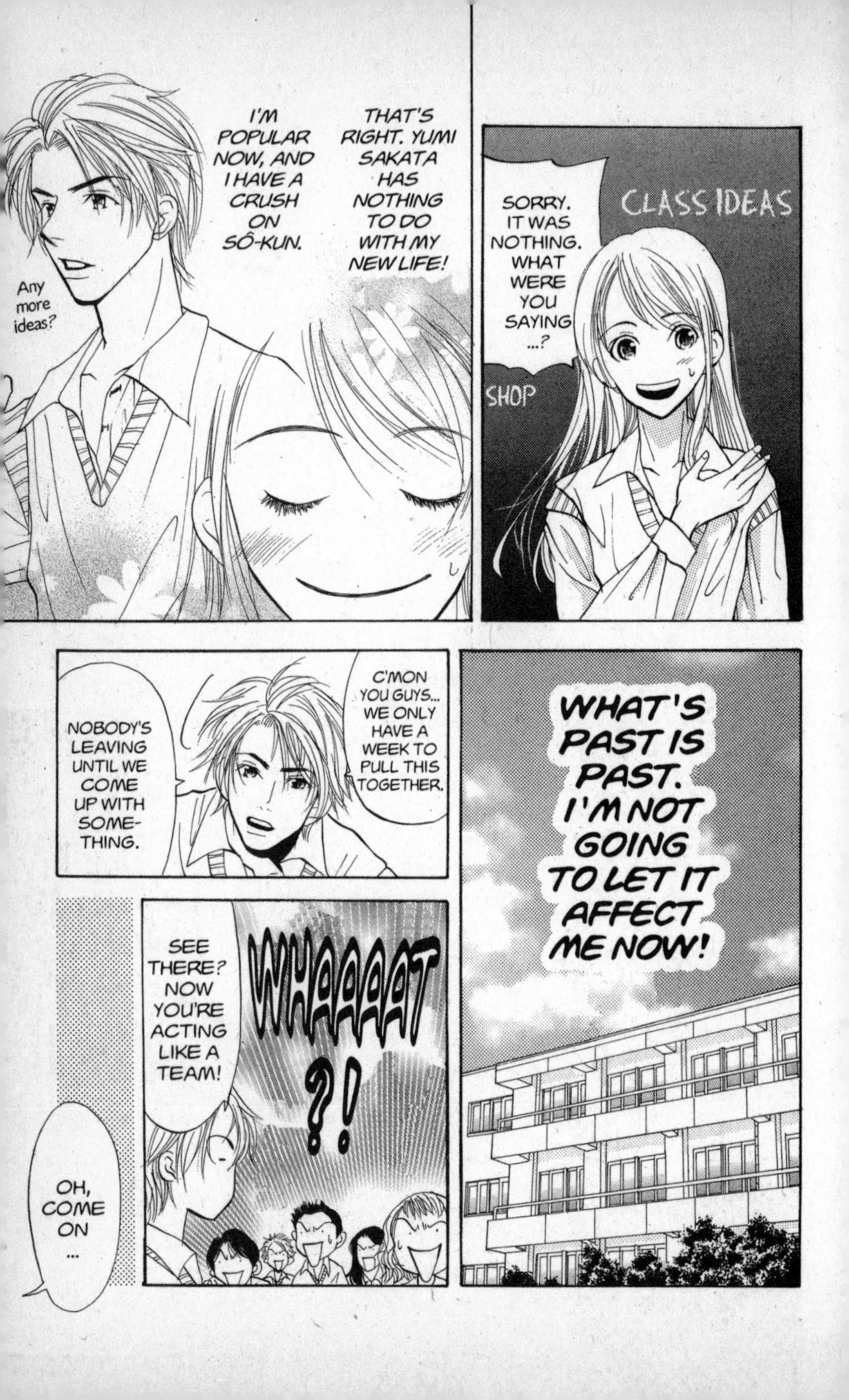
CLASS IDEAS
SORRY. IT WAS NOTHING. WHAT WERE YOU SAYING ...?
SHOP
THAT'S RIGHT. YUMI SAKATA HAS NOTHING TO DO WITH MY NEW LIFE!
I'M POPULAR NOW, AND I HAVE A CRUSH ON SÔ-KUN.
Any more ideas?
WHAT'S PAST IS PAST. I'M NOT GOING TO LET IT AFFECT ME NOW!
C'MON YOU GUYS... WE ONLY HAVE A WEEK TO PULL THIS TOGETHER.
NOBODY'S LEAVING UNTIL WE COME UP WITH SOME-THING.
SEE THERE? NOW YOU'RE ACTING LIKE A TEAM!
WHAAAAT ?!
OH, COME ON ...

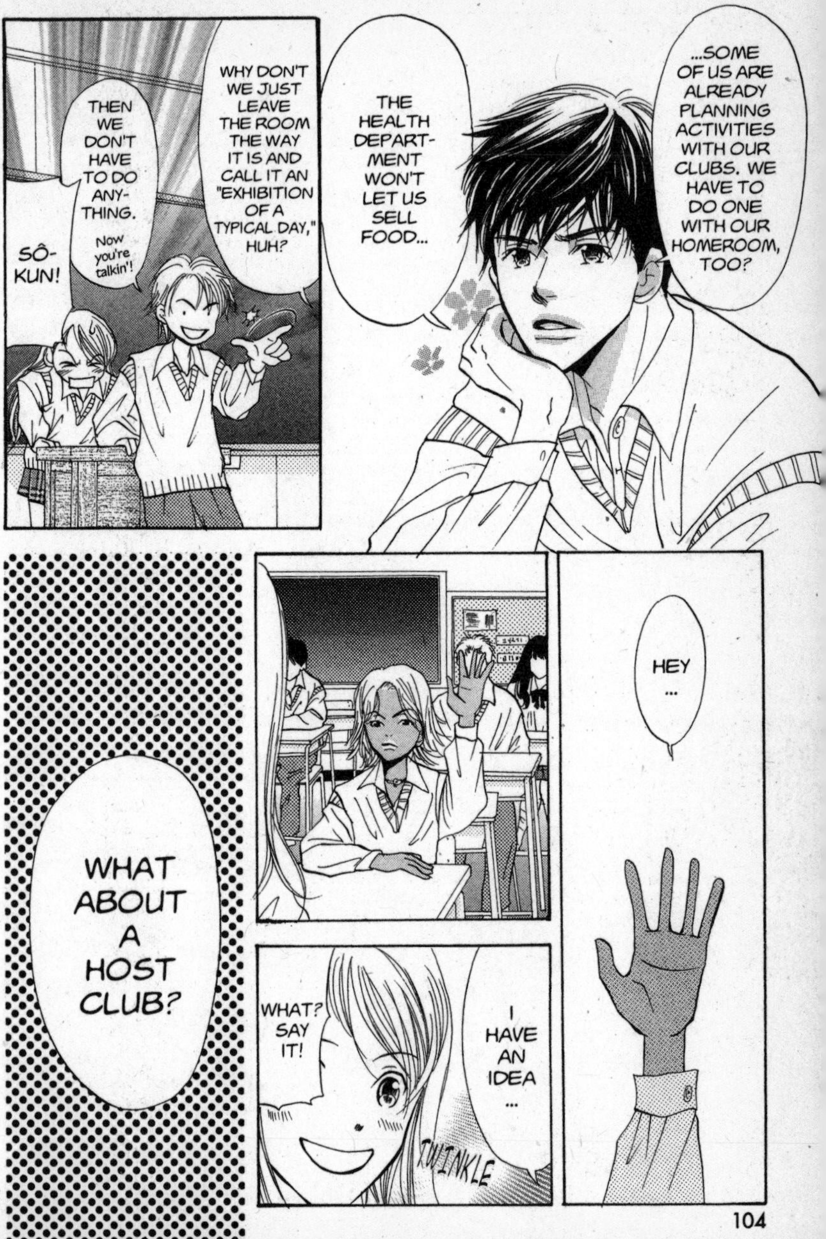
...SOME OF US ARE ALREADY PLANNING ACTIVITIES WITH OUR CLUBS. WE HAVE TO DO ONE WITH OUR HOMEROOM, TOO?
THE HEALTH DEPARTMENT WON'T LET US SELL FOOD...
WHY DON'T WE JUST LEAVE THE ROOM THE WAY IT IS AND CALL IT AN "EXHIBITION OF A TYPICAL DAY," HUH?
THEN WE DON'T HAVE TO DO ANYTHING.
Now you're talkin'!
SÔ-KUN!
HEY ...
I HAVE AN IDEA ...
WHAT? SAY IT!
TWINKLE
WHAT ABOUT A HOST CLUB?

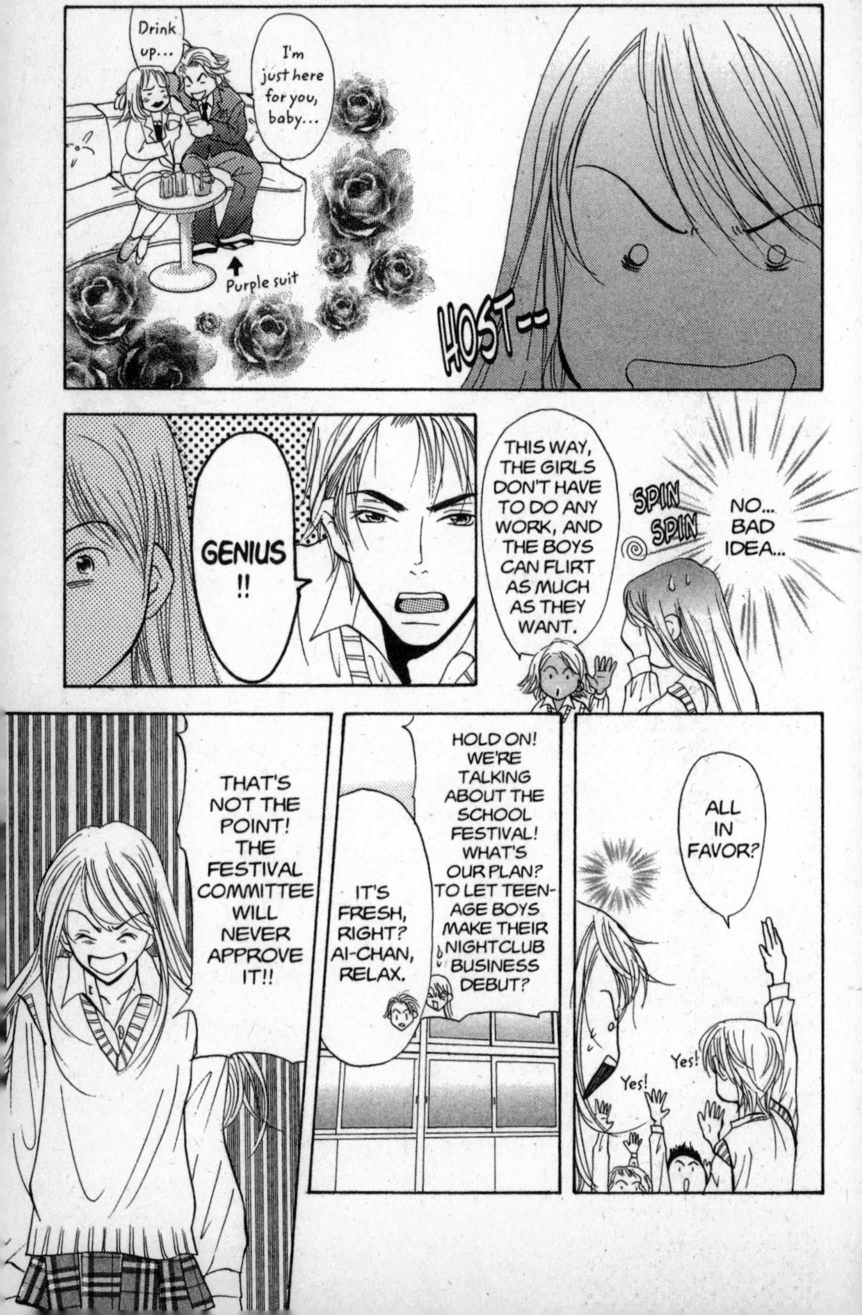
HOST--
I'm just here for you, baby...
Drink up...
Purple suit
NO... BAD IDEA...
SPIN SPIN
THIS WAY, THE GIRLS DON'T HAVE TO DO ANY WORK, AND THE BOYS CAN FLIRT AS MUCH AS THEY WANT.
GENIUS!!
ALL IN FAVOR?
Yes!
Yes!
HOLD ON! WE'RE TALKING ABOUT THE SCHOOL FESTIVAL! WHAT'S OUR PLAN? TO LET TEEN-AGE BOYS MAKE THEIR NIGHTCLUB BUSINESS DEBUT?
IT'S FRESH, RIGHT? AI-CHAN, RELAX.
THAT'S NOT THE POINT! THE FESTIVAL COMMITTEE WILL NEVER APPROVE IT!!

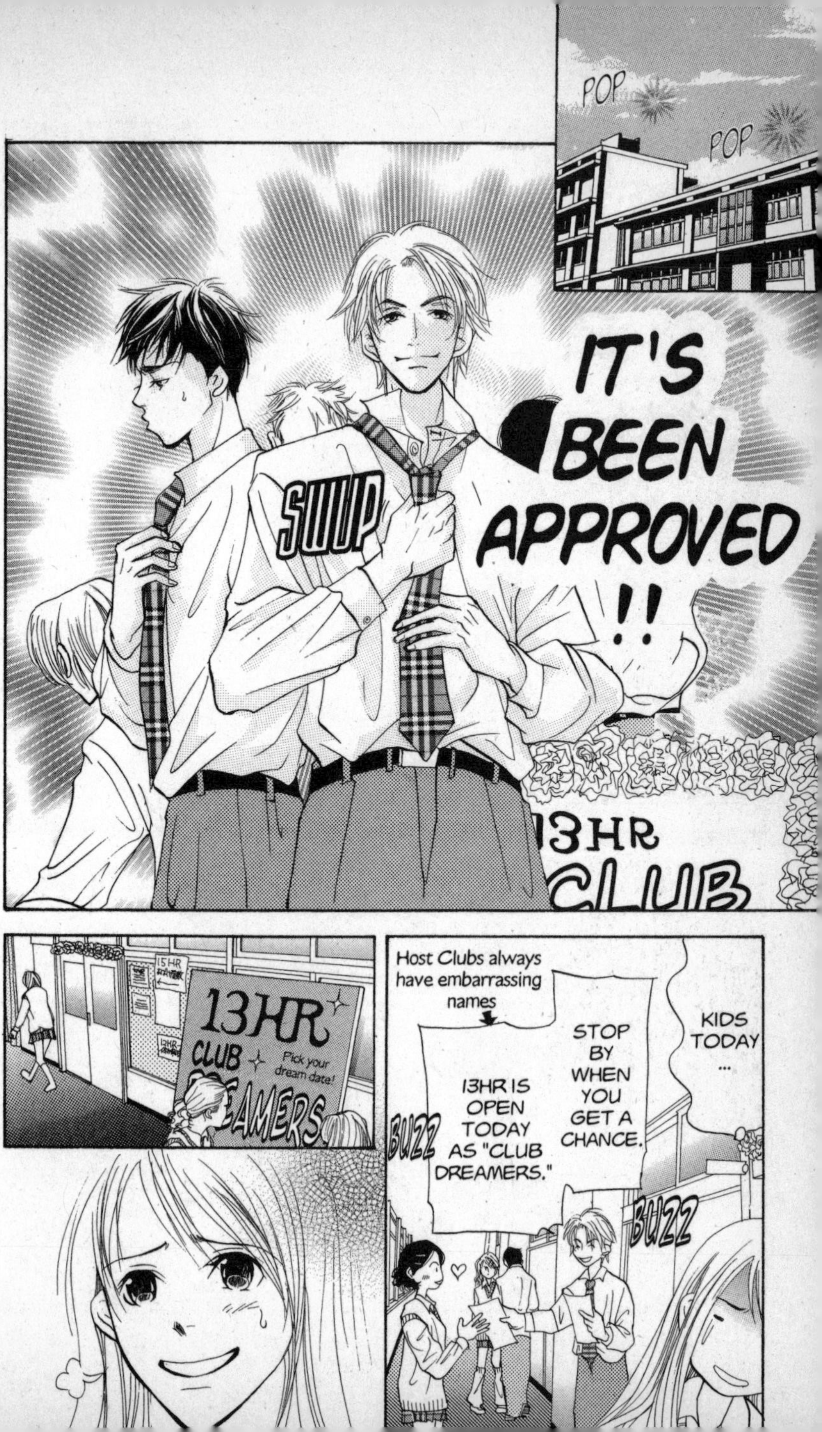

POP
POP
IT'S BEEN APPROVED!!
SWUP
13HR CLUB
KIDS TODAY...
STOP BY WHEN YOU GET A CHANCE.
13HR IS OPEN TODAY AS "CLUB DREAMERS."
Host Clubs always have embarrassing names
BUZZ
BUZZ
15HR
13HR
CLUB
Pick your dream date!
EAMERS

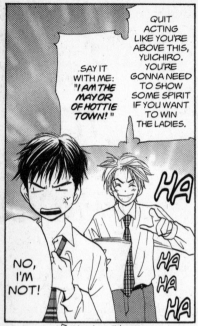

I MIGHT AS WELL TRY AND ENJOY MYSELF...
CAN I HELP?
Hey...
WILL YOU HAND OUT FLYERS? KATO'S NOT TRYING VERY HARD.
23HR
← RING TOSS
QUIT ACTING LIKE YOU'RE ABOVE THIS, YUICHIRO. YOU'RE GONNA NEED TO SHOW SOME SPIRIT IF YOU WANT TO WIN THE LADIES.
SAY IT WITH ME: "*I AM THE MAYOR OF HOTTIE TOWN!*"
HA
HA HA HA
NO, I'M NOT!
Not the wild type.
AI-CHAN, YOU DON'T HAVE TO BACK UP THIS MORON JUST BECAUSE YOU'RE HEAD GIRL.
I KNOW...
I'M DOING IT BECAUSE I WANT TO.

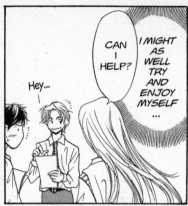

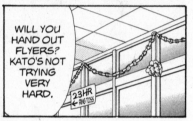

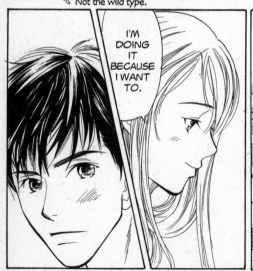

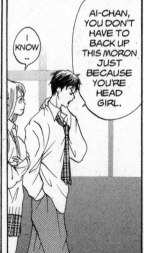

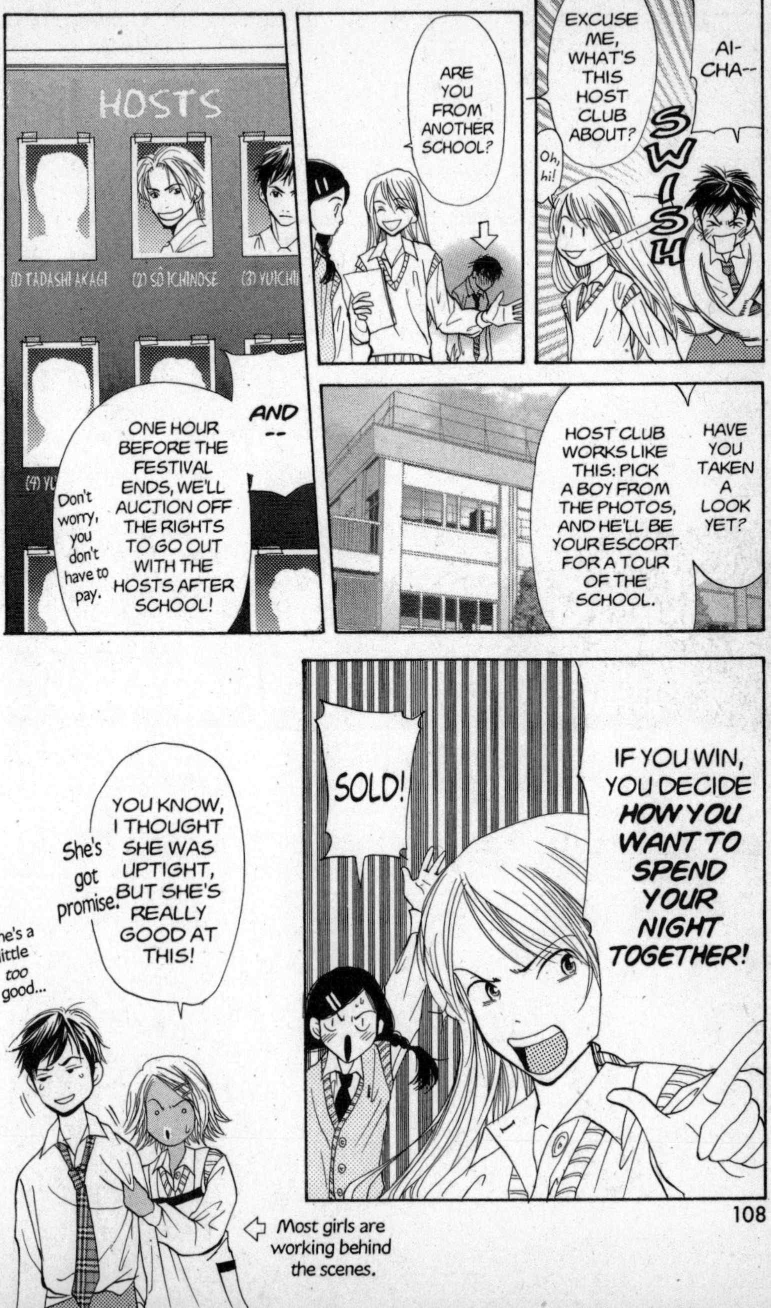
AI-CHA--
SWISH
EXCUSE ME, WHAT'S THIS HOST CLUB ABOUT?
Oh, hi!
ARE YOU FROM ANOTHER SCHOOL?
HAVE YOU TAKEN A LOOK YET?
HOST CLUB WORKS LIKE THIS: PICK A BOY FROM THE PHOTOS, AND HE'LL BE YOUR ESCORT FOR A TOUR OF THE SCHOOL.
HOSTS
(1) TADASHI AKAGI
(2) SÔ ICHINOSE
(3) YUICHI
AND --
ONE HOUR BEFORE THE FESTIVAL ENDS, WE'LL AUCTION OFF THE RIGHTS TO GO OUT WITH THE HOSTS AFTER SCHOOL!
Don't worry, you don't have to pay.
IF YOU WIN, YOU DECIDE HOW YOU WANT TO SPEND YOUR NIGHT TOGETHER!
SOLD!
YOU KNOW, I THOUGHT SHE WAS UPTIGHT, BUT SHE'S REALLY GOOD AT THIS!
She's got promise.
She's a little too good...
Most girls are working behind the scenes.

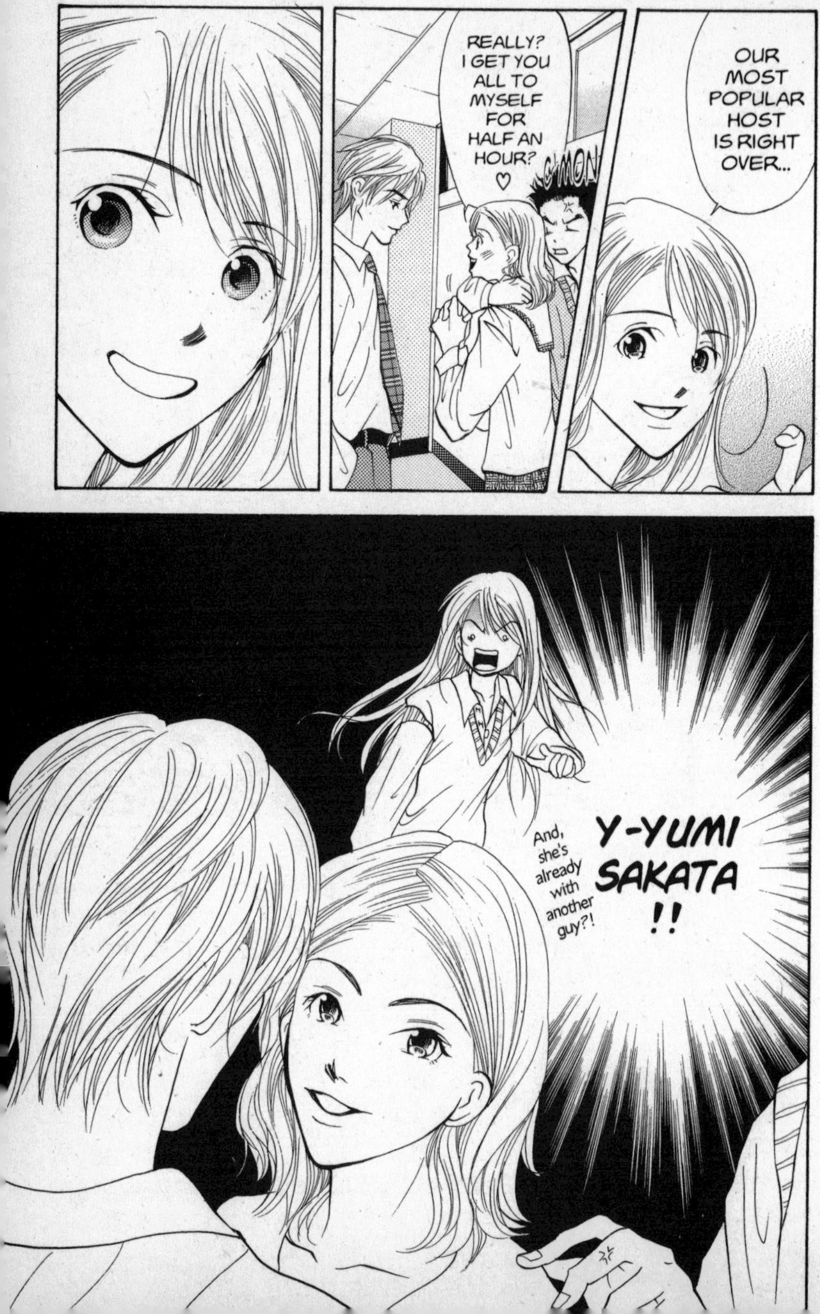
OUR MOST POPULAR HOST IS RIGHT OVER...
REALLY? I GET YOU ALL TO MYSELF FOR HALF AN HOUR? ♡
C'MON
Y-YUMI SAKATA !!
And, she's already with another guy?!

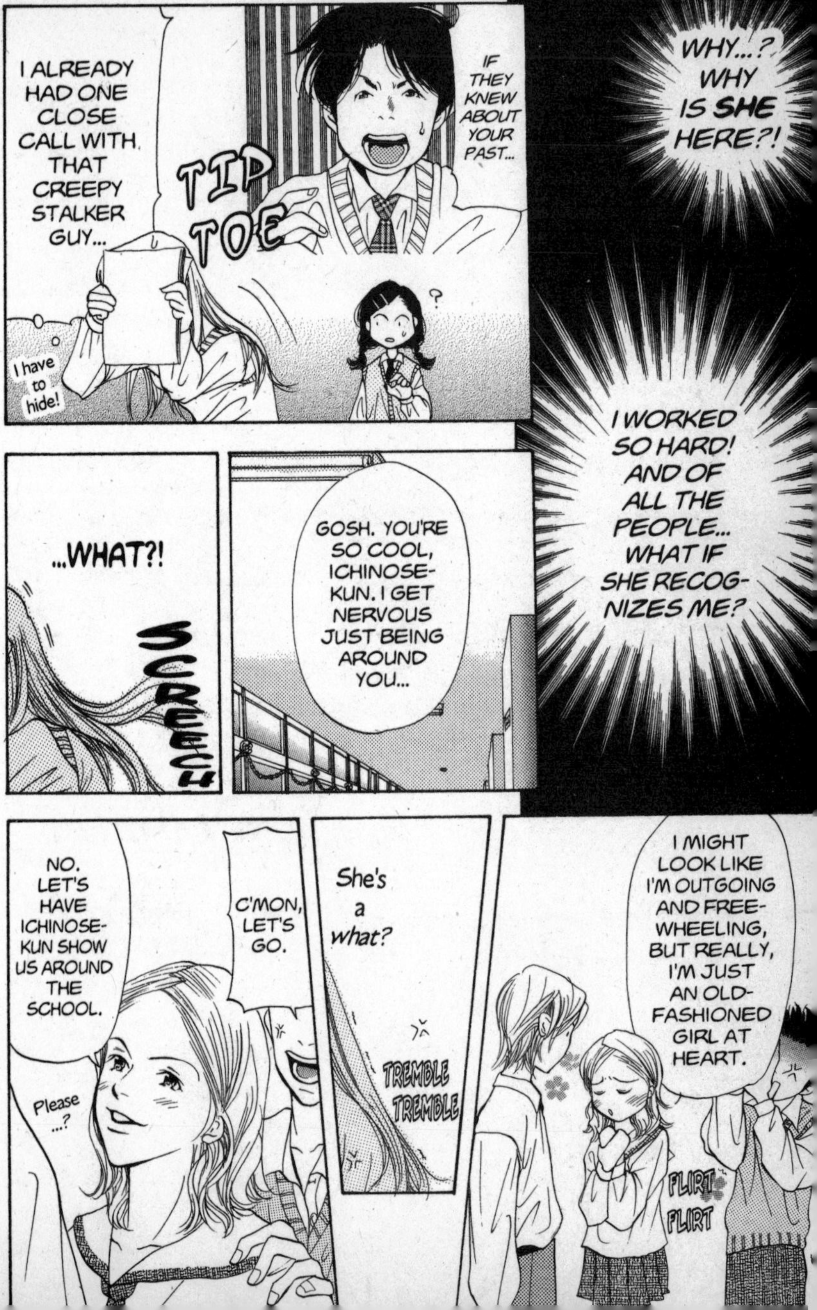
WHY...? WHY IS SHE HERE?!
I WORKED SO HARD! AND OF ALL THE PEOPLE... WHAT IF SHE RECOGNIZES ME?
IF THEY KNEW ABOUT YOUR PAST...
I ALREADY HAD ONE CLOSE CALL WITH THAT CREEPY STALKER GUY...
TIP TOE
?
I have to hide!
GOSH. YOU'RE SO COOL, ICHINOSE-KUN. I GET NERVOUS JUST BEING AROUND YOU...
...WHAT?!
SCREECH
I MIGHT LOOK LIKE I'M OUTGOING AND FREE-WHEELING, BUT REALLY, I'M JUST AN OLD-FASHIONED GIRL AT HEART.
FLIRT FLIRT
She's a what?
TREMBLE TREMBLE
C'MON, LET'S GO.
NO. LET'S HAVE ICHINOSE-KUN SHOW US AROUND THE SCHOOL.
Please ...?

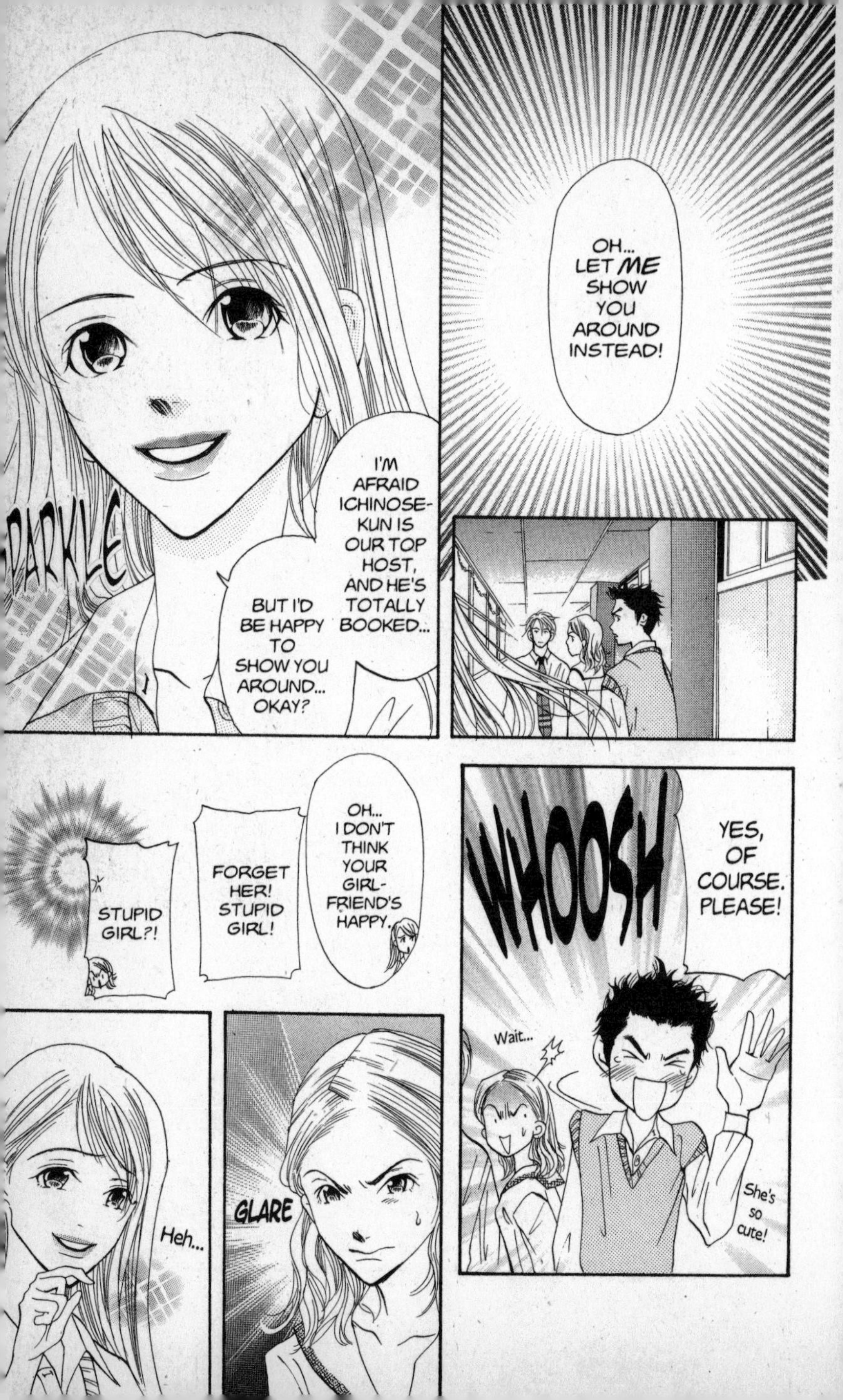
OH... LET ME SHOW YOU AROUND INSTEAD!
I'M AFRAID ICHINOSE-KUN IS OUR TOP HOST, AND HE'S TOTALLY BOOKED...
BUT I'D BE HAPPY TO SHOW YOU AROUND... OKAY?
PARKLE
WHOOSH
YES, OF COURSE. PLEASE!
Wait...
She's so cute!
OH... I DON'T THINK YOUR GIRL-FRIEND'S HAPPY.
FORGET HER! STUPID GIRL!
STUPID GIRL?!
GLARE
Heh...

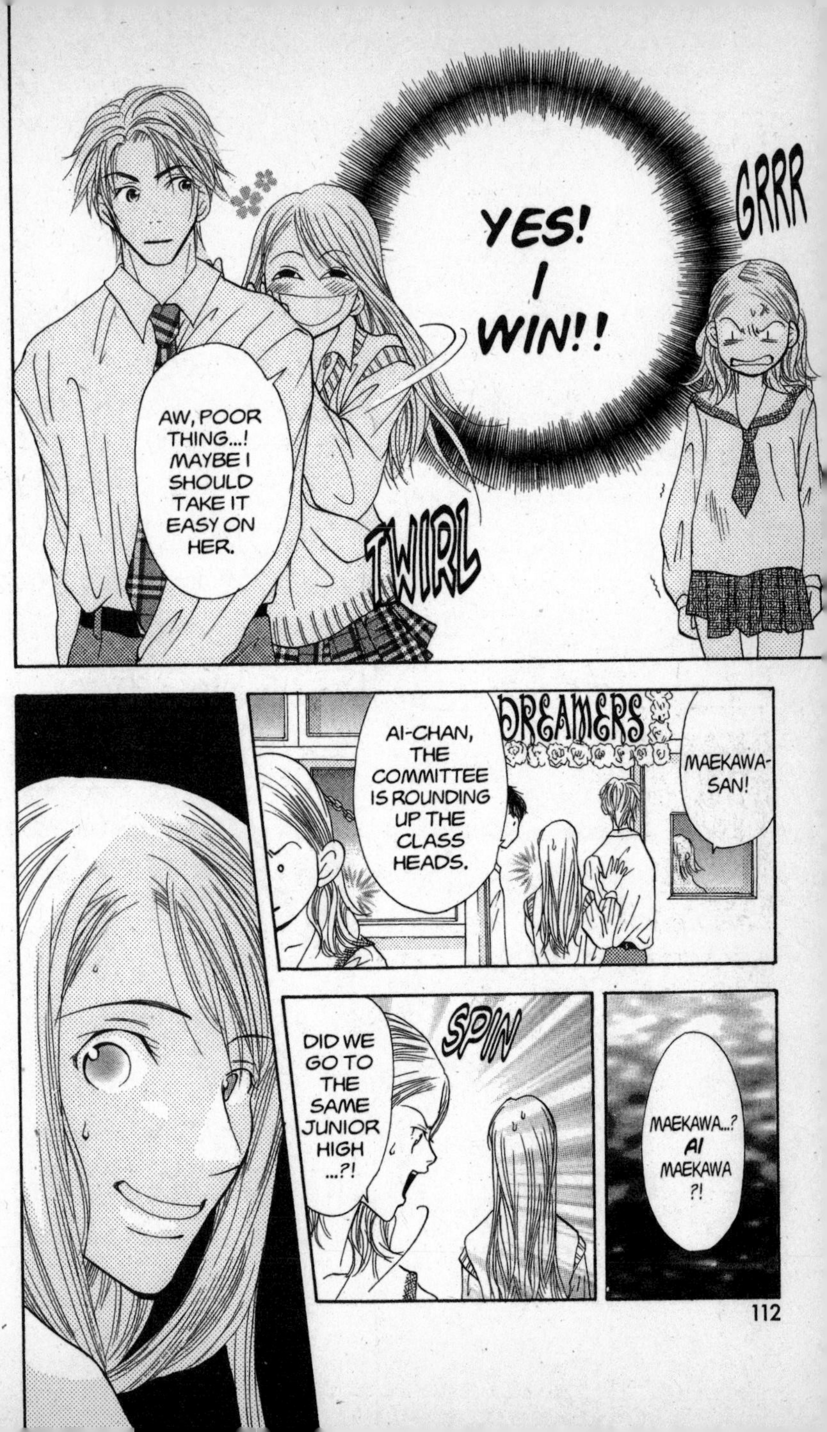
GRRR
YES! I WIN!!
AW, POOR THING...! MAYBE I SHOULD TAKE IT EASY ON HER.
TWIRL
DREAMERS
MAEKAWA-SAN!
AI-CHAN, THE COMMITTEE IS ROUNDING UP THE CLASS HEADS.
MAEKAWA...? AI MAEKAWA?!
SPIN
DID WE GO TO THE SAME JUNIOR HIGH ...?!

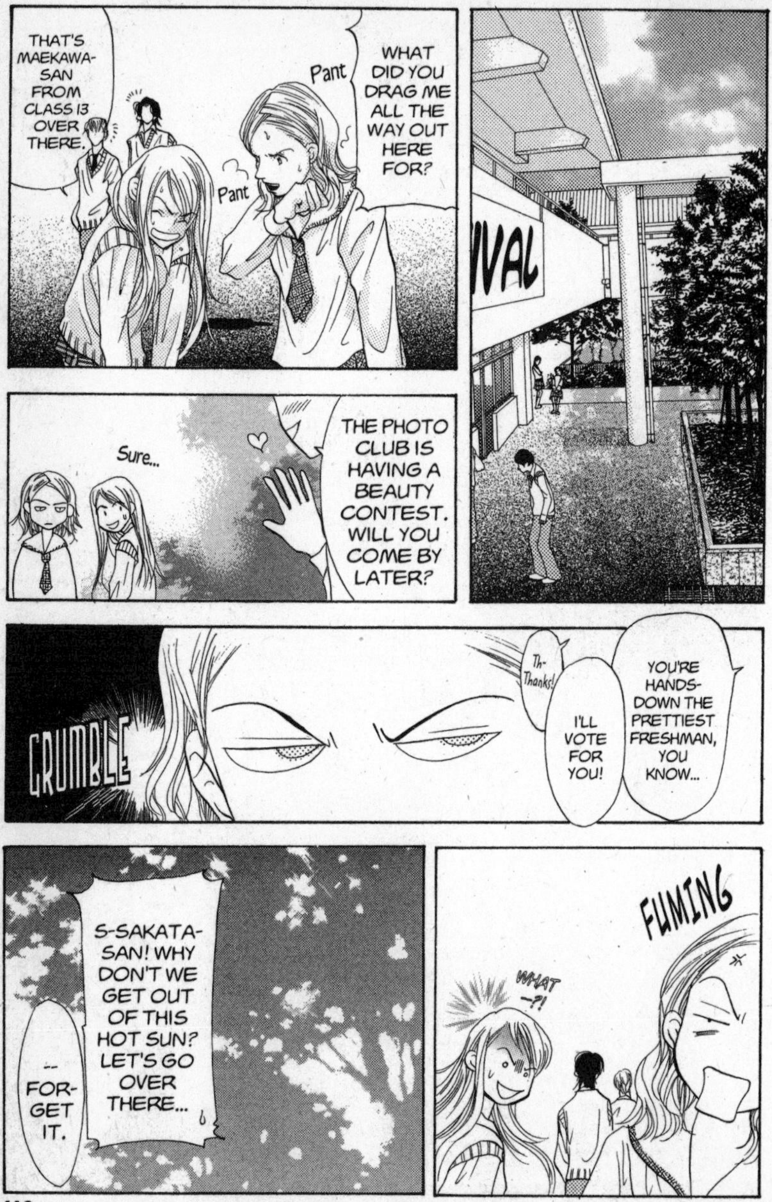
IVAL
WHAT DID YOU DRAG ME ALL THE WAY OUT HERE FOR?
Pant
Pant
THAT'S MAEKAWA-SAN FROM CLASS 13 OVER THERE.
THE PHOTO CLUB IS HAVING A BEAUTY CONTEST. WILL YOU COME BY LATER?
Sure...
YOU'RE HANDS-DOWN THE PRETTIEST FRESHMAN, YOU KNOW...
I'LL VOTE FOR YOU!
Th-Thanks!
GRUMBLE
FUMING
WHAT-?!
S-SAKATA-SAN! WHY DON'T WE GET OUT OF THIS HOT SUN? LET'S GO OVER THERE...
--FOR-GET IT.

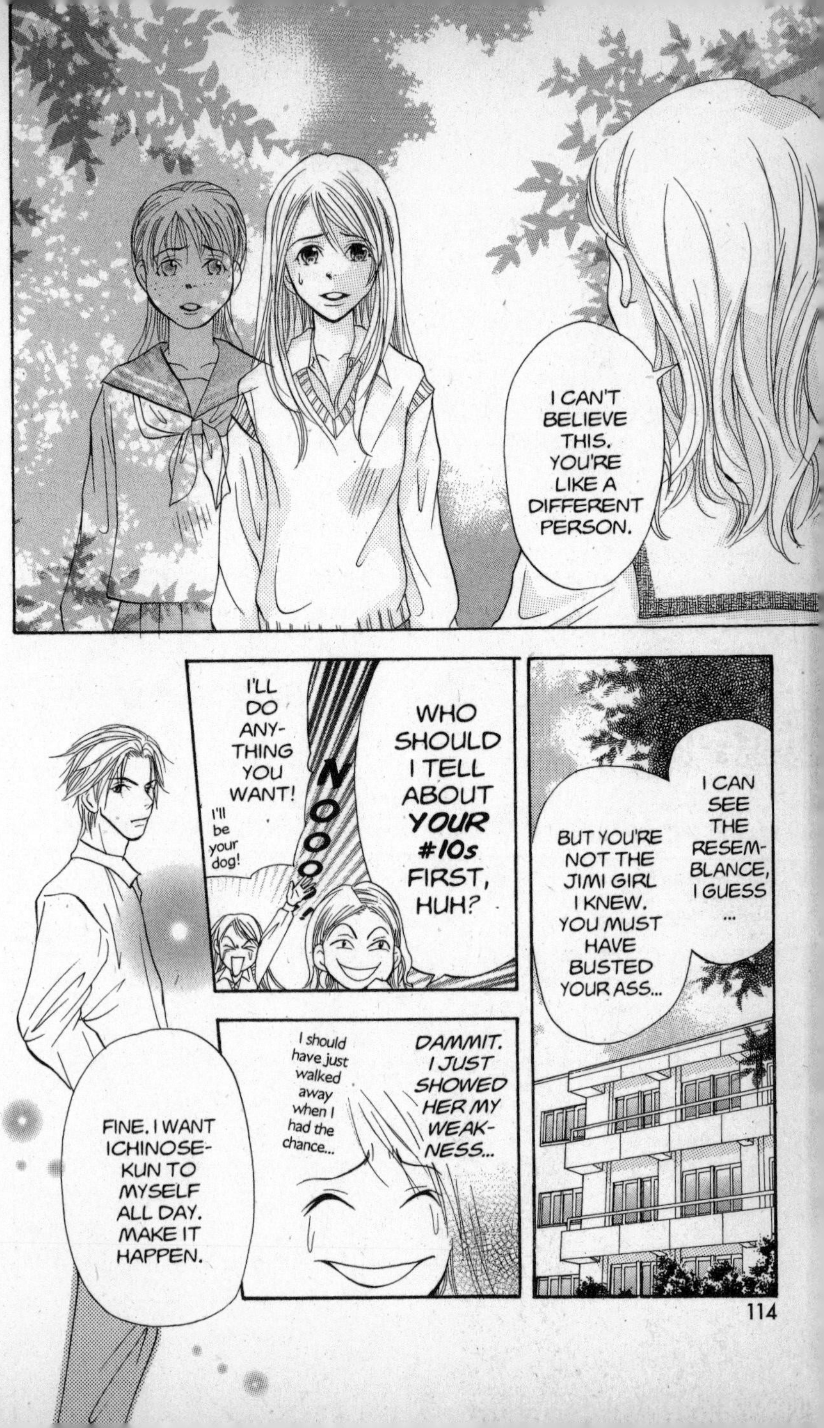
I CAN'T BELIEVE THIS. YOU'RE LIKE A DIFFERENT PERSON.
I CAN SEE THE RESEMBLANCE, I GUESS ...
BUT YOU'RE NOT THE JIMI GIRL I KNEW. YOU MUST HAVE BUSTED YOUR ASS...
WHO SHOULD I TELL ABOUT *YOUR* #10s FIRST, HUH?
I'LL DO ANYTHING YOU WANT!
I'll be your dog!
NOOOO?!
DAMMIT. I JUST SHOWED HER MY WEAKNESS...
I should have just walked away when I had the chance...
FINE. I WANT ICHINOSE-KUN TO MYSELF ALL DAY. MAKE IT HAPPEN.

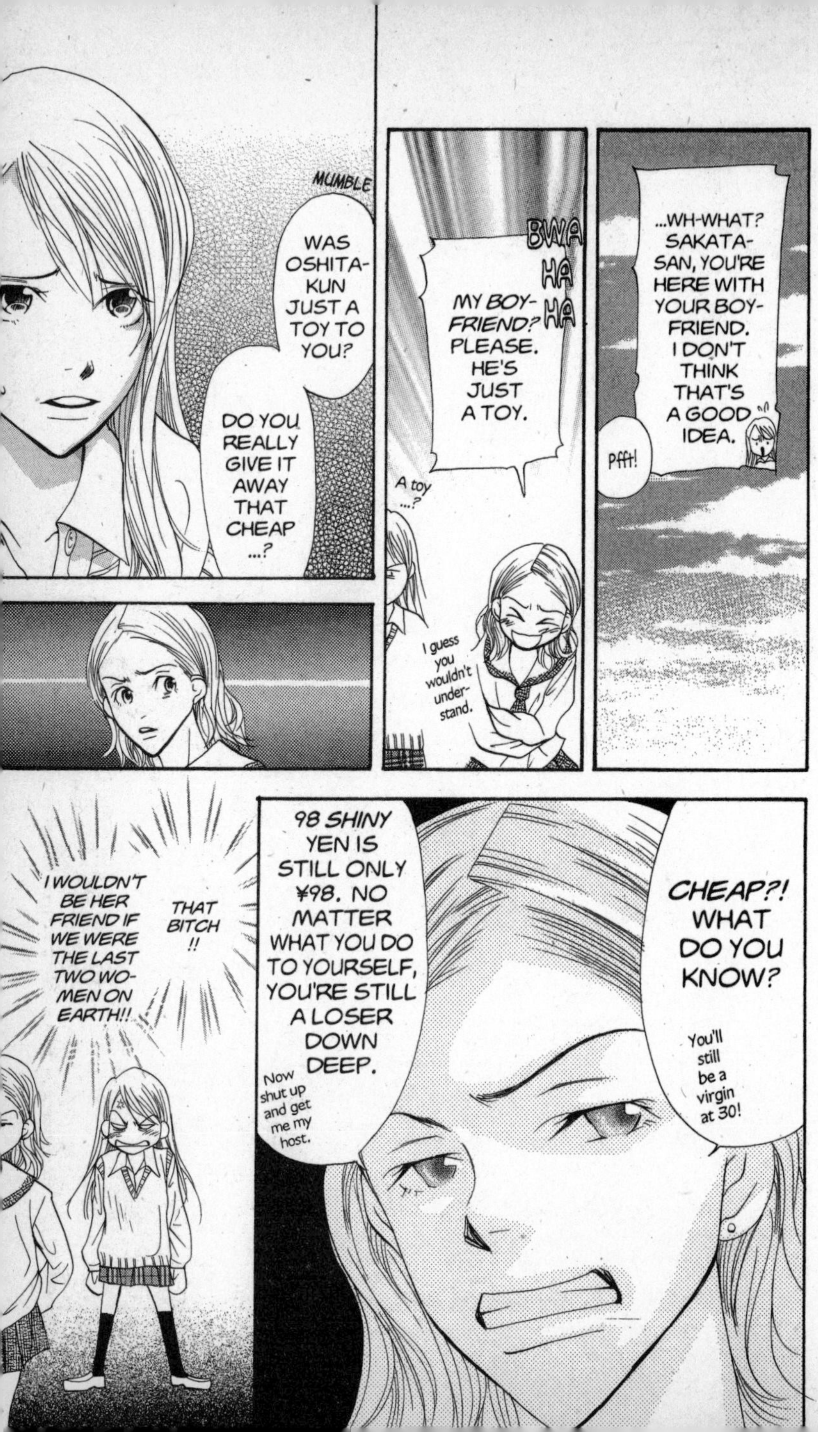
...WH-WHAT? SAKATA-SAN, YOU'RE HERE WITH YOUR BOY-FRIEND. I DON'T THINK THAT'S A GOOD IDEA.
Pfft!
BWA HA HA
MY BOY-FRIEND? PLEASE. HE'S JUST A TOY.
A toy ...?
I guess you wouldn't under-stand.
MUMBLE
WAS OSHITA-KUN JUST A TOY TO YOU?
DO YOU REALLY GIVE IT AWAY THAT CHEAP ...?
CHEAP?! WHAT DO YOU KNOW?
You'll still be a virgin at 30!
98 SHINY YEN IS STILL ONLY ¥98. NO MATTER WHAT YOU DO TO YOURSELF, YOU'RE STILL A LOSER DOWN DEEP.
Now shut up and get me my host.
THAT BITCH !!
I WOULDN'T BE HER FRIEND IF WE WERE THE LAST TWO WO-MEN ON EARTH!!

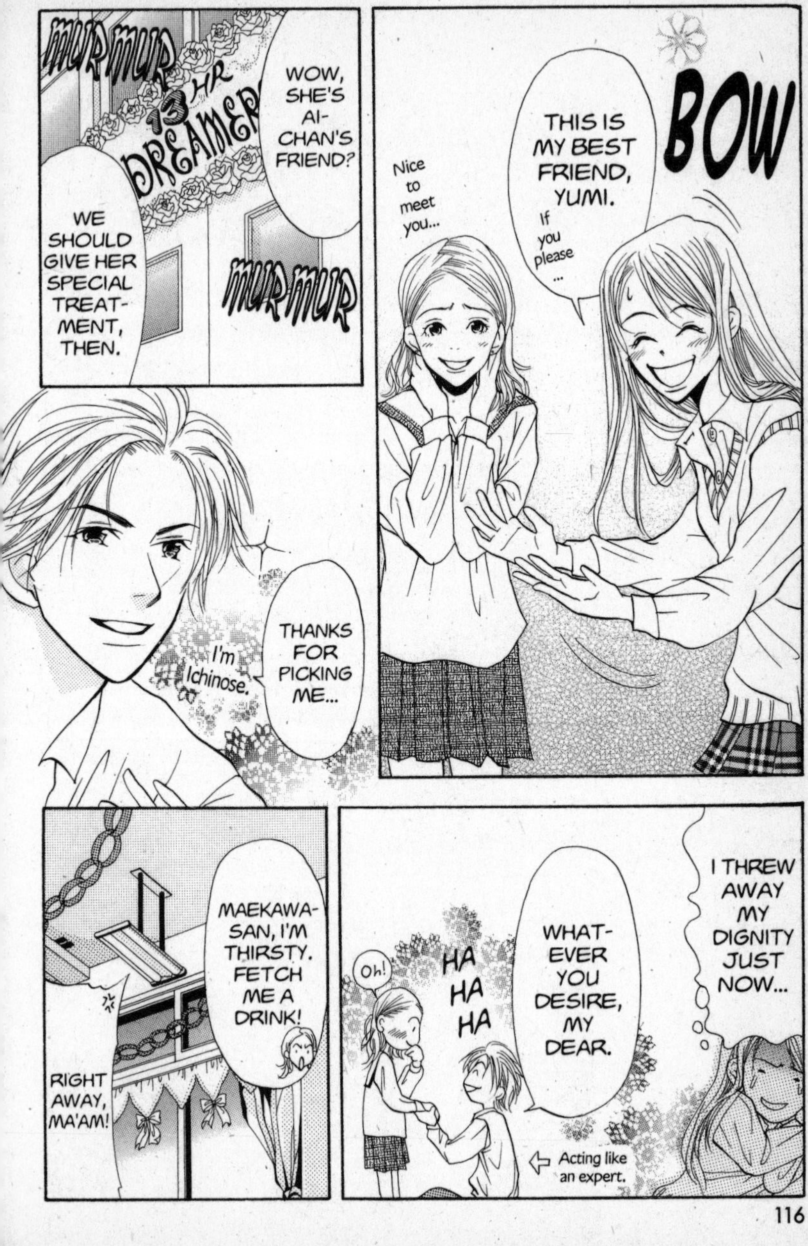
BOW
THIS IS MY BEST FRIEND, YUMI.
If you please ...
Nice to meet you...
MURMUR
WOW, SHE'S AI-CHAN'S FRIEND?
13 HR DREAMERS
WE SHOULD GIVE HER SPECIAL TREATMENT, THEN.
MURMUR
THANKS FOR PICKING ME...
I'm Ichinose.
I THREW AWAY MY DIGNITY JUST NOW...
WHATEVER YOU DESIRE, MY DEAR.
HA HA HA
Oh!
Acting like an expert.
MAEKAWA-SAN, I'M THIRSTY. FETCH ME A DRINK!
RIGHT AWAY, MA'AM!

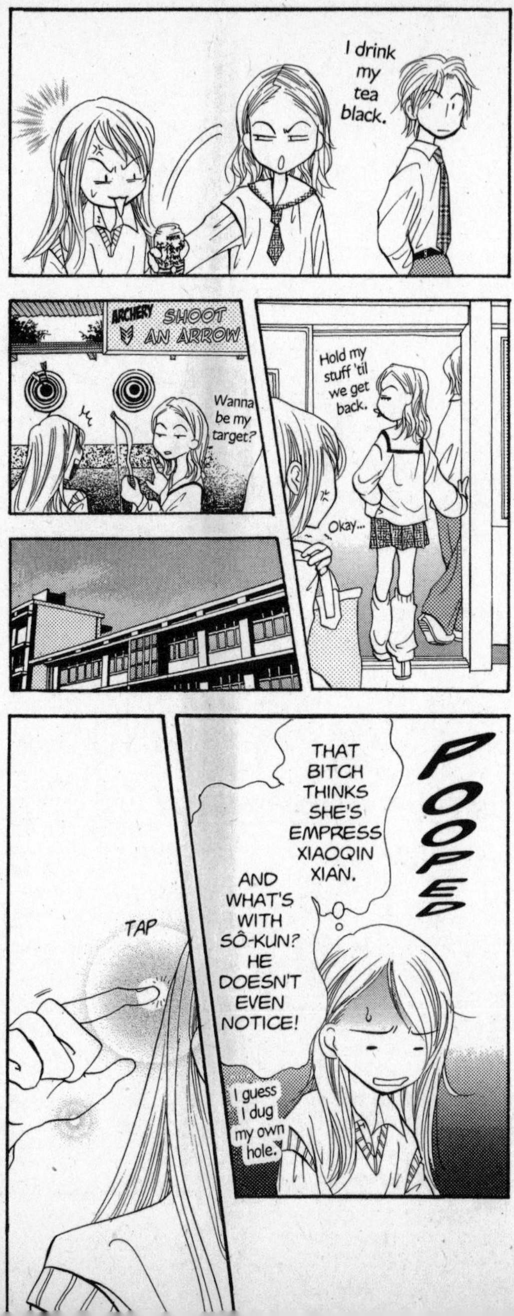
I drink my tea black.
Hold my stuff 'til we get back.
Okay...
ARCHERY
SHOOT AN ARROW
Wanna be my target?
POOPED
THAT BITCH THINKS SHE'S EMPRESS XIAOQIN XIAN.
AND WHAT'S WITH SÔ-KUN? HE DOESN'T EVEN NOTICE!
I guess I dug my own hole.
TAP

Exciting Encounters!
An Encyclopedia of Creatures

Part 3

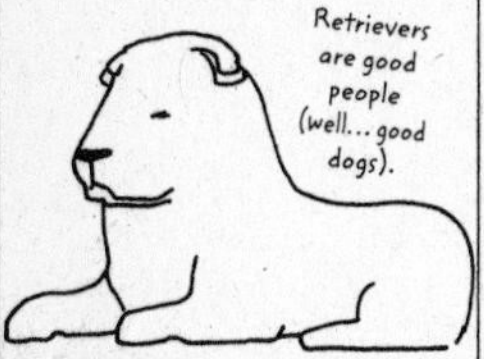
Retrievers are good people (well... good dogs).

Retriever (Dog)

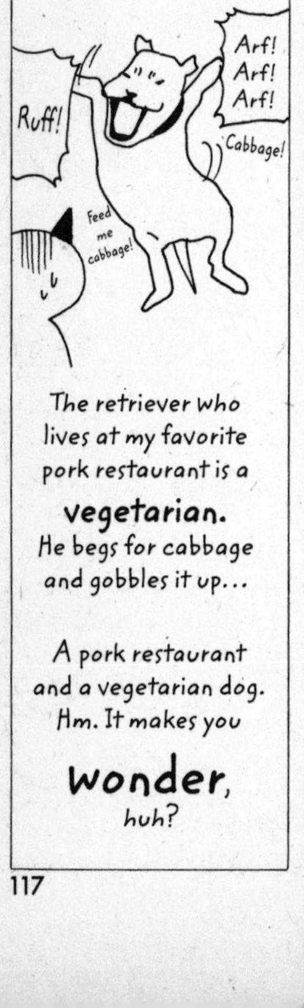
Arf! Arf! Arf!
Ruff!
Cabbage!
Feed me cabbage!

The retriever who lives at my favorite pork restaurant is a **vegetarian.** He begs for cabbage and gobbles it up...

A pork restaurant and a vegetarian dog. Hm. It makes you **wonder,** huh?

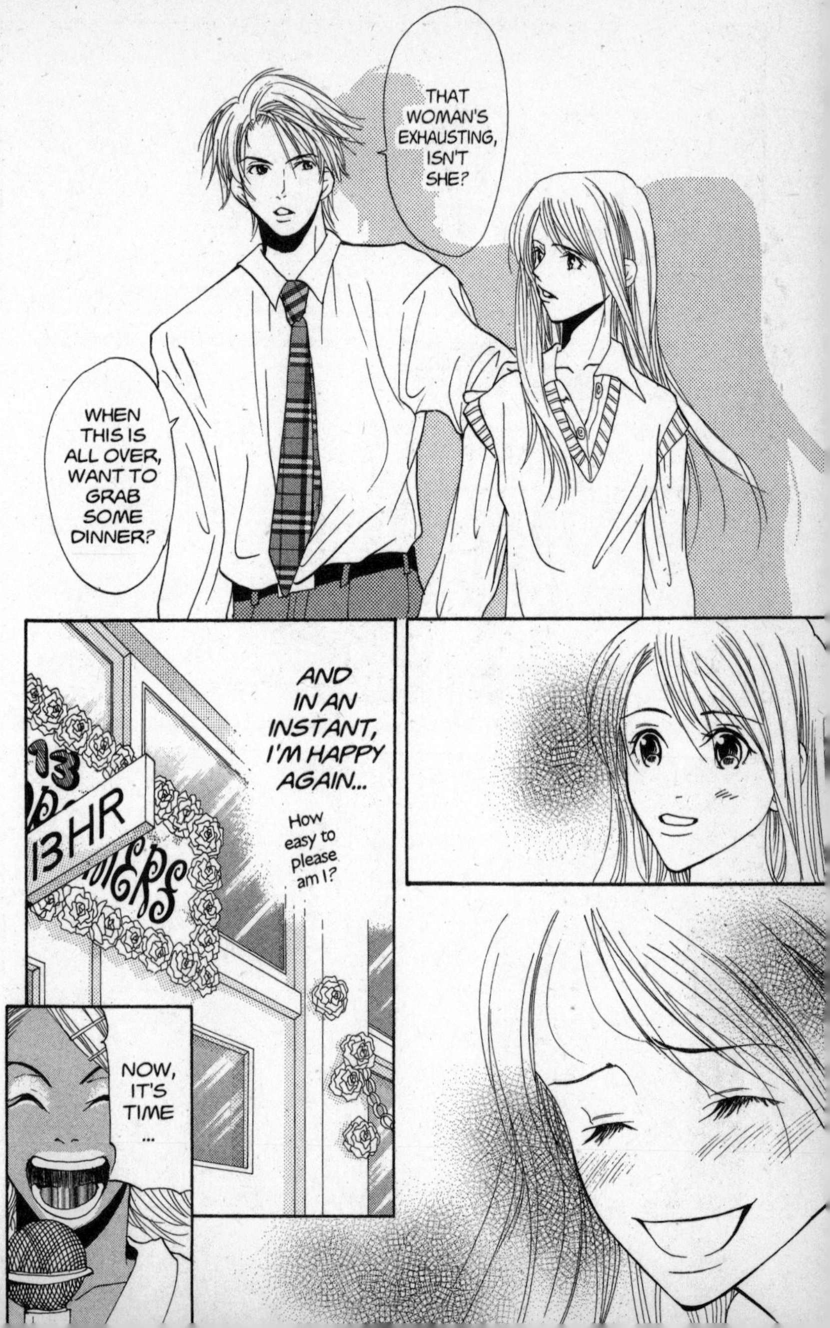
THAT WOMAN'S EXHAUSTING, ISN'T SHE?
WHEN THIS IS ALL OVER, WANT TO GRAB SOME DINNER?
AND IN AN INSTANT, I'M HAPPY AGAIN...
How easy to please am I?
13HR
NOW, IT'S TIME ...

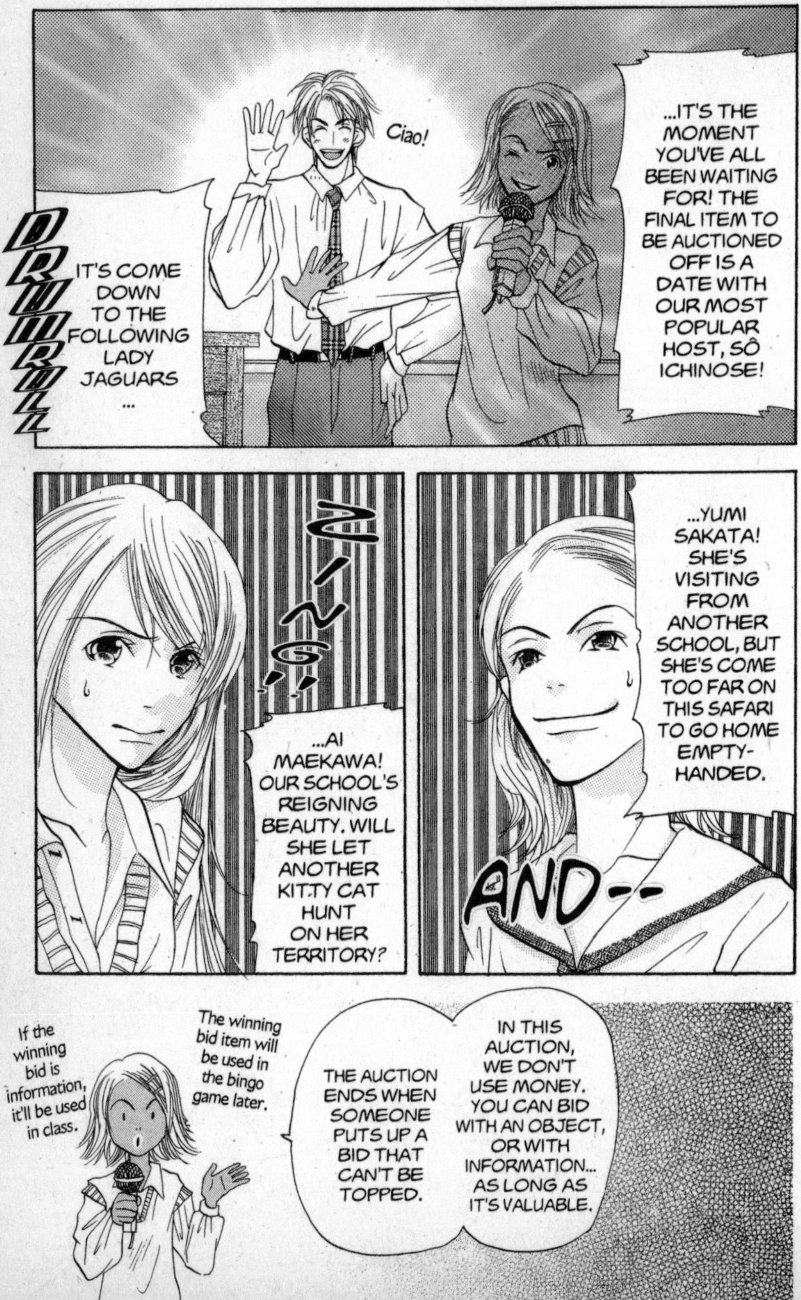
...IT'S THE MOMENT YOU'VE ALL BEEN WAITING FOR! THE FINAL ITEM TO BE AUCTIONED OFF IS A DATE WITH OUR MOST POPULAR HOST, SÔ ICHINOSE!
Ciao!
IT'S COME DOWN TO THE FOLLOWING LADY JAGUARS ...
DRUMROLL
...YUMI SAKATA! SHE'S VISITING FROM ANOTHER SCHOOL, BUT SHE'S COME TOO FAR ON THIS SAFARI TO GO HOME EMPTY-HANDED.
AND--
ZING!!
...AI MAEKAWA! OUR SCHOOL'S REIGNING BEAUTY. WILL SHE LET ANOTHER KITTY CAT HUNT ON HER TERRITORY?
IN THIS AUCTION, WE DON'T USE MONEY. YOU CAN BID WITH AN OBJECT, OR WITH INFORMATION... AS LONG AS IT'S VALUABLE.
THE AUCTION ENDS WHEN SOMEONE PUTS UP A BID THAT CAN'T BE TOPPED.
The winning bid item will be used in the bingo game later.
If the winning bid is information, it'll be used in class.

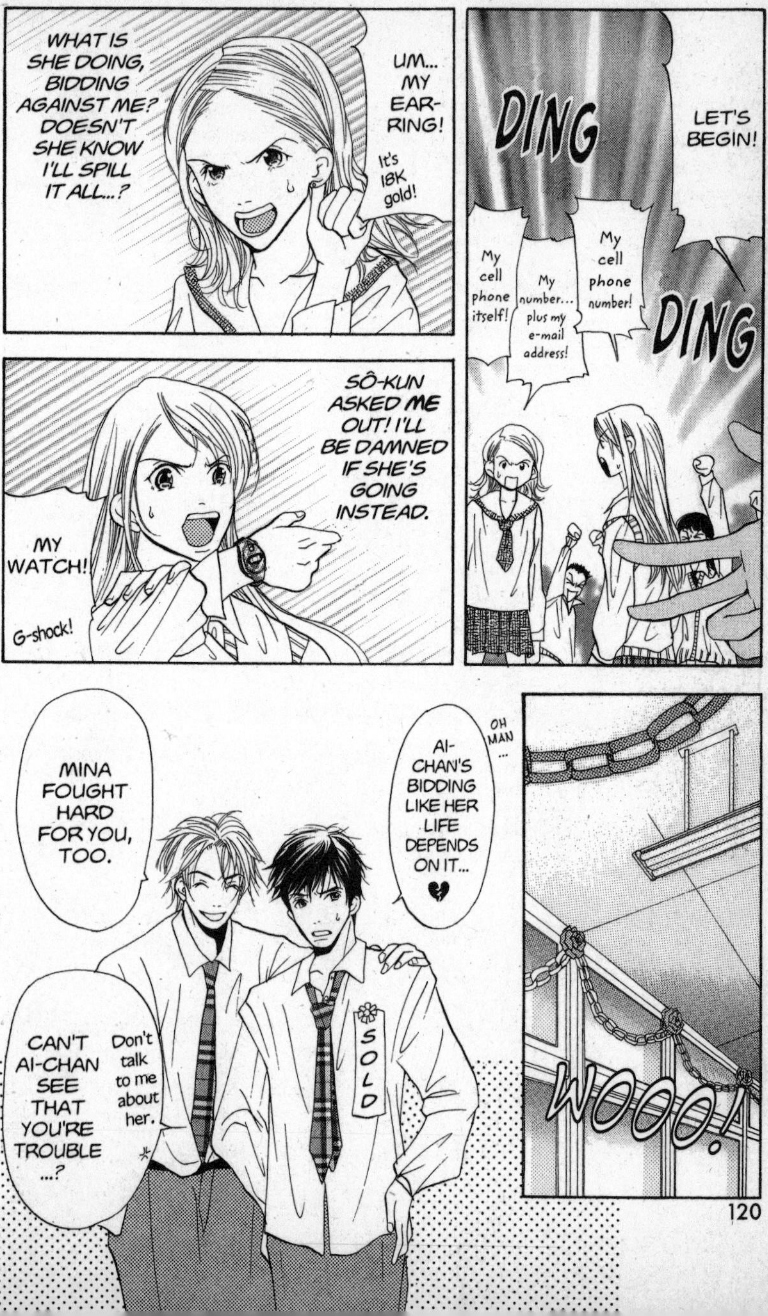
LET'S BEGIN!
DING
My cell phone number!
My number... plus my e-mail address!
My cell phone itself!
DING
UM... MY EAR-RING!
It's 18K gold!
WHAT IS SHE DOING, BIDDING AGAINST ME? DOESN'T SHE KNOW I'LL SPILL IT ALL...?
SÔ-KUN ASKED ME OUT! I'LL BE DAMNED IF SHE'S GOING INSTEAD.
MY WATCH!
G-shock!
WOOO!
OH MAN ...
AI-CHAN'S BIDDING LIKE HER LIFE DEPENDS ON IT...
MINA FOUGHT HARD FOR YOU, TOO.
SOLD
Don't talk to me about her.
CAN'T AI-CHAN SEE THAT YOU'RE TROUBLE ...?

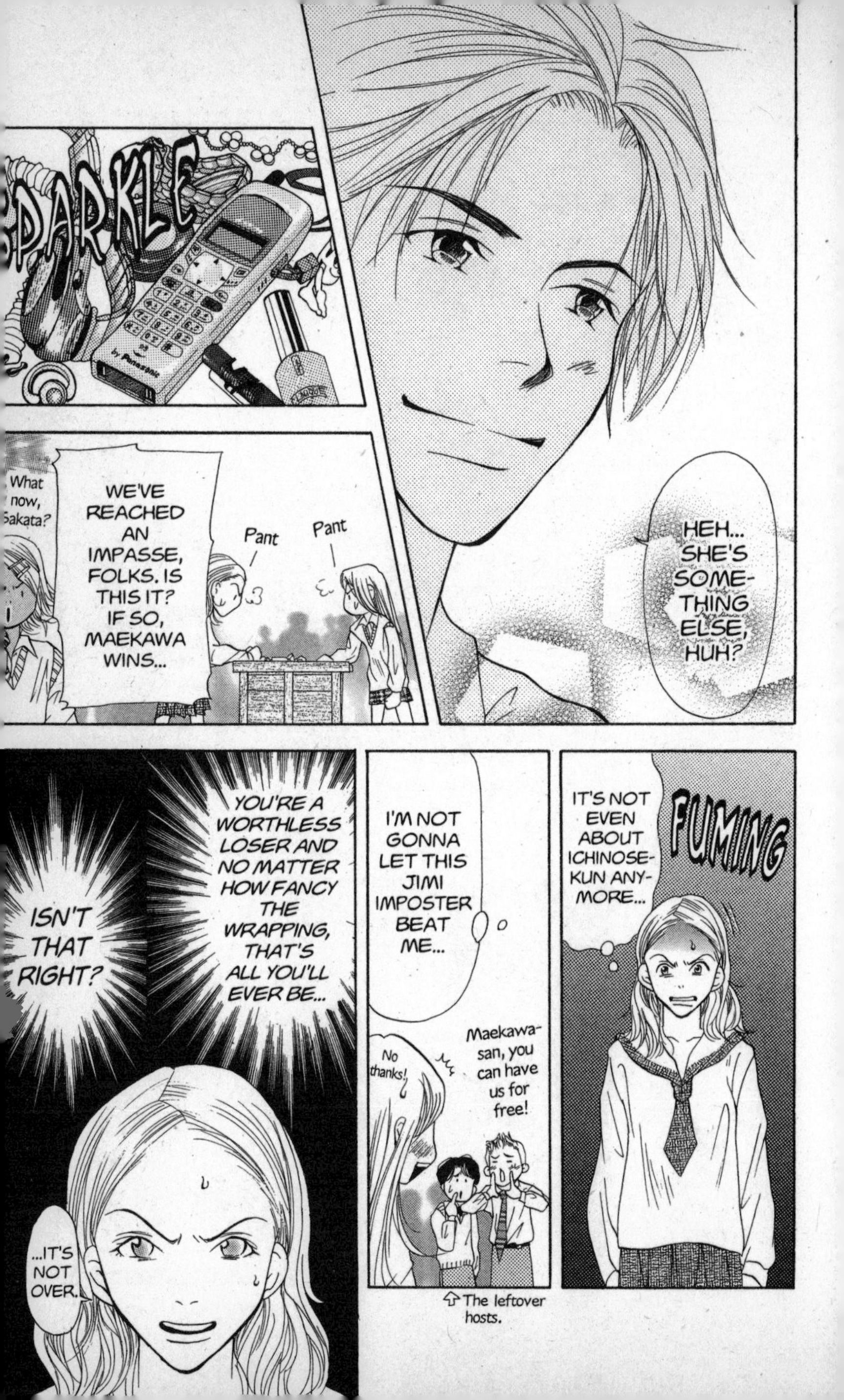
HEH... SHE'S SOME-THING ELSE, HUH?
SPARKLE
WE'VE REACHED AN IMPASSE, FOLKS. IS THIS IT? IF SO, MAEKAWA WINS...
Pant
Pant
What now, Sakata?
FUMING
IT'S NOT EVEN ABOUT ICHINOSE-KUN ANY-MORE...
I'M NOT GONNA LET THIS JIMI IMPOSTER BEAT ME...
Maekawa-san, you can have us for free!
No thanks!
The leftover hosts.
YOU'RE A WORTHLESS LOSER AND NO MATTER HOW FANCY THE WRAPPING, THAT'S ALL YOU'LL EVER BE...
ISN'T THAT RIGHT?
...IT'S NOT OVER.

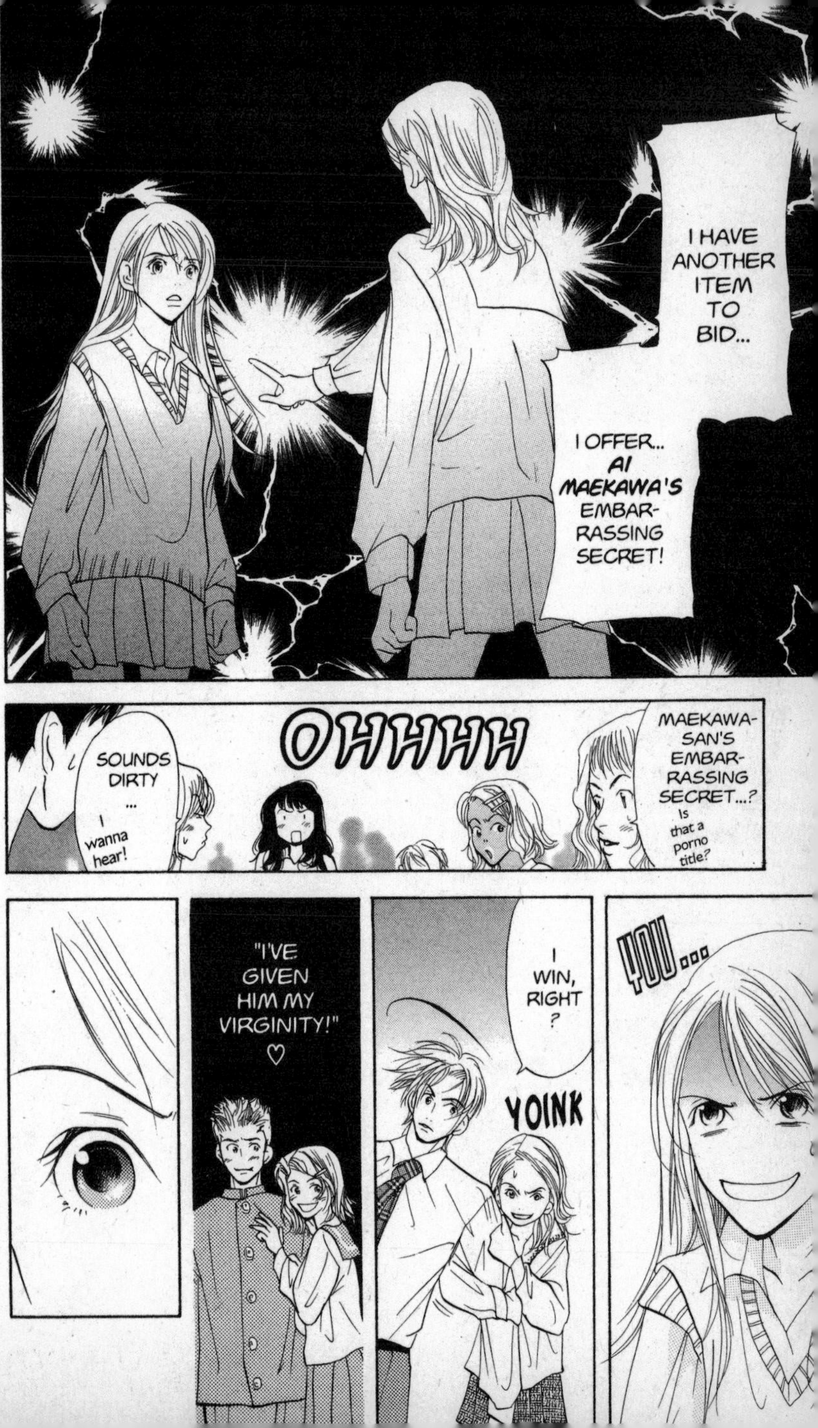
I HAVE ANOTHER ITEM TO BID...
I OFFER... AI MAEKAWA'S EMBARRASSING SECRET!
MAEKAWA-SAN'S EMBARRASSING SECRET...?
Is that a porno title?
OHHHHH
SOUNDS DIRTY ...
I wanna hear!
YOU...
I WIN, RIGHT?
YOINK
"I'VE GIVEN HIM MY VIRGINITY!" ♡

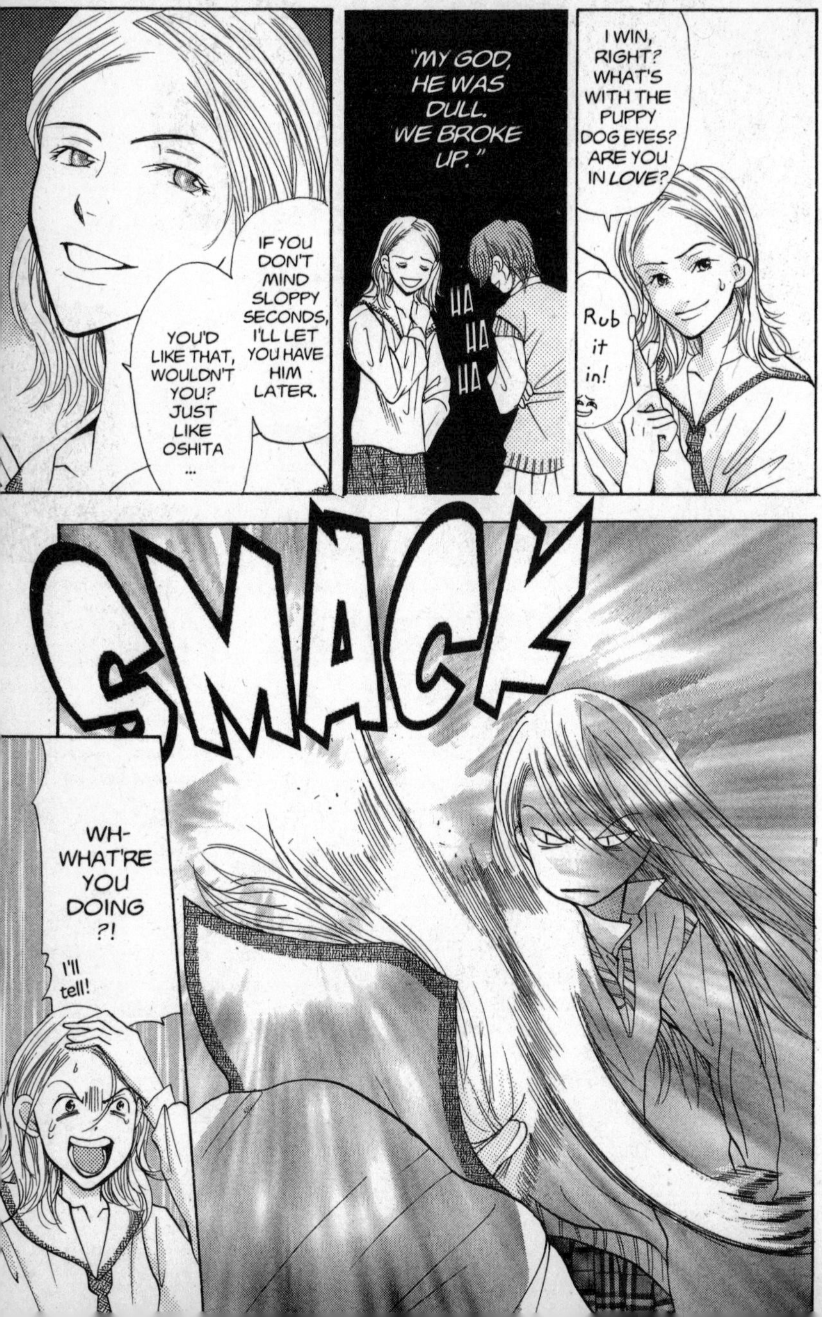
I WIN, RIGHT? WHAT'S WITH THE PUPPY DOG EYES? ARE YOU IN *LOVE*?
Rub it in!
"MY GOD, HE WAS DULL. WE BROKE UP."
HA HA HA
IF YOU DON'T MIND SLOPPY SECONDS, I'LL LET YOU HAVE HIM LATER.
YOU'D LIKE THAT, WOULDN'T YOU? JUST LIKE OSHITA ...
SMACK
WH-WHAT'RE YOU DOING ?!
I'll tell!

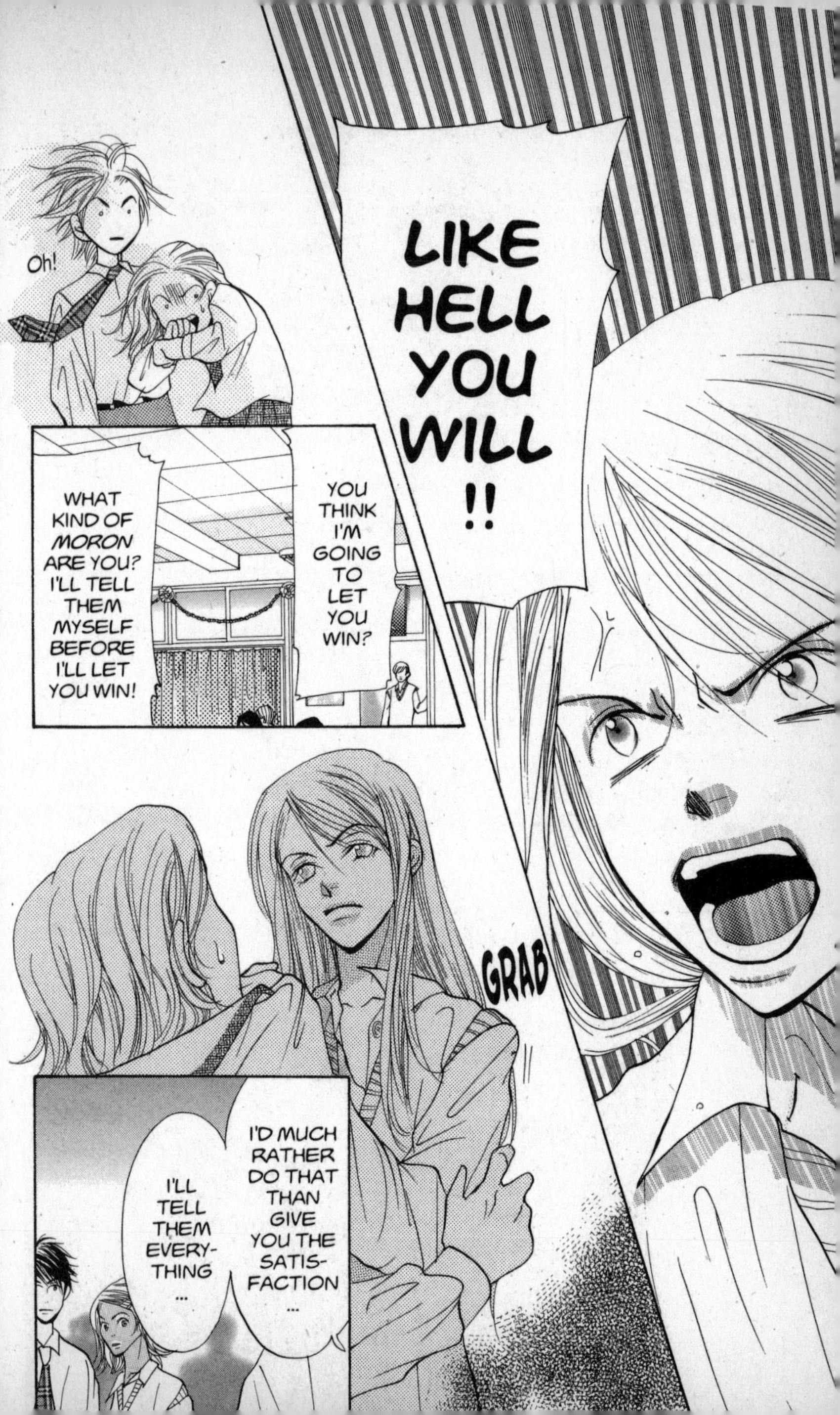
LIKE HELL YOU WILL!!
GRAB
Oh!
YOU THINK I'M GOING TO LET YOU WIN?
WHAT KIND OF *MORON* ARE YOU? I'LL TELL THEM MYSELF BEFORE I'LL LET YOU WIN!
I'D MUCH RATHER DO THAT THAN GIVE YOU THE SATIS-FACTION ...
I'LL TELL THEM EVERY-THING ...

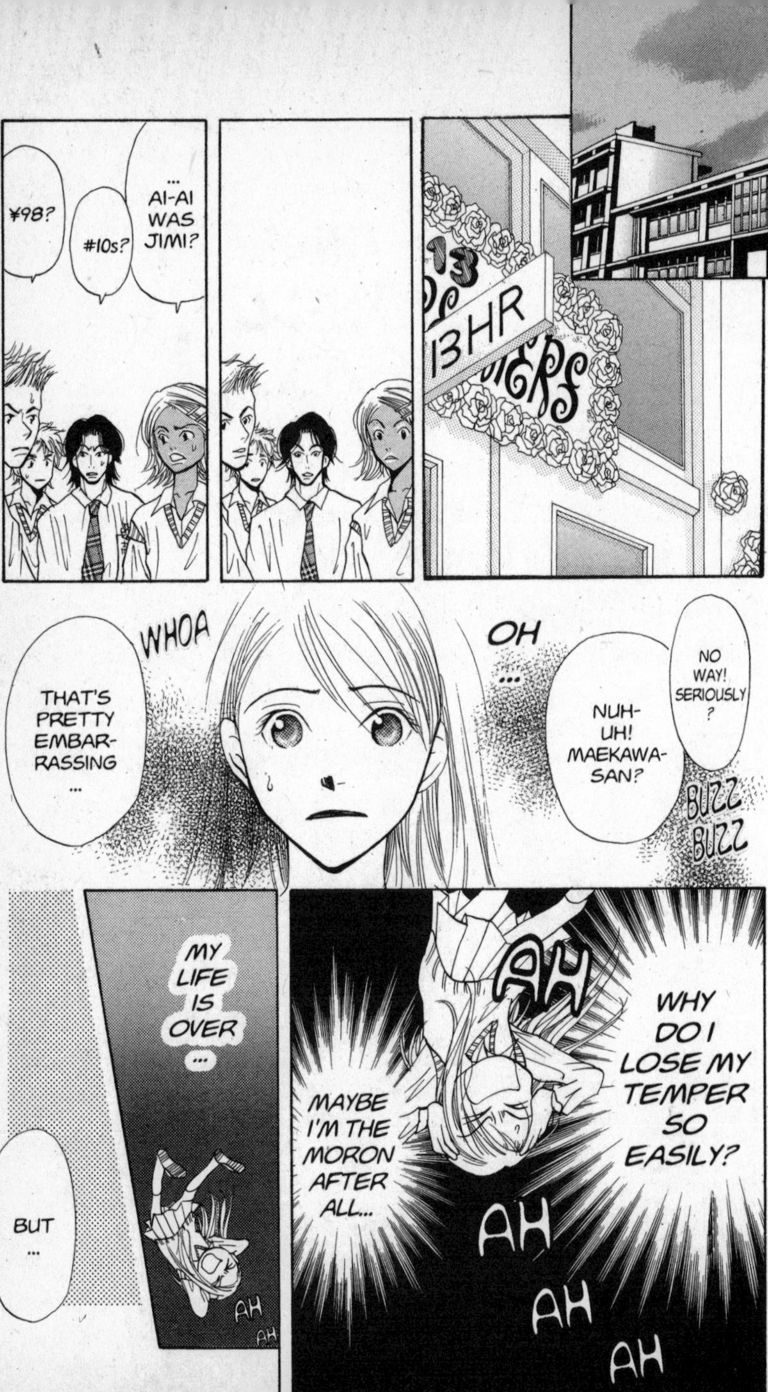
13HR
... AI-AI WAS JIMI?
#10s?
¥98?
NO WAY! SERIOUSLY?
NUH-UH! MAEKAWA-SAN?
BUZZ BUZZ
OH ...
WHOA
THAT'S PRETTY EMBARRASSING ...
AH
WHY DO I LOSE MY TEMPER SO EASILY?
MAYBE I'M THE MORON AFTER ALL...
AH
AH
AH
MY LIFE IS OVER ...
AH
AH
BUT ...

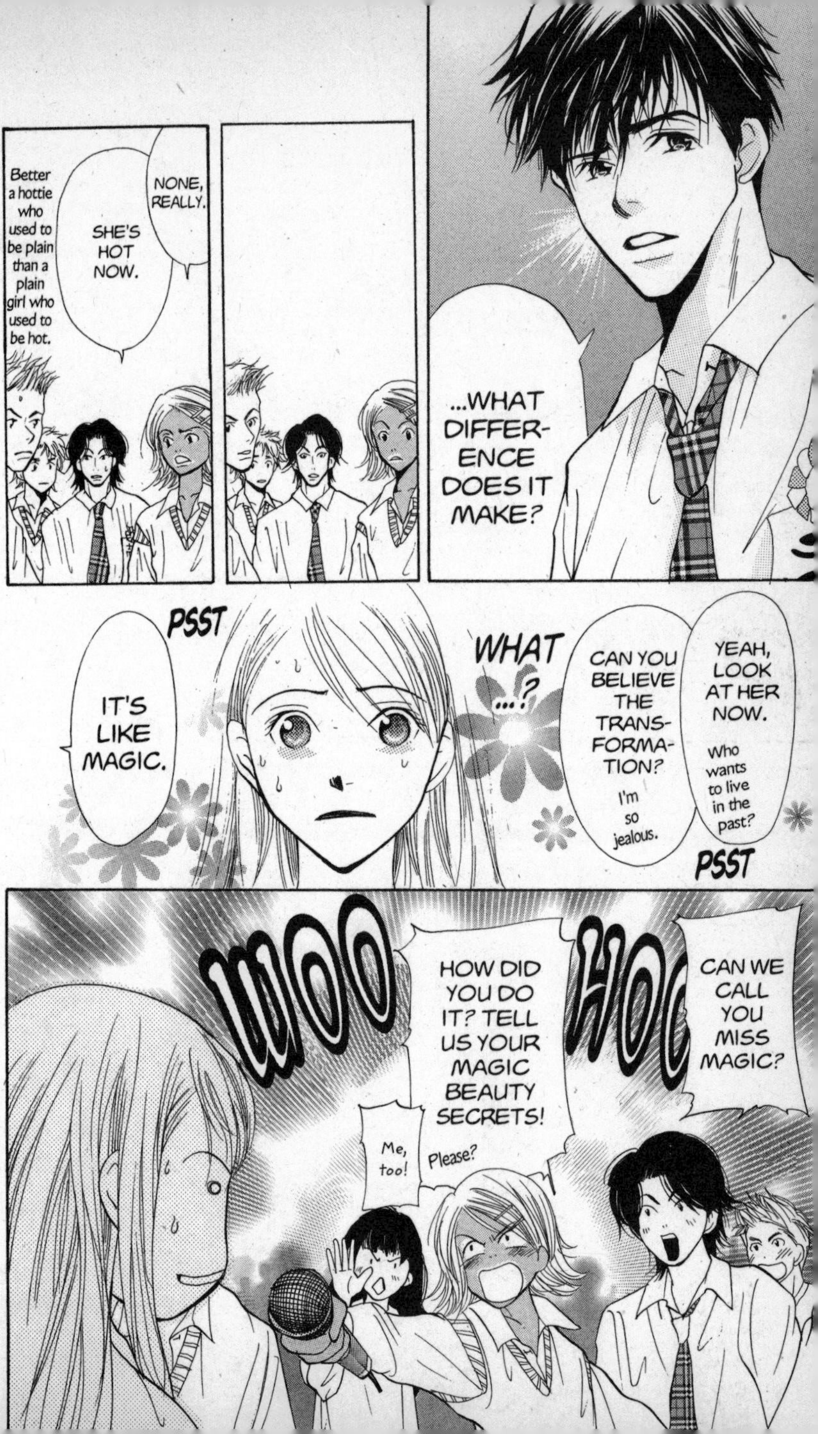
...WHAT DIFFERENCE DOES IT MAKE?
NONE, REALLY.
SHE'S HOT NOW.
Better a hottie who used to be plain than a plain girl who used to be hot.
PSST
YEAH, LOOK AT HER NOW.
Who wants to live in the past?
CAN YOU BELIEVE THE TRANSFORMATION?
I'm so jealous.
WHAT ...?
PSST
IT'S LIKE MAGIC.
CAN WE CALL YOU MISS MAGIC?
WOO HOO
HOW DID YOU DO IT? TELL US YOUR MAGIC BEAUTY SECRETS!
Please?
Me, too!

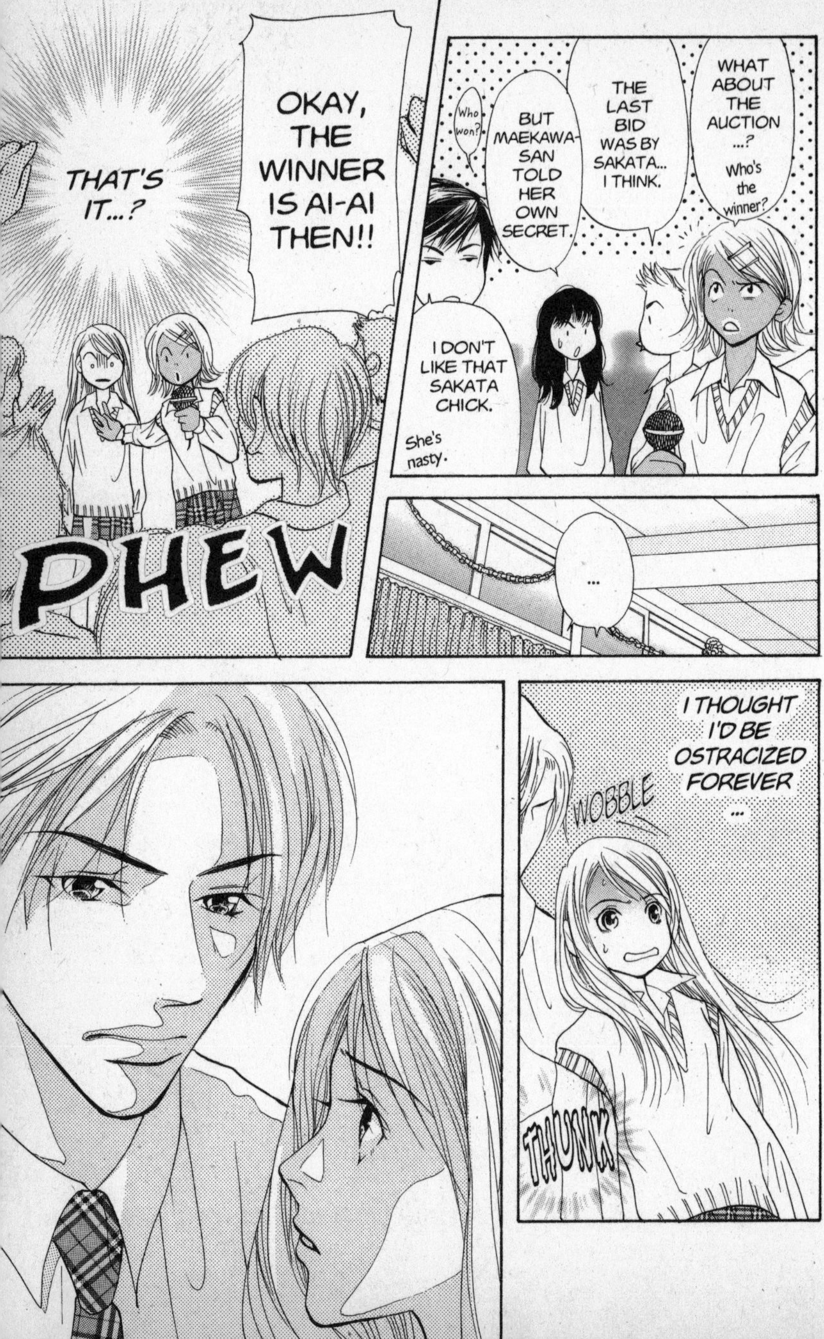
WHAT ABOUT THE AUCTION ...?
Who's the winner?
THE LAST BID WAS BY SAKATA... I THINK.
BUT MAEKAWA-SAN TOLD HER OWN SECRET.
Who won?
I DON'T LIKE THAT SAKATA CHICK.
She's nasty.
...
OKAY, THE WINNER IS AI-AI THEN!!
THAT'S IT...?
PHEW
I THOUGHT I'D BE OSTRACIZED FOREVER ...
WOBBLE
THUNK

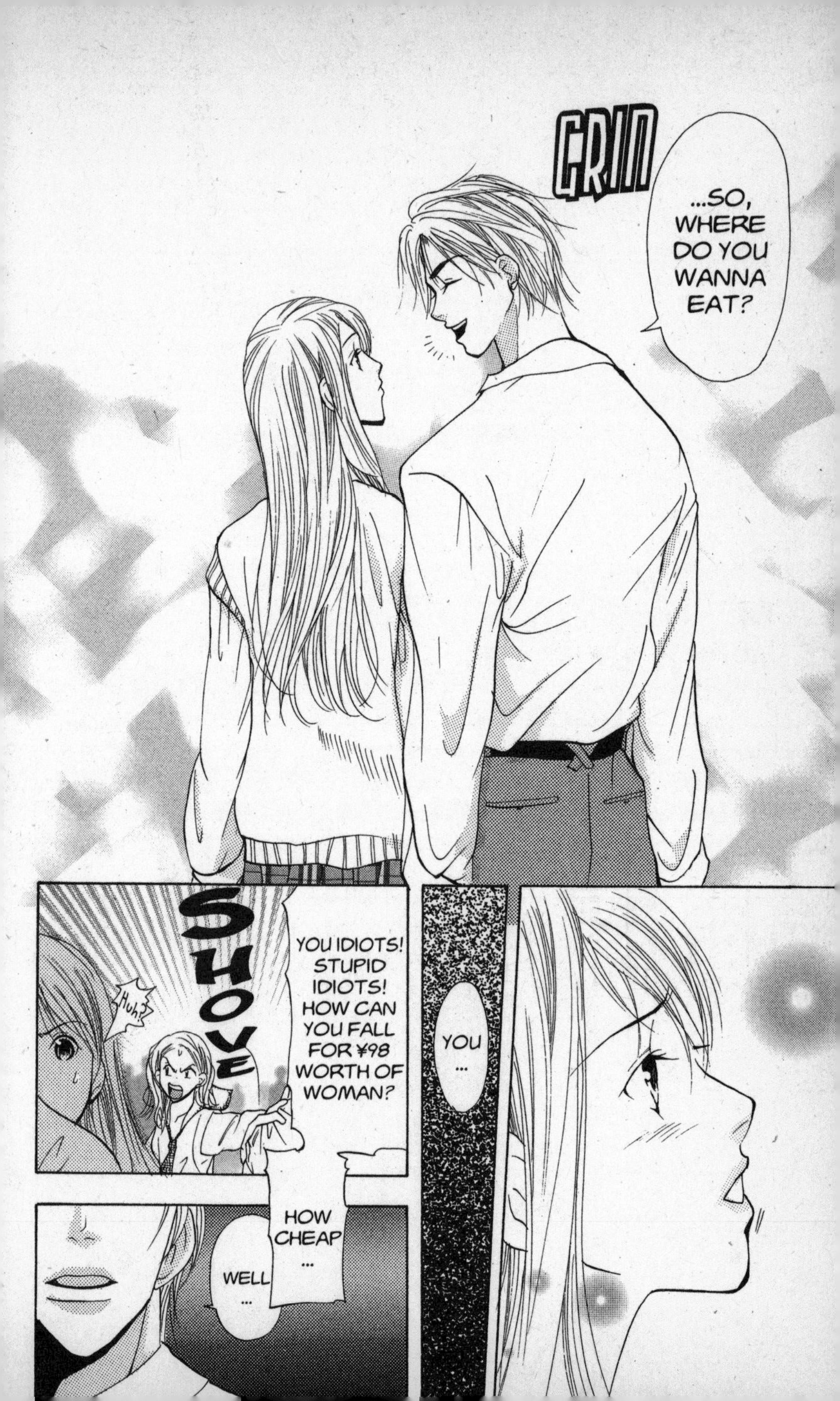
GRIN
...SO, WHERE DO YOU WANNA EAT?
YOU ...
SHOVE
Huh?
YOU IDIOTS! STUPID IDIOTS! HOW CAN YOU FALL FOR ¥98 WORTH OF WOMAN?
HOW CHEAP ...
WELL ...

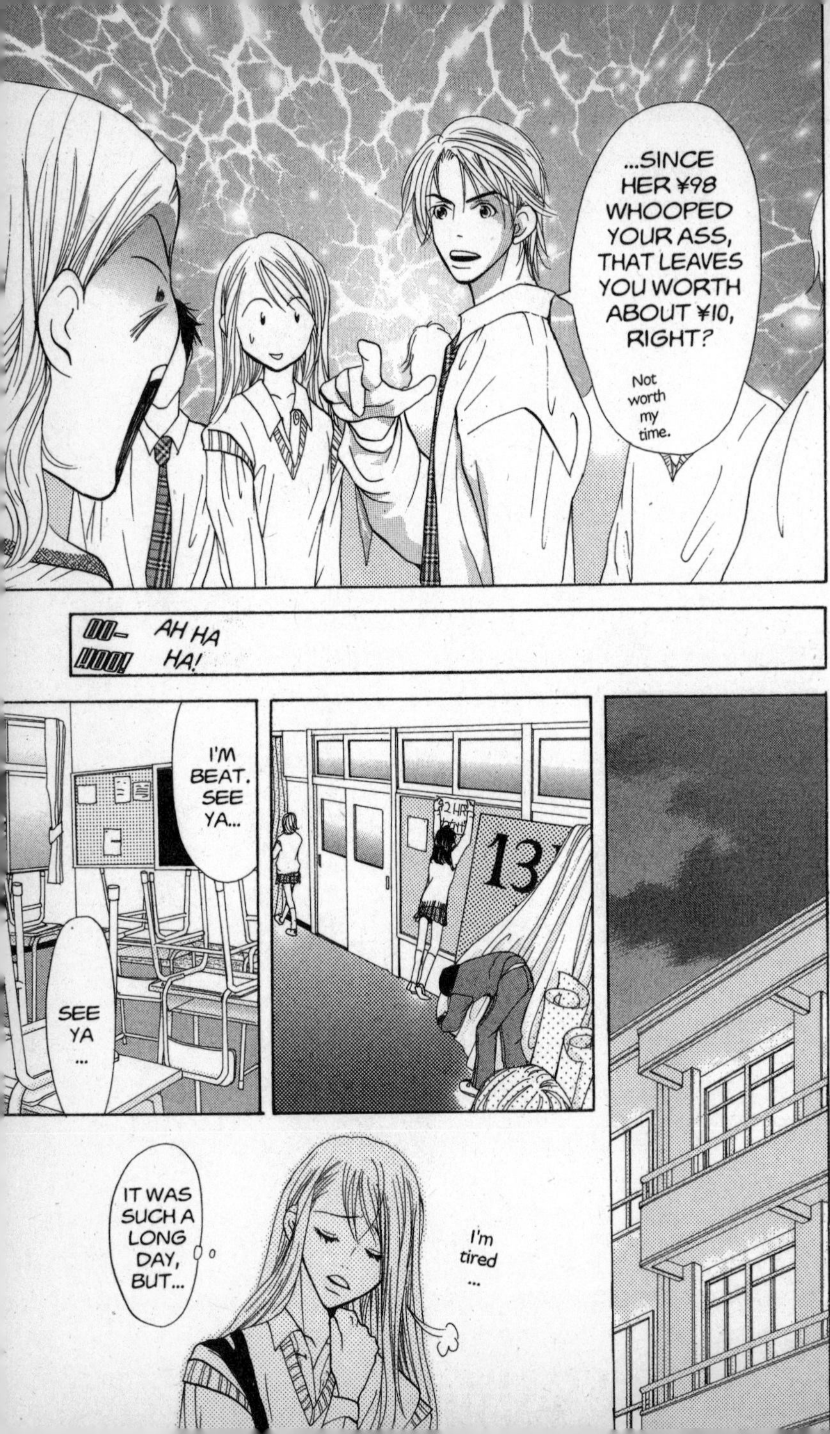
...SINCE HER ¥98 WHOOPED YOUR ASS, THAT LEAVES YOU WORTH ABOUT ¥10, RIGHT?
Not worth my time.
AH HA HA!
OO-HOO!
I'M BEAT. SEE YA...
SEE YA ...
I'm tired ...
IT WAS SUCH A LONG DAY, BUT...

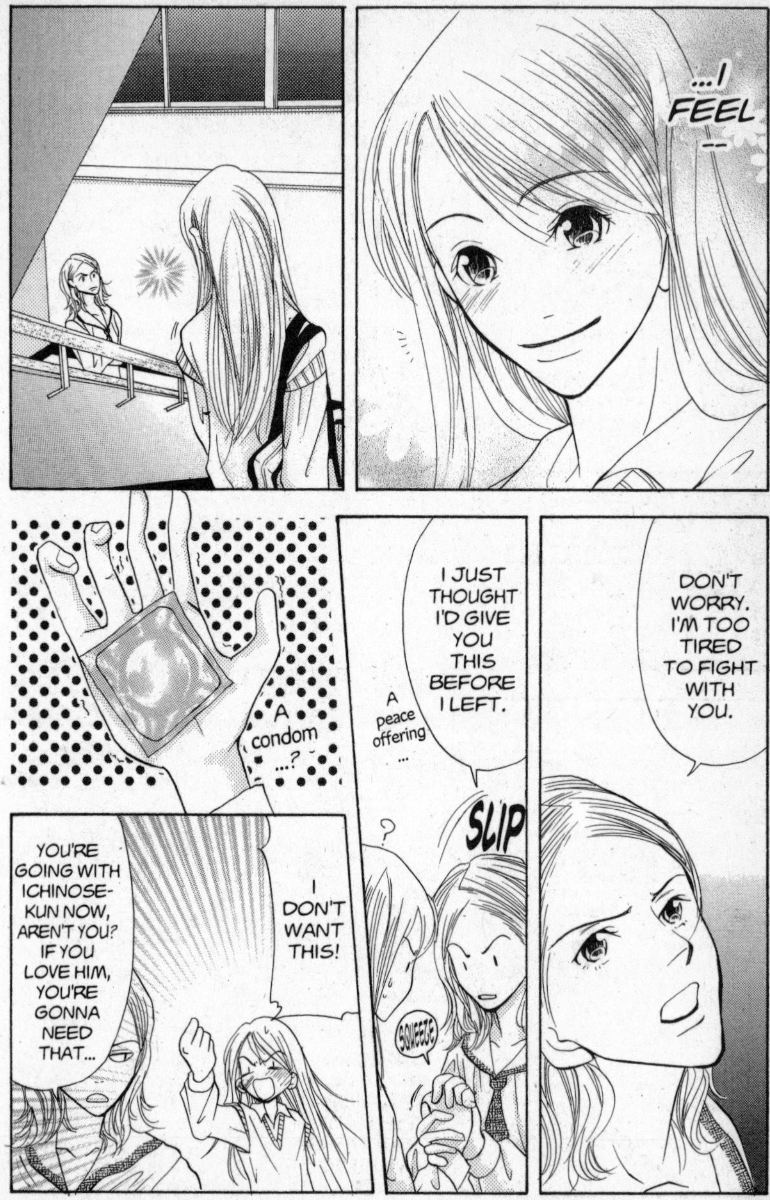
...I FEEL --
DON'T WORRY. I'M TOO TIRED TO FIGHT WITH YOU.
I JUST THOUGHT I'D GIVE YOU THIS BEFORE I LEFT.
A peace offering ...
SLIP
?
SQUEEZE
A condom ...?
I DON'T WANT THIS!
YOU'RE GOING WITH ICHINOSE-KUN NOW, AREN'T YOU? IF YOU LOVE HIM, YOU'RE GONNA NEED THAT...

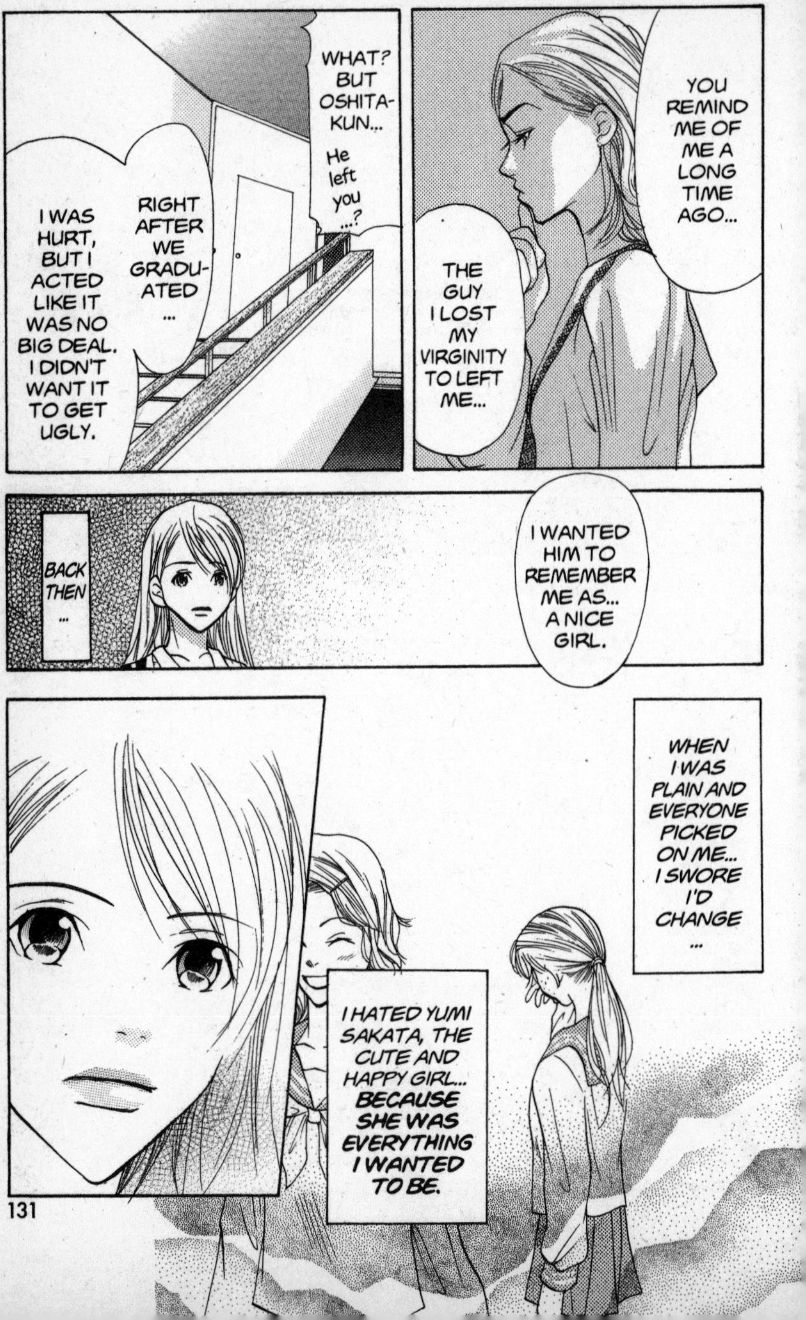
YOU REMIND ME OF ME A LONG TIME AGO...
THE GUY I LOST MY VIRGINITY TO LEFT ME...
WHAT? BUT OSHITA-KUN...
He left you ...?
RIGHT AFTER WE GRADUATED ...
I WAS HURT, BUT I ACTED LIKE IT WAS NO BIG DEAL. I DIDN'T WANT IT TO GET UGLY.
I WANTED HIM TO REMEMBER ME AS... A NICE GIRL.
BACK THEN ...
WHEN I WAS PLAIN AND EVERYONE PICKED ON ME... I SWORE I'D CHANGE ...
I HATED YUMI SAKATA, THE CUTE AND HAPPY GIRL... **BECAUSE SHE WAS EVERYTHING I WANTED TO BE.**

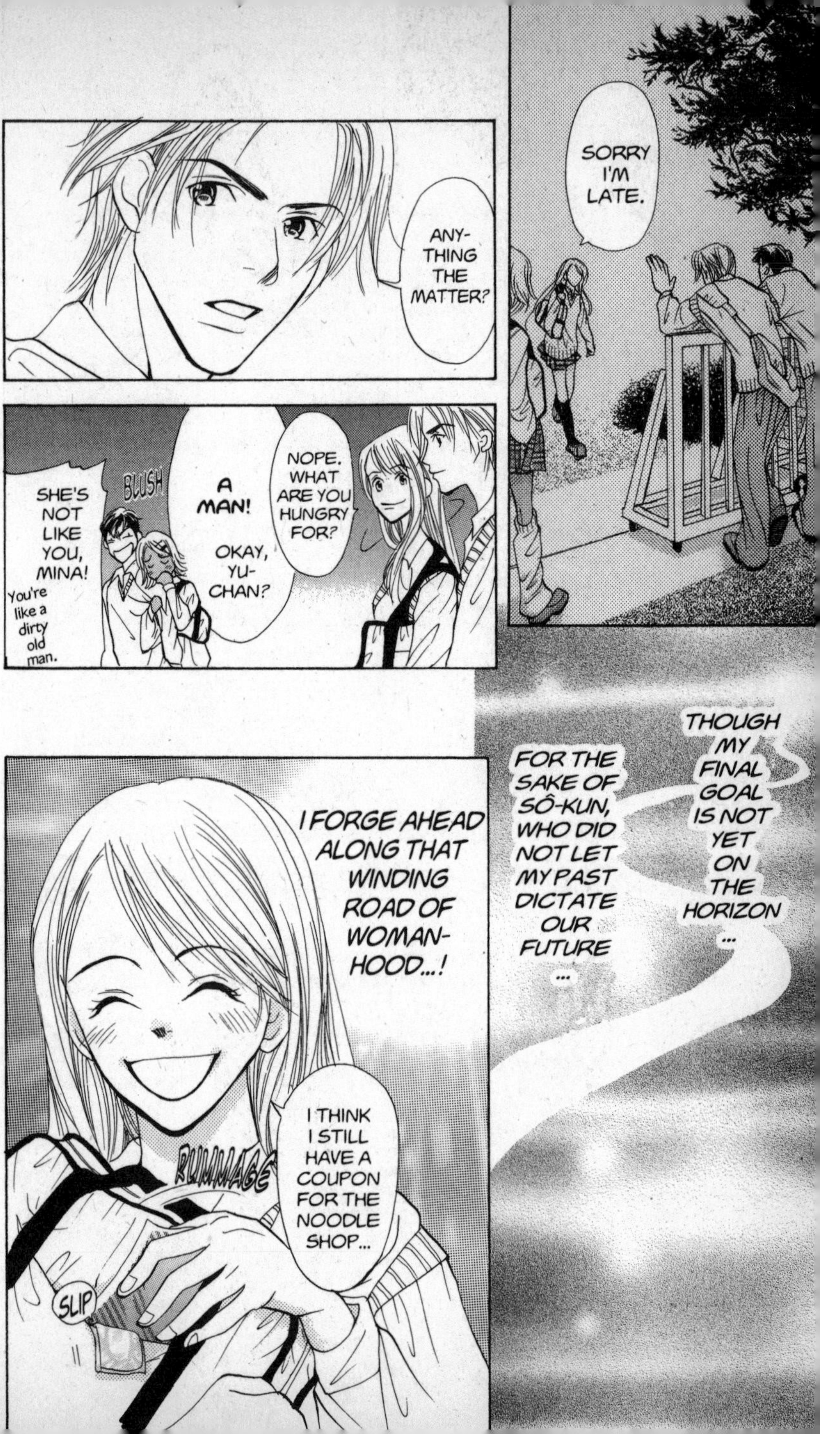
SORRY I'M LATE.
ANYTHING THE MATTER?
NOPE. WHAT ARE YOU HUNGRY FOR?
OKAY, YU-CHAN?
A MAN!
BLUSH
SHE'S NOT LIKE YOU, MINA!
You're like a dirty old man.
THOUGH MY FINAL GOAL IS NOT YET ON THE HORIZON...
FOR THE SAKE OF SÔ-KUN, WHO DID NOT LET MY PAST DICTATE OUR FUTURE...
I FORGE AHEAD ALONG THAT WINDING ROAD OF WOMANHOOD...!
I THINK I STILL HAVE A COUPON FOR THE NOODLE SHOP...
RUMMAGE
SLIP

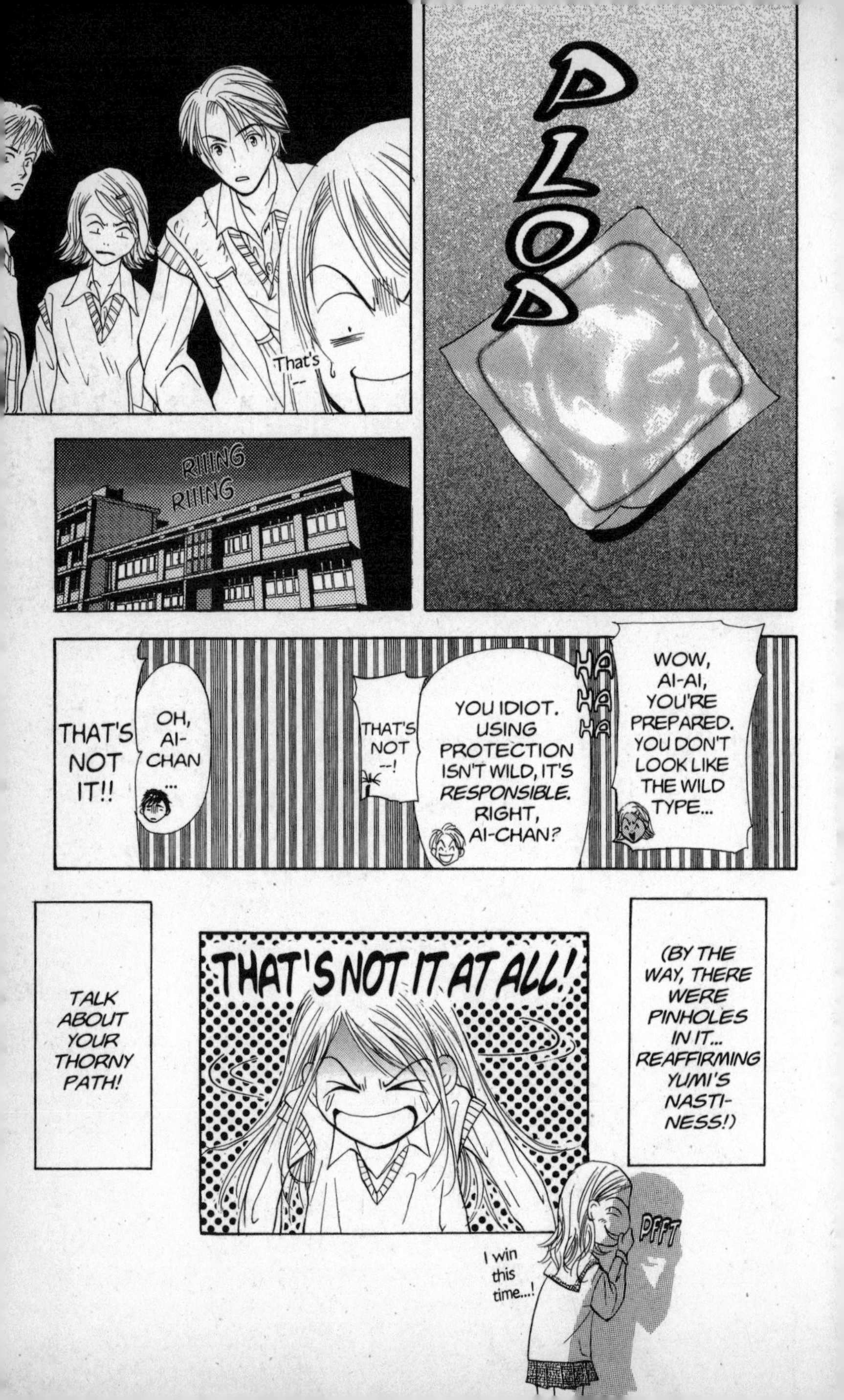
DPLOD
That's --
RIIING RIIING
WOW, AI-AI, YOU'RE PREPARED. YOU DON'T LOOK LIKE THE WILD TYPE...
HAHAHA
YOU IDIOT. USING PROTECTION ISN'T WILD, IT'S RESPONSIBLE. RIGHT, AI-CHAN?
THAT'S NOT --!
OH, AI-CHAN ...
THAT'S NOT IT!!
(BY THE WAY, THERE WERE PINHOLES IN IT... REAFFIRMING YUMI'S NASTI-NESS!)
THAT'S NOT IT AT ALL!
PFFT
I win this time...!
TALK ABOUT YOUR THORNY PATH!

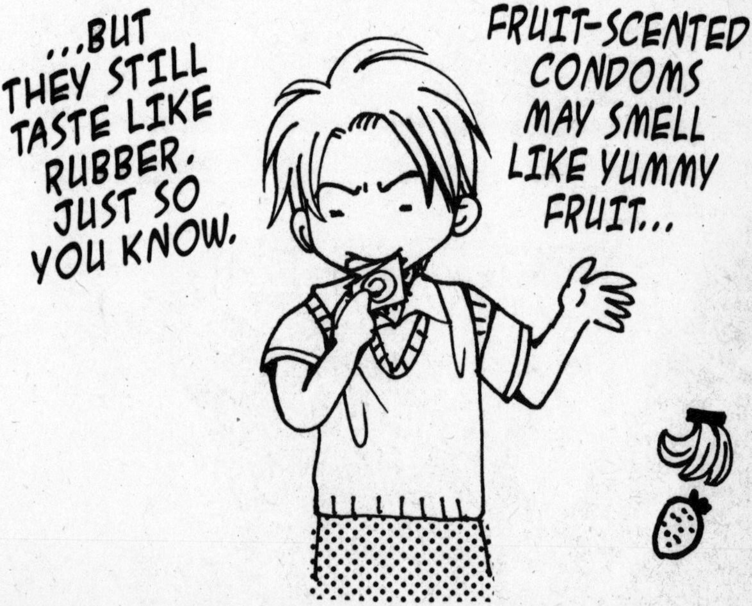
FRUIT-SCENTED CONDOMS MAY SMELL LIKE YUMMY FRUIT...
...BUT THEY STILL TASTE LIKE RUBBER. JUST SO YOU KNOW.

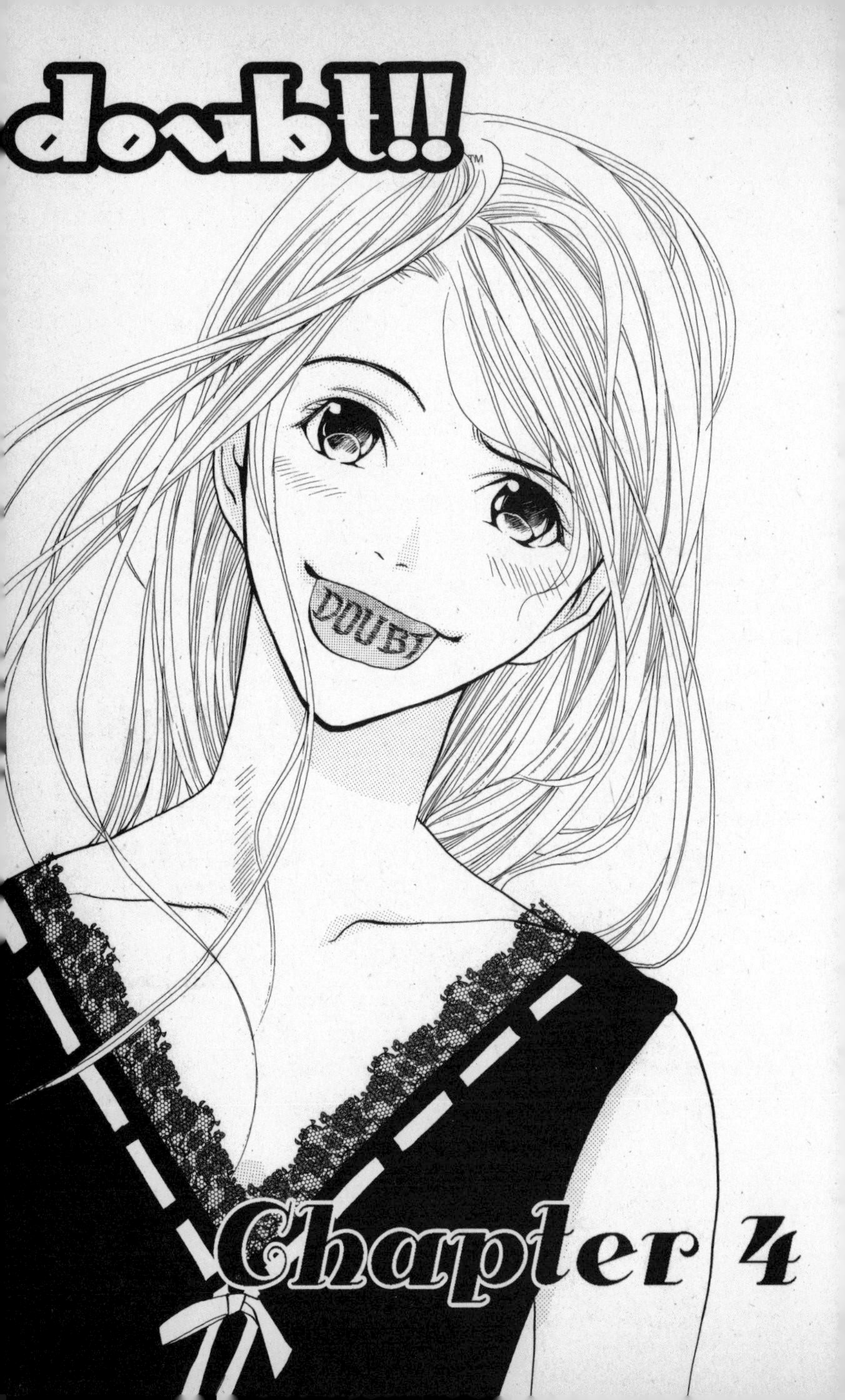
doubt!!™
DOUBT
Chapter 4

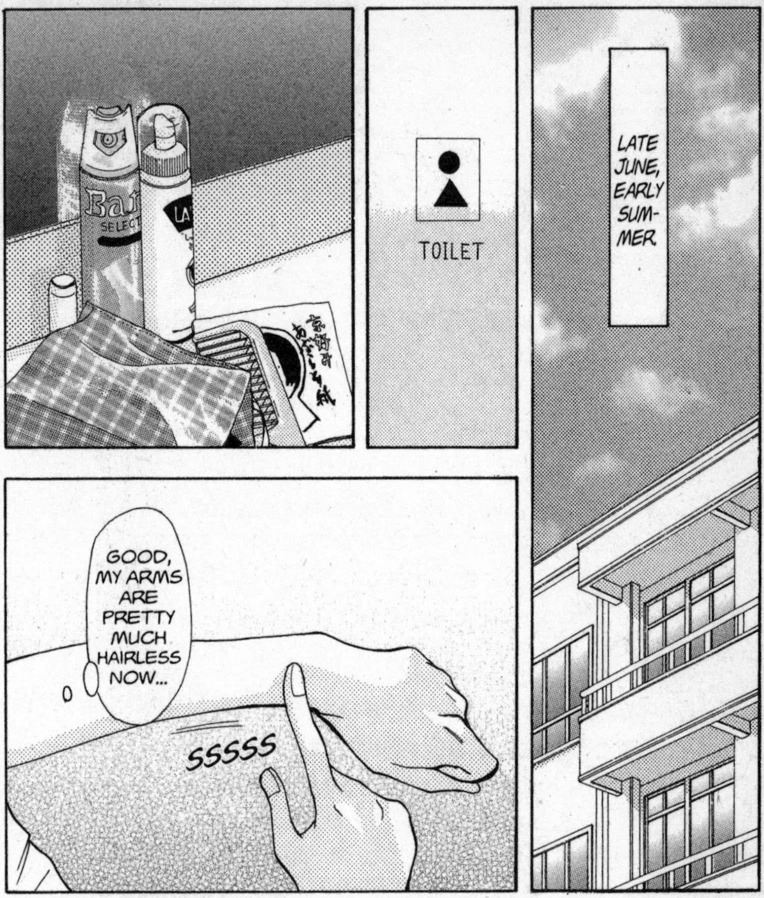
LATE JUNE, EARLY SUMMER.
TOILET
GOOD, MY ARMS ARE PRETTY MUCH HAIRLESS NOW...
SSSSS

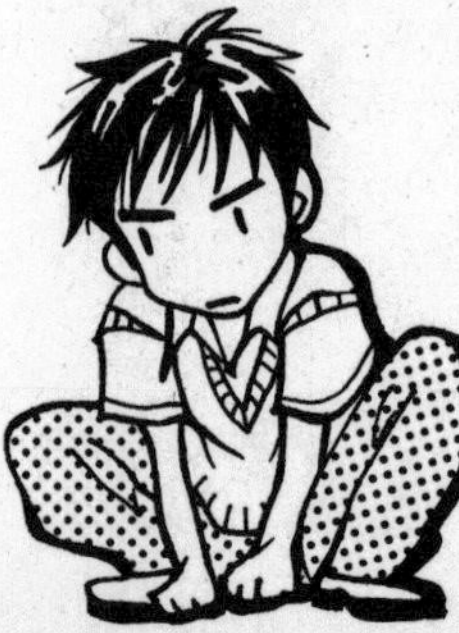

♡ Yuichiro Kato

Right now he's Sô's sidekick, but in volume 2 (if we make it that far), I'll be involving him more. You might hear a rumor that I don't use him as much because his hairstyle is hard to draw... but that's just a rumor.

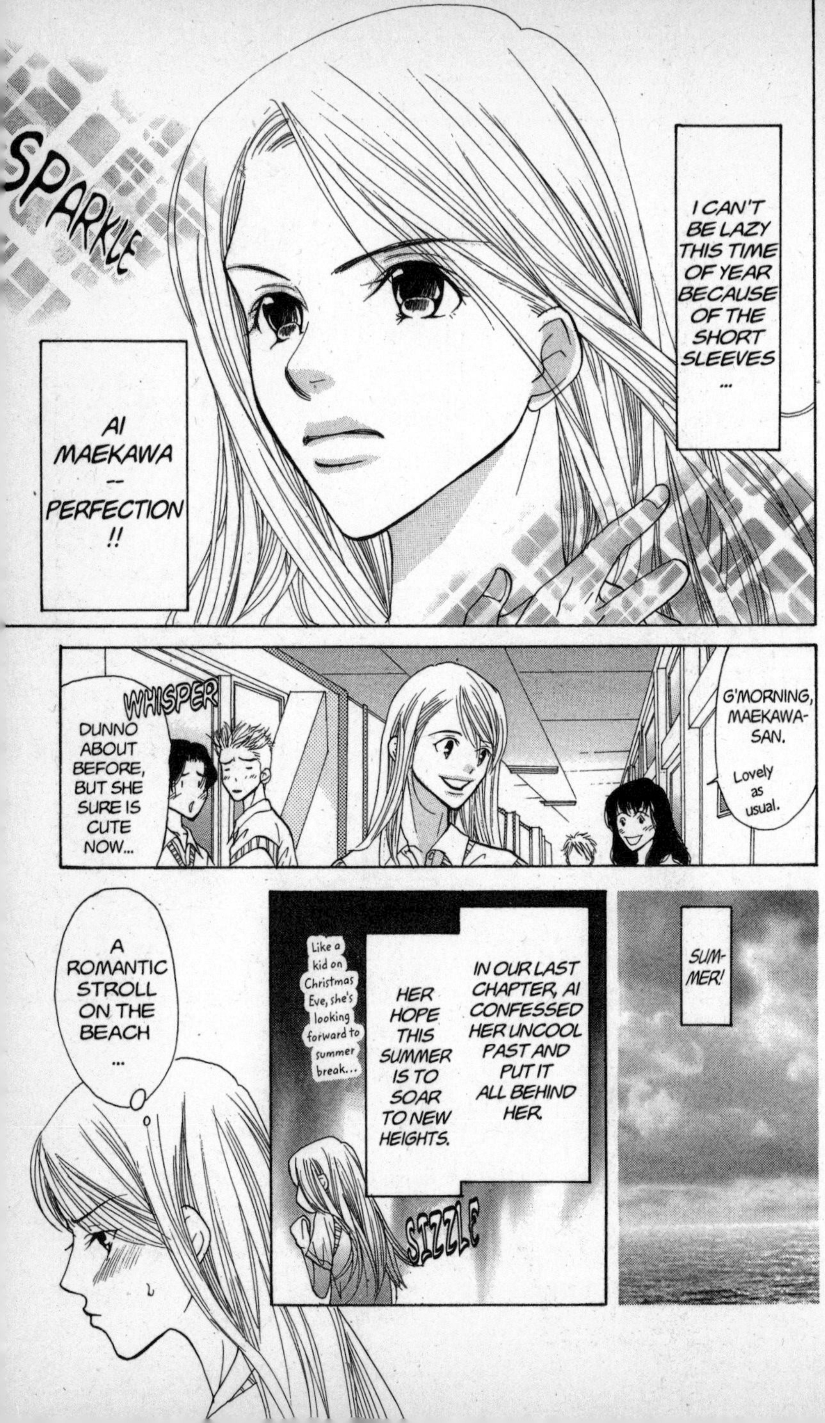
I CAN'T BE LAZY THIS TIME OF YEAR BECAUSE OF THE SHORT SLEEVES ...
SPARKLE
AI MAEKAWA -- PERFECTION !!
G'MORNING, MAEKAWA-SAN.
Lovely as usual.
WHISPER
DUNNO ABOUT BEFORE, BUT SHE SURE IS CUTE NOW...
SUMMER!
IN OUR LAST CHAPTER, AI CONFESSED HER UNCOOL PAST AND PUT IT ALL BEHIND HER.
HER HOPE THIS SUMMER IS TO SOAR TO NEW HEIGHTS.
Like a kid on Christmas Eve, she's looking forward to summer break...
SIZZLE
A ROMANTIC STROLL ON THE BEACH ...

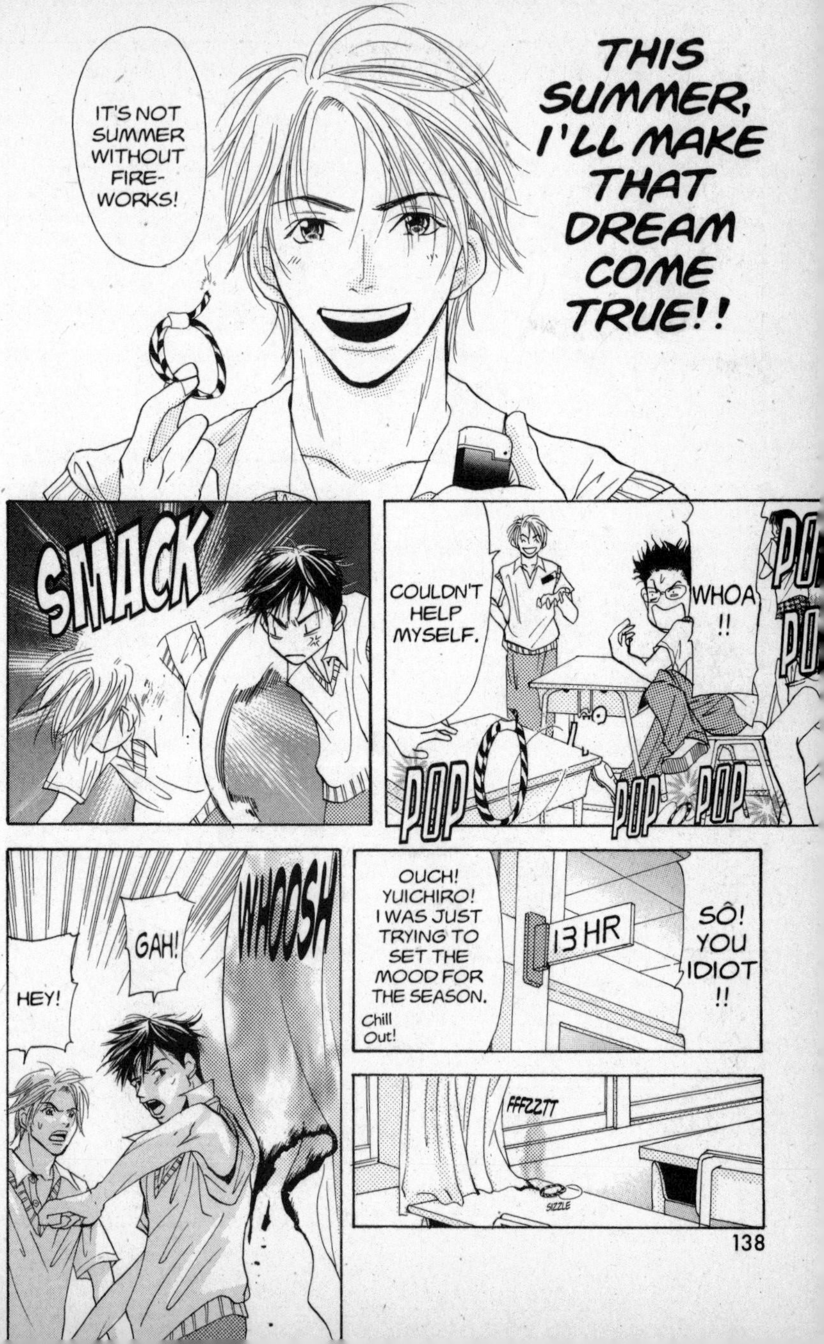

THIS SUMMER, I'LL MAKE THAT DREAM COME TRUE!!
IT'S NOT SUMMER WITHOUT FIRE-WORKS!
WHOA !!
COULDN'T HELP MYSELF.
PO PO
POP
POP
POP
SMACK
SÔ! YOU IDIOT !!
13 HR
OUCH! YUICHIRO! I WAS JUST TRYING TO SET THE MOOD FOR THE SEASON.
Chill Out!
FFFZZTT
SIZZLE
WHOOSH
GAH!
HEY!

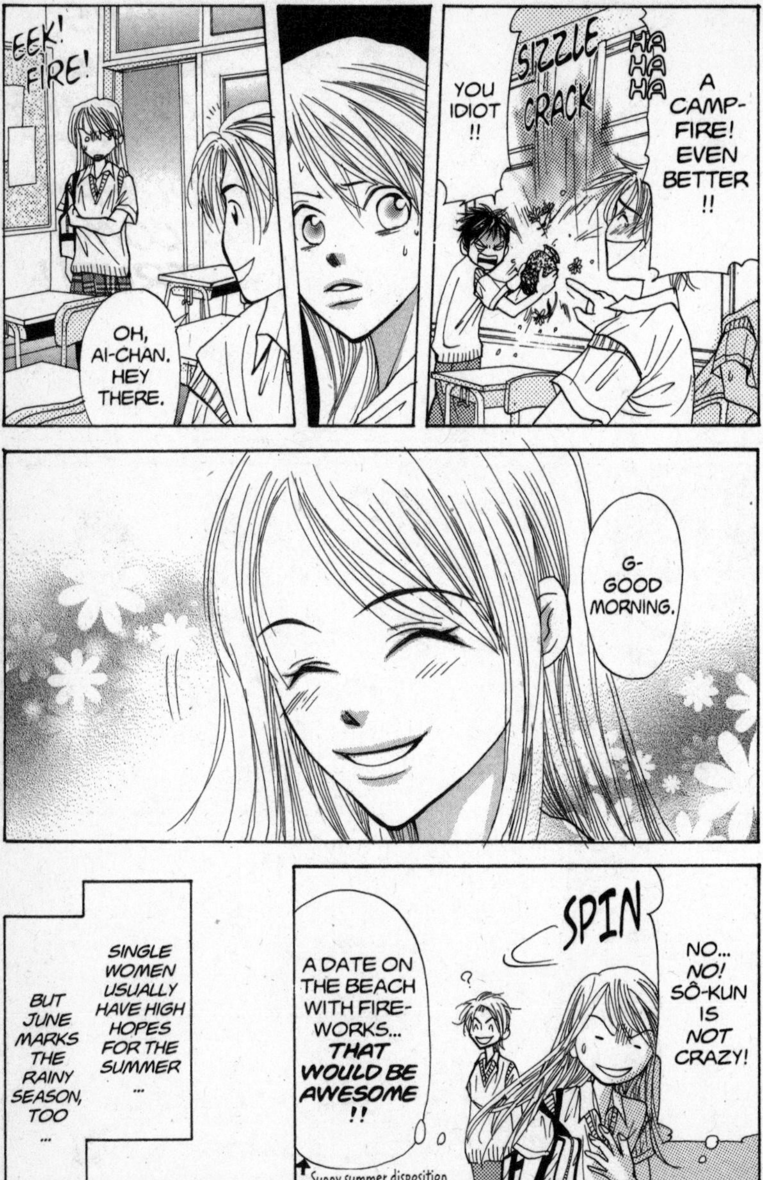
A CAMP-FIRE! EVEN BETTER!!
HA HA HA
SIZZLE CRACK
YOU IDIOT!!
EEK! FIRE!
OH, AI-CHAN. HEY THERE.
G-GOOD MORNING.
SPIN
NO... NO! SÔ-KUN IS NOT CRAZY!
A DATE ON THE BEACH WITH FIRE-WORKS... THAT WOULD BE AWESOME!!
Sunny summer disposition
SINGLE WOMEN USUALLY HAVE HIGH HOPES FOR THE SUMMER...
BUT JUNE MARKS THE RAINY SEASON, TOO...

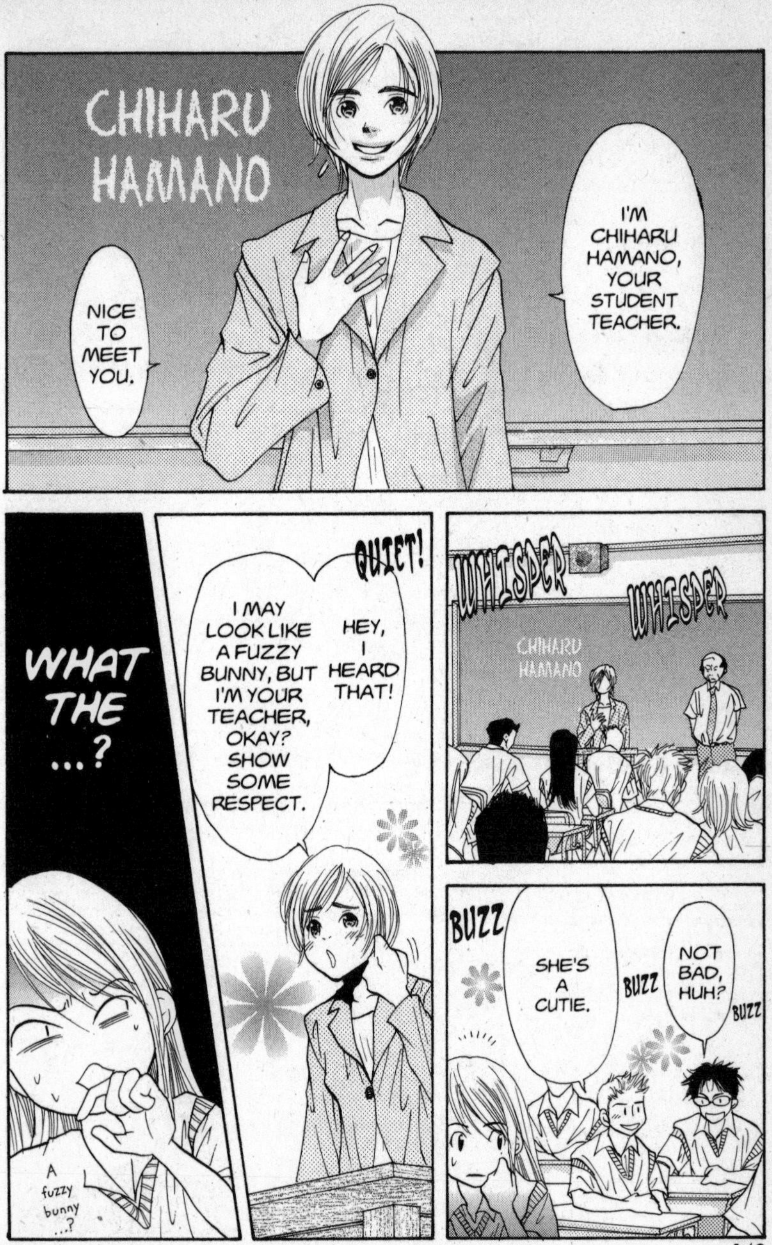
CHIHARU HAMANO
I'M CHIHARU HAMANO, YOUR STUDENT TEACHER.
NICE TO MEET YOU.
WHISPER
WHISPER
CHIHARU HAMANO
BUZZ
NOT BAD, HUH?
SHE'S A CUTIE.
BUZZ
BUZZ
QUIET!
HEY, I HEARD THAT!
I MAY LOOK LIKE A FUZZY BUNNY, BUT I'M YOUR TEACHER, OKAY? SHOW SOME RESPECT.
WHAT THE ...?
A fuzzy bunny ...?

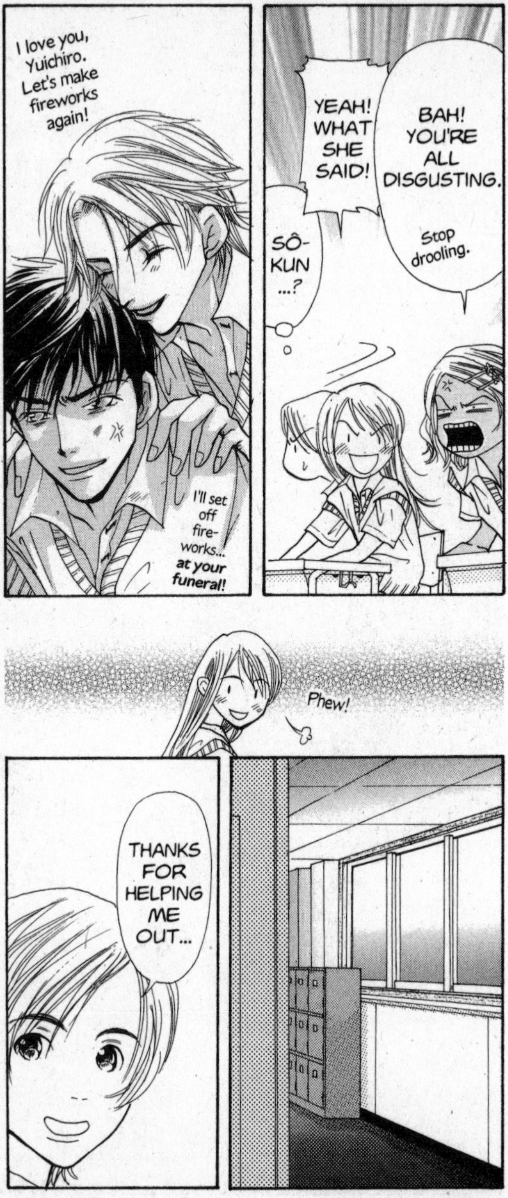
YEAH! WHAT SHE SAID!
BAH! YOU'RE ALL DISGUSTING.
Stop drooling.
SÔ-KUN ...?
I love you, Yuichiro. Let's make fireworks again!
I'll set off fire-works... **at your funeral!**
Phew!
THANKS FOR HELPING ME OUT...

Exciting Encounters!
An Encyclopedia of Creatures

Part 4

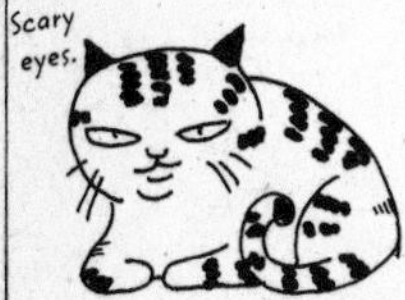
Scary eyes.

Fu-kun (Cat)

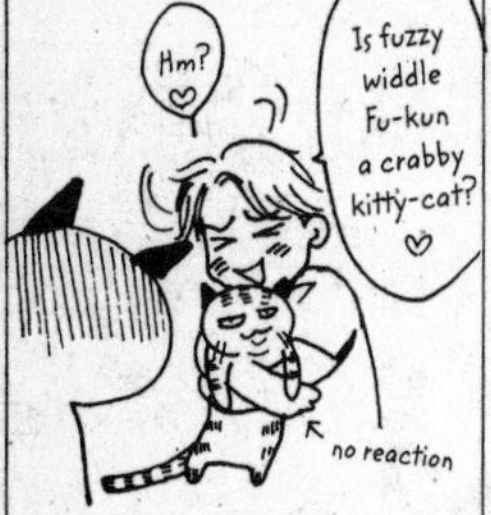
Is fuzzy widdle Fu-kun a crabby kitty-cat? ♡
Hm? ♡
no reaction

An animal with an amazing ability to make grown-ups resort to baby-talk. A man I used to date did that, and it **chilled me to the core of my being.** (I, too, like cats, but c'mon...) I told my friend about it later and we made fun of him behind his back, using the codename "**Fu.**"

Does that make me a bad person? Does it? What do you think?

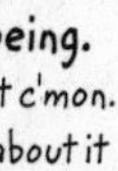

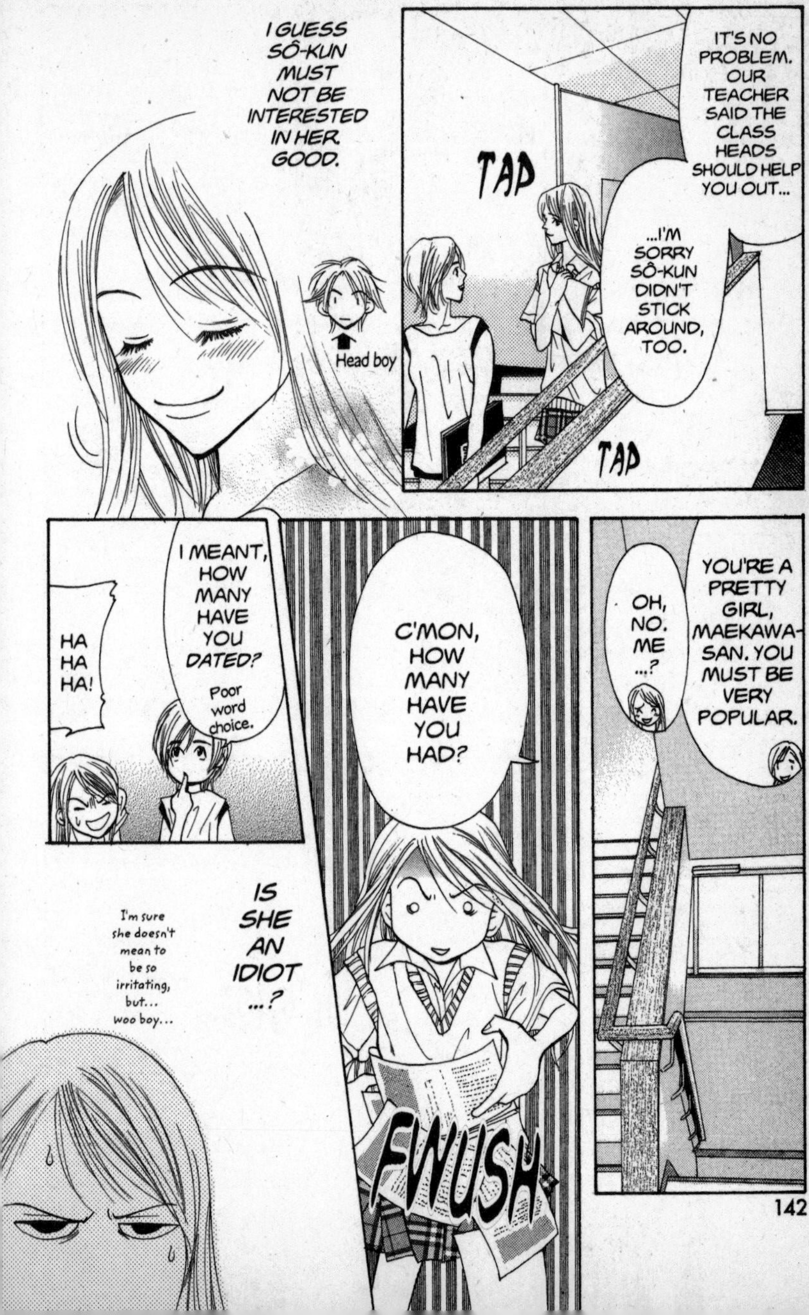
IT'S NO PROBLEM. OUR TEACHER SAID THE CLASS HEADS SHOULD HELP YOU OUT...
TAP
...I'M SORRY SÔ-KUN DIDN'T STICK AROUND, TOO.
TAP
I GUESS SÔ-KUN MUST NOT BE INTERESTED IN HER. GOOD.
Head boy
YOU'RE A PRETTY GIRL, MAEKAWA-SAN. YOU MUST BE VERY POPULAR.
OH, NO. ME ...?
C'MON, HOW MANY HAVE YOU HAD?
I MEANT, HOW MANY HAVE YOU DATED?
Poor word choice.
HA HA HA!
FWUSH
IS SHE AN IDIOT ...?
I'm sure she doesn't mean to be so irritating, but... woo boy...

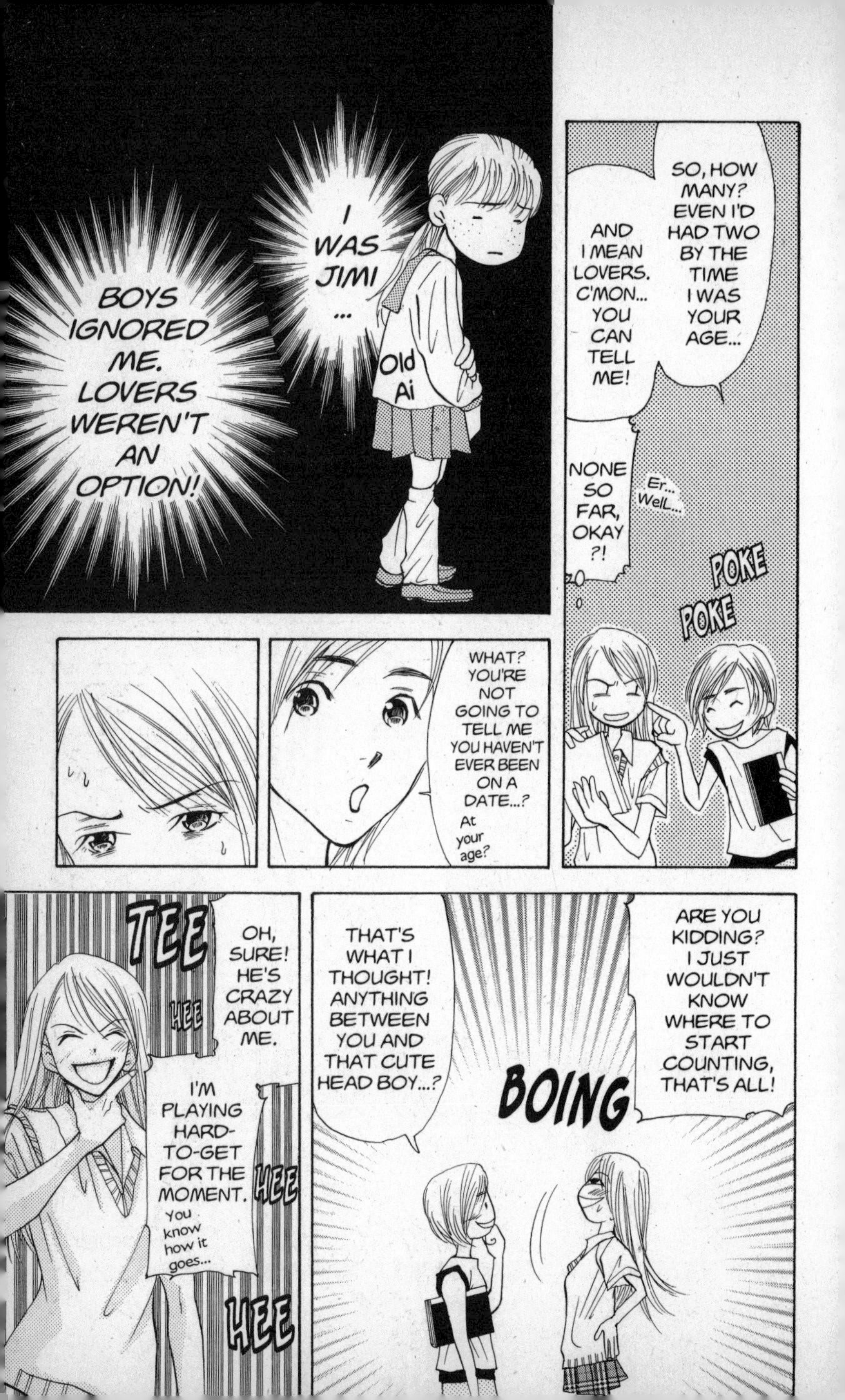
SO, HOW MANY? EVEN I'D HAD TWO BY THE TIME I WAS YOUR AGE...
AND I MEAN LOVERS. C'MON... YOU CAN TELL ME!
Er... Well...
NONE SO FAR, OKAY?!
POKE
POKE
I WAS JIMI...
Old Ai
BOYS IGNORED ME. LOVERS WEREN'T AN OPTION!
WHAT? YOU'RE NOT GOING TO TELL ME YOU HAVEN'T EVER BEEN ON A DATE...?
At your age?
ARE YOU KIDDING? I JUST WOULDN'T KNOW WHERE TO START COUNTING, THAT'S ALL!
BOING
THAT'S WHAT I THOUGHT! ANYTHING BETWEEN YOU AND THAT CUTE HEAD BOY...?
TEE
HEE
OH, SURE! HE'S CRAZY ABOUT ME.
I'M PLAYING HARD-TO-GET FOR THE MOMENT.
You know how it goes...
HEE
HEE

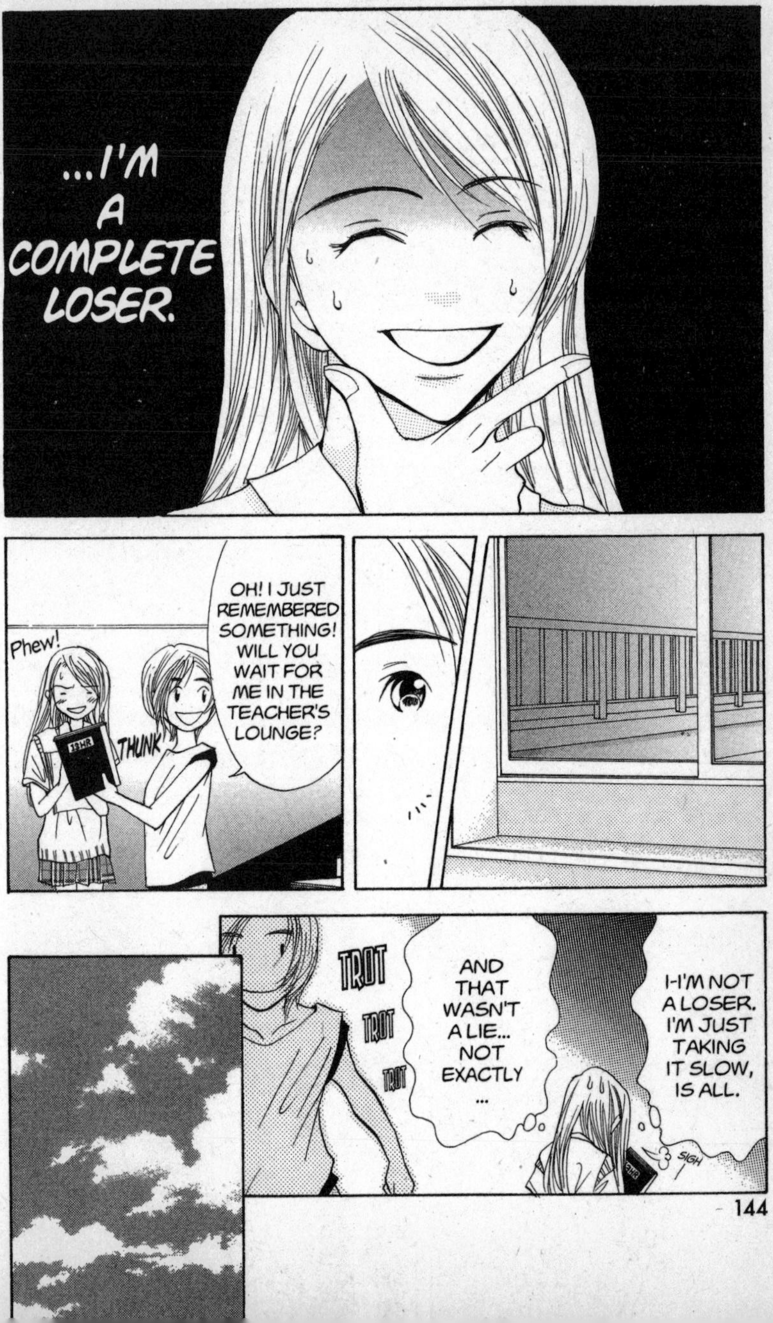
...I'M A COMPLETE LOSER.
OH! I JUST REMEMBERED SOMETHING! WILL YOU WAIT FOR ME IN THE TEACHER'S LOUNGE?
Phew!
THUNK
I-I'M NOT A LOSER. I'M JUST TAKING IT SLOW, IS ALL.
SIGH
AND THAT WASN'T A LIE... NOT EXACTLY ...
TROT
TROT
TROT

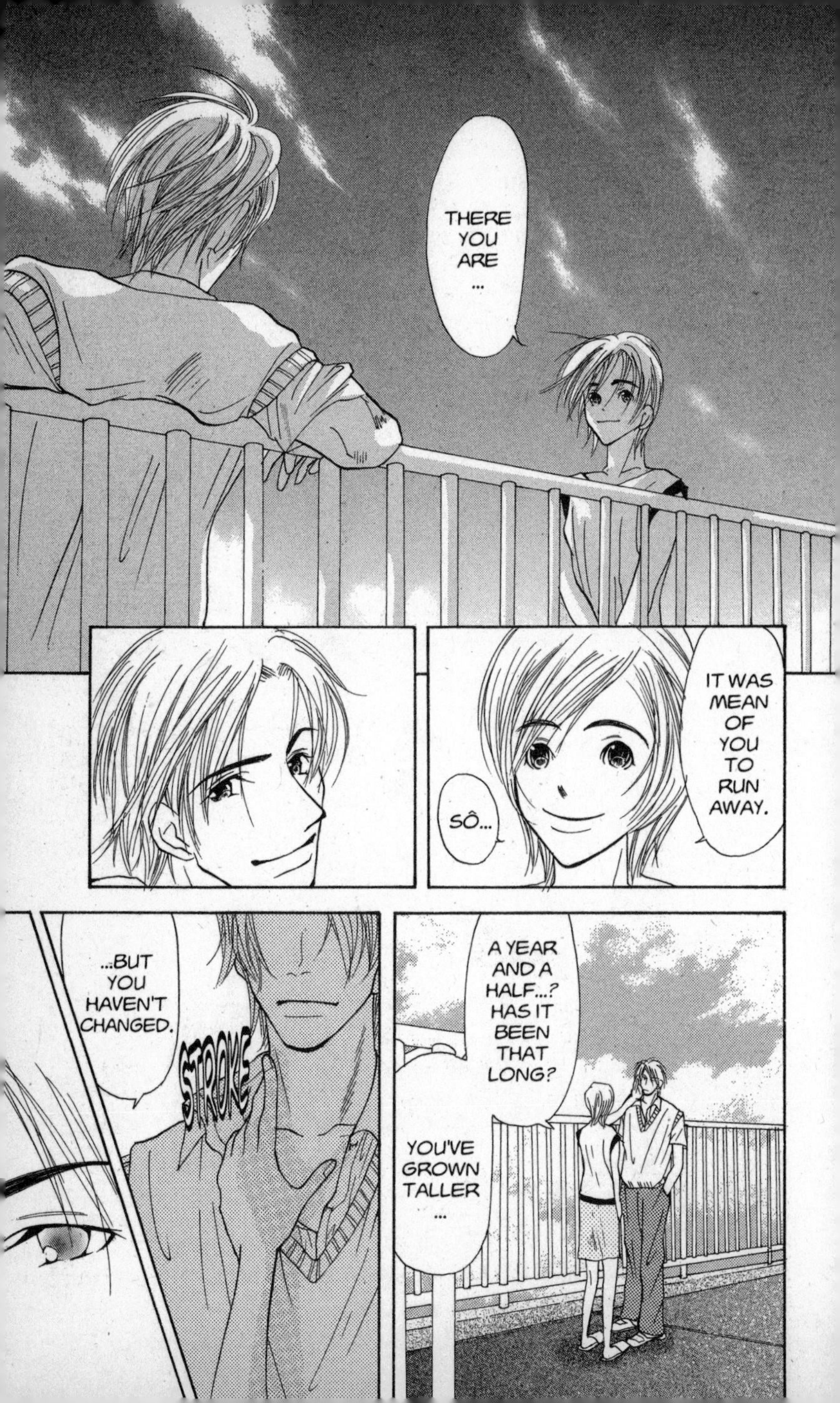
THERE YOU ARE ...
IT WAS MEAN OF YOU TO RUN AWAY.
SÔ...
A YEAR AND A HALF...? HAS IT BEEN THAT LONG?
YOU'VE GROWN TALLER ...
...BUT YOU HAVEN'T CHANGED.
STROKE

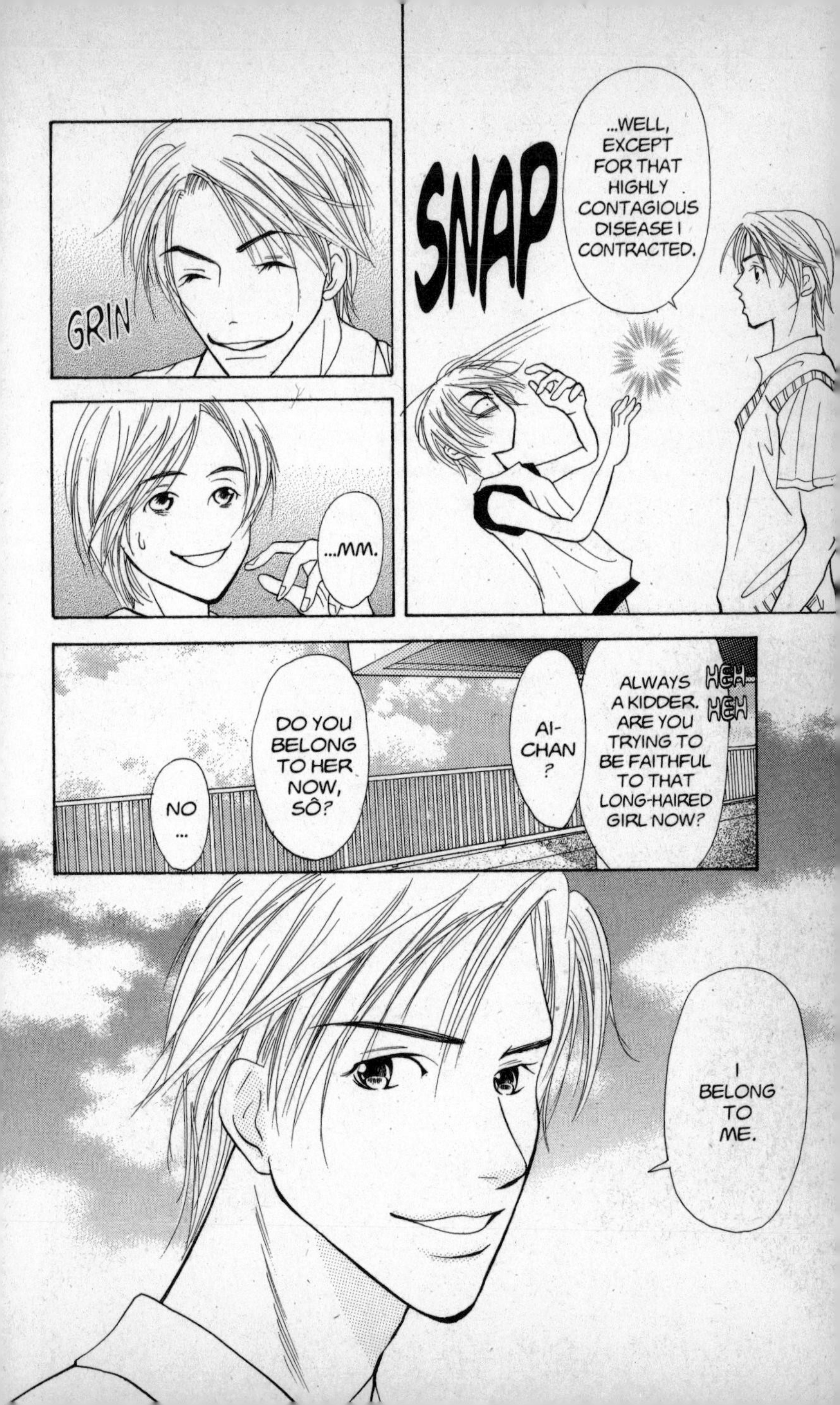
...WELL, EXCEPT FOR THAT HIGHLY CONTAGIOUS DISEASE I CONTRACTED.
SNAP
GRIN
...MM.
HEH HEH
ALWAYS A KIDDER. ARE YOU TRYING TO BE FAITHFUL TO THAT LONG-HAIRED GIRL NOW?
AI-CHAN?
DO YOU BELONG TO HER NOW, SÔ?
NO...
I BELONG TO ME.

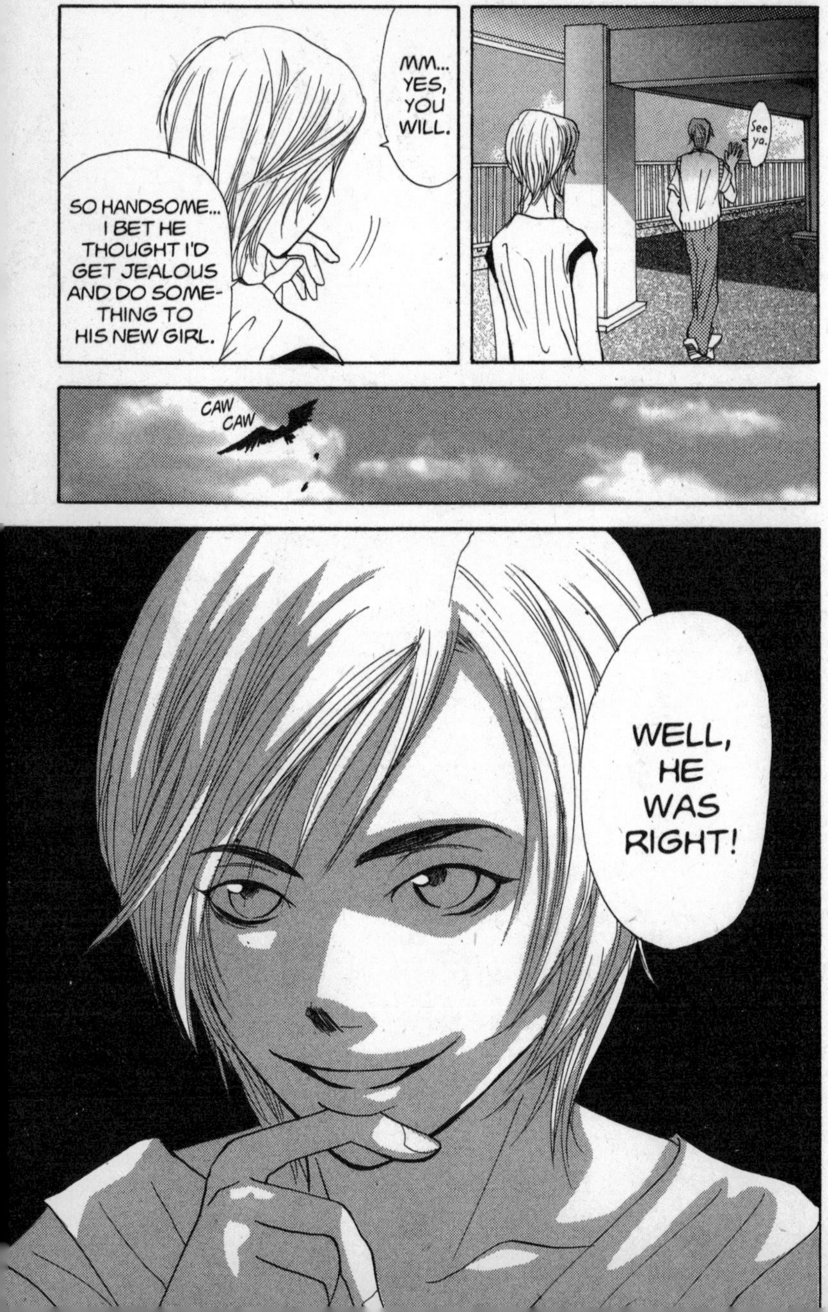
See ya.
MM... YES, YOU WILL.
SO HANDSOME... I BET HE THOUGHT I'D GET JEALOUS AND DO SOME-THING TO HIS NEW GIRL.
CAW CAW
WELL, HE WAS RIGHT!

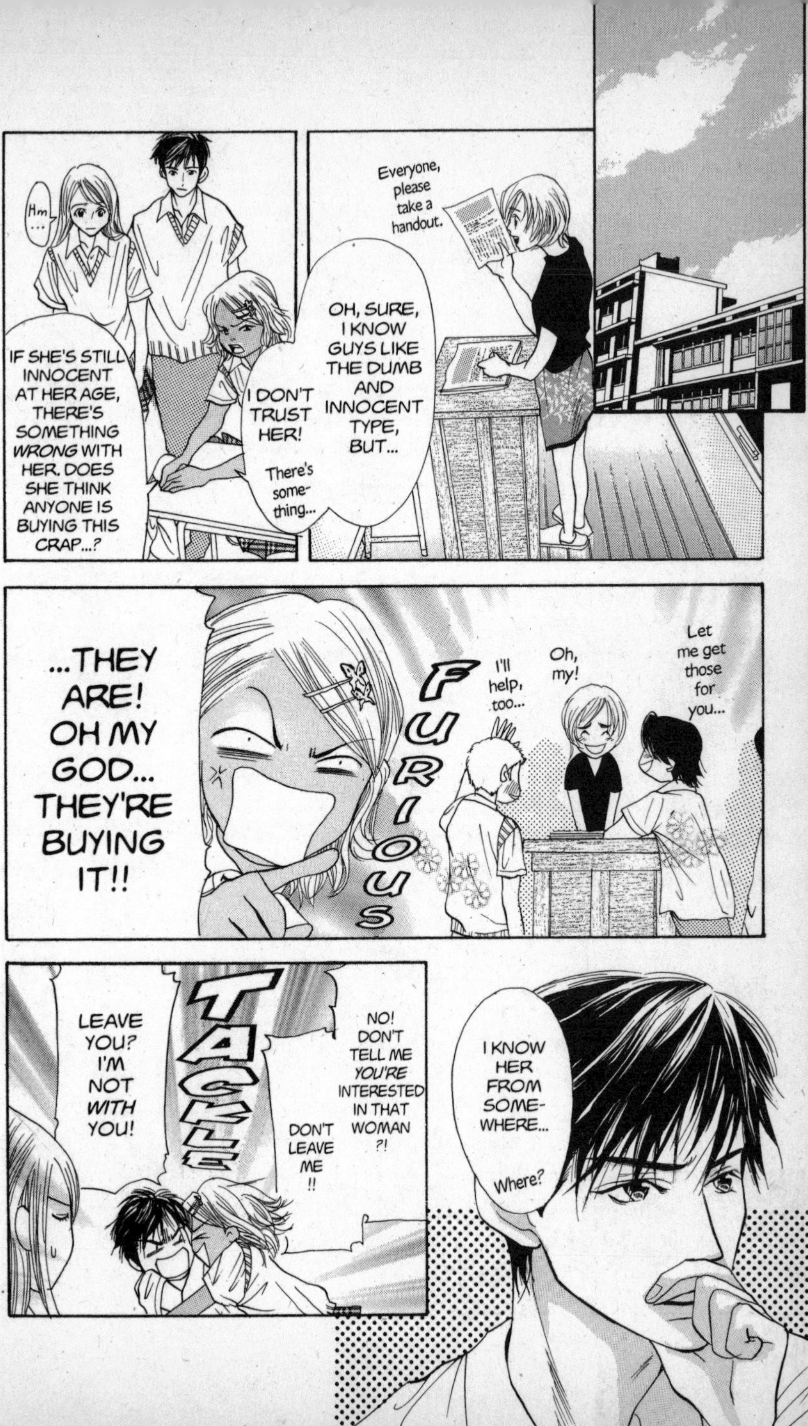
Everyone, please take a handout.
OH, SURE, I KNOW GUYS LIKE THE DUMB AND INNOCENT TYPE, BUT...
There's some-thing...
I DON'T TRUST HER!
Hm...
IF SHE'S STILL INNOCENT AT HER AGE, THERE'S SOMETHING *WRONG* WITH HER. DOES SHE THINK ANYONE IS BUYING THIS CRAP...?
Let me get those for you...
Oh, my!
I'll help, too...
FURIOUS
...THEY ARE! OH MY GOD... THEY'RE BUYING IT!!
I KNOW HER FROM SOME-WHERE...
Where?
NO! DON'T TELL ME *YOU'RE* INTERESTED IN THAT WOMAN?!
DON'T LEAVE ME!!
TACKLE
LEAVE YOU? I'M NOT *WITH* YOU!

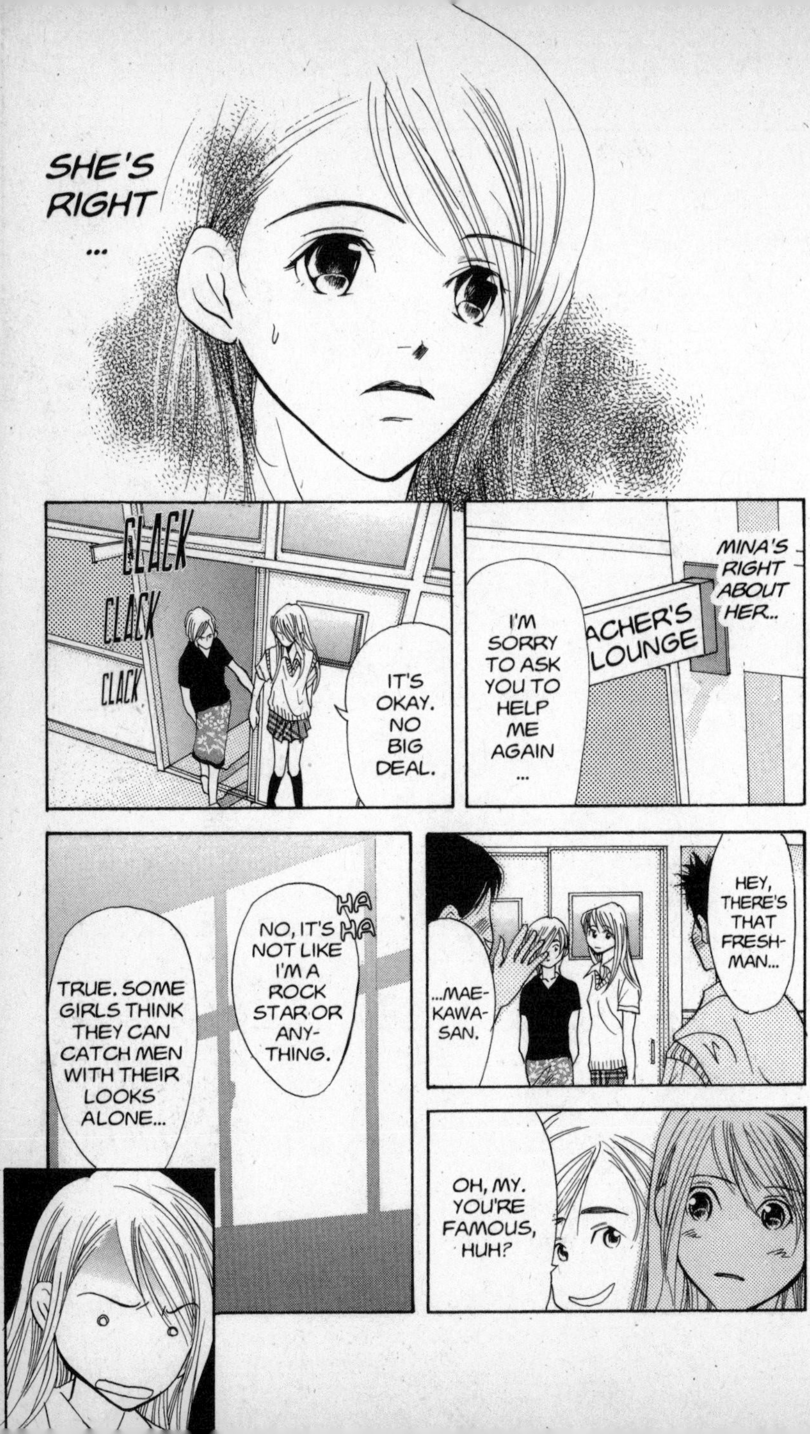
SHE'S RIGHT ...
MINA'S RIGHT ABOUT HER...
ACHER'S LOUNGE
I'M SORRY TO ASK YOU TO HELP ME AGAIN ...
CLACK
CLACK
CLACK
IT'S OKAY. NO BIG DEAL.
HEY, THERE'S THAT FRESH-MAN...
...MAE-KAWA-SAN.
OH, MY. YOU'RE FAMOUS, HUH?
HA HA
NO, IT'S NOT LIKE I'M A ROCK STAR OR ANY-THING.
TRUE. SOME GIRLS THINK THEY CAN CATCH MEN WITH THEIR LOOKS ALONE...

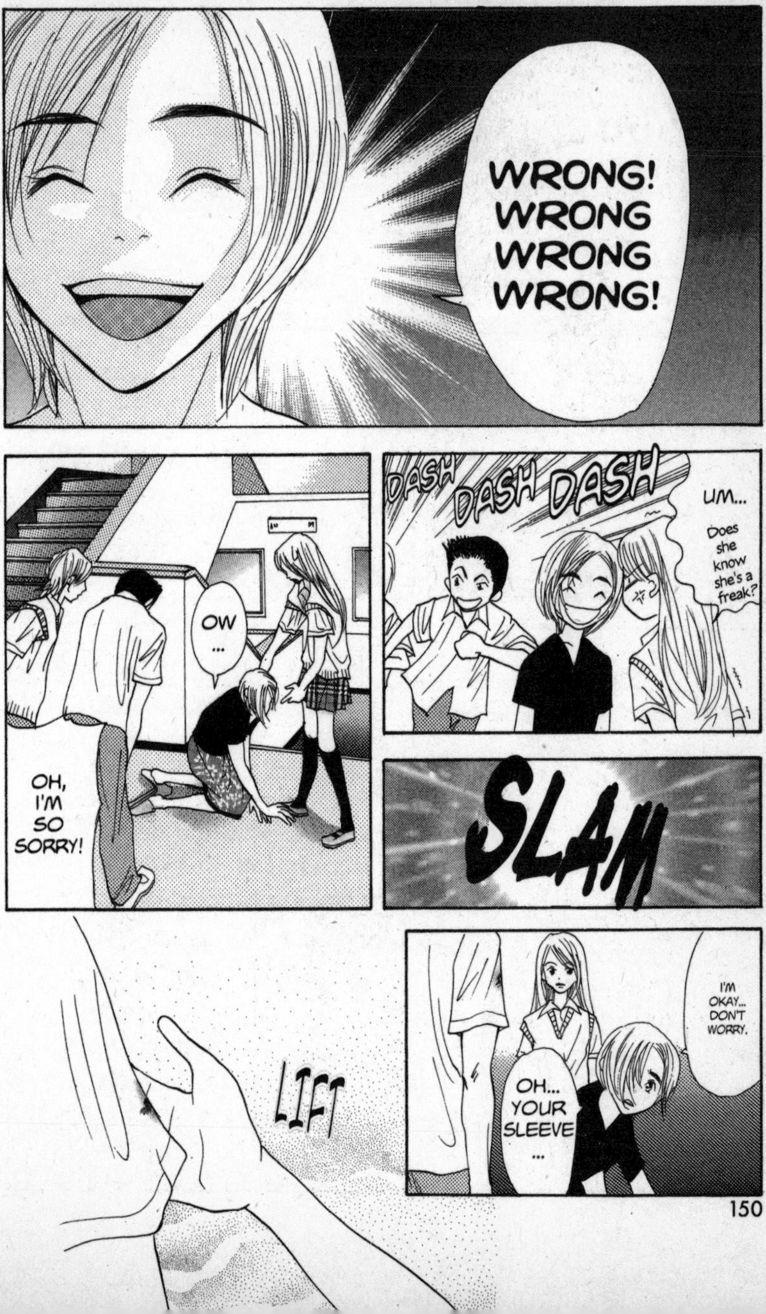
WRONG! WRONG WRONG WRONG!
DASH DASH DASH
UM...
Does she know she's a freak?
SLAM
OW ...
OH, I'M SO SORRY!
I'M OKAY... DON'T WORRY.
OH... YOUR SLEEVE ...
LIFT

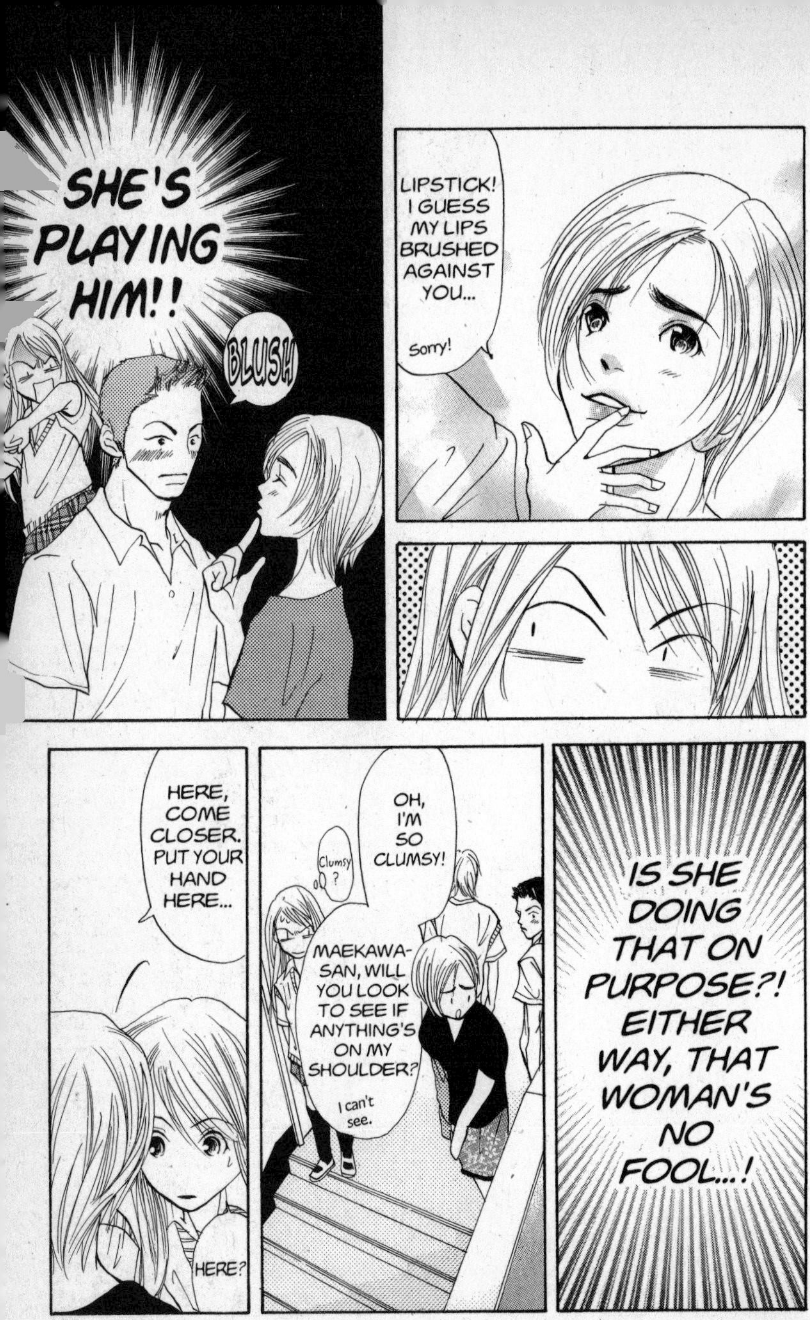
LIPSTICK! I GUESS MY LIPS BRUSHED AGAINST YOU...
Sorry!
SHE'S PLAYING HIM!!
BLUSH
IS SHE DOING THAT ON PURPOSE?! EITHER WAY, THAT WOMAN'S NO FOOL...!
OH, I'M SO CLUMSY!
Clumsy?
MAEKAWA-SAN, WILL YOU LOOK TO SEE IF ANYTHING'S ON MY SHOULDER?
I can't see.
HERE, COME CLOSER. PUT YOUR HAND HERE...
HERE?

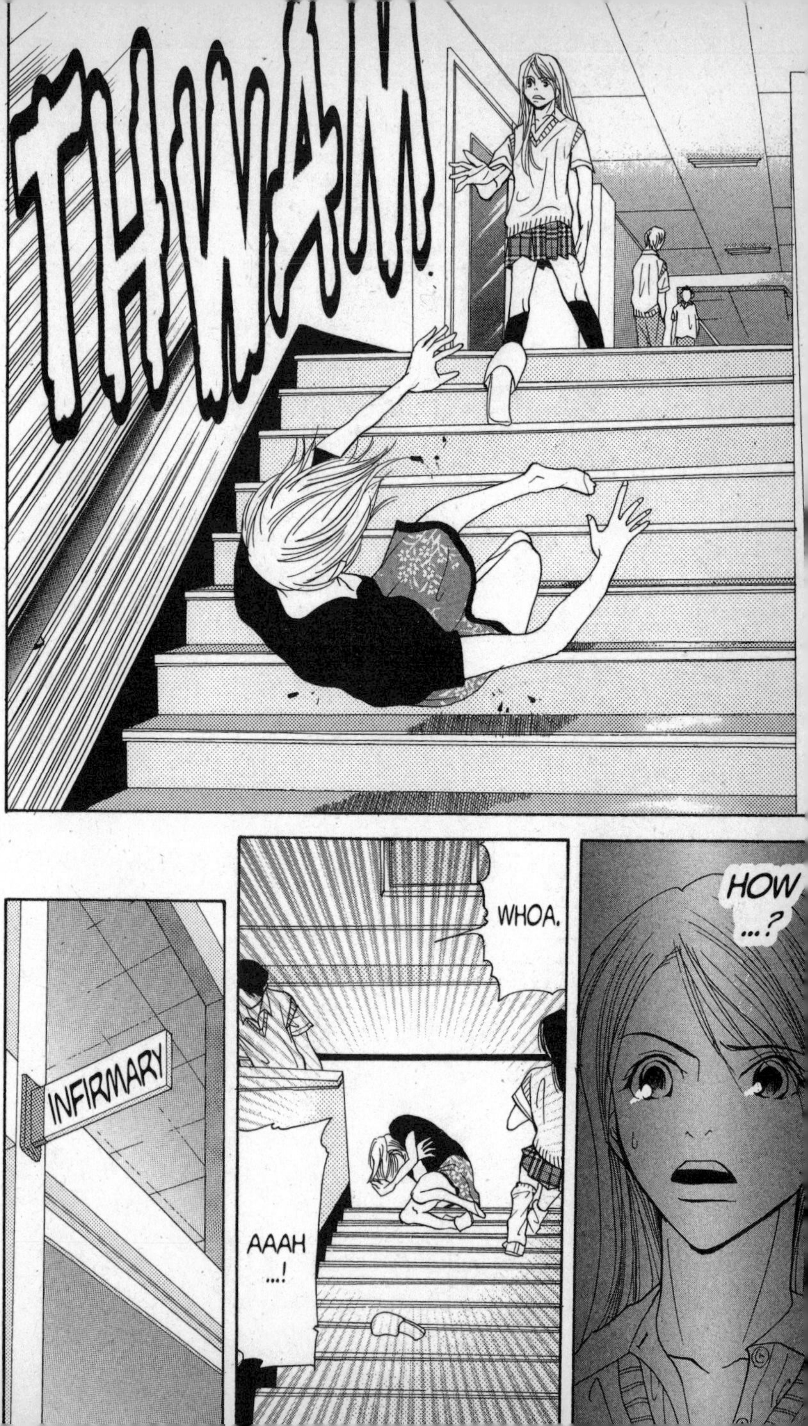
THWAUM
HOW ...?
WHOA.
AAAH ...!
INFIRMARY

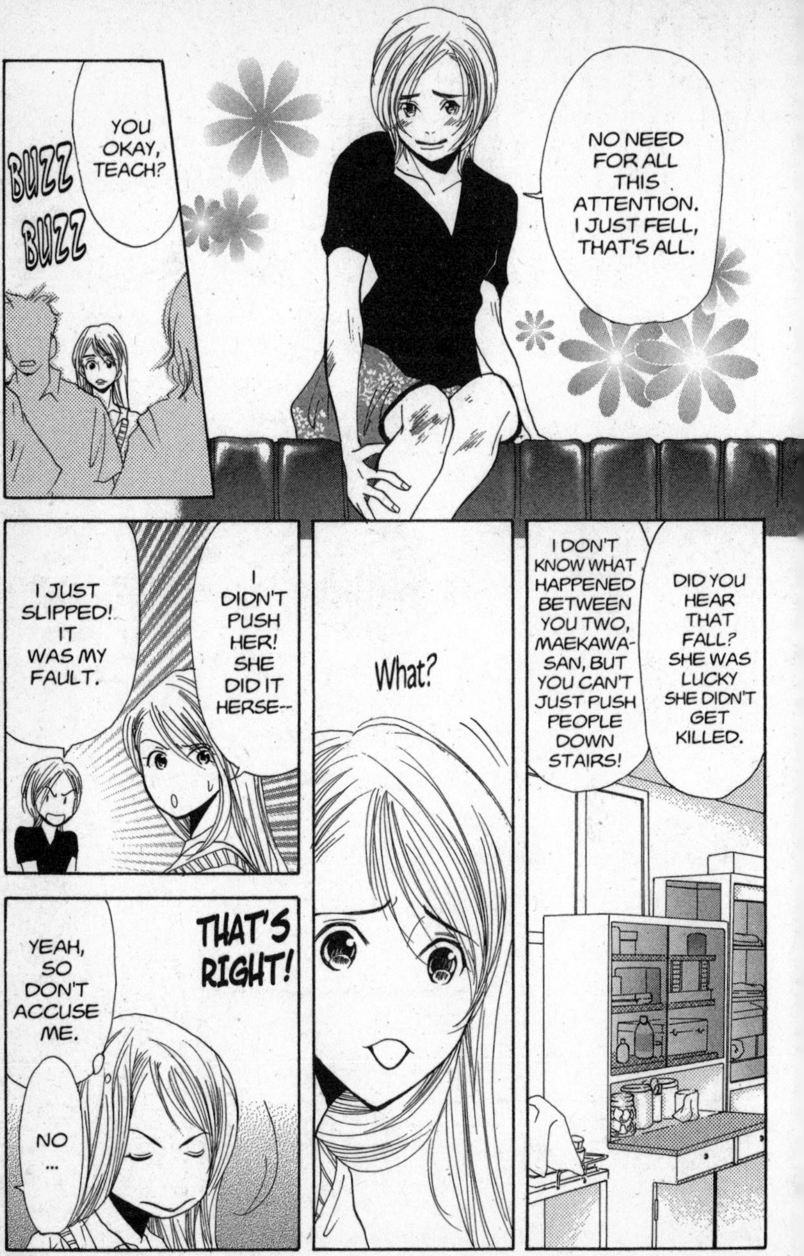
NO NEED FOR ALL THIS ATTENTION. I JUST FELL, THAT'S ALL.
YOU OKAY, TEACH?
BUZZ BUZZ
DID YOU HEAR THAT FALL? SHE WAS LUCKY SHE DIDN'T GET KILLED.
I DON'T KNOW WHAT HAPPENED BETWEEN YOU TWO, MAEKAWA-SAN, BUT YOU CAN'T JUST PUSH PEOPLE DOWN STAIRS!
What?
I DIDN'T PUSH HER! SHE DID IT HERSE--
I JUST SLIPPED! IT WAS MY FAULT.
THAT'S RIGHT!
YEAH, SO DON'T ACCUSE ME.
NO ...

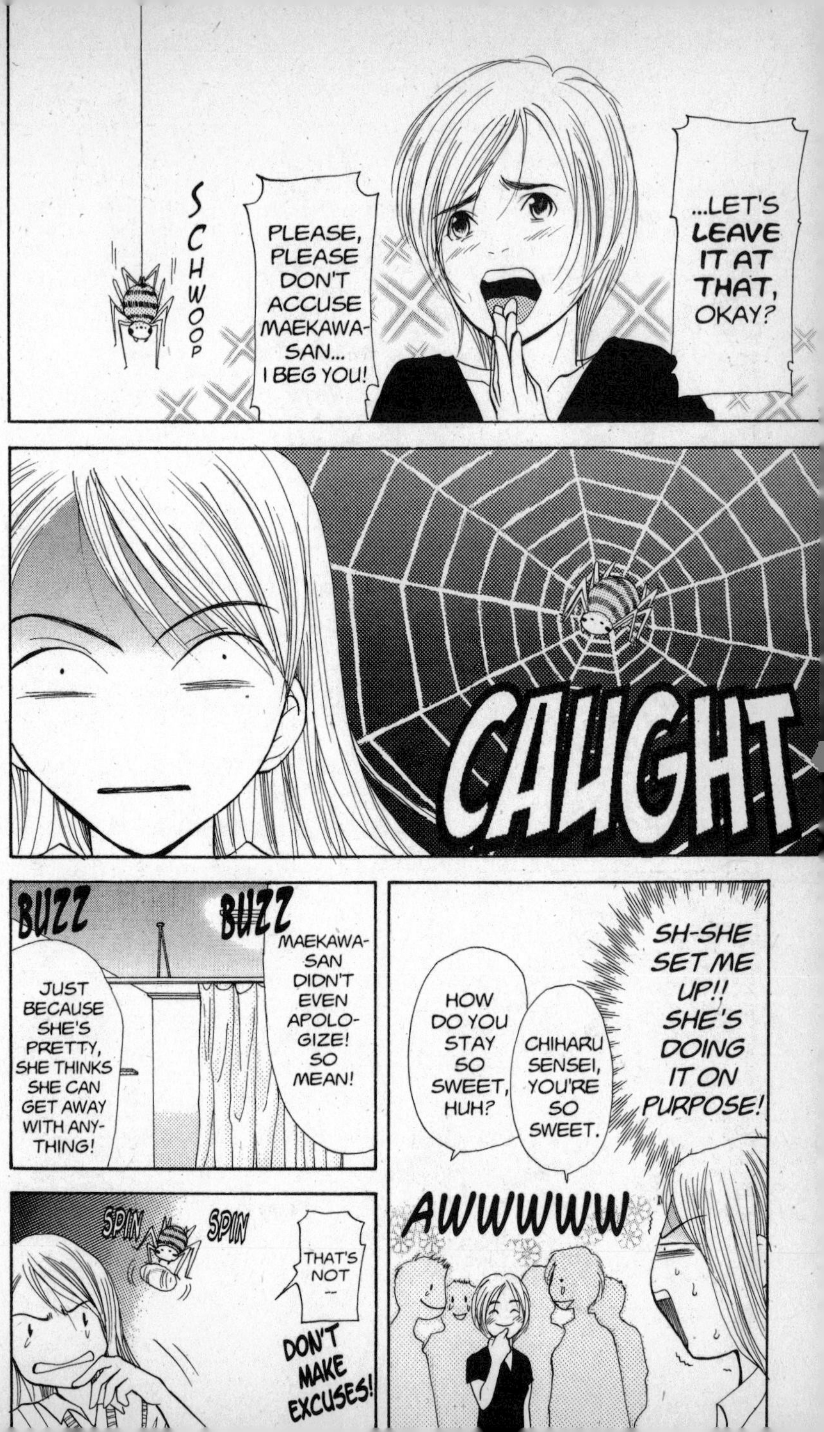

...LET'S LEAVE IT AT THAT, OKAY?
PLEASE, PLEASE DON'T ACCUSE MAEKAWA-SAN... I BEG YOU!
SCHWOOP
CAUGHT
SH-SHE SET ME UP!! SHE'S DOING IT ON PURPOSE!
CHIHARU SENSEI, YOU'RE SO SWEET.
HOW DO YOU STAY SO SWEET, HUH?
BUZZ
BUZZ
MAEKAWA-SAN DIDN'T EVEN APOLO-GIZE! SO MEAN!
JUST BECAUSE SHE'S PRETTY, SHE THINKS SHE CAN GET AWAY WITH ANY-THING!
AWWWWW
SPIN
SPIN
THAT'S NOT --
DON'T MAKE EXCUSES!

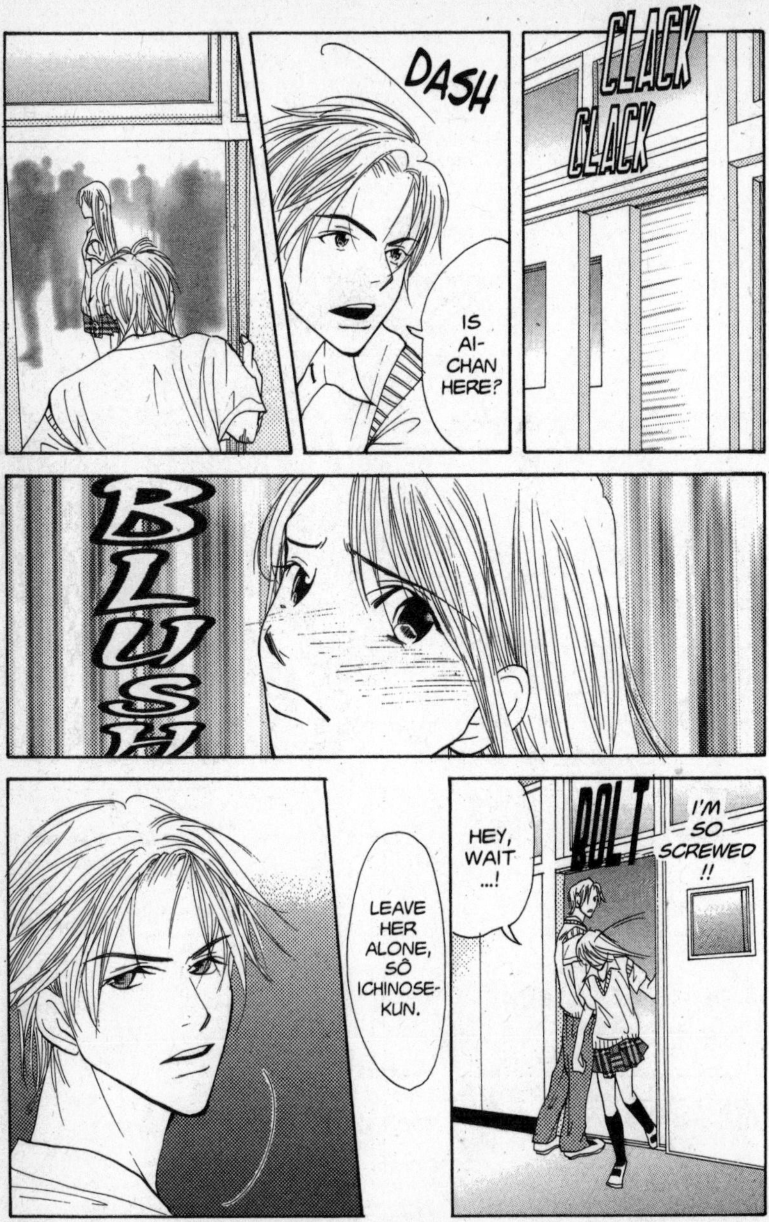
CLACK
CLACK
DASH
IS AI-CHAN HERE?
BLUSH
I'M SO SCREWED!!
BOLT
HEY, WAIT ...!
LEAVE HER ALONE, SÔ ICHINOSE-KUN.

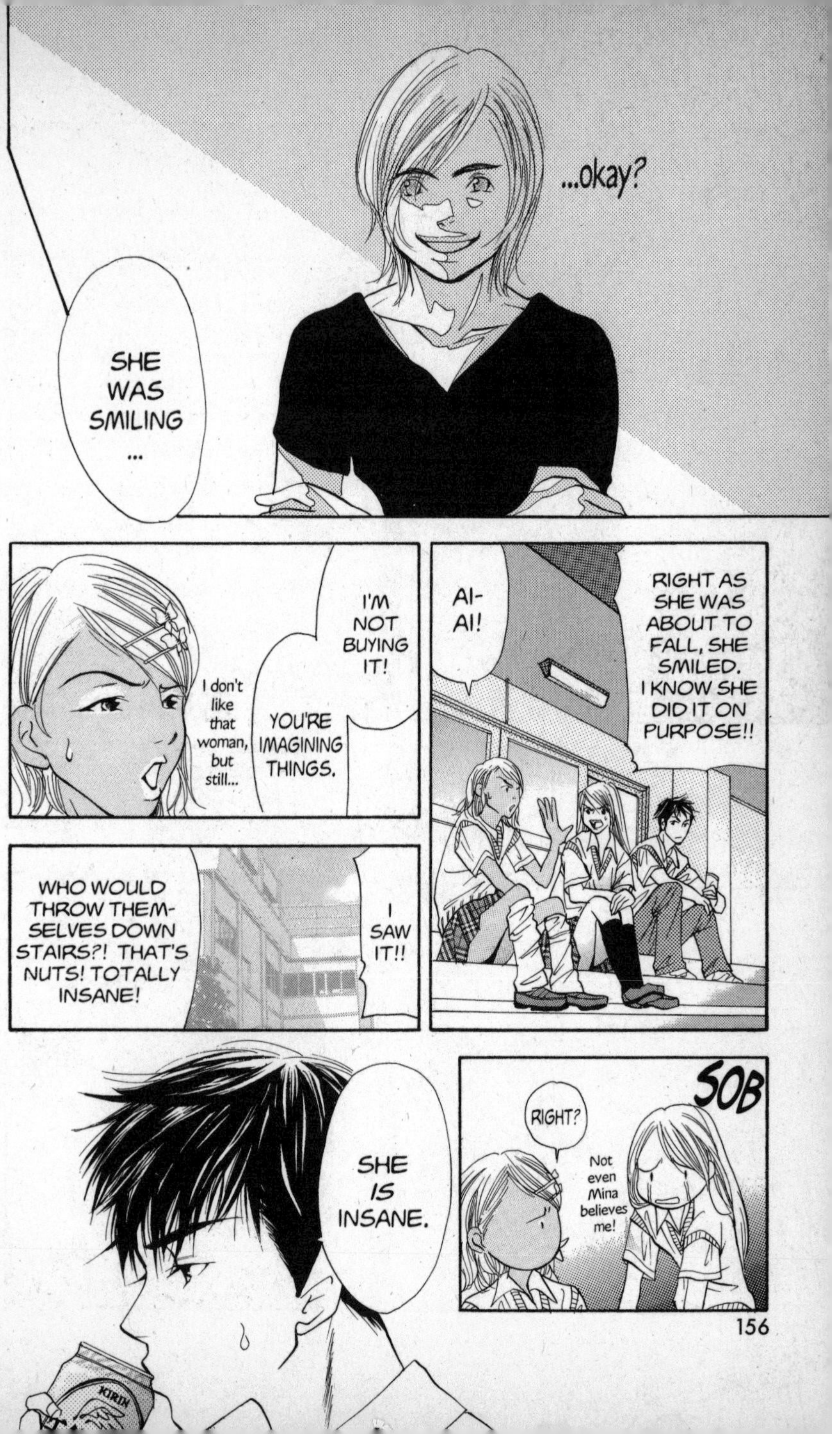
...okay?
SHE WAS SMILING ...
RIGHT AS SHE WAS ABOUT TO FALL, SHE SMILED. I KNOW SHE DID IT ON PURPOSE!!
AI-AI!
I'M NOT BUYING IT!
YOU'RE IMAGINING THINGS.
I don't like that woman, but still...
I SAW IT!!
WHO WOULD THROW THEMSELVES DOWN STAIRS?! THAT'S NUTS! TOTALLY INSANE!
SOB
RIGHT?
Not even Mina believes me!
SHE IS INSANE.
KIRIN

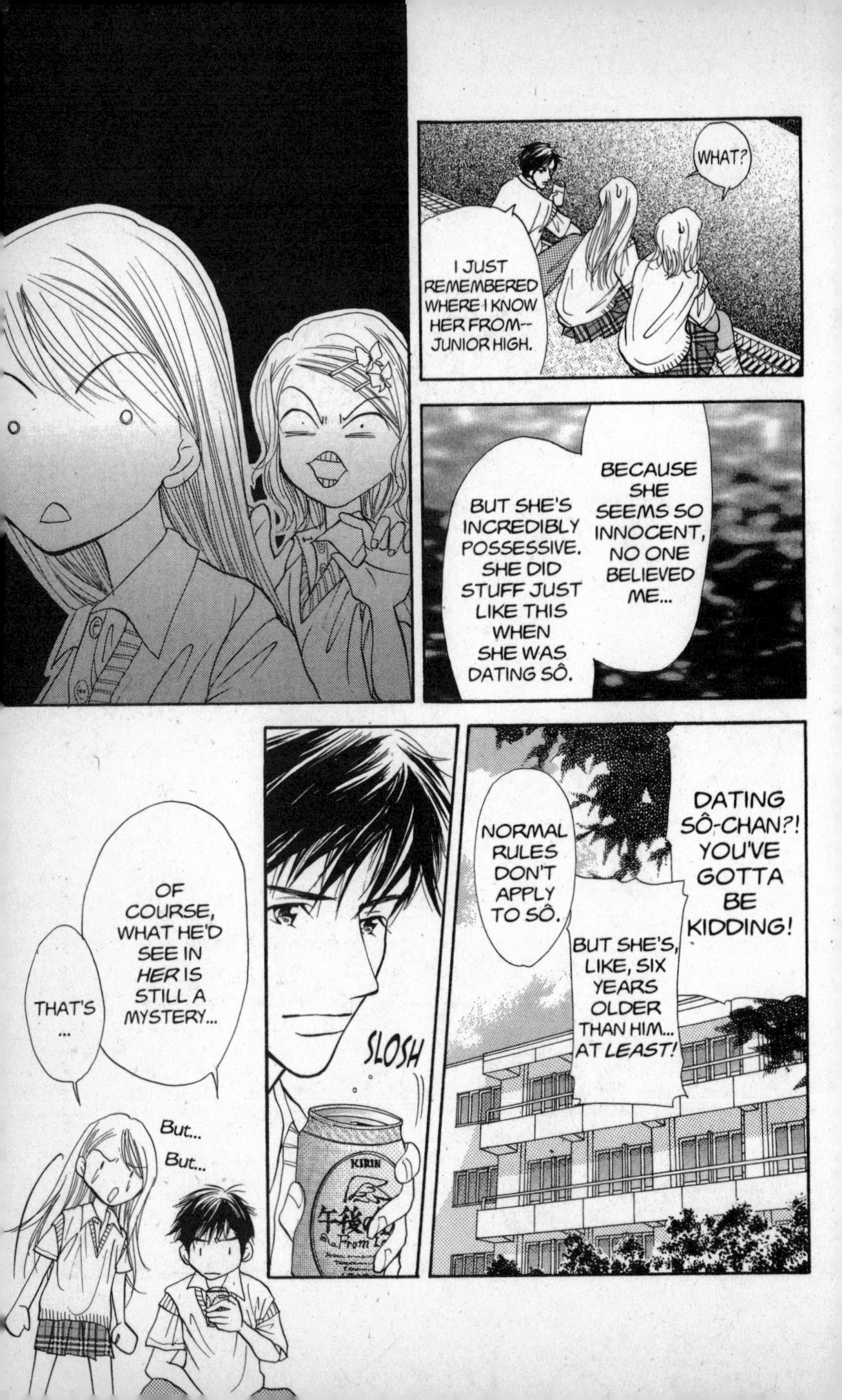

WHAT?
I JUST REMEMBERED WHERE I KNOW HER FROM-- JUNIOR HIGH.
BECAUSE SHE SEEMS SO INNOCENT, NO ONE BELIEVED ME...
BUT SHE'S INCREDIBLY POSSESSIVE. SHE DID STUFF JUST LIKE THIS WHEN SHE WAS DATING SÔ.
DATING SÔ-CHAN?! YOU'VE GOTTA BE KIDDING!
BUT SHE'S, LIKE, SIX YEARS OLDER THAN HIM... AT LEAST!
NORMAL RULES DON'T APPLY TO SÔ.
SLOSH
OF COURSE, WHAT HE'D SEE IN HER IS STILL A MYSTERY...
THAT'S ...
But...
But...

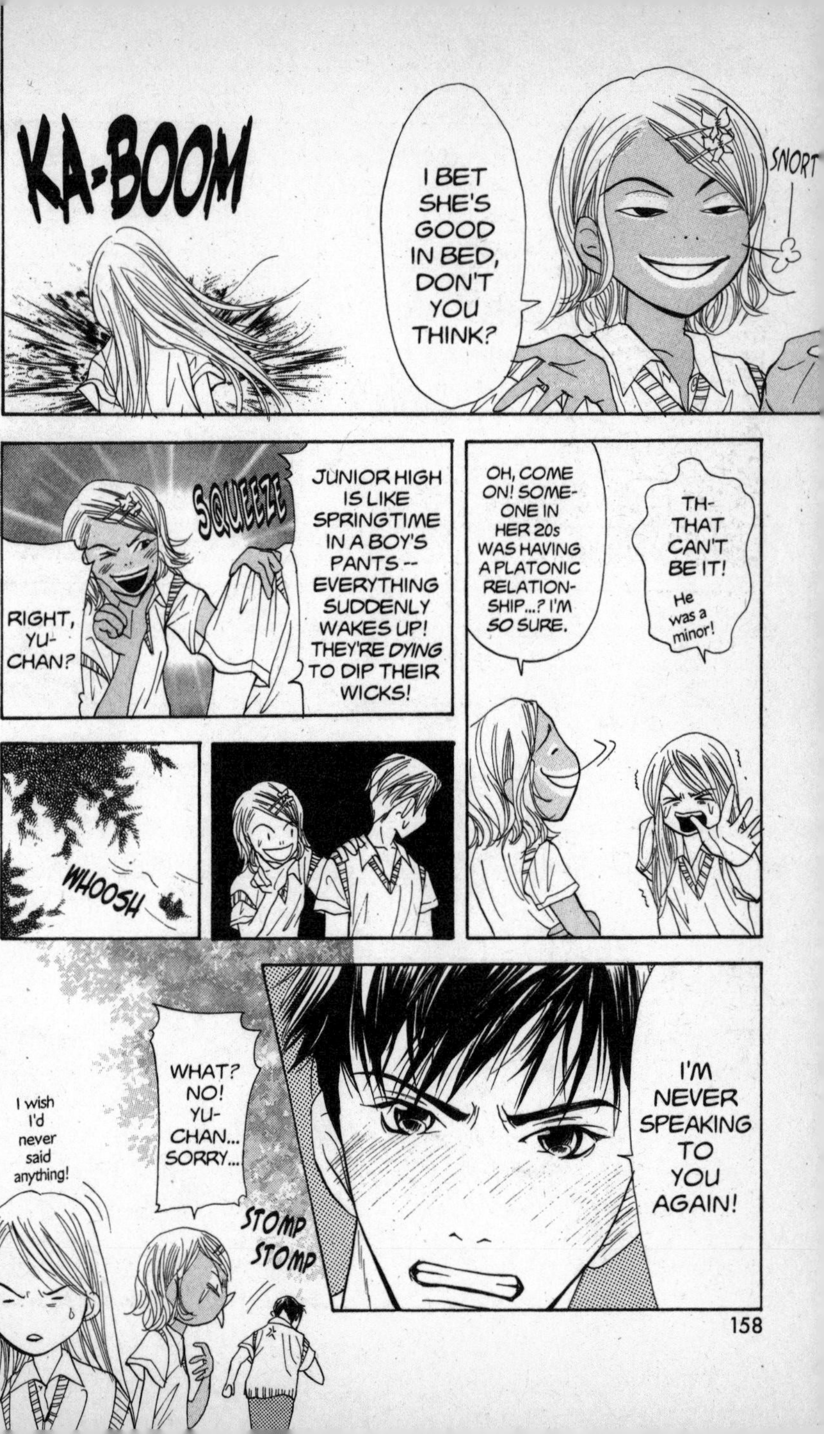
SNORT
I BET SHE'S GOOD IN BED, DON'T YOU THINK?
KA-BOOM
OH, COME ON! SOME-ONE IN HER 20s WAS HAVING A PLATONIC RELATION-SHIP...? I'M *SO SURE.*
TH- THAT CAN'T BE IT!
He was a minor!
JUNIOR HIGH IS LIKE SPRINGTIME IN A BOY'S PANTS -- EVERYTHING SUDDENLY WAKES UP! THEY'RE *DYING* TO DIP THEIR WICKS!
S@UEEZE
RIGHT, YU-CHAN?
WHOOSH
I'M NEVER SPEAKING TO YOU AGAIN!
WHAT? NO! YU-CHAN... SORRY...
STOMP STOMP
I wish I'd never said anything!

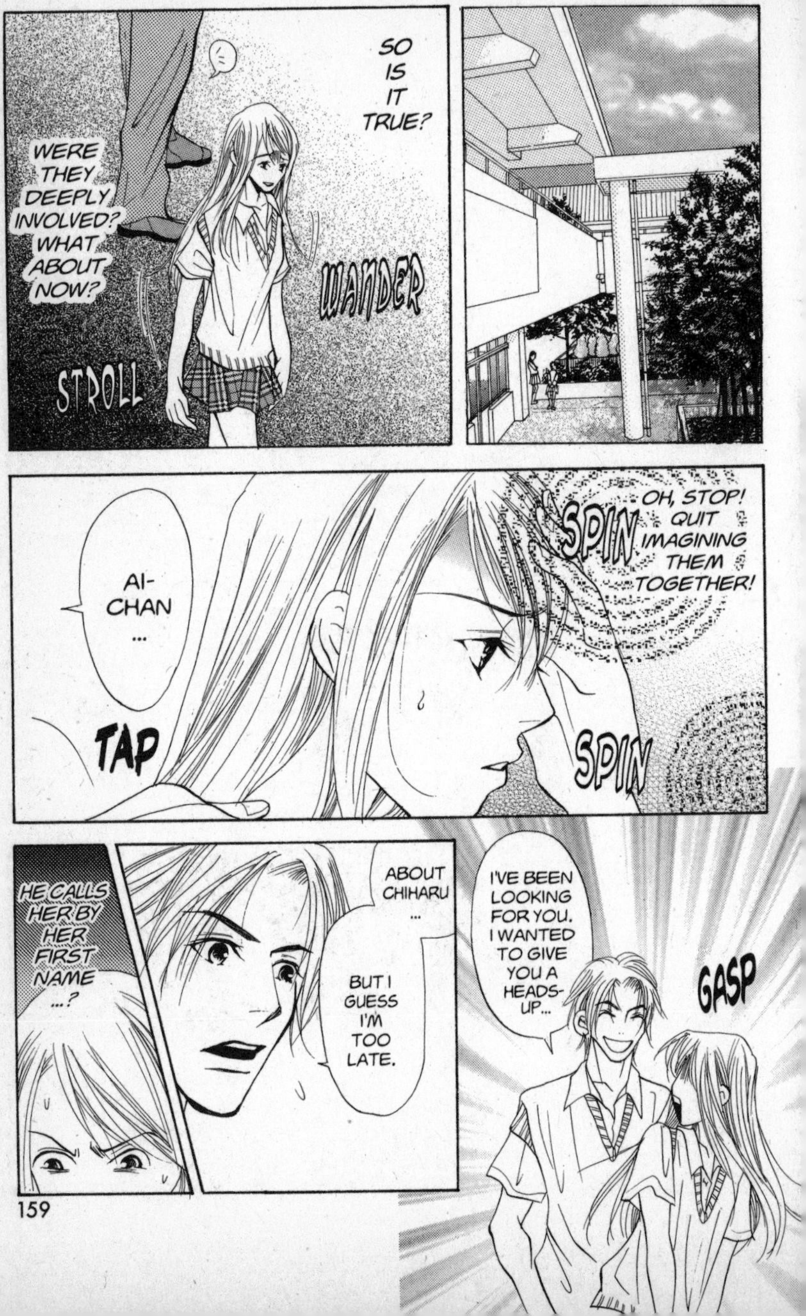
SO IS IT TRUE?
WANDER
WERE THEY DEEPLY INVOLVED? WHAT ABOUT NOW?
STROLL
OH, STOP! QUIT IMAGINING THEM TOGETHER!
SPIN
SPIN
AI-CHAN ...
TAP
GASP
I'VE BEEN LOOKING FOR YOU. I WANTED TO GIVE YOU A HEADS-UP...
ABOUT CHIHARU ...
BUT I GUESS I'M TOO LATE.
HE CALLS HER BY HER FIRST NAME ...?

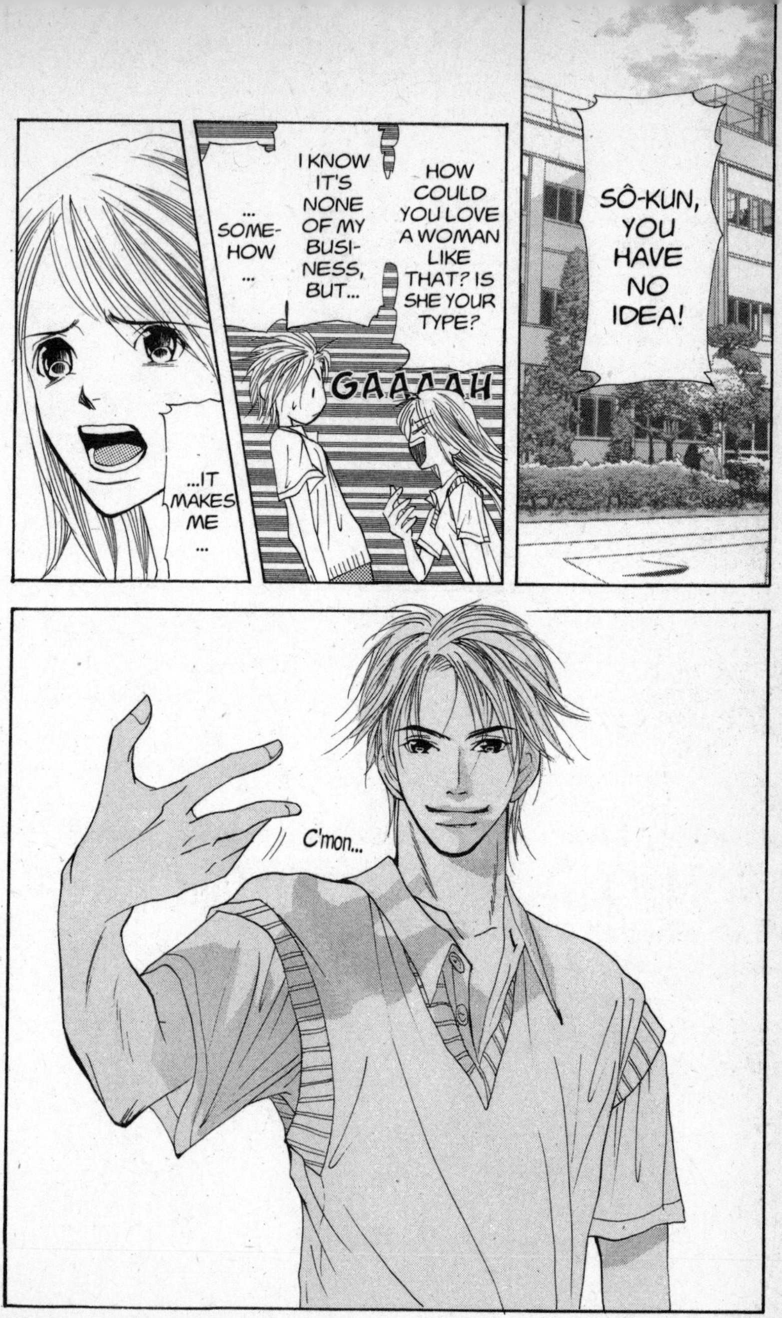
SÔ-KUN, YOU HAVE NO IDEA!
HOW COULD YOU LOVE A WOMAN LIKE THAT? IS SHE YOUR TYPE?
GAAAAH
I KNOW IT'S NONE OF MY BUSINESS, BUT...
... SOMEHOW ...
...IT MAKES ME ...
C'mon...

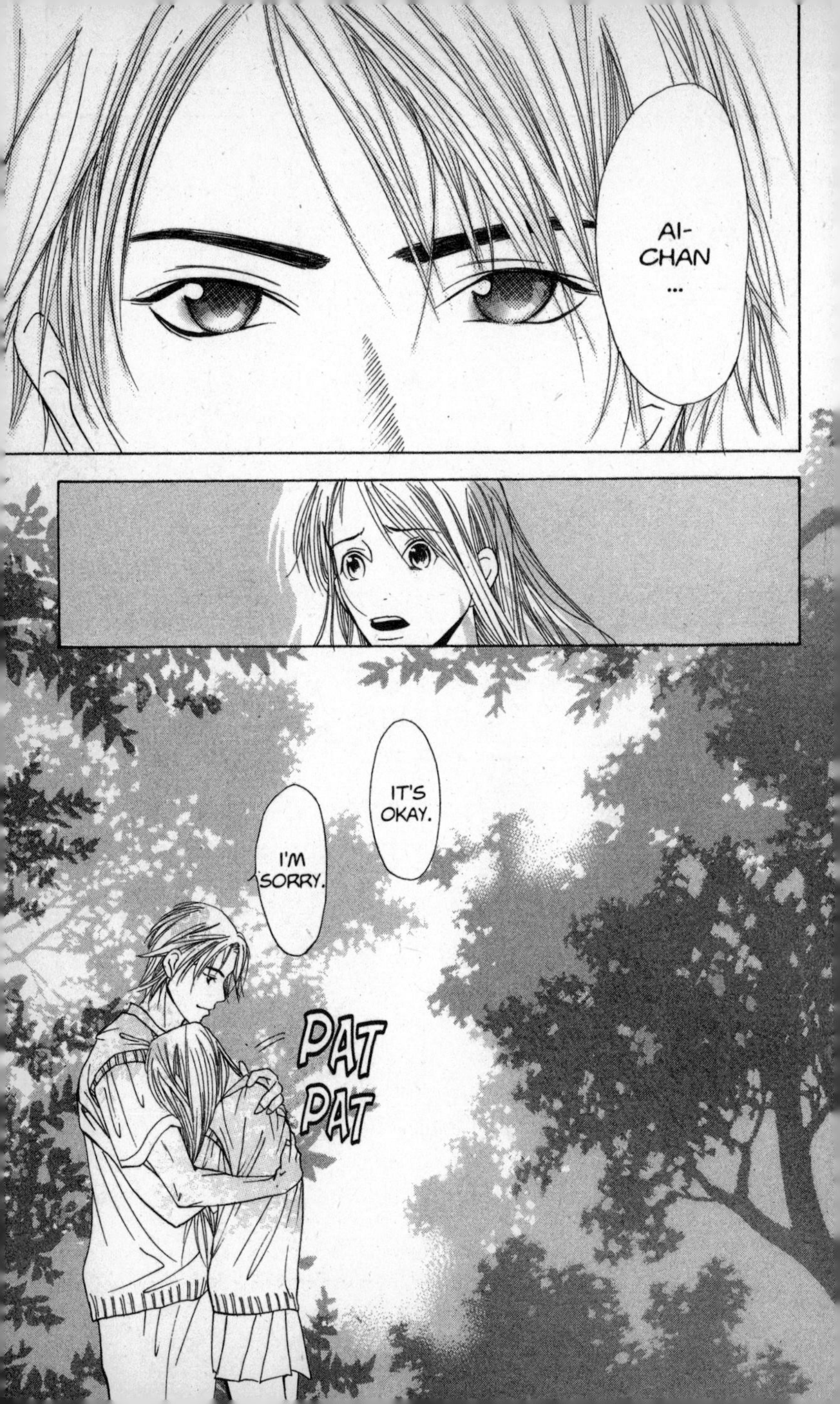
AI-CHAN ...
IT'S OKAY.
I'M SORRY.
PAT PAT

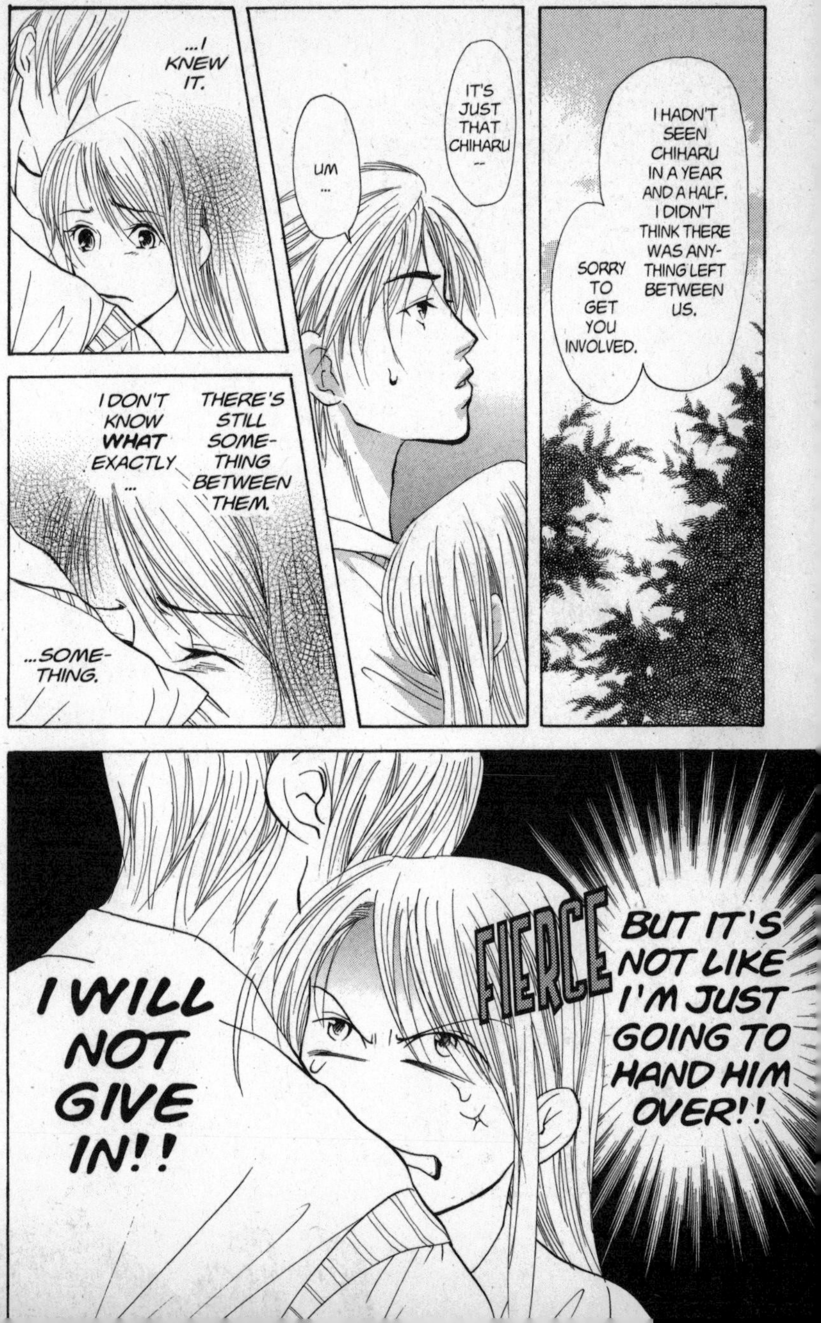
I HADN'T SEEN CHIHARU IN A YEAR AND A HALF. I DIDN'T THINK THERE WAS ANYTHING LEFT BETWEEN US.
SORRY TO GET YOU INVOLVED.
IT'S JUST THAT CHIHARU --
UM ...
...I KNEW IT.
THERE'S STILL SOMETHING BETWEEN THEM.
I DON'T KNOW **WHAT** EXACTLY ...
...SOMETHING.
FIERCE
BUT IT'S NOT LIKE I'M JUST GOING TO HAND HIM OVER!!
I WILL NOT GIVE IN!!

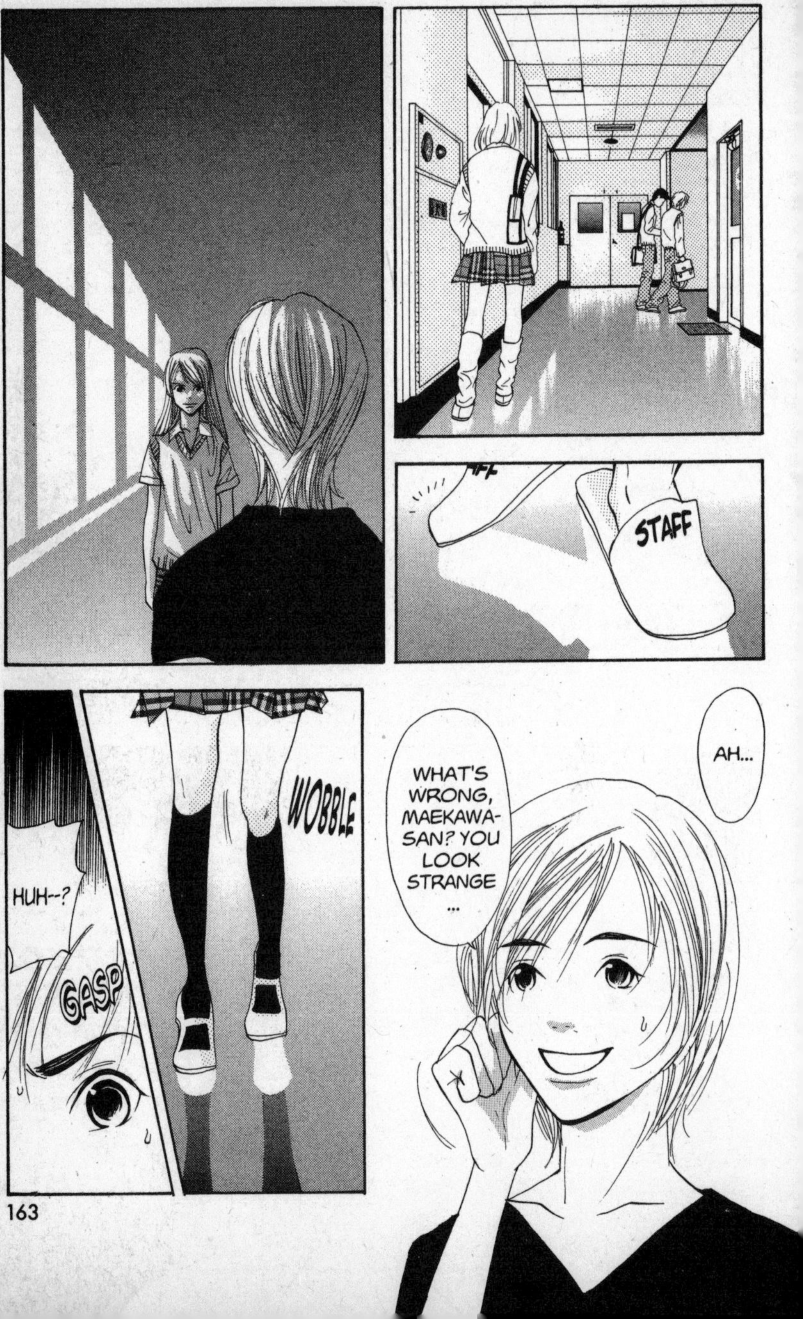
STAFF
AH...
WHAT'S WRONG, MAEKAWA-SAN? YOU LOOK STRANGE ...
WOBBLE
HUH--?
GASP

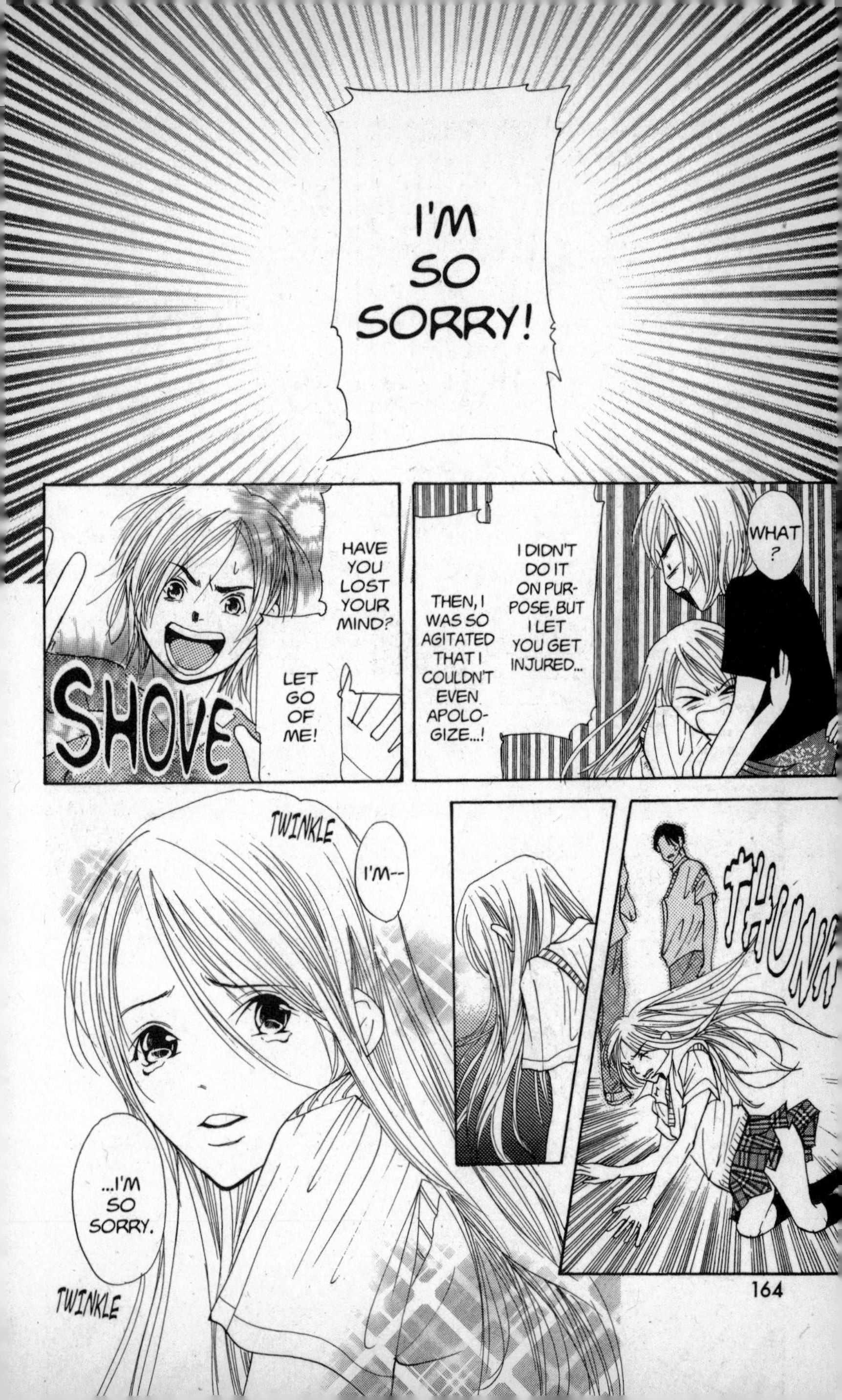
I'M SO SORRY!
WHAT?
I DIDN'T DO IT ON PURPOSE, BUT I LET YOU GET INJURED...
THEN, I WAS SO AGITATED THAT I COULDN'T EVEN APOLOGIZE...!
HAVE YOU LOST YOUR MIND?
LET GO OF ME!
SHOVE
THUNK
TWINKLE
I'M--
...I'M SO SORRY.
TWINKLE

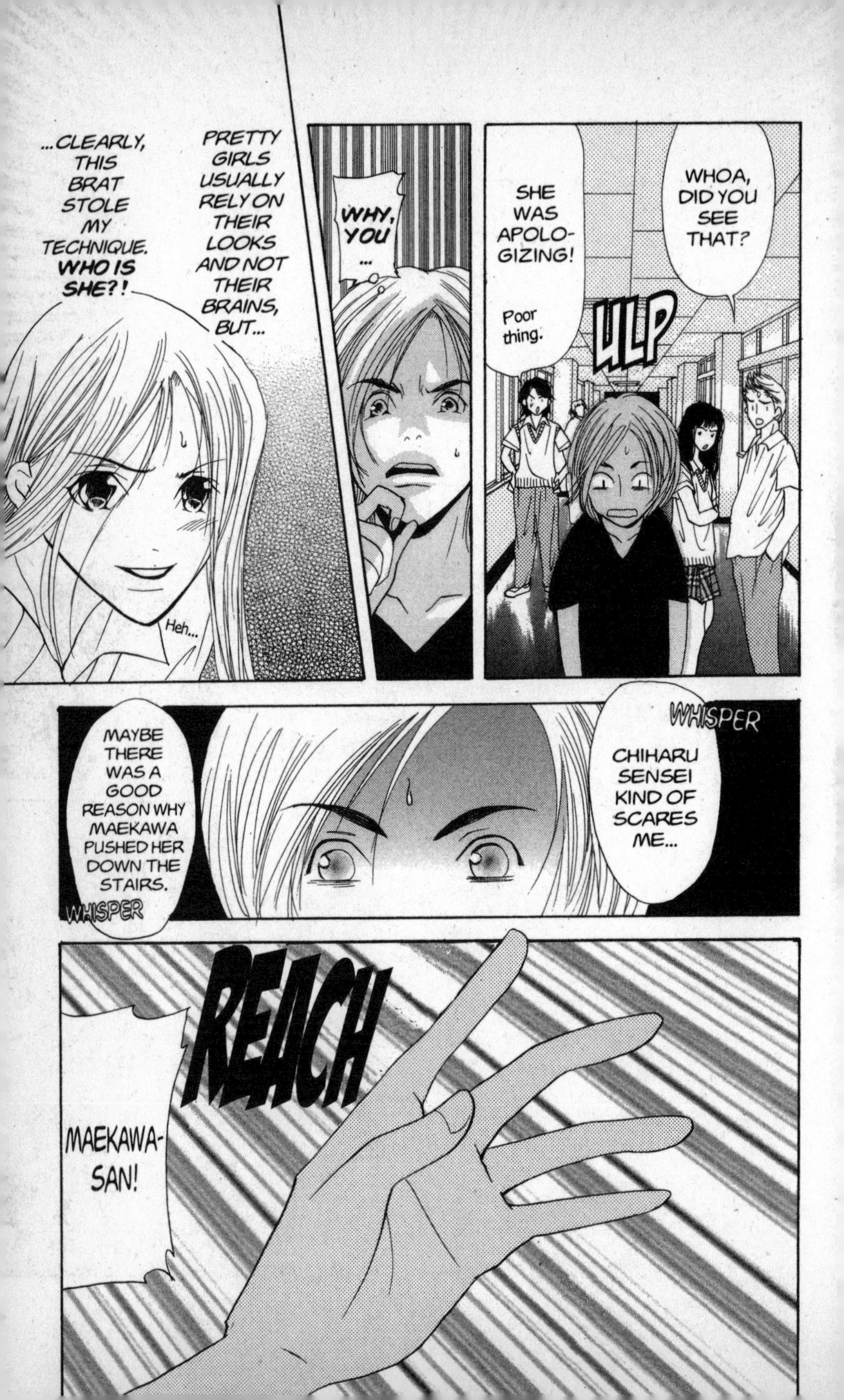
WHOA, DID YOU SEE THAT?
SHE WAS APOLOGIZING!
Poor thing.
ULP
WHY, YOU ...
PRETTY GIRLS USUALLY RELY ON THEIR LOOKS AND NOT THEIR BRAINS, BUT...
...CLEARLY, THIS BRAT STOLE MY TECHNIQUE. WHO IS SHE?!
Heh...
WHISPER
CHIHARU SENSEI KIND OF SCARES ME...
MAYBE THERE WAS A GOOD REASON WHY MAEKAWA PUSHED HER DOWN THE STAIRS.
WHISPER
REACH
MAEKAWA-SAN!

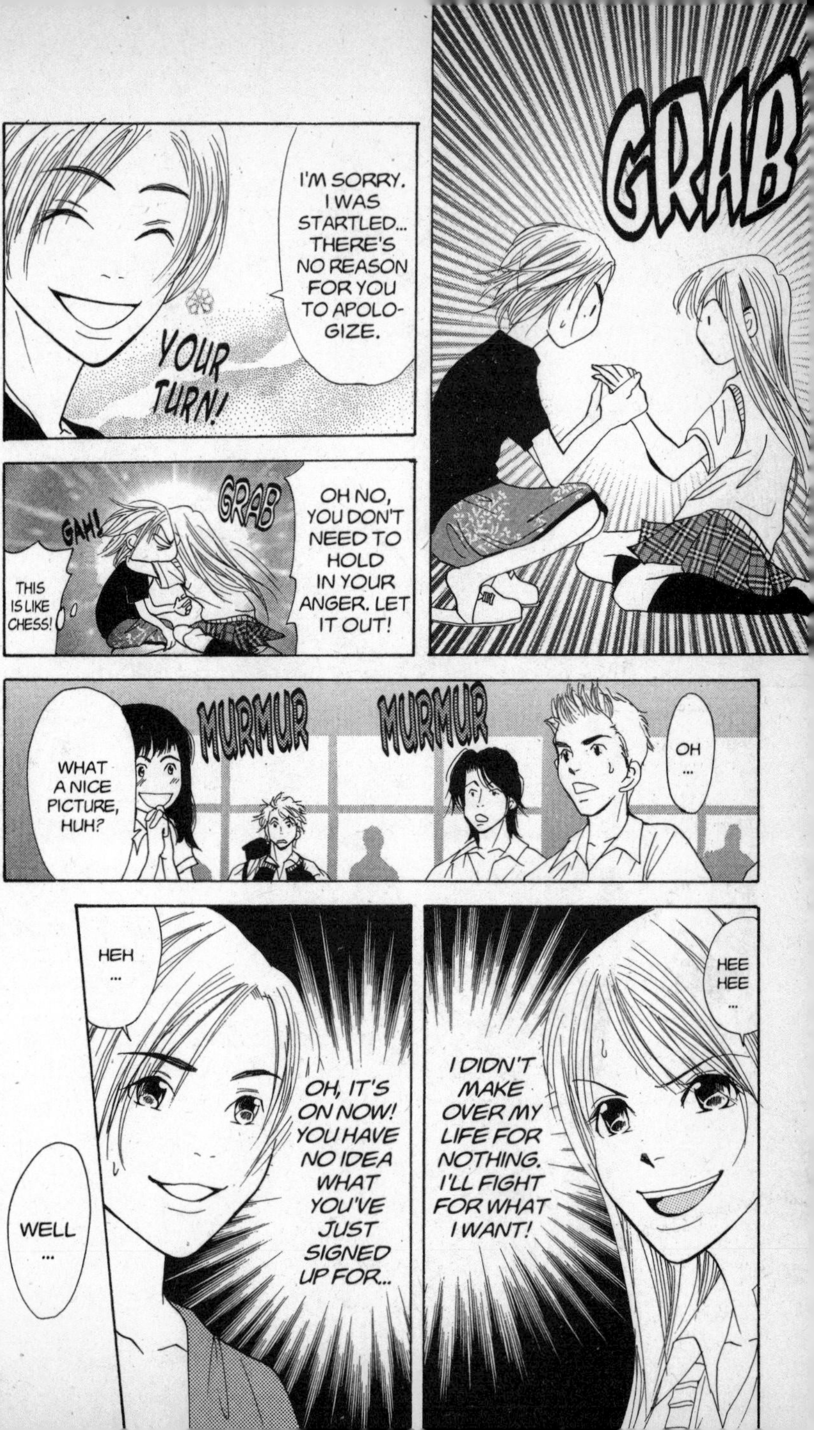
GRAB
I'M SORRY. I WAS STARTLED... THERE'S NO REASON FOR YOU TO APOLOGIZE.
YOUR TURN!
OH NO, YOU DON'T NEED TO HOLD IN YOUR ANGER. LET IT OUT!
GRAB
GAH!
THIS IS LIKE CHESS!
OH ...
MURMUR
MURMUR
WHAT A NICE PICTURE, HUH?
HEE HEE ...
I DIDN'T MAKE OVER MY LIFE FOR NOTHING. I'LL FIGHT FOR WHAT I WANT!
HEH ...
OH, IT'S ON NOW! YOU HAVE NO IDEA WHAT YOU'VE JUST SIGNED UP FOR...
WELL ...

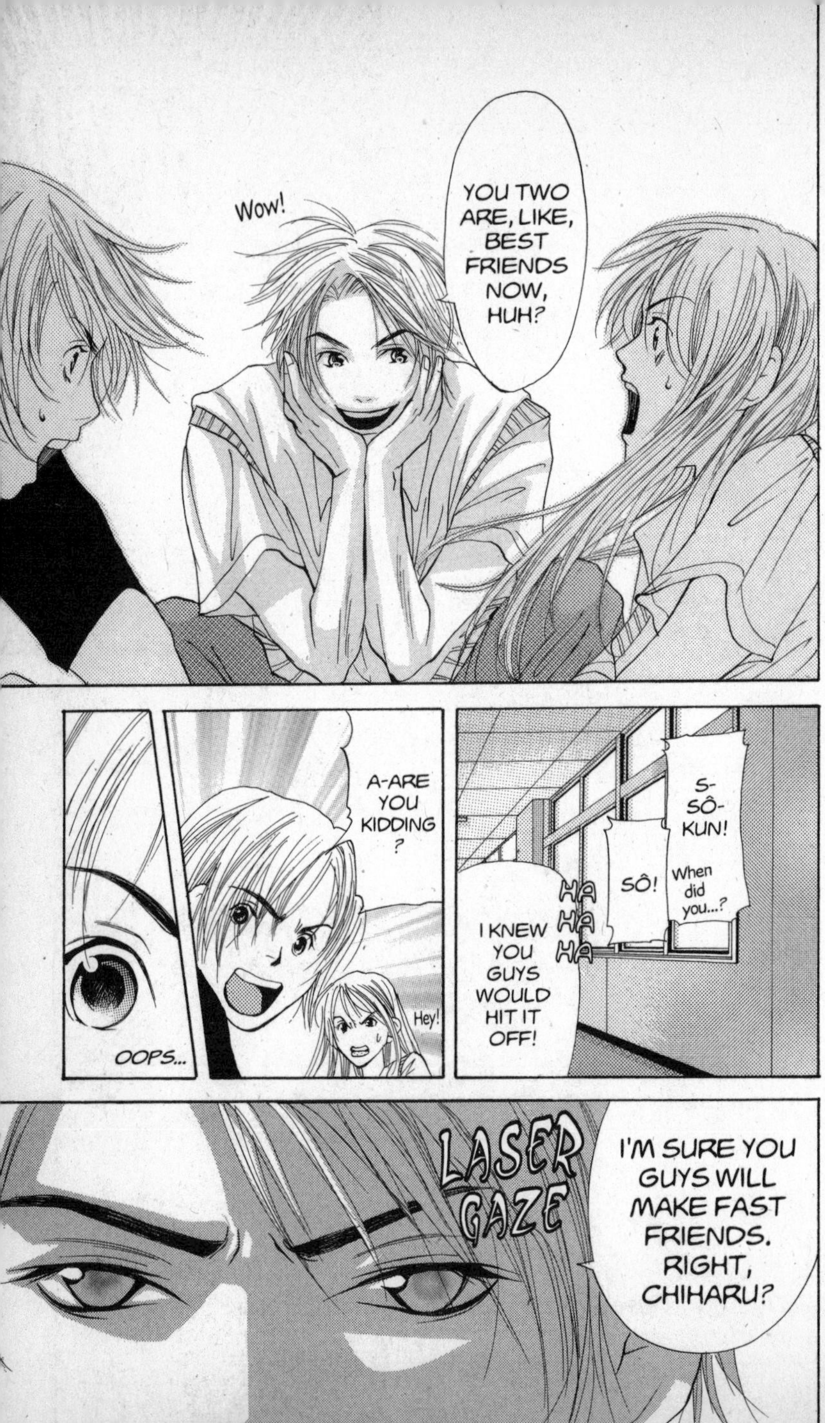
YOU TWO ARE, LIKE, BEST FRIENDS NOW, HUH?
Wow!
S-SÔ-KUN!
When did you...?
SÔ!
HA HA HA
I KNEW YOU GUYS WOULD HIT IT OFF!
A-ARE YOU KIDDING?
Hey!
OOPS...
LASER GAZE
I'M SURE YOU GUYS WILL MAKE FAST FRIENDS. RIGHT, CHIHARU?

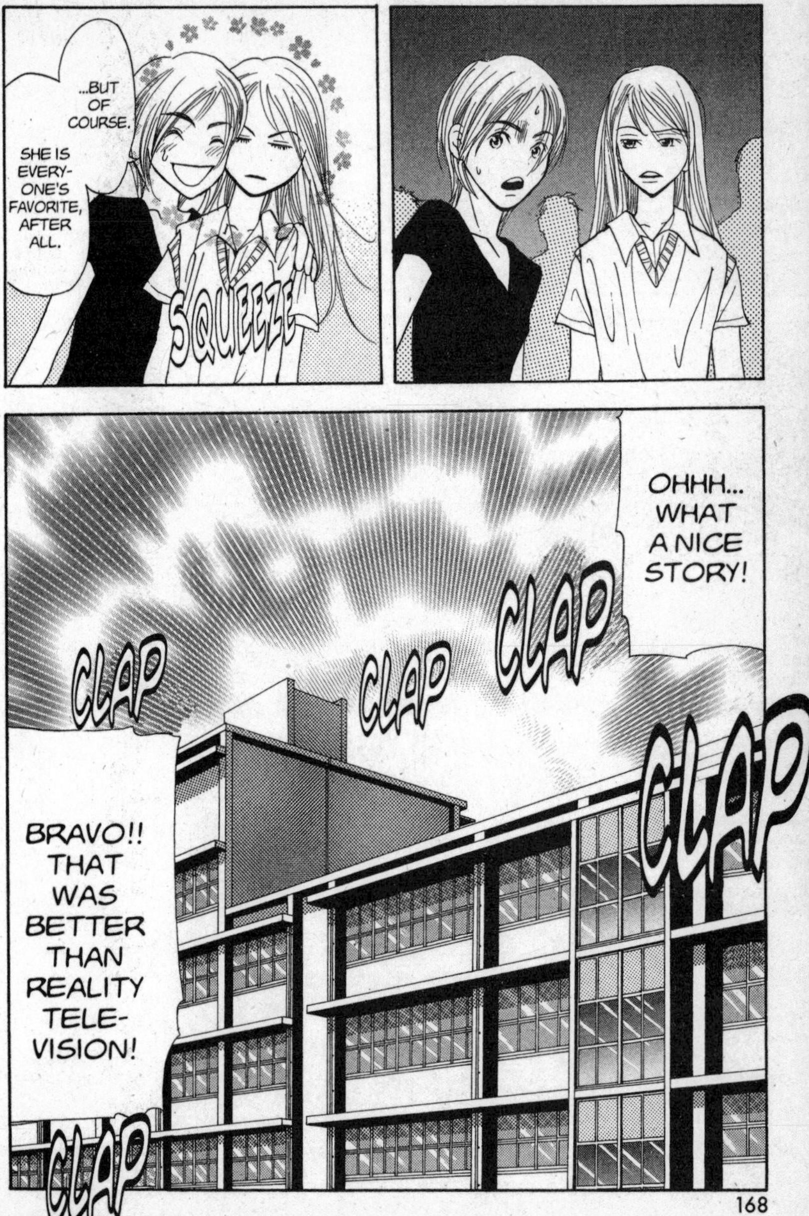
...BUT OF COURSE.
SHE IS EVERYONE'S FAVORITE, AFTER ALL.
SQUEEZE
OHHH... WHAT A NICE STORY!
CLAP
CLAP
CLAP
CLAP
BRAVO!! THAT WAS BETTER THAN REALITY TELEVISION!
CLAP

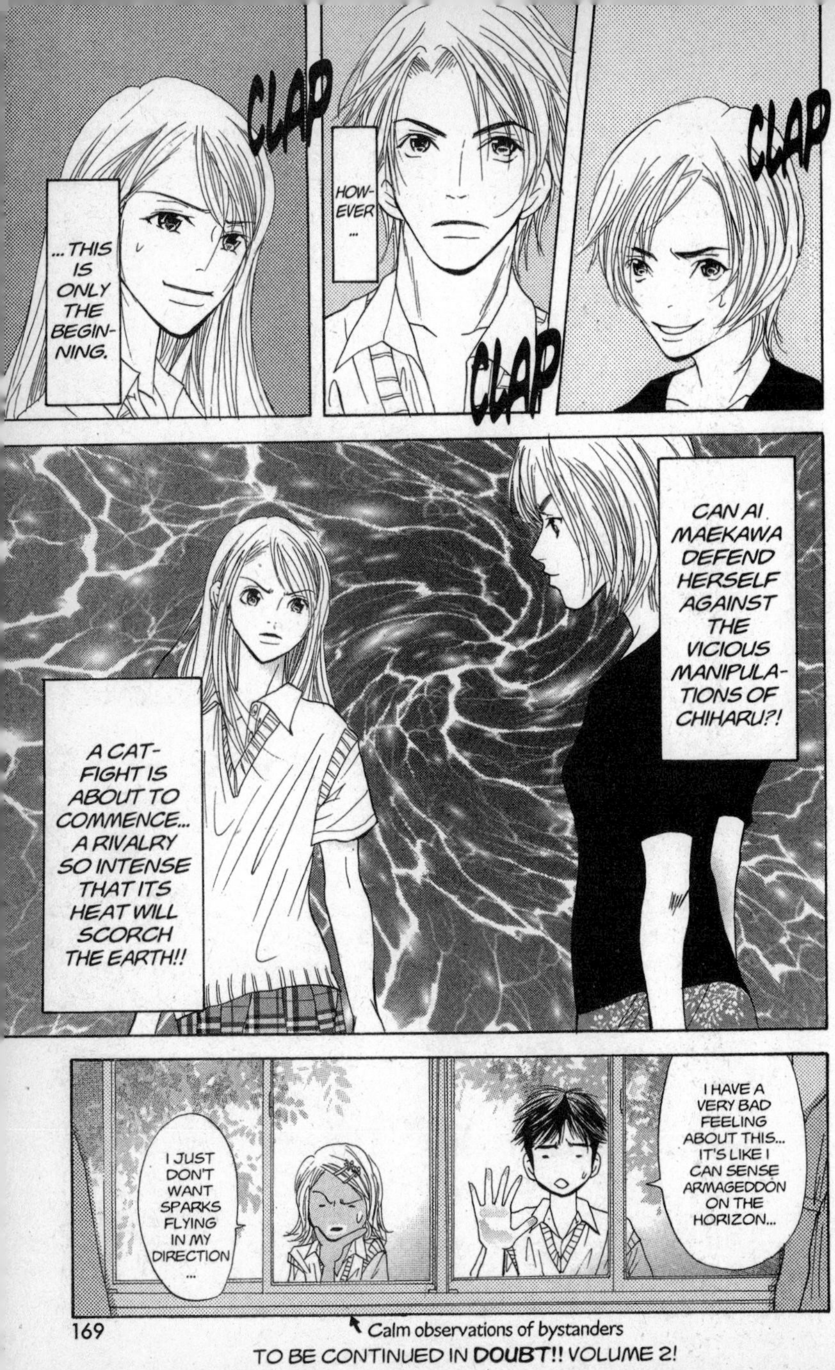
CLAP
CLAP
HOW-EVER...
CLAP
...THIS IS ONLY THE BEGIN-NING.
CAN AI MAEKAWA DEFEND HERSELF AGAINST THE VICIOUS MANIPULA-TIONS OF CHIHARU?!
A CAT-FIGHT IS ABOUT TO COMMENCE... A RIVALRY SO INTENSE THAT ITS HEAT WILL SCORCH THE EARTH!!
I HAVE A VERY BAD FEELING ABOUT THIS... IT'S LIKE I CAN SENSE ARMAGEDDON ON THE HORIZON...
I JUST DON'T WANT SPARKS FLYING IN MY DIRECTION...

↖ Calm observations of bystanders

TO BE CONTINUED IN **DOUBT!!** VOLUME 2!

Commentary on "The Day of Finals"

Finals... Yes, finals.

When I was a student, the only thing I liked about finals was the fact that we could go home earlier than usual. When you're studying in the middle of the night, preparing for exams, do you ever get the sudden urge to scream and go berserk because everything is just so horrible? (Or is it just me?)

This manga is centered on that kind of emotion. It's not particularly smart or elegant, but it's full of...

passion. That's all.

16 pages of idiotic manga.
Make sure to fasten the

seatbelt of your heart

when you read this.

Man can live on passion alone!

The Day of Finals

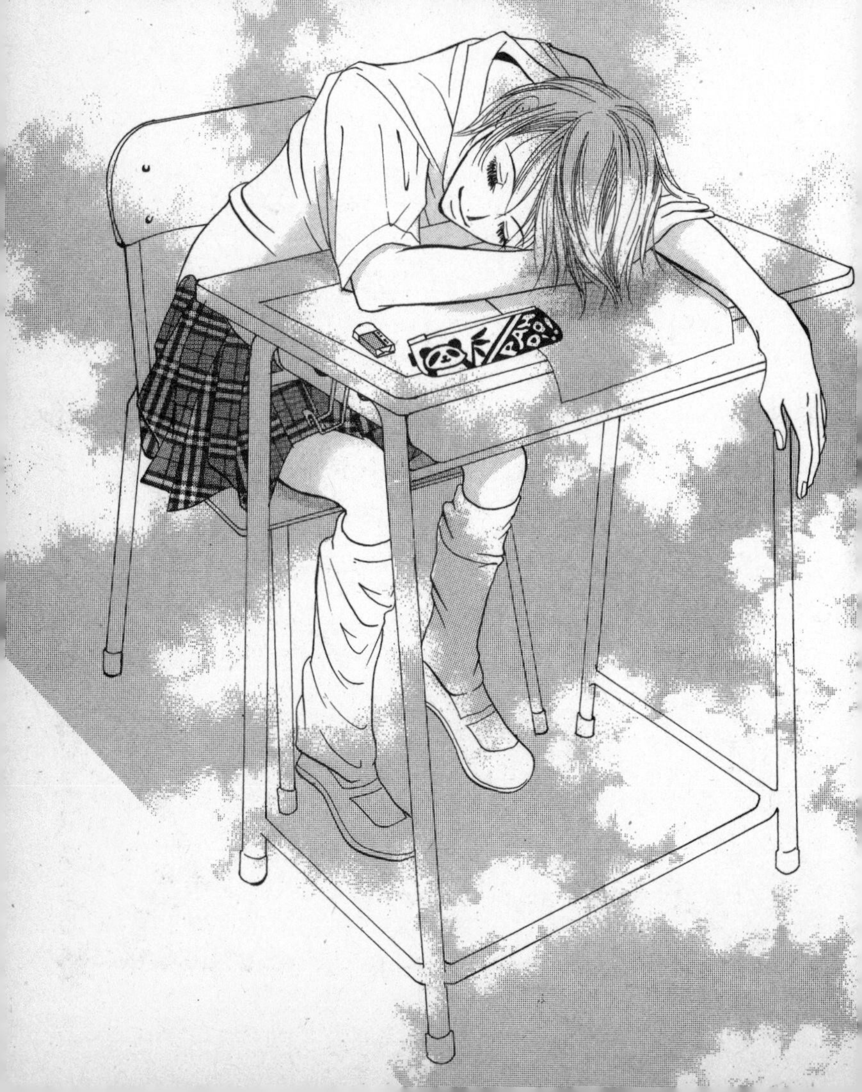

SECOND TERM FINAL EXAM

CLASSIC JAPANESE

AFTER READING THE FOLLOWING EXCERPT FROM THE TALE OF GENJI

<20>

いたくふけゆく
になるままに澄
残りなく
心づかひ、後の
この女のあり
おぼえなき世
神・仏のあ
A

①

SIZZLE
SIZZLE

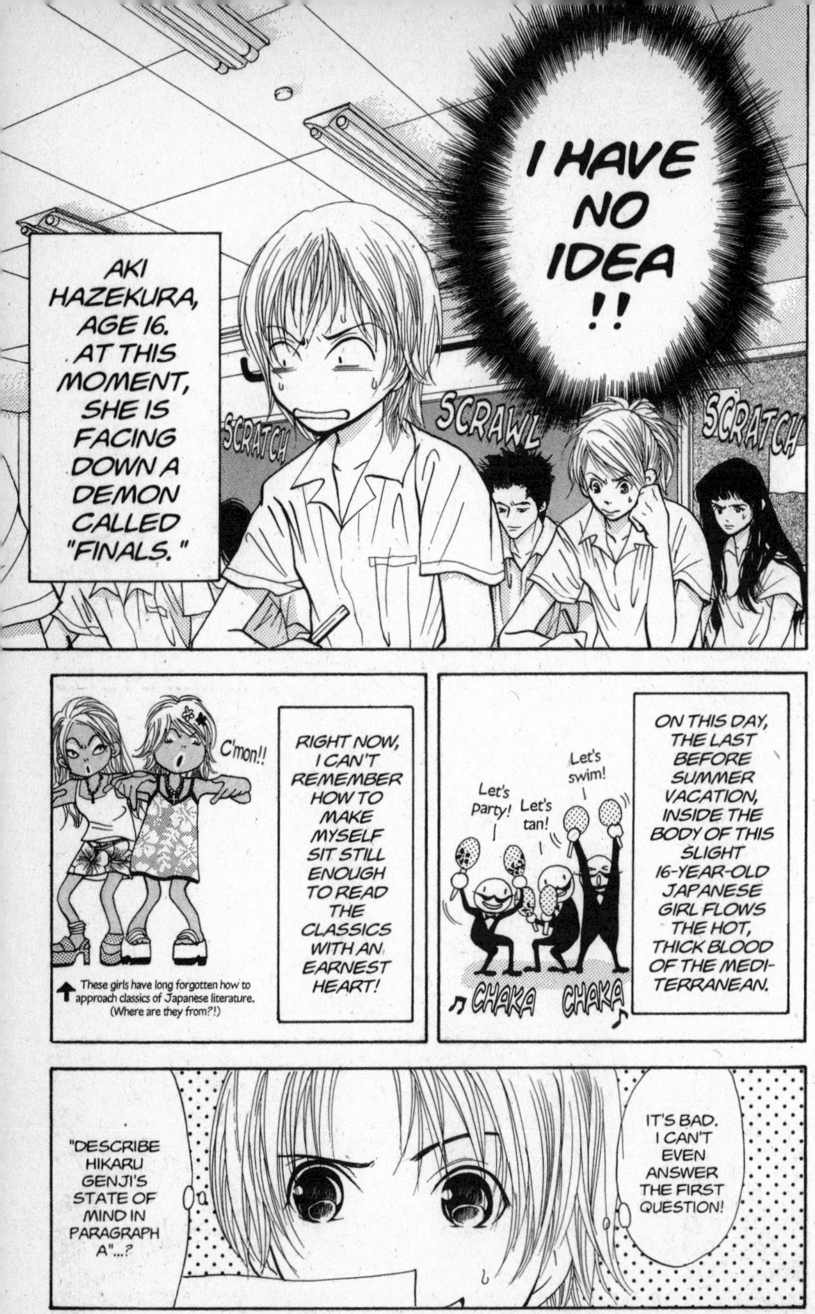

I HAVE NO IDEA!!
AKI HAZEKURA, AGE 16. AT THIS MOMENT, SHE IS FACING DOWN A DEMON CALLED "FINALS."
SCRATCH
SCRAWL
SCRATCH
ON THIS DAY, THE LAST BEFORE SUMMER VACATION, INSIDE THE BODY OF THIS SLIGHT 16-YEAR-OLD JAPANESE GIRL FLOWS THE HOT, THICK BLOOD OF THE MEDI-TERRANEAN.
Let's swim!
Let's tan!
Let's party!
CHAKA CHAKA
RIGHT NOW, I CAN'T REMEMBER HOW TO MAKE MYSELF SIT STILL ENOUGH TO READ THE CLASSICS WITH AN EARNEST HEART!
C'mon!!
These girls have long forgotten how to approach classics of Japanese literature. (Where are they from?!)
IT'S BAD. I CAN'T EVEN ANSWER THE FIRST QUESTION!
"DESCRIBE HIKARU GENJI'S STATE OF MIND IN PARAGRAPH A"...?

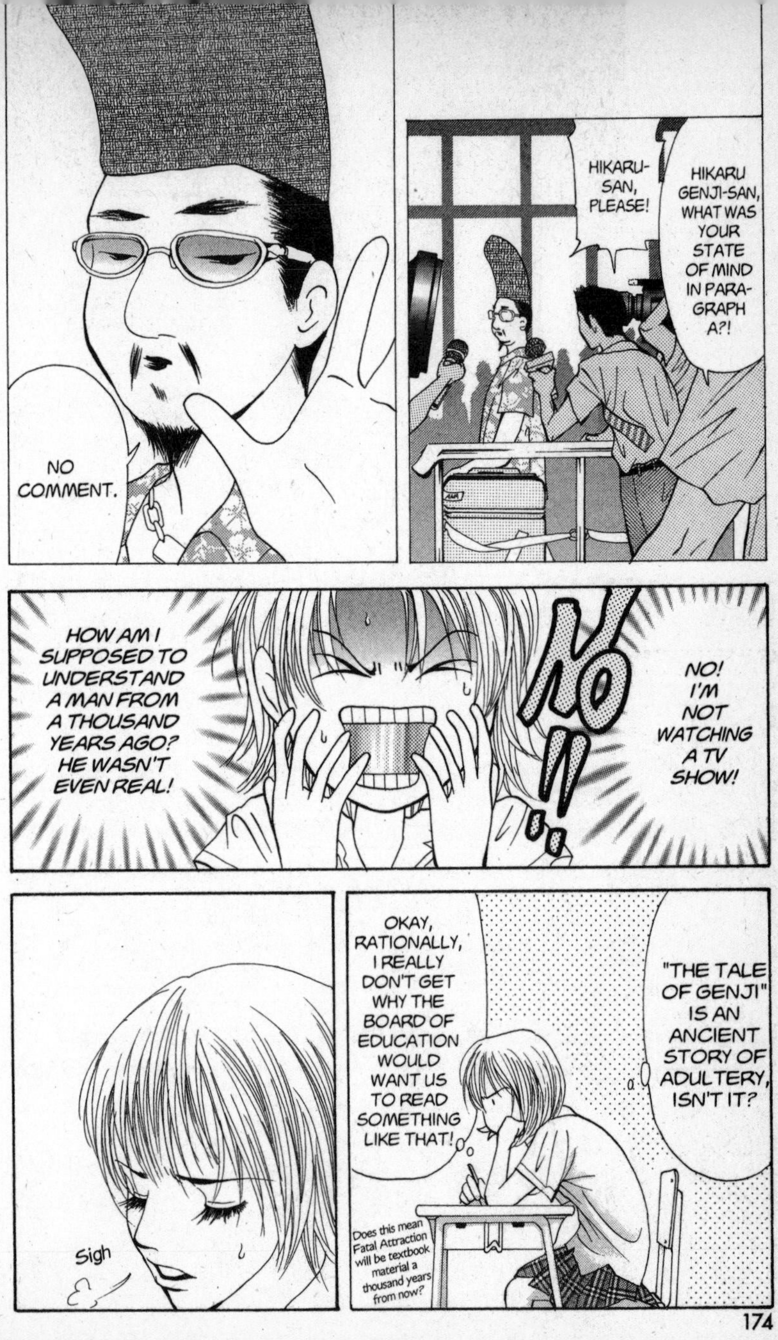
HIKARU GENJI-SAN, WHAT WAS YOUR STATE OF MIND IN PARAGRAPH A?!
HIKARU-SAN, PLEASE!
NO COMMENT.
NO! I'M NOT WATCHING A TV SHOW!
NO!!
HOW AM I SUPPOSED TO UNDERSTAND A MAN FROM A THOUSAND YEARS AGO? HE WASN'T EVEN REAL!
"THE TALE OF GENJI" IS AN ANCIENT STORY OF ADULTERY, ISN'T IT?
OKAY, RATIONALLY, I REALLY DON'T GET WHY THE BOARD OF EDUCATION WOULD WANT US TO READ SOMETHING LIKE THAT!
Does this mean Fatal Attraction will be textbook material a thousand years from now?
Sigh

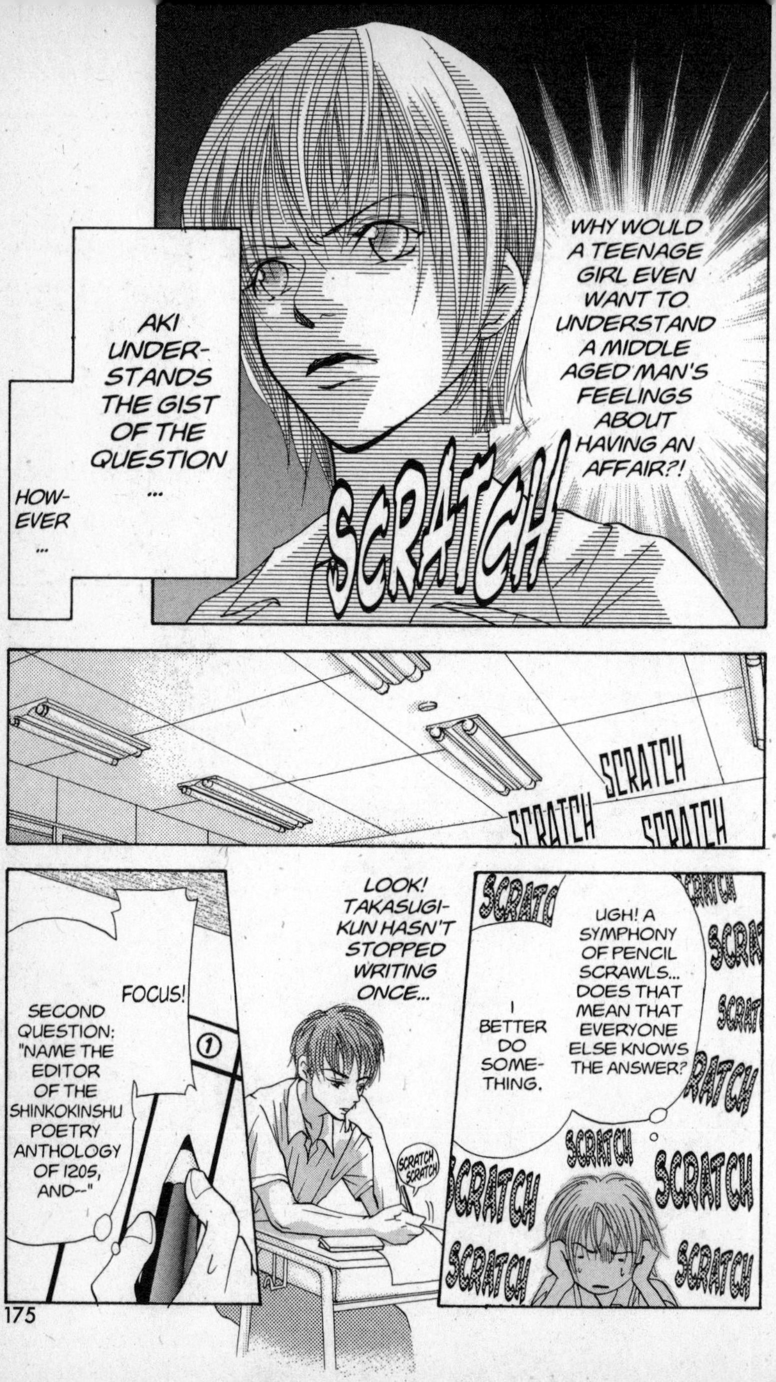
WHY WOULD A TEENAGE GIRL EVEN WANT TO UNDERSTAND A MIDDLE AGED MAN'S FEELINGS ABOUT HAVING AN AFFAIR?!
AKI UNDER-STANDS THE GIST OF THE QUESTION ...
HOW-EVER ...
SCRATCH
SCRATCH
SCRATCH
SCRATCH
SCRATCH
UGH! A SYMPHONY OF PENCIL SCRAWLS... DOES THAT MEAN THAT EVERYONE ELSE KNOWS THE ANSWER?
I BETTER DO SOME-THING.
SCRATCH
SCRATCH
SCRATCH
SCRATCH
SCRATCH
SCRATCH
SCRATCH
SCRATCH
LOOK! TAKASUGI-KUN HASN'T STOPPED WRITING ONCE...
SCRATCH SCRATCH
FOCUS!
SECOND QUESTION: "NAME THE EDITOR OF THE SHINKOKINSHU POETRY ANTHOLOGY OF 1205, AND--"
1

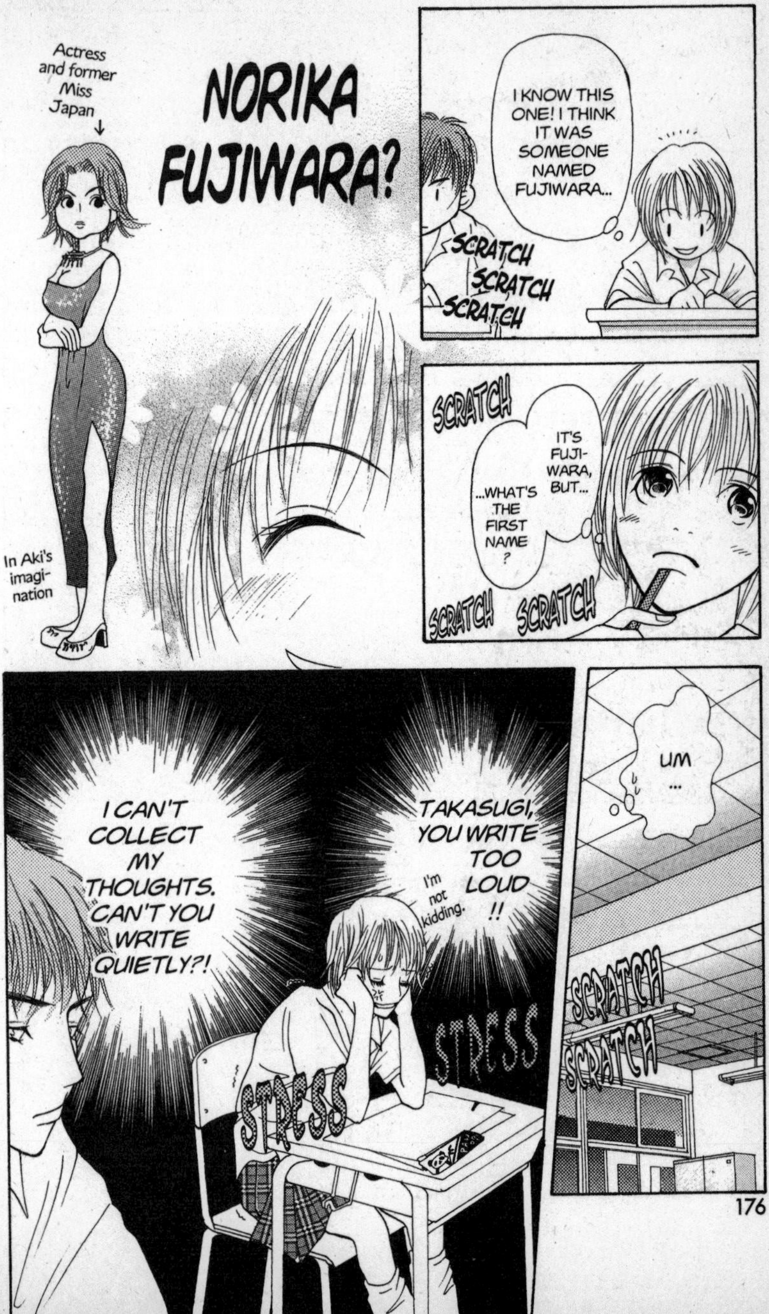

I KNOW THIS ONE! I THINK IT WAS SOMEONE NAMED FUJIWARA...
SCRATCH SCRATCH SCRATCH
SCRATCH
IT'S FUJI-WARA, BUT...
...WHAT'S THE FIRST NAME ?
SCRATCH SCRATCH
NORIKA FUJIWARA?
Actress and former Miss Japan
In Aki's imagi-nation
UM ...
SCRATCH SCRATCH
TAKASUGI, YOU WRITE TOO LOUD !!
I'm not kidding.
I CAN'T COLLECT MY THOUGHTS. CAN'T YOU WRITE QUIETLY?!
STRESS
STRESS

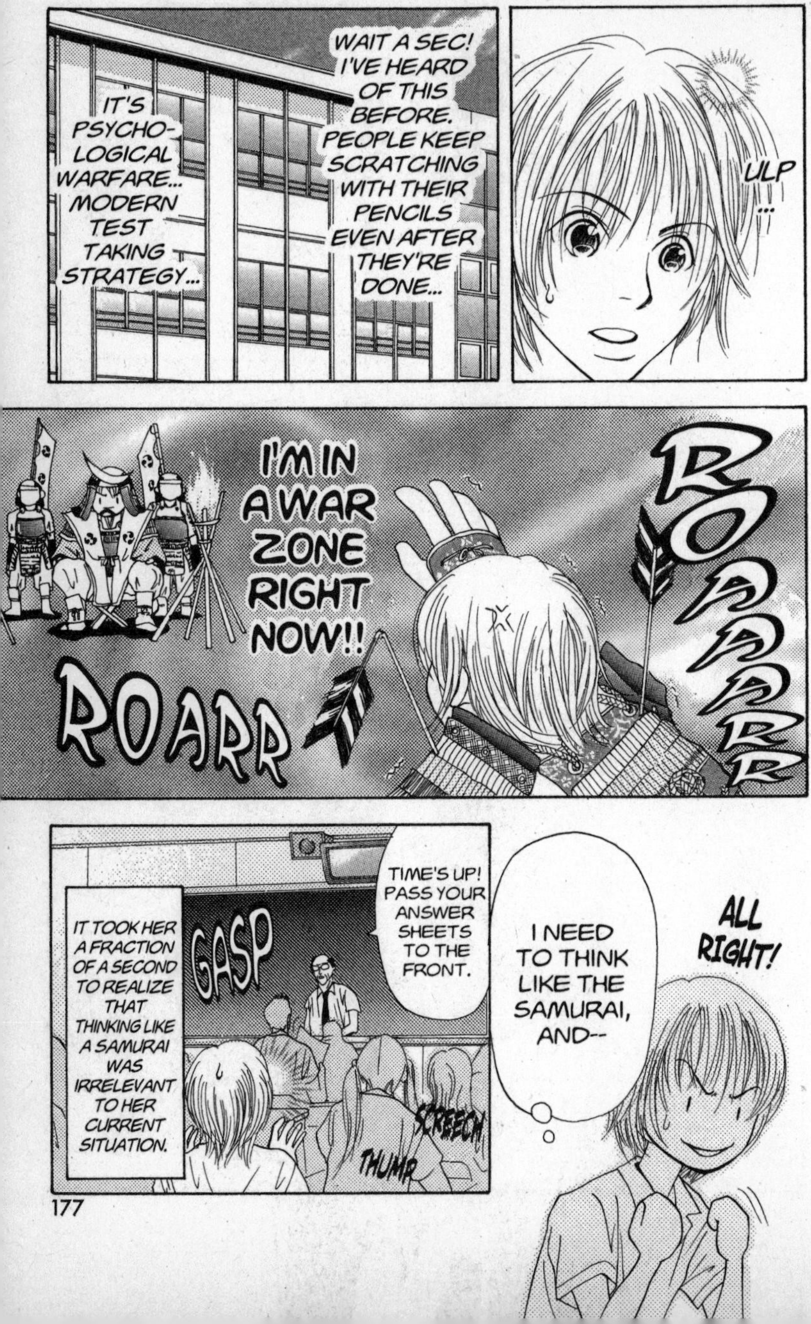
ULP...
WAIT A SEC! I'VE HEARD OF THIS BEFORE. PEOPLE KEEP SCRATCHING WITH THEIR PENCILS EVEN AFTER THEY'RE DONE...
IT'S PSYCHOLOGICAL WARFARE... MODERN TEST TAKING STRATEGY...
ROARRR
I'M IN A WAR ZONE RIGHT NOW!!
ROARR
ALL RIGHT!
I NEED TO THINK LIKE THE SAMURAI, AND--
TIME'S UP! PASS YOUR ANSWER SHEETS TO THE FRONT.
GASP
IT TOOK HER A FRACTION OF A SECOND TO REALIZE THAT THINKING LIKE A SAMURAI WAS IRRELEVANT TO HER CURRENT SITUATION.
SCREECH
THUMP

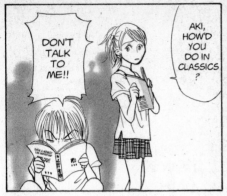

AKI, HOW'D YOU DO IN CLASSICS?
DON'T TALK TO ME!!
EVEN A MONKEY CAN UNDERSTAND BIOLOGY!
I'VE GOT TO MAKE UP FOR BOMBING CLASSICS BY ACING BIOLOGY NEXT...
THIS 15-MINUTE BREAK IS KEY.
EVEN A MONKEY CAN UNDERSTAND BIOLOGY!
GIVE IT UP! IT'S TOO LATE NOW.
HEY, BE NICE, TAKASUGI!
IT'S NEVER TOO LATE!

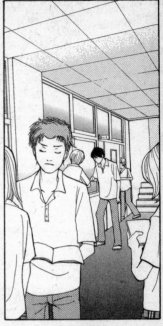

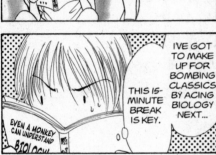

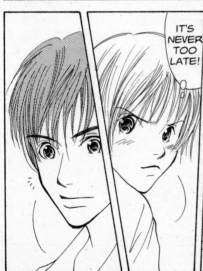

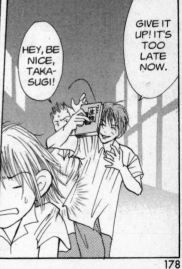

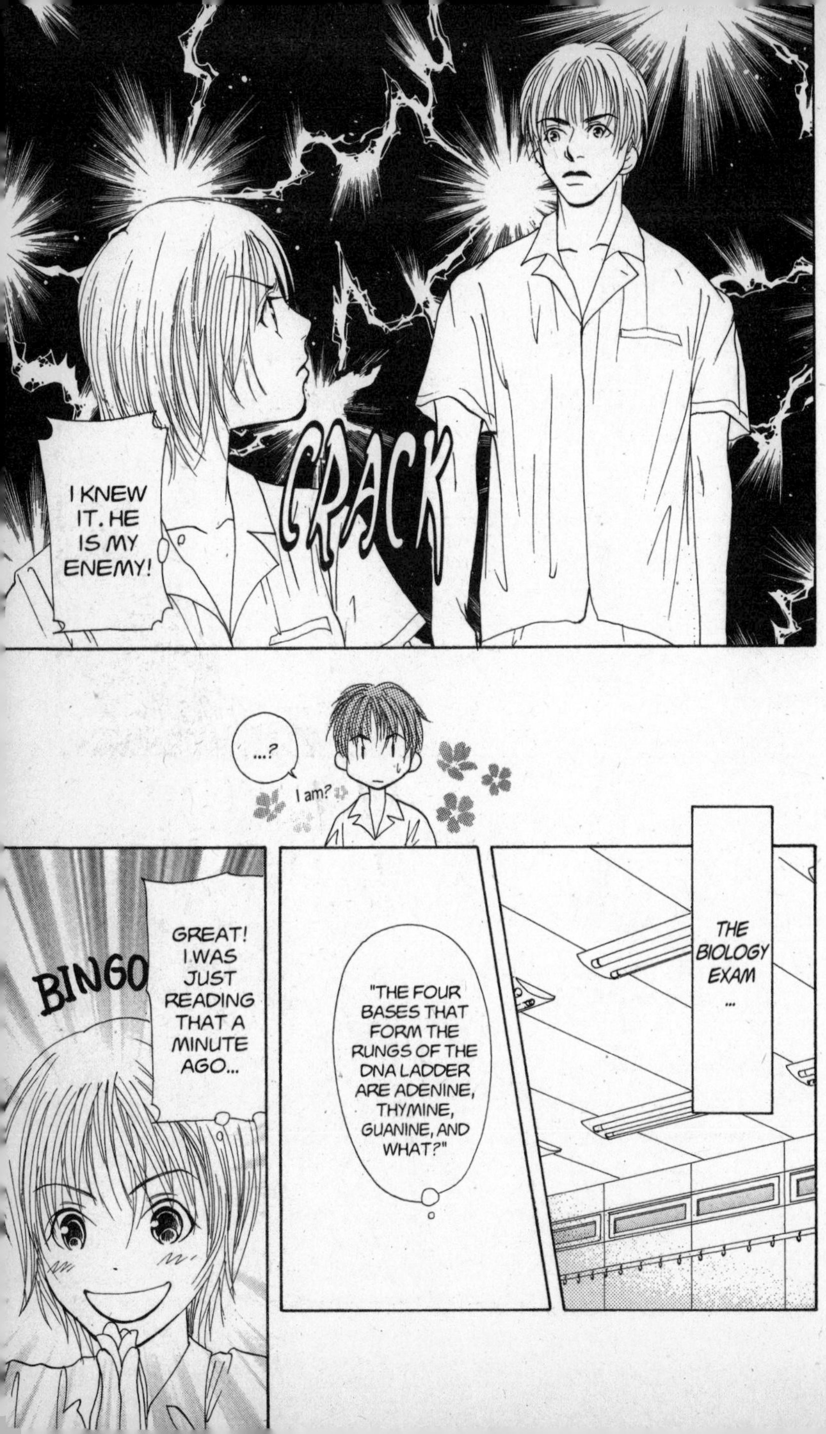
I KNEW IT. HE IS MY ENEMY!
CRACK
...?
I am?
THE BIOLOGY EXAM ...
"THE FOUR BASES THAT FORM THE RUNGS OF THE DNA LADDER ARE ADENINE, THYMINE, GUANINE, AND WHAT?"
BINGO
GREAT! I WAS JUST READING THAT A MINUTE AGO...

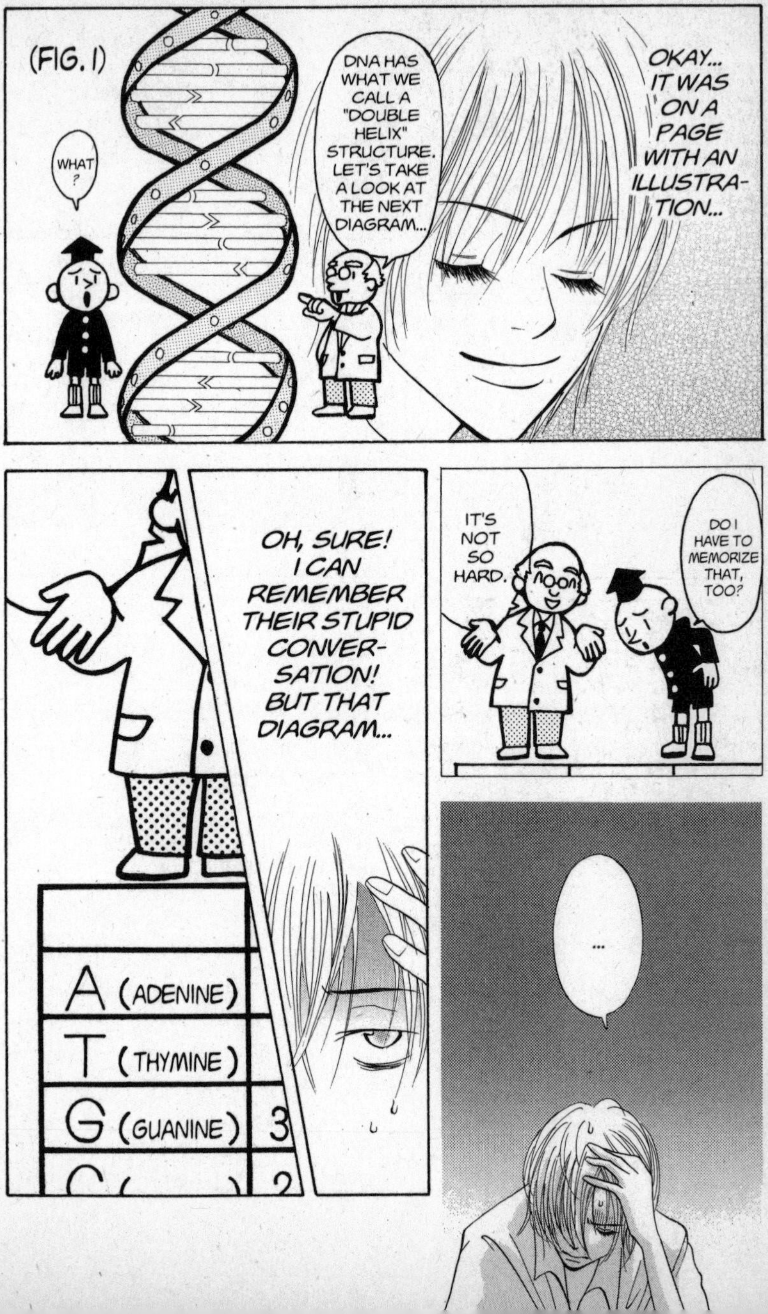

OKAY... IT WAS ON A PAGE WITH AN ILLUSTRATION...
DNA HAS WHAT WE CALL A "DOUBLE HELIX" STRUCTURE. LET'S TAKE A LOOK AT THE NEXT DIAGRAM...
WHAT?
(FIG. 1)
DO I HAVE TO MEMORIZE THAT, TOO?
IT'S NOT SO HARD.
...
OH, SURE! I CAN REMEMBER THEIR STUPID CONVERSATION! BUT THAT DIAGRAM...
A (ADENINE)
T (THYMINE)
G (GUANINE) 3
2

BE QUIET, TAKASUGI!!

Not once, but twice...

THE ONE RIGHT AFTER THE G...

SCRATCH

(ADENINE)	1
T (THYMINE)	2
G (GUANINE)	3
C (CYTOSINE)	2

SCRATCH SCRATCH SCRATCH

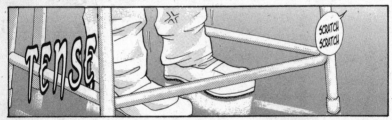

TENSE

SCRATCH SCRATCH

I DEDICATE MYSELF TO BATTLE...

THIS IS WARFARE, AND I AM A WARRIOR...

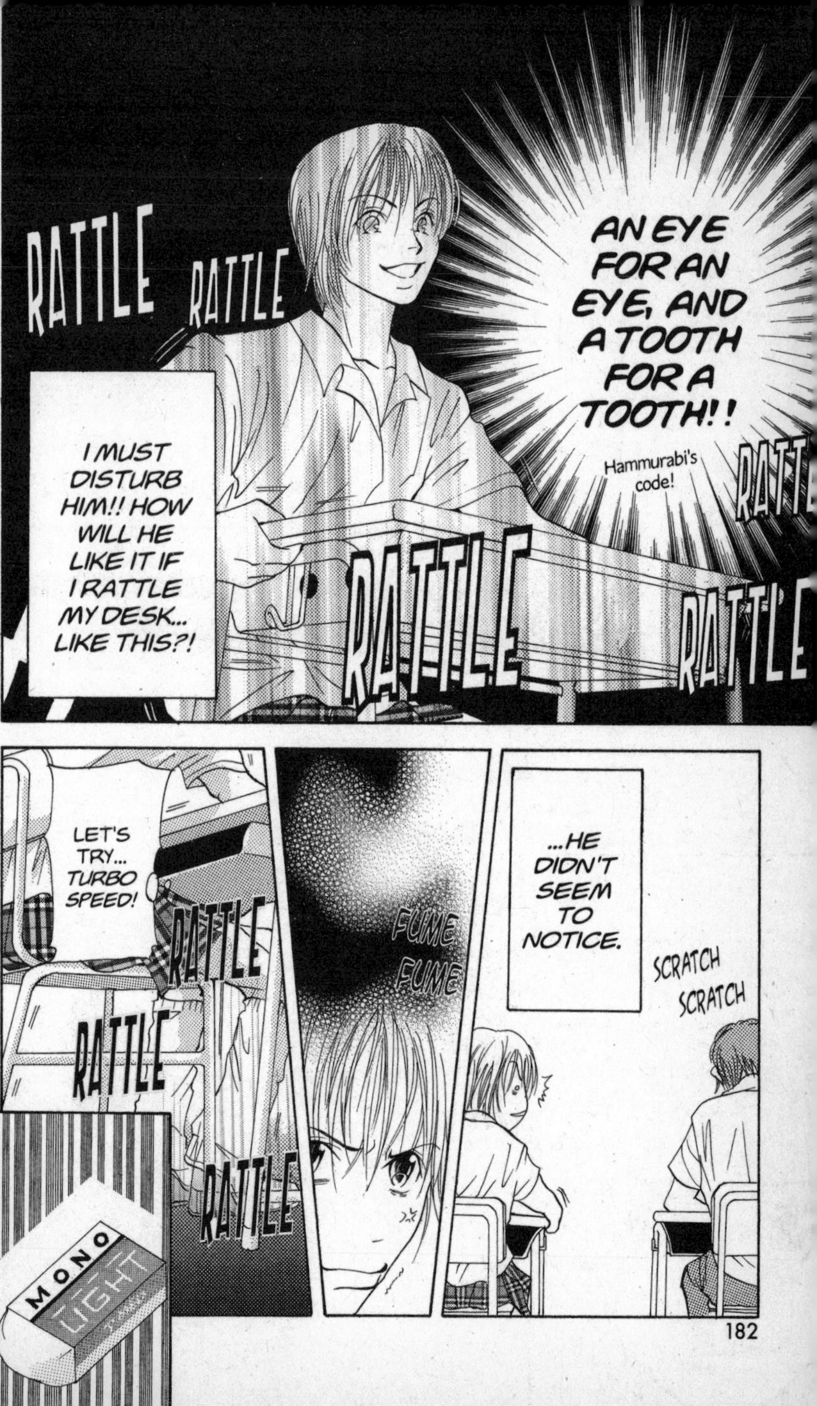
AN EYE FOR AN EYE, AND A TOOTH FOR A TOOTH!!
Hammurabi's code!
RATTLE
RATTLE
RATTLE
RATTLE RATTLE
I MUST DISTURB HIM!! HOW WILL HE LIKE IT IF I RATTLE MY DESK... LIKE THIS?!
...HE DIDN'T SEEM TO NOTICE.
SCRATCH SCRATCH
FUME FUME
LET'S TRY... TURBO SPEED!
RATTLE
RATTLE
RATTLE
MONO
LIGHT

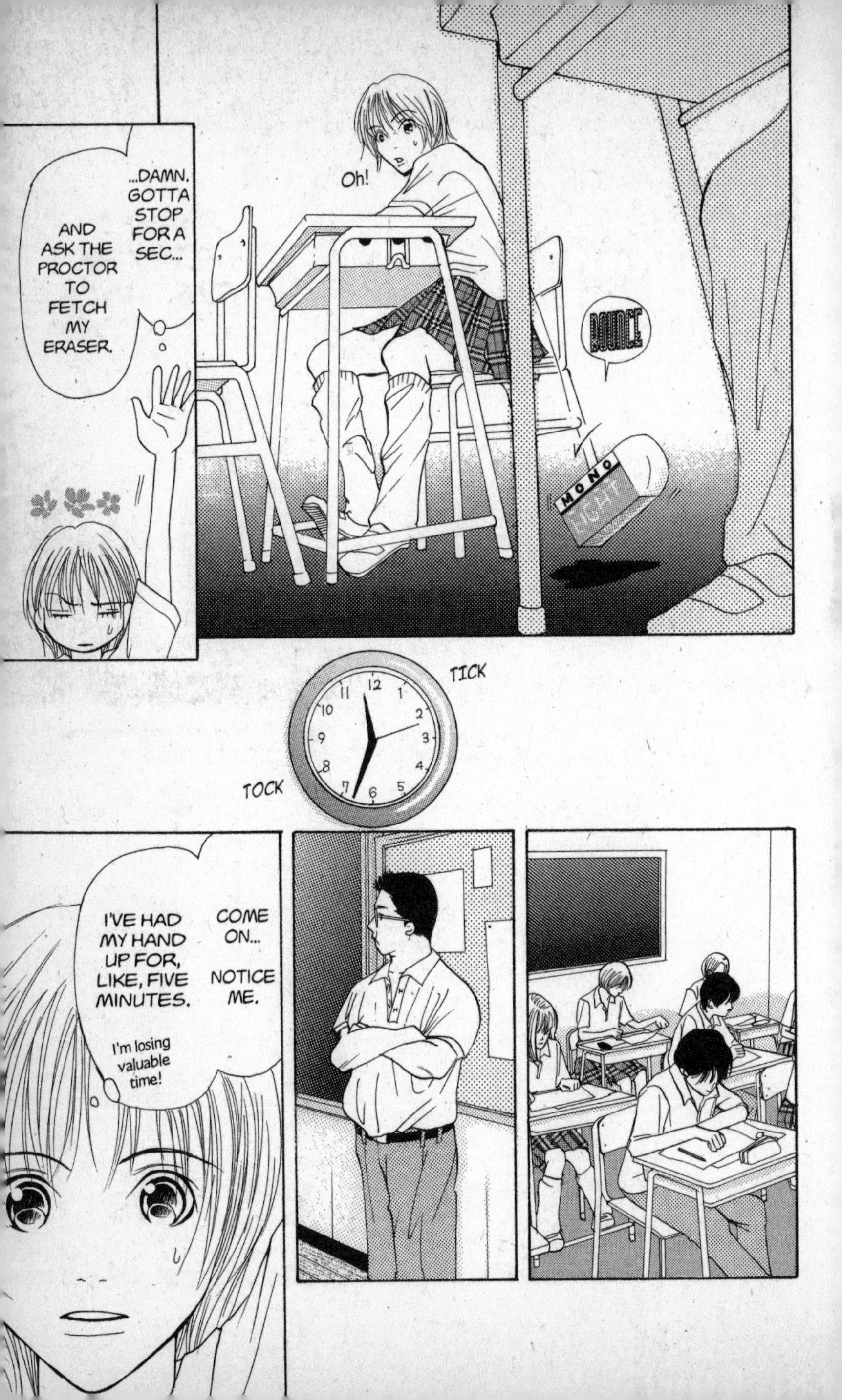
Oh!
BOUNCE
MONO
...DAMN. GOTTA STOP FOR A SEC...
AND ASK THE PROCTOR TO FETCH MY ERASER.
TICK
TOCK
COME ON... NOTICE ME.
I'VE HAD MY HAND UP FOR, LIKE, FIVE MINUTES.
I'm losing valuable time!

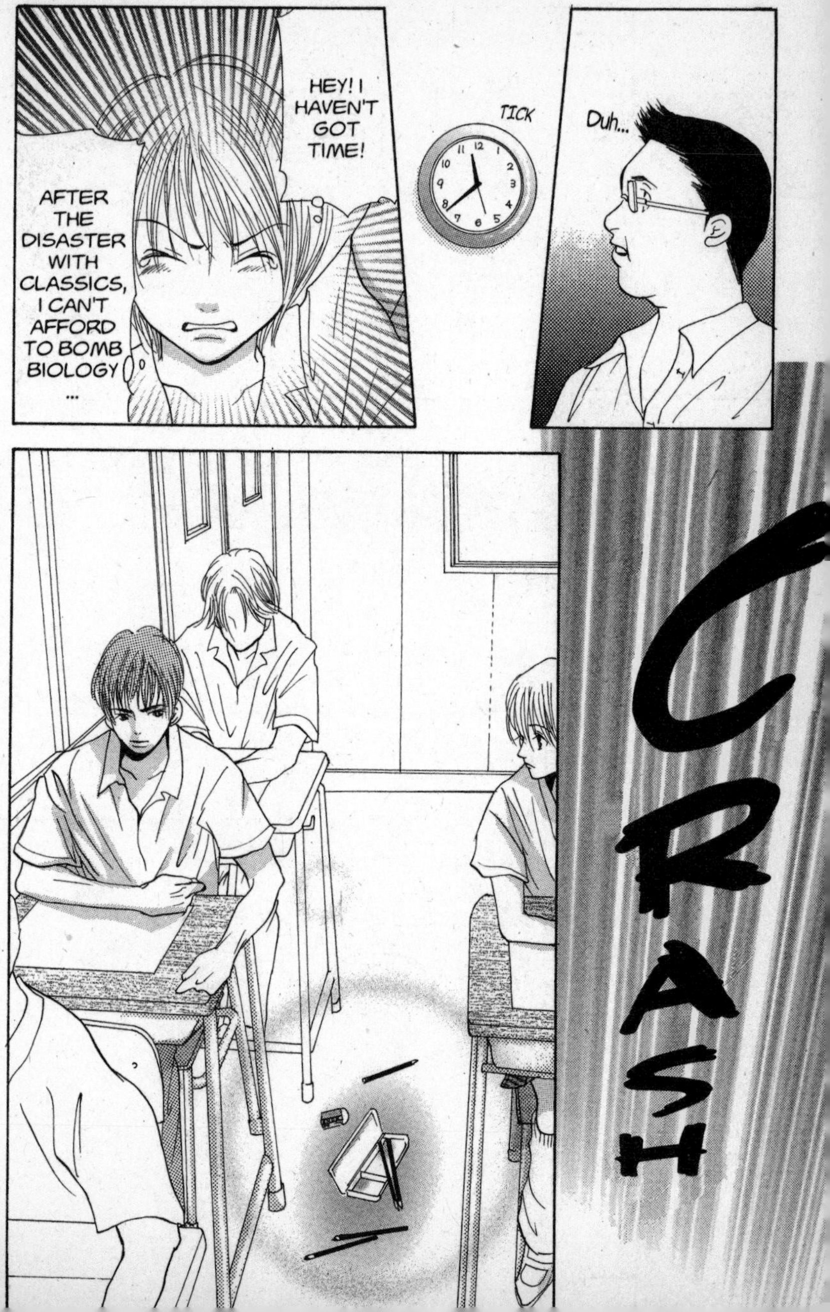
Duh...
TICK
HEY! I HAVEN'T GOT TIME!
AFTER THE DISASTER WITH CLASSICS, I CAN'T AFFORD TO BOMB BIOLOGY ...
CRASH

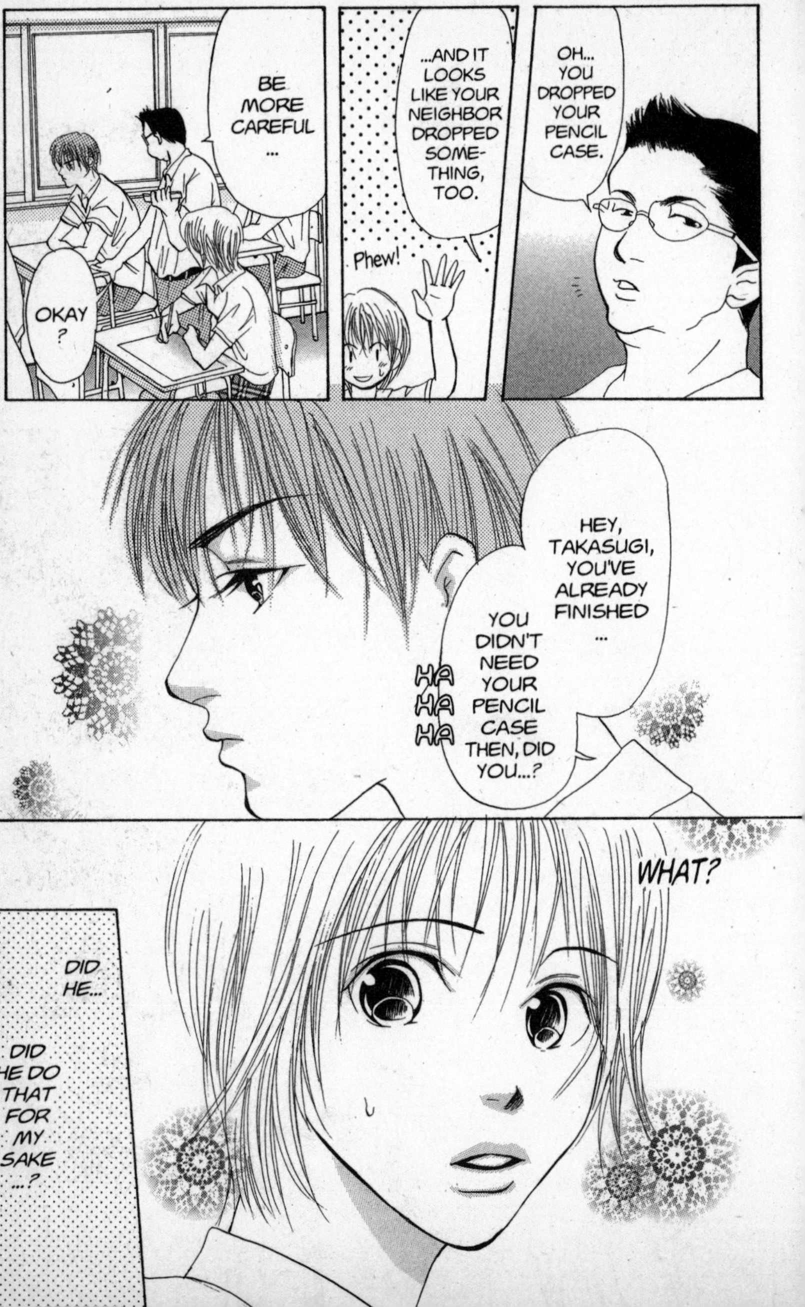
OH... YOU DROPPED YOUR PENCIL CASE.
...AND IT LOOKS LIKE YOUR NEIGHBOR DROPPED SOME-THING, TOO.
Phew!
BE MORE CAREFUL ...
OKAY ?
HEY, TAKASUGI, YOU'VE ALREADY FINISHED ...
YOU DIDN'T NEED YOUR PENCIL CASE THEN, DID YOU...?
HA HA HA
WHAT?
DID HE...
DID HE DO THAT FOR MY SAKE ...?

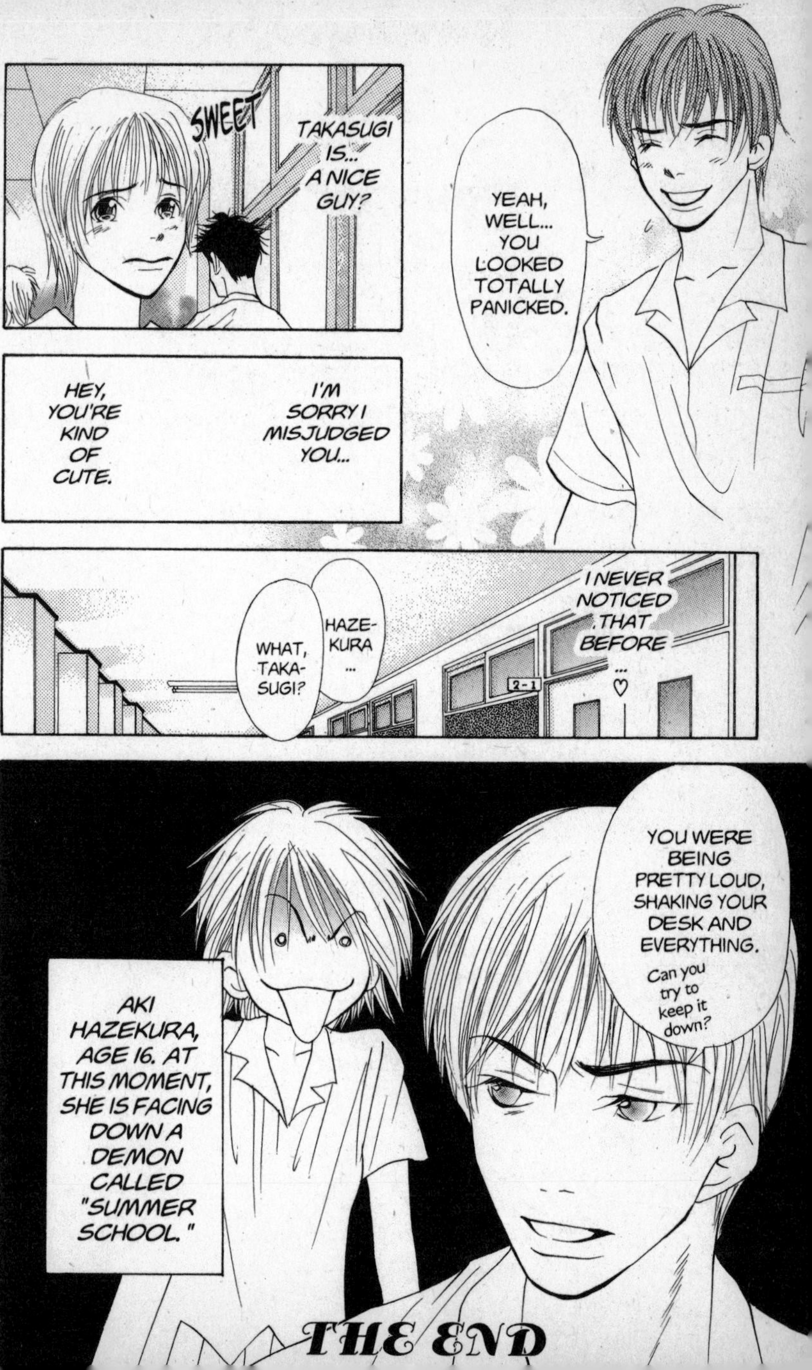
YEAH, WELL... YOU LOOKED TOTALLY PANICKED.
SWEET
TAKASUGI IS... A NICE GUY?
I'M SORRY I MISJUDGED YOU...
HEY, YOU'RE KIND OF CUTE.
I NEVER NOTICED THAT BEFORE ... ♡
HAZE-KURA ...
WHAT, TAKA-SUGI?
2-1
YOU WERE BEING PRETTY LOUD, SHAKING YOUR DESK AND EVERYTHING.
Can you try to keep it down?
AKI HAZEKURA, AGE 16. AT THIS MOMENT, SHE IS FACING DOWN A DEMON CALLED "SUMMER SCHOOL."
THE END

kaneyoshi izumi

MESSAGE FROM THE AUTHOR

According to my life plan, I was supposed to be married by now, living in a white house with a white dog as my pet. However, the reality is, I live in a black house with a black bird that sits on my shoulder. I'm a loser...

ABOUT THE AUTHOR

Kaneyoshi Izumi's birthday is April 1st and her blood type is probably type A (but she hasn't actually had it checked yet). Her debut story "Tenshi" ("Angel") appeared in the September 1995 issue of Bessatsu Shôjo Comics and won the 36th Shogakukan Shinjin ("newbie") Comics Award. Her hobbies include riding motorcycles, playing the piano, and feeding stray cats, and she continues to work as an artist for Bessatsu Shôjo Comics.

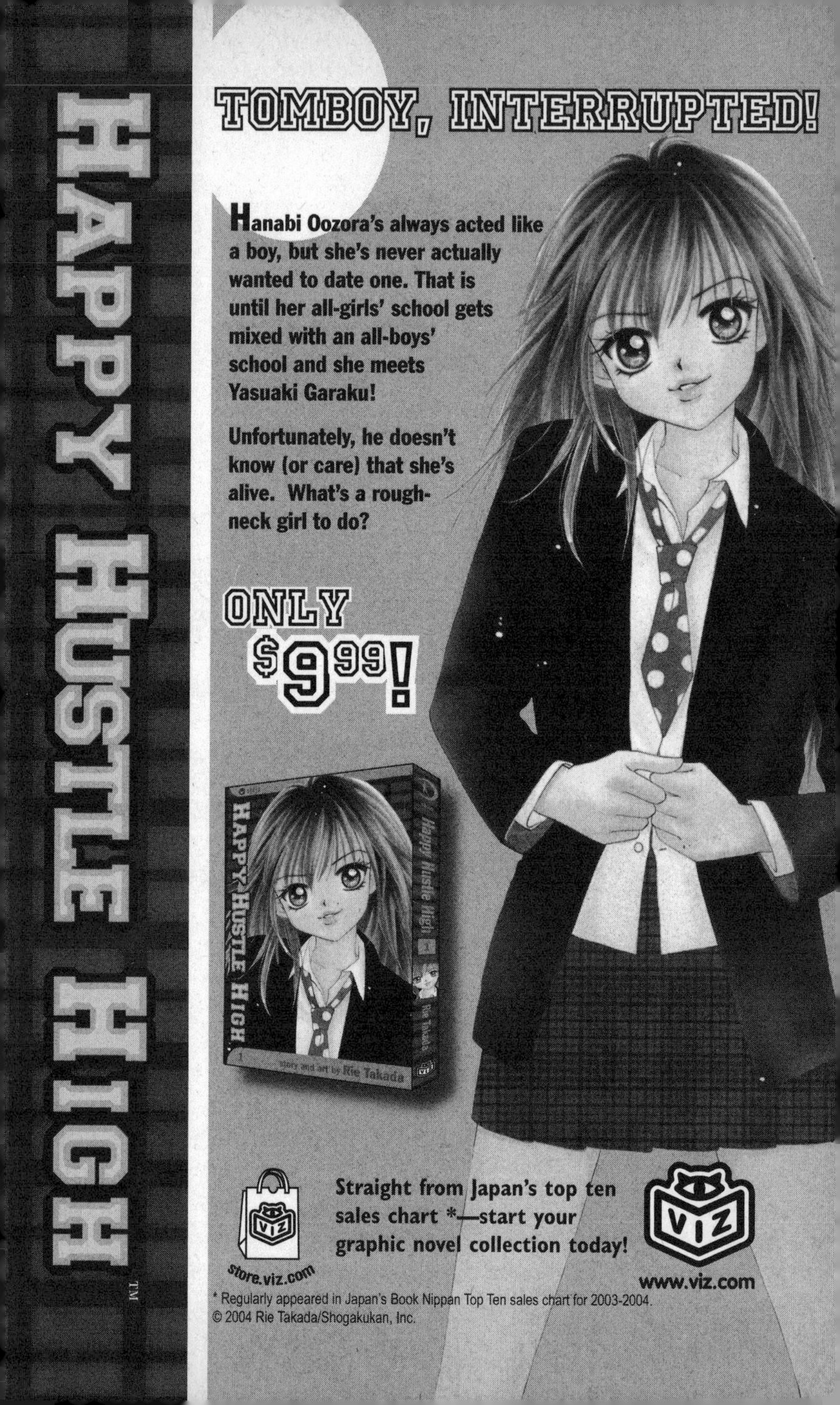

COMPLETE OUR SURVEY AND LET US KNOW WHAT YOU THINK!

☐ Please do NOT send me information about VIZ products, news and events, special offers, or other information.

☐ Please do NOT send me information from VIZ's trusted business partners.

Name: _____

Address: _____

City: _____ **State:** _____ **Zip:** _____

E-mail: _____

☐ Male ☐ Female **Date of Birth** (mm/dd/yyyy): ___/___/_____ (Under 13? Parental consent required)

What race/ethnicity do you consider yourself? (please check one)

☐ Asian/Pacific Islander ☐ Black/African American ☐ Hispanic/Latino

☐ Native American/Alaskan Native ☐ White/Caucasian ☐ Other: _____

What VIZ product did you purchase? (check all that apply and indicate title purchased)

☐ DVD/VHS _____

☐ Graphic Novel _____

☐ Magazines _____

☐ Merchandise _____

Reason for purchase: (check all that apply)

☐ Special offer ☐ Favorite title ☐ Gift

☐ Recommendation ☐ Other _____

Where did you make your purchase? (please check one)

☐ Comic store ☐ Bookstore ☐ Mass/Grocery Store

☐ Newsstand ☐ Video/Video Game Store ☐ Other: _____

☐ Online (site: _____)

What other VIZ properties have you purchased/own? _____

_____

How many anime and/or manga titles have you purchased in the last year? How many were VIZ titles? **(please check one from each column)**

ANIME	MANGA	VIZ
☐ None	☐	
☐ 1-4		☐ -4
☐ 5-10	☐ 5-10	☐ 5-10
☐ 11+	☐ 11+	☐ 11+

I find the pricing of VIZ products to be: (please check one)

☐ Cheap ☐ Reasonable ☐ Expensive

What genre of manga and anime would you like to see from VIZ? (please check two)

☐ Adventure ☐ Comic Strip ☐ Science Fiction ☐ Fighting

☐ Horror ☐ Romance ☐ Fantasy ☐ Sports

What do you think of VIZ's new look?

☐ Love It ☐ It's OK ☐ Hate It ☐ Didn't Notice ☐ No Opinion

Which do you prefer? (please check one)

☐ Reading right-to-left

☐ Reading left-to-right

Which do you prefer? (please check one)

☐ Sound effects in English

☐ Sound effects in Japanese with English captions

☐ Sound effects in Japanese only with a glossary at the back

THANK YOU! Please send the completed form to:

VIZ Survey
42 Catharine St.
Poughkeepsie, NY 12601

All information provided will be used for internal purposes only. We promise not to sell or otherwise divulge your information.